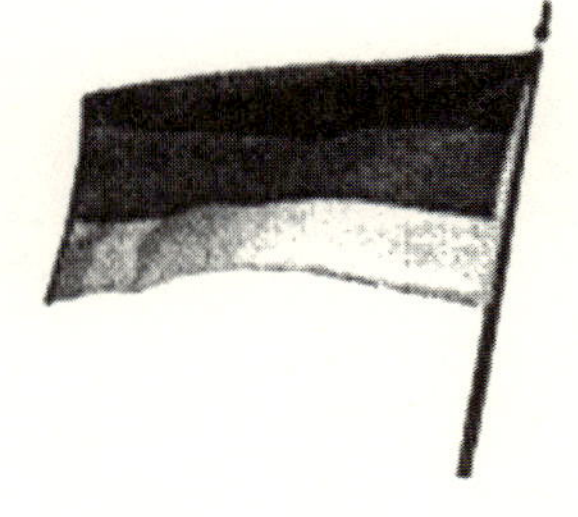

Encyclopedia of
Warrior Peoples and Fighting Groups

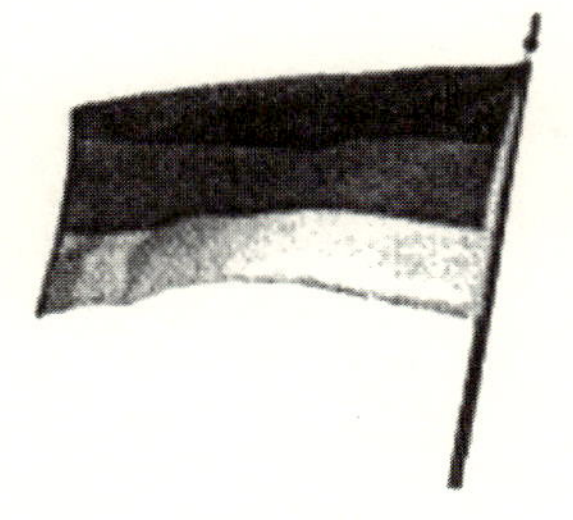

Encyclopedia of *Warrior Peoples and Fighting Groups*

Paul K. Davis
and Allen Lee Hamilton

ABC-CLIO

Santa Barbara, California
Denver, Colorado
Oxford, England

Library of Congress Cataloging-in-Publication Data

Davis, Paul K., 1952–
Encyclopedia of warrior peoples and fighting groups / Paul K. Davis and Allen Lee Hamilton.
p. cm.
Includes bibliographical references and index.

1. Military history. I. Hamilton, Allen Lee. II. Title.
D25.9.D38 1998
355'.003--dc21 98-36079
CIP

ISBN 0-87436-961-4 (hc)
ISBN 1-57607-046-8 (pbk)

02 01 00 99 98 10 9 8 7 6 5 4 3 2 1

ABC-CLIO, Inc.
130 Cremona Drive, P.O. Box 1911
Santa Barbara, California 93116-1911

This book is printed on acid-free paper.
Manufactured in the United States of America

For Jerri and Suzanne, whose patience and support have sustained us in more than just the writing of this book.

Contents

Preface

Ever since mankind began organizing military forces, some have excelled in their craft. This came about either by fortuitous circumstances, outstanding leadership, or specialized instruction or training. In some cases, entire societies were geared toward military excellence. It is these populations and units that are the focus of this work.

We have selected four criteria for inclusion in this book: (1) Populations that dedicated themselves to a military structure in order to maintain societal discipline or dominate their neighbors. For example, the Spartans of ancient Greece or the Zulus of nineteenth-century Africa fit this criterion. (2) Soldiers who, through specialized training in the use of particular weapons or fighting styles, dominated the military forces of their times. Under this definition we would include knights, who controlled the military and social structure of medieval Europe, or submariners, who in modern times are carefully selected for their physical and psychological characteristics in operating undersea craft. (3) Units that did not necessarily set out to be noteworthy but who, through leadership or circumstance, made themselves famous. Here we include units such as the Minutemen of the American Revolution and Merrill's Marauders of World War II. (4) Units that recruit only high-quality soldiers with the intent of creating an elite force. The Varangian Guard of the Byzantine Empire and the Special Air Service of modern Great Britain fit into this category.

Some units that are well known are mentioned as subgroups of other topics. The famous Black Watch regiment of the British Army, for example, is included in the Highlanders entry, and the Comanche tribe is included with the Plains Indians. Certainly some readers will have personal favorites they feel we have overlooked; perhaps a second edition could expand to include such suggestions. It has been our intent to include as many topics over as wide an area as possible, in terms both of eras and of parts of the world. No unit or group has been left out intentionally, but only as a matter of oversight.

We would like to thank several contributors who have eased our writing burden in the production of this work: Robert Burke of St. Philip's College, Steve Davis of St. Mary's University, John Drake of the University of Texas at San Antonio, and Michael Forbes and Melvin C. (Mel) Wheat, free-lance historians.

A

Afghans

A population of Afghanistan known for hostile and effective resistance to outside occupation.

For a few thousand years, Afghanistan was a crossroad for conquerors, with the countryside being overrun by Aryans, Greeks, Indians, Persians, Arabs, and Mongols. Over time this constant influx of conquerors created a population of tough, independent-minded fighters that adopted a policy of maximum resistance to invaders. After the Sassanid Persians were removed from power, a local ruler, Ahmad Shah Durani, assumed control in 1747. He founded a ruling family that remained in power for 100 years before they—as do so many dynasties—became complacent and vulnerable. In 1824 Dost Mohammed overthrew this dissolute dynasty and became amir of Afghanistan. He soon began to feel pressure from major international powers both north and south of him.

The Persians, supported by the Russians, invaded Afghanistan in the 1830s. By chance, Eldred Pottinger, a British spy operating in Afghanistan, broke his cover, offered his assistance to the amir, and led the Afghan army in a successful defense of the country. Rather than bring closer ties with Great Britain, which currently dominated India to the south, this incident instead provoked a British invasion. Britain did not fear Afghanistan itself, but feared that its domination by Russia would pose a potential threat to India. When Dost Mohammed refused to grant Britain the concessions it demanded, the British decided to place a more amenable ruler in his stead. Shah Shuja, Britain's chosen nominee, was of the ruling line Dost Mohammed had overthrown, but he was weak and therefore despised by the Afghan population. British forces invaded in late 1838 and by August 1839 Dost Mohammed was in exile and Shah Shuja was on the throne. The British army proceeded to put down pockets of resistance around the capital city of Kabul, and the tribes they did not defeat they pacified with bribery. When in 1841 the bribes stopped, so did tribal cooperation. The British forces in Afghanistan found themselves surrounded in isolated forts and the Afghans proved themselves able snipers, picking off unwary defenders. This uprising, coupled with the murder of the British ambassador, provoked another invasion.

The British in Kabul decided to flee for India. In January 1843 4,500 British and Indian soldiers, civilians, women, and children, along with some 10,000 Afghan supporters abandoned the city. Only one British soldier made it to the border fort at Jelalabad. The rest were killed by the Afghans. The First Afghan War (as it came to be known) set a pattern for future intervention in the rugged country. A relief army from India forced the Khyber Pass, a feat no other power had ever accomplished, relieved the besieged Jelalabad, and then marched on Kabul. They released British prisoners held in Afghan confinement and burned the Great Bazaar, then marched home. Afghanistan was once again free of outside occupation, and Dost Mohammed returned to power.

The British failed to learn from history. In 1879 they once again attempted to place an envoy in Kabul, hoping to direct Afghanistan's foreign policy and keep out yet another Russian threat. One of Dost Mohammed's sons, Shere Ali, refused Britain's demands and, like his father, fled another army that marched into Kabul. Shere Ali died escaping to Russia, but one of his brothers, Yakub Khan, was installed as amir with British sufferance. By bowing to British pressure Yakub Khan incurred the wrath of his people who once again rose up, slaughtering the envoy and the British soldiers in the Residence of the British representative in the capital. Another relief force from India made its way to Kabul and exacted justice for the British envoy, then soon found itself surrounded and cut off from communication with India. A relief force from the fortress town of Kandahar fought through to Kabul, then learned that Kandahar had been besieged in their absence. Troops from Kabul marched back and recaptured the town. Now seemed like a good time to take everyone home, and the British retreated.

Once again rid of foreigners, the new Amir Abd-ar-Rahman Khan created a standing army and by diplomacy settled his borders with both Russia and British India. All was peaceful until 1919 when a new amir, supported by Afghan nobles, declared war on Britain. As the British were busy with Indian independence movements, they quickly negotiated a settlement whereby Great Britain recognized Afghan sovereignty. Free from outside threats, the Afghans turned upon each other. Rulers came and went over the next several years, all overthrown and either killed or forced into exile. Although the Afghans established friendly relations with Germany, Italy, and Japan in the 1930s when World War II broke out they declared themselves neutral. After the war they joined the United Nations.

In 1947 another border dispute flared. The newly formed nation of Pakistan had a large ethnic Pathan population, people closely related to Afghans. When Pakistan would not allow the Pathans a referendum on self-rule, Afghanistan protested and began supporting Pathan insurgents demanding their own homeland, Pashtunistan (or Pathanistan). When the United States established friendly relations with Pakistan and offered them military aid, Afghanistan began leaning toward the Soviet Union. With Soviet financial aid, the Afghan government began modernizing the country, but famine in the late 1960s and early 1970s brought aid from around the globe. Internal political squabbling led to more changes of government, still through violent means, until a revolutionary council established a socialist-style republic in 1978. When devout Muslims (the country is predominantly Shi'ite) revolted, the new government sought Soviet military assistance. In December 1979 a Soviet-supported coup killed Afghan Prime Minister Hafizullah Amin and Soviet troops occupied the country. Their experience, a hundred years after the last British incursion, would be no more successful.

As many as 118,000 Soviet troops were sent to Afghanistan, but they could do little more than hold the major cities and roadways. The Afghan tribesmen, who had harassed and ultimately embarrassed the British, proceeded to do the same to the Soviets. With covert military aid from the United States, the Muslim tribesmen controlled the mountainous countryside and the best Soviet attempts could not break them. In 1989 the disillusioned Soviet government withdrew all its combat troops, and once again the Afghans continued to fight among themselves. The blood of centuries of conquerors seems to have bred in the Afghan people the ability to fight; history has forced on them an ample opportunity to exercise that ability.

References: Adamec, Ludwig, *Dictionary of Afghan Wars, Revolutions, and Insurgencies* (Lanham, MD: Scarecrow Press, 1996); Bilgrami, Ashgar,

Afghanistan and British India (New Delhi: Sterling Press, 1972); Farwell, Byron, *Queen Victoria's Little Wars* (New York: Harper and Row, 1972).

Afrika Korps

An outstanding unit of the Nazi army in North Africa in World War II.

Geography and terrain are always important when armies meet on the battlefield, and this was especially clear in North Africa during World War II. The desert environment determined the way war was fought in that campaign. Soldiers not only fought the enemy; they fought the elements as well. Temperatures rose above 100 degrees in the daytime and fell below freezing at night. Sand permeated everything from equipment to food and clothing. The fierce sun bleached uniforms and caused heat waves to dance on the sand, which sometimes prevented seeing farther than 1,000 yards.

The Mediterranean coastline with its sparkling waters was beautiful, but inland was a sterile, desolate, and foreboding desert. Rather than sand dunes, a hard crusty ground littered with rocks and boulders was typical. Maps were unreliable and the absence of landmarks made navigation difficult; men separated from their units could become lost and perish. Some parts of the desert rose in impassable escarpments or sunk in depressions many miles across. Desert warfare employed new tactics using mechanized equipment—the tank, armored car, and self-propelled gun—in swift attacks. To take and hold territory required large quantities of supplies, so the main objective was simply to destroy the enemy. The opposing armies had to maneuver quickly, trying to flank their opponents and attack from the rear or side. The main consideration was always supply. If an army raced forward too quickly, it might outrun its supply lines and become immobilized, which would lead to a counterattack.

Soldiers fought the desert and the enemy. They shared the desert with snakes, scorpions, lizards, and millions of flies and sand fleas. Dust was a big problem. Large movements of vehicles and troops stirred up the dust and gave away their positions. The dust got into the men's eyes, noses, and mouths. It penetrated into the food and water. Worse, it fouled engines and equipment, including rifles and cannons. Sandstorms were fierce and would stop most advances, causing the men to seek shelter in tents or vehicles until the storm passed. The sand, whipped by winds of 60 miles per hour or more, could strip the paint from vehicles and feel like millions of pinpricks on the skin. It could reduce visibility to a few feet and make breathing impossible without covering the mouth and nose. Despite these conditions, the men of the German Afrika Korps under Field Marshall Erwin Rommel conducted a war in North Africa that almost beat the Allies.

The men of the German Afrika Korps had been given no desert training and became hardened to the desert conditions as they fought. They were supplied at most only one gallon of water per man per day for drinking, cooking, and washing. They then saved the dirty water to be used in the vehicles. The army did not issue equipment for protection from the sun, such as sunglasses or lotion to protect the skin. Soldiers were originally issued pith helmets, but they soon discarded these in favor of cloth caps. They also wore shorts as part of the standard uniform. Soldiers soon found their skin chapped by the desert winds. Their lips

Nazi General Erwin Rommel on the battlefield in Africa, 1942

cracked and their eyes became bloodshot from the piercing sunlight. Everyone was sunburned. Night brought no relief. The men, having sweated all day would now shiver with the cold. Flies tormented the men by day, and sand fleas emerged at night to swarm the men. Their biting caused sores that were slow to heal.

The need for speed and mobility meant long, fast drives to reach a battle. Soldiers often steered their vehicles in a daze for lack of sleep. Sleeping at the wheel might only be interrupted by hitting another vehicle or a random boulder or being stuck in loose sand found off the main track. The sleepy soldier would then be admonished for not staying awake. Moonless nights and the policy of driving without headlights caused men to lose sight of vehicles ahead of them and become lost in the vast desert. They would then be at the mercy of enemy air attacks when daylight came.

Supplies were always a problem. German soldiers were fed meager rations consisting of biscuits, cheese, and canned sardines. Canned meat was occasionally available, but was tough and tasteless. There was never enough water, and thirst was a constant companion; there were periods when water was rationed to one half cup per day. The Afrika Korps captured food and supplies from the enemy. Fuel was also obtained from enemy fuel dumps captured in battle. Both armies used captured vehicles, and cannibalized parts from vehicles that were no longer usable.

The equipment was as susceptible to the harsh conditions as the men. Tanks required an overhaul in only one fourth the time of those in a normal environment. The average tank went only 1,500 miles before requiring an entire overhaul. Vehicles bogged down in sand and the men had to wrestle with machines that the sun rendered too hot to touch with unprotected hands. The heat required columns to halt in order to allow engines to cool, and there were delays while crews cleaned clogged air and fuel filters. After a long night's drive and a daytime battle, men would refurbish their equipment and prepare for the next day's battle. The average soldier might get three hours of sleep in every 24.

The desert's lack of cover made fighting very dangerous. Men in armored equipment had some protection, but the supporting infantries were at the mercy of enemy fire. Barbed wire and trenches surrounded emplacements. Mines were laid in minefields that stretched for miles with only a few clear paths through them. Infantry advanced with armor, and in the confusion of battle the soldiers had to be alert to keep from being run over by their own tanks. Infantry also tried to avoid the tanks because they invited enemy fire. The tank provided cover, but an exploding tank could kill everyone around it.

Tank crews, although better protected than infantry, were not immune to destruction. Survival depended on the thickness of the tank's armor versus the shell being shot at it. A penetrating shell could ignite the ammunition or fuel in the vehicle, and all inside would perish. Tank crews fought in steel ovens. The big gun would add to the heat, and tremendous noise required crews to talk with each other by intercom. At midday, the sun sent shimmering heat waves over the desert, cutting visibility, so the armies fought most battles at dawn or dusk. Fighting caused smoke and dust to obscure the battlefield. In addition, identification of the enemy was confusing because both armies used captured vehicles. Tank commanders needed good visibility so they often opened the hatch and stood up in their turrets, risking death.

After nightfall, with the battle over, commanders shot flares into the sky to show lost units where to regroup. This was a time for tank crews to do maintenance or repair on the tanks and to rearm and refuel. There would also be guard duty or other duties to perform. This limited the sleeping time of the troops to just a few hours because they frequently had to go back into action before dawn the next day. The British tank crews were usually on the line for a week before becoming exhausted, but Rommel kept his men in action for two weeks at a time or longer.

The Afrika Korps was an elite group led by an unusual leader. Rommel was revered by his men and acquired the nickname "Desert Fox." He had no compunctions about visiting the front and his men frequently saw him. During one engagement, he piloted a light plane over the battlefield alone to understand the battle for himself. Rommell's assumption of command in North Africa changed the entire nature of the war there. The British, who had easily dominated the Italians and had success against earlier commanders, found Rommel's audacious moves almost impossible to counter. For example, the port city of Tobruk, which had resisted Axis capture for 26 months, fell to the Afrika Korps under Rommel in 26 hours. Repeatedly, Rommel defeated the Allied armies and caused England's prime minister, Winston Churchill, to remark that he was a formidable general. Rommel would not be stopped until September 1942 when a lack of supplies from Germany doomed his final drive on Alexandria and Cairo that threatened the Suez Canal. The combination of better-supplied British forces in Egypt and the arrival in early November 1942 of American forces to his rear doomed the Desert Fox to a fighting withdrawal and doomed the Axis plans to control North Africa.

—John Drake

References: Barnett, Correlli, *The Desert Generals* (Bloomington: Indiana University Press, 1982); Bianco, Richard L., *Rommel, the Desert Warrior* (New York: Julian Messner, 1982); Mitcham, Samuel W., *Rommel's Desert War: the Life and Death of the Afrika Korps* (New York: Stein and Day, 1982).

Akkadians

An ancient population that created through conquest the first known empire during the late third millennium B.C.

The people of the city of Akkad, or Agade, were Sumerians. The origin of the Sumerians, like many peoples of the ancient world, is somewhat hypothetical. They probably came from the area around the Caspian Sea, although there is no indication that they were Indo-European, like many later invaders from the north. They arrived in the fourth millennium B.C. and settled the Tigris and Euphrates valleys, establishing the cities of Ur, Eridu, Mari, Nippur, Uruk, Kish, and Lagash. These communities collectively made up the population of Sumer, although they formed more a confederation than a nation. They developed the cuneiform style of writing and were best known architecturally for the construction of ziggurats, step pyramids used as temples or altars. They also developed a monarchy, with a king in each city-state. The king was originally chosen for his military abilities, but over time the post became a permanent, and then a hereditary, position. As military commander, the king commanded forces that fought in a phalanx-type formation, 11 men wide and six ranks deep. Most of the time the city-states fought among themselves in ever-shifting power struggles, or united against outside threats. That ended, however, with the monarchy of Sargon.

As with many ancient figures, Sargon's early years are somewhat of a mystery. He was born around 2350 B.C. of undetermined parentage, though some theorize either a pastoral upbringing or that he was the child of a temple prostitute because he did not know his father. According to legend, Sargon began life as Moses did: cast adrift on a river by his mother—in this case, the river Euphrates. He was then reputedly rescued and raised by another, although it was a farm family and not a royal one. He did manage, however, to become cupbearer to Ur-Zababa, the king of Kish. He came to power either by overthrowing the king himself or assuming the king's throne when Ur-Zababa was killed by the invading king of Sumer. Either way, at this point he took the name Sargon, meaning "King of Universal Dominion," and made war against Sumer.

Sargon united his Semitic people into history's first empire, the Akkadians. Sargon went about conquering and was quite successful at it. He captured cities up the Euphrates River, then crossed to the Tigris and worked his way up that river to Ashur. From there he conquered eastward to the Persian hills, then south to defeat Sumer, possibly gaining revenge for the death of Ur-Zababa. He symbolically washed his weapons in the Persian Gulf, marking the limit of his conquests in that direction. After consolidating his hold on Sumer, he marched west to conquer Mesopotamia and possibly as far as Syria and Lebanon, with rumors of conquests in lands as far flung as Egypt, Asia Minor, and India.

In order to control this vast territory, Sargon appointed representatives of the conquered peoples to governing positions, answerable only to him. He stationed troops in posts around the empire, garrisoning them with forces of all nations, although some soldiers were forced to join his armies. Sargon was successful in battle because he initiated new tactics. He abandoned the standard tight phalanx-style formation in favor of a looser one, and he adopted the use of javelins and arrows shot from compound bows. He also maintained the first standing army, a force of 5,400 men.

With so much land under one ruler, previously uncooperative peoples became more likely to open relations with neighboring tribes and the freer exchange of goods and ideas resulted. New gods and religions were adopted from conquered peoples, as were cuneiform writing and art. The Akkadians were the first to use writing for more than keeping temple records. Because of this, we have the first recorded actions of royalty; hence, Sargon is regarded as the first clearly identified individual in history. He set an example for later royal chroniclers, as seen here: "He spread his terror-inspiring glamour over all the countries. He crossed the Sea in the East and he, himself, conquered the country of the West.... He marched against the country of Kazalla and turned Kazalla into ruin-hills and heaps of rubble. He even destroyed there every possible perching place for a bird" (Starr, 1965).

Having acquired vast amounts of land, Sargon's empire was exceedingly wealthy, controlling the known world's gold, silver, copper, and stone. With the abundant agriculture of Mesopotamia and abundant forage to the north, Sargon seemingly had it all. He maintained control by appointing loyal governors and visiting parts of his empire on occasion to let the people know he was interested in them. He ruled for 56 years but ended his reign with parts of his empire in revolt. The Akkadian empire lasted some 200 years—only to be overthrown by its first conquest, a resurgent Sumerian society.

References: Edwards, I. E. S., ed., *The Cambridge Ancient History* (Cambridge: Cambridge University Press, 1980); Gabriel, Richard, *The Culture of War* (New York: Greenwood Press, 1990); Gabriel, Richard, *From Sumer to Rome* (New York: Greenwood Press, 1991); Starr, Chester, *A History of the Ancient World* (New York: Oxford University Press, 1965).

Almoravids

A Saharan Desert tribe known for its aggressive spread of fundamentalist Islam during the eleventh and twelfth centuries.

The nomads of the western Sahara, most notably the Sanhaja tribes, dominated the gold trade between Ghana and the Mediterranean in the eleventh century. This was a profitable pastime until Ghana seized control of the town of Awdaghust, at the southern end of the trade route. Owing to internal dissent, the Sanhaja tribes were unable to respond to this loss of revenue and power. The king of the tribes believed something needed to be done to unite his people, and he thought that religion was the key. Although Islam had been spread throughout western Africa since the eighth century, it was practiced with irregular piety. Among the Sanhaja tribes of the Sahara, the people seemed to be only nominally Moslem. When their king went on his pilgrimage to Mecca, he returned with the desire to increase his people's faithfulness. He brought with him a teacher, Ibn Yasin, to motivate his tribes to become better Moslems—a task Ibn Yasin was unable to accomplish.

Disgusted at the intransigence of the nomads, Ibn Yasin went into retreat along the west coast of Africa (some say near the mouth of the Senegal River, some say Mauritania or an island off the coast). Here he established a ribat, a fortified center for the study of religion and warfare, which attracted a following of people pious to the point of fanaticism. These "men of the ribat" came to be known as Almoravids (in Arabic, al-muributun). When Ibn Yasin had about a thousand followers, mostly from the Sanhaja tribes, he declared a jihad, or holy war. Returning to the territory of the Sanhaja, he told his recruits to convert their people to a stronger belief or to visit God's wrath upon them. After a few defeats, the Sanhaja tribes embraced Ibn Yasin's fundamentalist stand and joined his forces, not just for religious reasons but for the promise of booty. With enlarged forces, Ibn Yasin moved north to Morocco, defeating the Berber inhabitants in 1054–1055. Here, in Ibn Yasin's homeland, the Almoravid state was established. After Ibn Yasin's death in battle in 1059 a dynasty was founded by Yusuf ibn Tashufin.

As the main Almoravid force was conquering Morocco, a smaller force attacked south with the intent of recapturing Awdaghust. They accomplished this in 1054 and ultimately attacked deeper into Ghanan territory, where they captured the capital in 1076. For a while the Almoravids instituted a strict Moslem rule in the west African state, forcing tribute and the payment of a head tax for non-Moslems. This control lasted only a few years, as the Almoravids were more concerned with pillage and profit than local improvement. Even though they controlled both ends of the trans-Saharan trade route, they did not take advantage of it. When the Almoravids withdrew, Ghana remained disrupted, giving an opportunity for the expansion of Mali into the gold territory.

Meanwhile, the Almoravids in Morocco extended their campaign for Moslem fundamentalism into Spain. They attempted to revive the lethargic religious practices of the Islamic Spaniards and were welcomed by them to provide protection from the approaching Christian forces from Europe.

At their height, the Almoravids controlled territory from Spain through western Africa. That rule was short-lived, however. The Almoravids were in turn overthrown by another fundamentalist movement, the Almohads, who declared a jihad against them in 1122 and ultimately overthrew them in 1163. That defeat in Morocco, coupled with the inability to make a profit at the southern extreme of their holdings in the gold region of Ghana, brought the Almoravids to a rather abrupt end. The legacy of the Almoravid reign is mixed. It did not introduce Islam into Ghana, but it did accelerate the spread of the religion into the interior of western Africa along the Niger River to Mali and the Songhay empires. The Almoravids also acted as a solidifying influence for the tribes of the Maghrib in northwest Africa. By building their capital at Marrakesh, they laid the foundation for the modern nation of Morocco. Both in Morocco and in the Sahara, the tribes were firm in their Islamic faith, but the fundamentalism the Almoravids preached did not last much past their demise.

References: Fage, J. D., *A History of West Africa* (London: Cambridge University Press, 1969); Hallett, Robin, *Africa to 1875* (Ann Arbor: University of Michigan Press, 1970); Trimingham, J. S., *Islam in West Africa* (London: Oxford University Press, 1962).

Amazons

A legendary tribe of warrior women reported in ancient accounts.

No account of female warriors could exist without reference to the stories of the Amazons. Amazons appear in the earliest Greek legends, predating Homer and the Trojan War. The most famous Amazon population supposedly resided in the Caucasus between the Black and Caspian Seas along the Thermidon River. Concrete evidence of their existence is lacking, but a society of female warriors in this region was also referred to in Chinese and Cherkessian folklore. If they were indeed mythical, an amazing amount of detail concerning their lifestyle is extant, differing mainly in detail rather than substance.

It is assumed by some that the society first appeared in the wake of warfare that seriously depleted the male population. The females, apparently trained for combat, turned away from a male-dominated society to establish a matriarchy in which males were either completely excluded or existed only around the edges of society. The most popular version of the fashion in which they maintained their population was that they would make annual forays into neighboring areas in order to engage in sexual activity strictly for the purposes of procreation. Female children born of these assignations would be retained while male children were either sent to their fathers, crippled and kept as slaves, or killed, depending on which account of the society one reads. The females reputedly were raised by the crippled slaves and nursed by mares, the mothers never feeding their children. At age eight they would have their right breasts seared by hot irons so that no mammary glands would grow. The reason for this was either to sublimate any masculine tendencies (which were believed to emanate from the right side) or to remove any obstacle to the use of a bow (assuming, one supposes, that all were right-handed). Hunters, Amazons nourished themselves by a diet of mare's milk, honey, blood, raw meat, and reeds. They apparently never acquired a taste for grain; indeed, one possible derivation of the word "amazon" is from the Greek *A-Maza,* meaning "no barley bread" or "one who lives without bread."

The Amazon society was supposedly ruled by a dual monarchy, one queen to command the armies and one to rule at the capital. They fought with double-headed axes *(sagaris),* a small crescent-shaped shield, bows and arrows, and short swords. They apparently adopted the lance after combat against the Greeks.

Greek folklore tells of a war with the Amazons waged by Theseus, one of the founders of Athens. He led an attack on the Amazon capital city of Themiscyra to acquire the queen's crystal and gold sword belt, the loss of which would symbolize the queen's ravishment. In one version of the story, Hercules aids Theseus in his attack on the capital while the Amazon army under Oreithyia is away defending its borders. The raiders overcame the city garrison and stole Queen Hippolyte's belt. Hercules seduced or kidnaped the queen's sister, Antiope. Oreithyia immediately launched a punitive expedition against Athens and occupied the Areopagus, besieging the Greeks on the Acropolis. The outcome of the battle is disputed, but after negotiations, the Amazons departed without having destroyed Athens. Later Greek historians located a number of sites where important events in the battle supposedly took place or where important casualties were buried.

Apparently, this marked the beginning of the end of Thermodontine Amazon power. They retained an eternal hatred of the Greeks and supposedly sent a detachment to King Priam to aid in the defense of Troy. Later populations that traveled or campaigned in western Asia reported stories of Amazon-style societies, fighting in Persia against Rome or in Russia against the Muscovites. These later descriptions often match the dress and fighting ability of the ancient Amazons, but no direct contact was ever established.

An earlier Amazon society was supposed to have existed in North Africa, the Libyan Amazons, although they did not live in the area of modern Libya, but along the Atlas Mountains of Morocco. According to legend, they derived much of their culture from a mainland colony of Atlantis. These women wore red leather armor and supposedly conquered as far as Ethiopia, Syria, and Phyrigia. There were two Amazon tribes, the Libyans and the Gorgons, who supposedly fought each other over the Atlantean colony. The Libyans under Myrine prevailed and the funeral pyres of the slain were the sites of monuments at the time of Diodorus. After this conflict, Myrine led the Libyans on campaigns into the Middle East. During their conquests, they established cities and conquered the Mediterranean islands of Samos, Lesbos, Pathmos, and Samothrace. They lost these lands later to a combined Thracian-Scythian force during which time Myrine was killed.

Strabo discussed the Amazon society of his day as maintaining a female-oriented military, but mainly for show rather than conquest. They did, however, still remove their right breast and had to remain unmarried while in the military. The society included men and marriage, but the men were relegated to domestic roles. Modern Berber and Tuareg societies emulate these practices in some ways.

Other Amazon-type societies have been reported around the world. The Gagans also lived in North Africa and killed baby boys until the group was converted to Christianity. They maintained a female-dominated government. Arabian sources describe a Hamitic Amazon tribe between the Nile and the Red Sea who fought with wonderfully wrought lances. Herodotus wrote of the Sauromatians on the far side of the Don River in Russia, a mixture of Amazon and Scythian, whose offspring, the Sarmatians, practiced Amazon ways. Pliny said they could not have children until they had first killed three male enemies. The earliest of the Amazon societies could have been an army led by Euryple, capturing Babylon in 1760 B.C. Pope Pius II, before he reached the pontificate, wrote in his *Historia Bohemica* of the kingdom of Libussa and Valeska in central Europe, describing a Bohemian girls' war. Finally, the Amazon River supposedly got its name from the resistance of a female army encountered by Portuguese explorers in the 1500s.

Did Amazons really exist? That can probably never be proven, but the multiple mentions throughout history and literature, with details overlapping in so many cultural references, imply the existence of some sort of female-dominated society as the basis for such a legend.

References: Diner, Helen, *Mothers and Amazons* (New York: The Julian Press, 1965); Herodotus, *The Histories,* trans. Aubrey de Selincourt (Baltimore: Penguin, 1954); Strabo, *Geography,* trans. Horace Leonard Jones (Cambridge: Harvard University Press, 1966).

ANZACs

Soldiers from Australia and New Zealand whose name derived from the words "Australia and New Zealand Army Corps."

When World War I began on 4 August 1914 Great Britain called on its empire for assistance. One of the first and largest responses came from Australia, which immediately promised 20,000 men. The number of volunteers was so much higher, however, that the authorities were able to select the cream of the crop of young Australian manhood. This meant that the members of the army, which came to be called the Australian Imperial Force (AIF), were in peak physical condition. By 21 September the troops were in uniform, organized into units, equipped, and ready to travel. It took until early November before sufficient transport could be arranged, however. When the AIF left western Australia it had acquired a large number of New Zealand volunteers as well.

As the convoy approached the Suez Canal en route to Britain, force commander Major General Sir W. T. Bridges received word from London that the Ottoman Empire had just entered the war on the side of the Central Powers. General Bridges was instructed to debark in Egypt for training and to await orders for action against the Turks. The forces from the two nations of the British empire were combined into the Australia and New Zealand Army Corps, hence the acronym "ANZAC." The use of the acronym as a description for the soldiers themselves is supposed to have been started by the new commander sent from India, General Sir William Birdwood, who called the men ANZACs. The ANZACs trained in the desert outside Cairo and adapted themselves to the drier climate of the Mediterranean. They were physically ready for action when orders came in the spring of 1915 to go into combat against the Turks.

The Turks had focussed most of their attention on their traditional enemy, Russia, and the Russian government appealed to Britain and France to do something to ease the pressure. Britain already had an expedition in Mesopotamia working its way up the Tigris River. This diverted some Turkish troops, but a larger diversionary attack was necessary. Furthermore, the fighting in France had quickly turned from the rapid attack and response of the early weeks of the war into the stalemate of trench warfare. First Lord of the Admiralty Winston Churchill proposed a plan to both aid the Russians and accomplish a dramatic victory in the Mediterranean, a feat that was seemingly impossible in France. Churchill believed that a naval assault on the Dardanelles, the straits that connected the Mediterranean with the Ottoman capital of Constantinople, could possibly force Turkey out of the war completely and rob Germany of an ally. Although the naval bombardment of the forts guarding the Dardanelles was initially successful, minefields turned the ships back. The Allied governments then decided to send in the army to secure the area that the navy could not sail past. It was on the beaches of the Gallipoli peninsula, the western flank of the Dardanelles straits, to which the ANZACs were committed.

The invasion force, under the command of General Sir Ian Hamilton, consisted of a British and a French division as well, but it was the ANZACs who formed the bulk of the force and became the most famous force in the battle. The landings took place 25 April 1915. The ANZACs were landed a mile north of their assigned target beach. They landed on a narrow strand at the foot of a cliff from which well-placed Turkish machine guns swept the soldiers. The earlier naval assault had caught the Turks by surprise, but they were well prepared for the arrival of the army troops. Unable to return to their boats and unwilling to stand and be slaughtered, the ANZACs scaled the bluffs and dislodged the Turks from the top. They quickly followed the retreating Turks onto still higher ground a few hundred yards inland, and elements of the ANZAC force actually reached the highest elevation about a half mile inland, from where they could see the waters of the straits. However, the disarray caused by the mistake in the landings, as well as the almost individual nature of the fighting, caused the ANZAC commanders to order a withdrawal of the most forward elements in order for the force to regroup and prepare for Turkish reinforcements. Had the forward elements been reinforced instead, the invasion probably would have been a success. Instead, the Turks were allowed to bring in their reserves to the highest ground and the quick operation turned into a eight-month stalemate reminiscent of the fighting taking place in France.

The Australians and New Zealanders who fought at Gallipoli suffered from the weather as well as enemy assaults, and heavy casualties were reported. The poor logistical planning by the British commanders, as well as the difficulties of the rocky terrain, conspired against them. Their determination and courage were so impressive to the Turks, however, that many of the positions the ANZACs defended retain to this day the names given to them by the foreigners during the battle. For example, the landing area where the men came ashore is still called ANZAC Cove. Colonel (later General) John Monash, a brigade commander at Gallipoli, wrote about the Australians in the force: "I have had plenty of opportunity of comparing them with the troops of British regular units and Territorials, and the British officers are the first to admit that for physique, dash, enterprise and sublime courage, the Australians are head and shoulders above any others.... In spite, however, of our heavy losses (a total of over half the brigade) the men, as I say, are cheerful, not to say jolly, and are only too eagerly awaiting the next advance. I am convinced that there are no troops in the world equal to the Australians in cool daring, courage and endurance" (Firkins, 1972). The New Zealanders performed no less well, and suffered no less.

The most successful part of the entire Gallipoli operation from the Allied standpoint, however, was the withdrawal. Although the Turks had mounted a stout defense and were not unaware of the Allied retreat, the ANZACs withdrew from their positions, assembled on the beaches, and were ferried out to the transports, all without the loss of a single soldier. The casualties had been high: the New Zealanders lost approximately 3,000 dead and 5,000 wounded of the 10,000 men in the ANZAC force, while the Australians lost some 7,000 combined casualties. The anniversary of the landing, 25 April, is called ANZAC Day and is a national holiday in both Australia and New Zealand, with memorial services and wreath-laying in almost every town in both countries.

The ANZACs were not through fighting after the Gallipoli fiasco. Some were posted to France and fought in the trenches, where they unfortunately came under the command of General Sir Hubert Gough, a particularly unimaginative commander with little regard for any soldiers who were not English. They continued to suffer heavy casualties, as did every unit in France during the war. Other Australians were sent to Mesopotamia where they were involved in the relief operations around the besieged Indian Army Sixth Division at Kut-al-Amara and for the rest of the campaign in that theater. The Australian First Light Horse Brigade served in Palestine and their charge at Beersheba in October 1918 was one of the last battles of World War I.

When World War II broke out in 1939 the empire again rapidly responded to Britain's call for aid. The Australians and New Zealanders who fought in North Africa in that war also came to be called ANZACs, but the term best denotes the World War I force. ANZAC Day observations, first practiced in 1916 in London, became annual soon thereafter and following World War II achieved the same importance as Memorial Day in the United States as an occasion to remember the dead of all the wars in which each country fought.

In one of history's tragic ironies, the Turkish republic established in 1924 joined the nations fighting the Axis in World War II and became an ally of Australia and New Zealand. The "father" of modern Turkey, Mustapha Kemal Ataturk, commanded the Turkish forces on the Gallipoli Peninsula. He oversaw the construction of a monument to the ANZACs and every year ANZAC Day is observed in Turkey, with Turkish, Australian, and New Zealand officials in attendance. A 1934 quote of Ataturk is inscribed on the Turkish ANZAC memorial: "Those heroes that shed their blood and lost their lives; you are now lying in the soil of a friendly country. Therefore rest in peace. There is no difference between Johnnies and Mehemets to us where they lie side by side here in this country of ours. You, the mothers, who sent their sons from far-away countries, wipe away your tears; your sons are now lying in our bosom and are at peace. After having lost their lives on this land they have become our sons as well."

References: Firkins, Peter, *The Australians in Nine Wars* (London: Robert Hale & Co., 1972); Moorehead, Alan, *Gallipoli* (London: H. Hamilton, 1956); Thomson, Alastair, *ANZAC Memories* (New York: Oxford University Press, 1994).

Army of Northern Virginia

The primary military force of the Confederate States of America (1861–1865).

The 11 states of the United States that seceded from the Union in 1860–1861 faced an almost impossible task. Creating a successful country with the governmental form of a confederation is difficult enough, but by firing on Union troops at Fort Sumter in

Charleston Harbor the seceding states provoked a war that they almost certainly could not win. The Confederacy's economy, based almost exclusively on agriculture, lacked the resources necessary to fight an industrialized enemy, yet with a motivation that drew on the inspiration of the American Revolution, the rebellious states willingly engaged in what we know as the Civil War. Whatever the wisdom of their cause, the armies they fielded displayed remarkable courage and tenacity, with the Army of Northern Virginia leading the effort. The Confederacy named its armies after their theater of operations, hence their two primary forces were this and the Army of Tennessee. It was the leadership of its commander, Robert E. Lee, that imparted special status to the Army of Northern Virginia. Lee led that force from June 1862 through the final surrender in April 1865.

Lee was regarded by U.S. Army commanding general Winfield Scott as the most talented of American military leaders, and he encouraged President Abraham Lincoln to appoint Lee commander of the Union armies. Lee, after extreme soul-searching, decided he could not make war against his home state of Virginia, so he resigned his commission and joined the Confederate army. He served in the background for the first year of the war, but upon the wounding of General Joseph Johnston in the Peninsular Campaign of June 1862 Lee was appointed commander of the Army of Northern Virginia. He initially had a poor reputation with the Confederate troops owing to his dedication to digging defenses for the capital city of Richmond, Virginia—a project that brought him the nickname "King of Spades" and "Granny" Lee. Once having taken over from Johnston, however, Lee proved himself anything but conservative.

He knew his opponent, George McClellan, from West Point, and was aware of his overly cautious temperament. Lee therefore attacked McClellan's far larger force. Lee lost the opening battle, but McClellan withdrew. In the Seven Days Campaign that followed, Lee lost four of five battles, yet it was McClellan who retreated from the outskirts of Richmond back to the port city of Yorktown. By sheer aggression and audacity, Lee had convinced McClellan that the Union faced an overwhelming force. Lee's knowledge of his opponents, gathered from years serving alongside them or knowing them from the U.S. Military Academy, enabled him time and again to outthink opposing generals. His daring, which he showed by attacking with smaller forces, dividing his forces in the face of the enemy, and launching surprise attacks, continually baffled his opponents and turned Lee into an icon of the Confederate army.

Lee's leadership emboldened his men who, like their enemies, came to believe Lee could perform any feat and outsmart any enemy. His men responded by fighting with ferocity born of confidence and loyalty. As the war progressed, however, that was the mainstay of the Confederate effort, for the effective Union blockade of Southern harbors made maintenance of the army increasingly difficult. The Confederacy's defensive strategy forced its armies to fight and live off its own land, which soon became unable to support them. Victories over Union generals John Pope in August 1862, Ambrose Burnside in December 1862, and Joseph Hooker in May 1863, as well as the inability of McClellan to operate effectively when opposed to Lee at Antietam in September 1862 all served to enhance the status of Lee's army. However, continued fighting without steady supplies made the army increasingly ragged. After his defeat of Hooker at Chancellorsville in 1863 Lee stated that feeding his men caused him much more concern than did fighting Union armies.

It was that need for supplies that convinced Lee to take the war to the North in June 1863 both to live off the enemy's land for a while and hopefully to encourage the Northern peace advocates as well as potential European allies. The Army of Northern Virginia marched through Maryland into Pennsylvania in late June. The residents of both states were appalled at the state of the Confederate troops and unbelieving that such a rabble could defeat their Union soldiers. Rumors of a supply of shoes at the small town of Gettysburg, Pennsylvania, brought about a skirmish that led to the battle that changed the fortunes of the Confederacy. Lee was once again outnumbered, and finally the steadiness of new Union General Gordon Meade allowed that numerical superiority to tell. Unable to turn the flanks of the Union position on 2 July Lee gambled that the attacks had weakened the Union center sufficiently to allow a breakthrough there. He ordered some 10,000 men under the command of George Pickett to assault the Union position on Cemetery Ridge in a frontal assault. His men unhesitatingly followed his orders into the teeth of overwhelming artillery fire that caused almost 75 percent losses. When Lee openly wept and apologized to the survivors for ordering the assault, their response was to apologize to him for their failure and to volunteer to try again.

Lee withdrew from Gettysburg on 4 July back to defensive positions in Virginia. More than half of the 75,000 men he had taken into Gettysburg had failed to return with him to Virginia. He had failed in his plan to exploit northern supplies, but his army was allowed to recover by cautious Union generalship. Through the remainder of 1863 and into 1864 Lee labored to rebuild his shattered forces, while the legendary army held the Northern forces at bay by reputation alone. Only with the arrival of Ulysses Grant in May 1864 did Union caution come to an end. Grant brought more than 100,000 men into Virginia, almost double Lee's strength, and throughout the month of May lost battle after battle, yet continued to maneuver ever closer to Richmond. At the Wilderness, Spotsylvania, the North Anna River, and Cold Harbor, Confederate forces exacted a terrible toll on Union armies, yet Grant had replacements while Lee did not. In June, Grant was stymied at Petersburg, south of Richmond, and obliged to lay siege for nine months. Lee's army fought to maintain the railroad lines into Petersburg that brought whatever meager sustenance they received, but when the last line fell to Union troops in April 1865 the Army of Northern Virginia, down to less than 10,000 men, had no choice but to flee westward. Finally surrounded on 8 April, Lee met with Grant to surrender at Appomattox Courthouse on 9 April 1865.

Robert E. Lee, 1865

By the end of the war, the Army of Northern Virginia was fighting almost on courage alone, and in many cases even that failed. Desertions after Gettysburg and during the siege at Petersburg hurt the Confederate cause, but in reality had little effect on the final outcome. Still, Lee inspired almost fanatical devotion and even his opponents could not help but respect and praise him. His men came to call themselves "Lee's Miserables," referring to the recently published Hugo novel. They had suffered privations caused not only by the nature of warfare itself but also by the inability of a confederation-style government to harness national resources and cooperation. In every battle the Army of Northern Virginia fought, it was outnumbered, but almost always inflicted greater casualties on its enemies than it received itself. Had Lee decided not to surrender but to disperse his men into the Virginia hills and fight a guerrilla war, those remaining would certainly have followed him. As one Texas soldier said of Lee after the battle of the Wilderness, "I'd charge Hell itself for that old man."

In Arlington National Cemetery, built on the grounds of Robert E. Lee's confiscated estate, stands a memorial to the Confederate dead. "Not for fame or reward, not for place or rank, not lured by ambition or goaded by necessity, but in simple obedience to duty as they understood it, these men suffered all, sacrificed all, endured all...and died."

References: Foote, Shelby, *The Civil War, a Narrative*, 3 vols. (New York: Vintage Books, 1958–1972); MacPherson, James, *Ordeal by Fire* (New York: McGraw-Hill, 1982); Smith, Page, *Trial by Fire* (New York: McGraw-Hill, 1982).

Aryans

An ancient Indo-European population that conquered and settled in India during the second millennium B.C.

The earliest known civilization in India was that of the Harappans, who established well-organized cities in the valley of the Indus River in the third millennium B.C. By about 2000 B.C. that civilization was beginning to fade, probably because of climatic changes that brought about shifts in the rivers and resultant widespread flooding. By sheer coincidence, as the Harappans were weakening, a group of invaders appeared from the steppes of the Caucasus. The Aryans were mostly nomadic, herding sheep, horses, and cattle, and (like most nomadic peoples) were more warlike than the agricultural inhabitants of northern India. Both by migration and by force of arms, they came to dominate the area of the upper Indus valley and over time spread eastward down the Ganges.

The Aryans took their name from the word in their language, Sanskrit, that means "noble." The Aryans themselves are identified as a language, not a racial, group. The fact that their area of origin made them lighter skinned than the people they conquered has nothing to do with the language they spoke, so equating "Aryan" with "white" is an incorrect, nineteenth-century concept made worse by some twentieth-century racists. The original Aryans did, however, institute a practice that called for separation of their peoples from that of the conquered. The Aryans had a society based on four basic classes: priests, warriors, merchant/artisans, and laborers. This class division did not include the conquered peoples of India, and this attitude was the basis of the caste system that dominates India to this day; hence the terms "outcasts," or the "untouchables" of modern India.

Aryan weaponry included bows and arrows, hurling spears, and battle axes. Aryans probably fought from chariots, thus easily overwhelming whatever type of foot soldier that may have opposed them in India. They did not conquer in order to spread culture, but to acquire wealth, especially cattle. In fact, their word for "war" translated as "desire for more cows." Once they established themselves in India, each region was ruled by a king who was somewhat limited in his power by an advisory council of warriors. At the top of the society they imposed were the warriors, or Kshatriyas, who (like the Vikings) believed that the ultimate honor was to die in battle; and the ultimate disgrace, to die in bed. Their primary god was Indra, whose hard-fighting and hard-living ways mirrored the Aryan warrior ideal. Contemporary literature described "the Aryans as a rowdy crew fond of beer, who engaged in bragging about their gambling, fighting, horse-racing and womanizing" (Stearns et al., 1992).

The Aryans ultimately settled down to an agricultural way of life, but their early years in India were characterized by their primary herding ways. The plains of northern India provided good grazing land and their horse and cattle herds grew. Cattle became the most valuable of commodities, possibly foreshadowing the sacredness of cattle in the Hindu faith. The Aryans' horsemanship was famous and was the reason for their military successes, as the Harappans had neither cavalry nor chariots. Considering the Aryans' Indo-European heritage, their common use of the horse is to be expected, as later steppe peoples like the Scythians were master riders as well.

The greatest legacy of the Aryans are the religious works passed down originally through the priesthood. The Vedas are a collection of religious rituals handed down through the oral tradition and finally committed to writing when that skill was introduced about 700 B.C. The ceremonies practiced and the gods worshipped through the Vedas laid the groundwork for the introduction of the Hindu faith, the dominant religion of India for some 2,000 years.

As conquerors of northern India early in the second millennium B.C., and of the northeastern plains and Ganges River valley between 1000 and 500 B.C. the Aryans became the dominant inhabitants of India as they settled into agricultural pursuits. This less mobile pursuit bred—as it almost always does—a less martial society, but, thanks to their mountainous frontiers, the Indians managed to remain fairly isolated from later conquerors. Alexander the Great spent two years fighting and negotiating in northwestern India, installing a Greek administration in some areas. After his death, however, Chandragupta Maurya overthrew the bureaucracy and established an Indian empire. Not until the Islamic invasion of India in the 800s a.d. did outside forces have much luck in penetrating the subcontinent.

References: Gokhale, Balkrishna, *Ancient India: History and Culture* (Bombay and New York: Asia Publishing House, 1959); Stearns, Peter, et al., *World Civilizations* (New York: HarperCollins, 1992); Wheeler, Radha, *Early India and Pakistan* (New York: Praeger, 1959); Wolpert, Stanley, *India* (Englewood Cliffs, NJ: Prentice-Hall, 1965).

Ashanti

A West African tribe in the nineteenth century, known for its local dominance and resistance to European colonization.

The predecessors of the population that inhabits modern-day Ghana in northwestern Africa were the Akan tribe, probably descended from immigrants from the western Sudan region. They mined the gold available in the region and engaged in profitable trade with both Moslem and later European merchants. The cross-Sahara trade in gold to the Mediterranean coast made the source of that wealth almost mythical. When the Portuguese began exploring southward along the African continent's western shore, the area of the Akan people came to be called the Gold Coast.

The dominant tribe among the southern Akan peoples were the Ashanti (or Asante). In the mid-1600s the Ashanti expanded from their homeland around Lake Bosumtwi to encompass most of the central forest region of the country. The primary military leader in this era was Oti Akenten (reigned circa 1630–1660), who either conquered his neighbors or brought them into a confederation as allies. Under his descendant, Osei Tutu, at the end of the century, the confederacy was transformed into an empire, with its capital established at Kumasi. Osei Tutu took the title *asantehene,* or "King of the Ashanti." Osei Tutu allowed the subordinate tribes to retain their local customs and took the chief of each into a tribal council, both practices creating a relatively easy assimilation into the empire. The assimilated tribes exercised local autonomy, but in times of outside threat united under the asantehene's direction. By the 1820s the Ashanti held sway over a huge area that encompassed three subordinate tribes and abutted the coastal possessions of the Fanti and other tribes that carried on trade with the Europeans.

The first Europeans, the Portuguese, built forts on the coast to protect their trading interests, which at first was gold but soon came to include slaves. Over time the Portuguese were joined or supplanted by Dutch, Danish, and even Swedish interests. However, by the 1820s the primary European power along the coast was Great Britain. All the Europeans stayed along the coast and traded with the interior tribes through local representatives. As long as the goods came to them, the Europeans were happy to leave the interior jungle well enough alone. The British bought out other European business interests and forts until, by the 1870s, they controlled the coastline completely and declared the Gold Coast a British colony. It was the decades-old British ban on slavery, however, that began to bring the British into affairs in the interior. That, coupled with the traditional Ashanti expansionist policies, guaranteed conflict.

In the first quarter of the nineteenth century, the Europeans dealt with the Ashanti peacefully, recognizing the preeminence of their inland empire. As long as trade goods arrived at the coast with a minimum of trouble, the Ashanti were free to do as they liked with their neighbors. It was when the British attempted to recruit coastal tribes to aid in the suppression of the slave trade that fighting started. Governor Charles MacCarthy tried to rouse the coastal Fanti and Ga tribes to resist Ashanti power, but in 1824 MacCarthy died leading native troops in a disastrous defeat. When the Ashanti attacked again in 1826 they were turned back, but their power was hardly diminished. The British attempted to consolidate the coastal tribes into a protectorate, which was formalized by the signing of the Bond of 1844. This gave the British judicial authority over serious crimes, a greater voice in local administration, and a greater role in local defense. The British purchase of Elmina Castle, the last Dutch trading post, upset the Ashanti. They had viewed the Dutch as allies and good trading partners and saw the British acquisition of Elmina as a closing of the Ashanti coastal trade outlet.

The Ashanti launched attacks on the coastal tribes and gained early successes, but the arrival of British reinforcements under command of Major General Sir Garnet Wolseley set off what came to be called the Ashanti War. Wolseley brought with him an outstanding group of subordinates, most of whom later reached general's rank. He convinced the British government to supply him with battalions from three British regiments to supplement the First and Second West India Regiments and the few native troops he managed to coerce into accompanying him. As European troops fared notoriously badly in the climate of the Gold Coast, Wolseley planned his campaign to punish the Ashanti to take place in the dry months of December 1873 through February 1874. He planned on sending three columns to converge on the Ashanti capital at Komasi, but only his command encountered Ashanti forces and did any fighting; the other two columns served as little more than diversions. The single trail leading to Komasi ran through dense jungle, the occasional open ground being quite swampy. The track had, through years of use in wet weather, been worn as deep as a trench.

Wolseley tried to maintain his units in an open square formation, but the terrain kept them from holding their positions very well. Some 30 miles short of Komasi, the British encountered their first major Ashanti force, before the village of Amoafu. Ashanti forces numbered possibly 40,000 and were positioned on the crests of low hills in a crescent formation. Their plan was to lure the British down the road into the open end of their position, then use their traditional enveloping tactics. The Ashanti used the high grass and tall trees to great advantage, but their muskets were not up to the quality of the rifles carried by Wolseley's men. Although the Ashanti warriors remained concealed, the smoke from their muskets gave away their positions and drew rifle, artillery, and rocket fire, for the British had four Congreve rocket launchers. Still, the Ashanti did have the advantage of superior numbers and knowledge of the terrain, and were also able at one point to send a body of men around the British rear. They were in turn outflanked by the British rear guard.

The two flanking forces of the British square made their way forward through dense jungle to take the high ground and blunt the Ashanti flanking units with rocket fire. The artillery in the center killed hundreds of Ashanti warriors. In spite of confusion (made worse by the echoing of the gunfire giving the impression of being attacked from all sides) the British and West Indian troops beat back the Ashanti force and captured Amoafu. They suffered some 250 casualties (although only three Europeans and one African dead) while inflicting possibly 2,000 casualties on the Ashanti, who had no fear of closing with their enemy if need be. The Ashanti could not, however, stand up to the artillery fire. The Ashanti continued to harass the British column as it progressed northward, attacking at times in such great numbers that it seemed as if the entire jungle were moving. The British were able to take advantage of the deep-rutted track for cover and drove off all the Ashanti assaults.

When Wolseley's men reached Komasi, the town had been abandoned. The asantehene had fled, but left much loot behind. He also left behind evidence of why the local tribes feared the Ashanti more than they did the British: a large pile of skulls told the tale of widespread human sacrifice. Henry Stanley, traveling with the column as a war correspondent, estimated that the bones of 120,000 victims lay scattered around the area. The British burned the town, blew up the palace, and withdrew. They returned to the coast almost unmolested. The British were able after this victory to enforce a peace treaty whereby the Ashanti abandoned all their claims to coastal territories. They were also obliged to keep the road to Komasi open for trade. Gold and palm oil flowed fairly steadily to British merchants at the coast, but the Ashanti had been warriors too long to go quietly into oblivion. A rebellion in 1896 brought another British punitive expedition that again occupied Komasi, then abolished the position of asantehene. The Ashanti tried again in 1900 but another defeat broke their power for good. In 1902 the British proclaimed all Ashanti lands to be under their control, included in the jurisdiction of the governor of the Gold Coast.

Their contacts with Moslems and Europeans for centuries through the gold trade had given the Ashanti enough superior weaponry to dominate their tribal neighbors, but in the face of European arms they could not stand. The Ashanti have been described as being an African version of the Prussians of nineteenth-century Europe in that they practiced universal military training and fielded a disciplined force that used the terrain and their numbers wisely. Had they been better armed, the outcome for them could have been quite different.

References: Farwell, Byron, *Queen Victoria's Little Wars* (New York: Harper & Row, 1972); Featherstone, Donald, *Colonial Small Wars* (Newton Abbot, Devon: David & Charles, 1973); Keegan, John, "Ashanti," in *War Monthly,* no. 7, 1974.

Assyrians

An ancient population known for its Middle Eastern empire built on terror and cruelty between the ninth and seventh centuries B.C.

Although many populations prior to the Assyrians engaged in war, the Assyrians were the first to make it a national pastime and the focus around which their society was built. Assyria's roots lay in four cities in the upper reaches of the Tigris River: Ashur, Arbela, Kalakh, and Nineveh. Their population was probably a mixture of Semites from the south, Hittites from the west, and Kurds from the north. They adopted the Sumerian language and artistic style, then further modified these by contact with Babylon. The cities grew up under the domination of the Kassites, with Shalmaneser regarded as the first Assyrian king. For the first few hundred years of their existence, the Assyrians depended on local levies to fill out the ranks of the army in time of need, with each city's governor having only a palace guard of perhaps 1,000 men as a standing force. These governors ultimately became the cadre of leaders when the Assyrians began to practice war more seriously.

The Assyrians first began to show aggressive tendencies in the latter half of the thirteenth century B.C. expanding westward toward the Euphrates and downriver to Babylon, which they held for a time. A hundred years later, Tiglath-Pileser I attacked as far as the Mediterranean, but could not hold his conquests. His successors fell into obscurity until the ninth century B.C. In the intervening 200 years, the Assyrians farmed, hunted, and defended themselves from their neighbors. King Adadnirari II began the return to expansionary ways and laid the groundwork for the coming Assyrian empire.

Through the administration of Adadnirari II's grandson, Ashurnasirpal II, the Assyrians raided downriver and westward, honing their army's skills. Babylon remained too strong in the south to conquer yet, and in the west Syria called on Phoenician and Israelite assistance to beat back an attack at the battle of Qarqar in 853 B.C. It was Tiglath-Pileser III (744–727 B.C.) who finally began to conquer widely. He defeated Babylon and had himself crowned king of that city, then captured Damascus and solidified his control. It was this king who really became the first emperor, not only of the conquered territories but of his own land. No longer did each of the four cities exercise autonomy. The palace guards of earlier days became the core of a new standing army that was in almost constant action for more than 100 years.

Sennacherib before the City of Lachish. Bas-relief in the Palace of Nineveh as depicted in a lithograph by Austen Henry Layard in The Monuments of Nineveh (London, 1853).

Tiglath-Pileser III maintained forces primarily of infantry, but also of cavalry and chariots, in a ratio of approximately 100 infantry to ten cavalry to one chariot. The infantry was primarily made up of Assyrian peasant stock, armed with spears and shields in a phalanx-type formation. The large rectangular shield was usually used to protect an archer, with the foot soldier and archer fighting in pairs. Carrying up to 50 arrows, massed archers could deliver extremely deadly fire. Lancers and slingers were also employed. The cavalry was both of heavy and light types and employed en masse riding horses often bred especially for them by the government. The cavalry frequently rode in pairs, one rider controlling both horses and using his shield or lance while the other rider used his bow. The chariots initially carried a crew of two, a driver and an archer. Later a third and then fourth man was added to carry shields for protecting the others. The chariots were used either in the attack as a shock force or around the flanks for harassment and pursuit.

When the Assyrians conquered a country, its surviving army was obliged to fight alongside them. This gave the Assyrian army a certain diversity in weaponry, depending on the nationality absorbed: Slingers, mounted archers, and light cavalry all joined the heavier-armed Assyrian forces. Perhaps the key element in Assyrian superiority, however, was the widespread use of iron, which had previously been less available and normally only used in the weapons of the nobility who could afford it. This gave the Assyrians a great edge over those societies still dependent on bronze. The Assyrians also perfected siege tactics that had been developed centuries earlier in other societies. Battering rams, along with sapping and mining of the city walls, were the preferred methods. Sometimes earthen ramps were constructed to allow the soldiers to overcome the walls.

Once a province was defeated, the Assyrians occupied it with a royally appointed governor and a garrison for whatever forts may have survived. All were under the direct control of the king, known to himself and his subjects as "the great king, the legitimate king, the king of the world, king of Assyria, king of all the four rims of the earth, king of kings, prince without rival, who rules from the Upper Sea to the Lower Sea." Kings were strong men, for they had to both lead their armies in battle and guard against palace intrigues. They also kept a tight rein on their governors by appointing family members or by stationing spies (openly or covertly) to their entourage.

The Assyrians ruled their conquered territories ruthlessly, extracting money, supplies, and manpower. Royal records brag on the number of enemy soldiers slain and prisoners tortured. For example, Ashurnasirpal II boasted, "I destroyed them, tore down the walls and burned the town with fire; I caught the survivors and impaled them on stakes in front of their towns" (Starr, 1965). It was this treatment that proved the Assyrians' ultimate undoing.

Successive kings spread Assyrian power southeastward down the Tigris and Euphrates as far as the Persian Gulf and southwestward past the Mediterranean coast into Egypt as far up the Nile as Thebes. In spite of the terror they spread, they also spread urbanization, the culture of Babylon (which they had adopted as their own), and the worship of their gods (primarily Ashur). Trade and industry expanded and Assyrians began to make profits other than by looting. These were not enough, however, to replace the great wealth that plunder brought in, so the still weak economy could not stand on its own. Nevertheless, it was Assyrian high-handedness that caused such resentment that when the army was not engaged in conquering new territory, it was putting down revolts in provinces already occupied.

The constant warfare both on the frontiers and against captured peoples proved too much of a drain on the army. The Assyrian peasant, who was its backbone, came to be too rare a commodity, and dependence on an increasing number of foreign troops proved unfeasible. It was just too difficult to maintain loyalty with terror and few troops were willing to voluntarily aid in the suppression of their own people. This weakening of the Assyrian army's quality, coupled with constant revolts against its rule, brought the Assyrians to a swift downfall. In 612 B.C. attacks by the Scythians from the Caucasus and the Medes to the east brought the Assyrian Empire down in a matter of weeks. The main beneficiary of the Assyrian rule proved to be Cyrus the Persian, whose benevolent manner was so radically different that cities and provinces often surrendered to his army without a fight in order to enjoy the relative blessings of his leadership. The Persian Empire inherited some of Assyria's military methods along with its imperial administration, and their establishment of control over what had been Assyria's dominion was swift, relatively painless, and profitable.

References: Starr, Chester, *A History of the Ancient World* (New York: Oxford University Press, 1965); Wise, Terence, *Ancient Armies of the Middle East* (London: Osprey Publishing, 1981); Wiseman, D. J., "The Assyrians," in John Hackett, ed., *Warfare in the Ancient World* (London: Sidgwick and Jackson, 1989).

Aztecs

The dominant population, conquering Mexico immediately prior to Spanish conquest and colonization of the fifteenth century.

Much of Central America was dominated by the Toltec peoples until their downfall about 1200 A.D. The power vacuum that followed was coincidental with the arrival of nomadic tribes from the north. One of these tribes was from Aztlan and came to be known as Aztecs, or People from Aztlan. They drifted south into the valley of central Mexico and became subject to whatever power was able to achieve temporary hegemony. The Aztecs ultimately settled on the western side of Lake Texcoco, where they began to adapt themselves to the already established practice of building "floating gardens" of built-up silt. Here they established the city of Tenochtitlan in the mid-fourteenth century. A second city, Tlatelolco, was built by a second Aztec faction. The two cities put themselves under the protection of rival powers: Tenochtitlan under Culhuacan, Tlatelolco under the Tepanecs.

Through the latter part of the fourteenth century, the Tepanecs came to dominate the valley and they expanded their power across the mountains to the west to encompass an area of perhaps 50,000 square kilometers. This consolidation was performed by the Tepanec king Tezozomoc, but after his death in 1423 the various city-states he had dominated began to rebel. Three powers joined together into a Triple Alliance to replace the Tepanecs, and one of those three was the Aztecs of Tenochtitlan. Despite the occasional disagreement, the three worked fairly well together and dominated central Mexico for 90 years. From 1431 to 1465 they consolidated their hold over the former Tepanec domain, and then began a period of expansion. The Aztecs came to be the dominant partner in the triumvirate, but the three tribes collectively spread the empire from the Atlantic to the Pacific and as far southward as the modern-day border of Mexico and Guatemala. Only two tribes remained recalcitrant, the Tlaxaltecs and the Tarascans. The Aztecs established garrisons along disputed borders and occasionally warred with them although they never subjugated them.

The Aztecs led the expansion for a number of reasons. Mainly they were expanding their trading routes while incorporating a larger tax base among the conquered peoples. They also fought for religious reasons. The Aztecs worshipped, among other gods, the god of the sun, Huitzilopochtli. The

Aztec priest performing the sacrificial offering of a living human heart to the war god Huitzilopochtli (From the Codex Magliabecchi, 1904)

Aztec religion taught that history moved in cycles, the end of which came with the destruction of the sun. To stay healthy and shining, the sun god required sacrifices to eat, and the Aztecs went conquering for sacrificial offerings. The pyramids that dominated the city of Tenochtitlan were large altars that saw the daily execution of prisoners of war. On days of special celebration, several thousand might be sacrificed. This need for offerings drove the Aztecs to conquest, but did not create loyal subjects.

The Aztecs developed a highly structured military organization, led by the nobility and the elite warriors. The warriors were in the front ranks, dressed in elaborate costumes festooned with feathers and animal skins. Their primary weapons were wooden swords with chunks of obsidian embedded along the edges to create a razor-sharp blade. Obsidian was also the primary material for spear heads and javelin points. The javelins were propelled by *atlatls* (spear throwers), which greatly increased their range. Slings and bows and arrows made up the missile weapons.

Peculiar to the Aztec society was the practice of "flower wars," or *xochiyaoyotl.* These were conflicts of relatively low intensity, in which small bands of warriors engaged in what was almost ritual combat. Both sides would agree in advance to fight at an appointed time and place and with an equal number of troops. Prior to the battle, ceremonies were performed to honor the gods. The two forces approached each other with battle cries and the pounding of swords on leather shields. Combat, once begun, broke into individual duels. The main object was not to inflict death and defeat but to wound and capture enemy soldiers to be used in sacrifices. Units would be rotated in and out of the battle every quarter hour or so and the battles could last for days.

Sometimes these flower wars were preludes to invasion and conquest, but they could also be used both for training young soldiers and exercising political influence without the costs of a major war. As the Aztec Empire stretched over too much territory to be ruled directly, the threat of retribution was the chief Aztec tool in maintaining sufficient control to keep the tribute flowing. By winning these flower wars the Aztecs could keep their warriors in shape and demonstrate their prowess to neighbors. Also, by using only a small number of troops in these conflicts, other units could be employed simultaneously capturing villages and towns allied to the formal enemy in the flower war. As the season for fighting in Central America was December to April, conquests generally had to be accomplished quickly. The Aztecs found that subversion of their opponents' allies, coupled with victory in the flower wars, was often the best way to keep potential rivals from growing too strong.

When needed, however, the Aztec army could fight serious wars of annihilation, as demonstrated against tribes ranging from 150 miles north of Tenochtitlan to the borders of modern-day Guatemala. When the Spanish arrived, Hernán Cortés found the Tlaxcallan people (living just east of Tenochtitlan) to be aggressive fighters that almost wiped out his small command. Only the discipline and fire power the Spaniards demonstrated kept them alive in several battles, and that impressed the Tlaxcallans enough to ally themselves with Cortés to fight against Montezuma and the Aztecs. Had they continued to harass the Spaniards to annihilation, the history of Spanish relations with Mesoamerica may have been quite different.

Once in control of their empire, the Aztecs expanded and beautified the city of Tenochtitlan. The city reached a population of perhaps 200,000, which may have numbered one fifth of the Aztec population. The total number of subject peoples might have taken the empire's population as high as six million at the start of the sixteenth century. The capital city was laid out in logical order with straight streets and many canals, along which trade moved by boats. When Montezuma II came to power in 1502 the Aztec empire was well established and he was responsible for much of the lavish architecture and decoration in the city. Tenochtitlan's sister city, Tlatelolco, which the Tenochtitlan Aztecs took under their control in 1475, became the commercial center and contained the largest market in central America. The Spaniards under Cortés, who arrived in the city in 1519, estimated that 60,000 people attended the market days. The constant need for sacrificial victims created a resentment among all the subject peoples, however, and when the Spaniards arrived they were able to gain allies to assist them in their attacks on the Aztec empire. Although the Aztecs were in many ways more advanced than the Europeans, they lacked the necessary weaponry and resistance to foreign diseases to defeat their invaders. The Aztecs created outstanding works of art and developed an extensive hieroglyphic writing system. However, their scientific knowledge was extremely limited. Even without the arrival of the Spaniards, it is questionable how much longer the tribes of central America would have accepted the military dominance and religious practices of the Aztecs.

References: Hassig, Ross, *Aztec Warfare: Imperial Expansion and Political Control* (Norman: University of Oklahoma Press, 1995); Sahagun, Bernardino de, *The War of Conquest,* trans. Arthur Anderson and Charles Dibble (Salt Lake City: University of Utah Press, 1978); Townsend, Richard, *The Aztecs* (London: Thames and Hudson, 1992).

B

Berserkers

Individual Viking warriors known during the eighth through eleventh centuries for their ferocity.

The berserkers are one of the most interesting and least understood aspects of the Viking warrior society. These were individuals who fought in such a blinding fury that they lost all sense of self and became unconscious killing machines without discrimination.

The term *berserker* has a disputed derivation. It has been suggested that it comes from the term "bare-sark," meaning "bare of shirt," or without armor. Many references to the berserkers mention their lack of body armor. The other primary suggestion is "bear-sark," describing the wearing of animal skins. Bear skin would seem to be the logical choice of fur, but in some of the sagas the berserkers are called "Wolf-Skins" or "wolf-coats" (ulfhedinn). The berserkers are often associated with the Norse god Odin, or Wodan, whose name possibly comes from the German wut, meaning "rage" or "fury," and the Gothic wods, meaning "possessed."

This kinship with the chief Norse god is illustrated in many of the legends concerning berserkers. One is that, like Odin, they could alter their form and become animals, or at least assume wolflike or bearlike qualities. *Hrolf's Saga* describes the hero Bjarki taking the shape of a bear during battle and killing more men than any five warriors. Georges Dumezil, in *Gods of the Ancient Northmen* (1973), describes this phenomenon as the *hamnigja,* the spirit or soul of the animal appearing in dreams or visions as well as (so the Vikings believed) in reality. The berserkers were also reputed to have had an immunity to weapons, either naturally or through the performance of incantations. This quality is described in many of the sagas. It could possibly be explained by the thickness of the animal skins they wore as protection or their blind rage that dulled any feeling of pain or wounding. Either way, the sight of berserker warriors receiving what should be mortal wounds and continuing to fight certainly had strong psychological effects on their enemies.

The berserkers may have belonged to a cult of Odin, whose practices and spells would have been revealed only to initiates. Emperor Constantine VII of Byzantium, who employed Vikings in his Varangian Guard, noted a dance his men engaged in while wearing animal skins. This could indicate the performance of cultish rites. Such a dance is also recorded in artwork on Swedish helmets, scabbards, and bracelets. A newly accepted member of the cult is sometimes described as having to undergo an initiation into a warrior band whereby he has to fight a bear. Such combats are also shown in artwork inscribed on Swedish helmets. In such a cult, a member probably would have learned the secrets of bringing on the fighting frenzy, and it has been suggested that the fury was a product of drugs or alcohol.

One drug proposed to bring about this condition is the hallucinogenic mushroom *Amanita mucaria.* Other researchers put the killing frenzy down to mental illness, epilepsy, or self-induced hysteria.

The appearance of the berserker was also important in instilling fear in the enemy. The animal skin itself, especially if the head was still attached and worn over the warrior's head, could present a frightening sight. This, along with an already established reputation as shape changers, provoked fear in the berserkers' own forces at times. Sagas tell of warriors who in the evening would become moody and quiet before going off by themselves, and many in camp saw in this hints of a werewolf. Berserkers are also often described as being particularly ugly, to the point of being mistaken for trolls. Whether this came from genetic makeup, or intentional actions to make themselves look worse, is unknown.

Once battle was joined, the warrior would go into his frenzy, called *berserkergang.* The flow of adrenaline must have been immense, because the aftermath of the fight always left the berserker drained. *Hrolf's Saga* describes it thus: "On these giants fell sometimes such a fury that they could not control themselves, but killed men or cattle, whatever came in their way and did not take care of itself. While this fury lasted they were afraid of nothing, but when it left them they were so powerless that they did not have half of their strength, and were as feeble as if they had just come out of bed from a sickness. This fury lasted about one day" (Fabing, 1956). The berserkers screamed like animals and showed incredible strength. This also over time could have contributed to their reputation as shape changers, who turned into bears. Indeed, many of these warriors would assume a "bear name," by adding "bjorn" or "biorn" to their given names, for example, Arinbjorn or Esbjorn. They also are reputed to have drunk bear or wolf blood in order to take on some of the animals' characteristics.

The berserkers were admired as warriors, and in battle they were often the vanguard. Their ties to Odin gave their commanders some elevated status as well, for Odin was seen in many societies as patron of rulers and chieftains. However, the potential for killing their own comrades was great. This put the berserkers in a kind of social limbo, for killing ones' fellows was looked upon in Norse society as the meanest of crimes. Thus, in many sagas the berserkers are portrayed as villains. They were often accused of raping maidens or even other mens' wives. It is probably this factor that brought about the end of the berserkers. In 1015 King Erik had them outlawed, along with duels. Prior to this reform, berserkers often challenged men to duels and then killed them while in berserkergang. They then took their victims' possessions and families, as was allowed under Viking law. In Iceland, the church outlawed the practice as well, stating that if anyone went berserk they would receive three years' banishment. Being a berserker was equated with being a heathen and practicing magic, neither of which a Christian church or society would allow. Finally succumbing to these civilizing pressures, berserkergang came to an end in the twelfth century.

References: Dumezil, Georges, *Gods of the Ancient Northmen* (Los Angeles: University of California Press, 1973); Fabing, Howard D., "On Going Berserk: A Neurochemical Inquiry," in *Scientific Monthly,* November 1956, vol. 83; Jones, Gwen, *Eirik the Red and Other Icelandic Sagas* (New York: Oxford University Press, 1961); Ward, Christy, "Description of the Berserk," (www.realtime.com/~gunnora).

Boers

Dutch South African population particularly known for its mastery of guerrilla warfare.

The southern portion of the African continent was the last to attract serious attention from Europeans. It is not surprising that the Dutch first settled people there, as they had most of the shipping going around the Cape of Good Hope en route to the East Indies.

They established a way station there in 1652 from which a colony began to grow. The victualing station needed farmers to provide the food and soldiers to provide protection, so a number of Dutch moved there to start a new life of farming, ranching, or hunting. The inhabitants called themselves *Boers,* Dutch for "farmer." Over time the Boers expanded their population and moved northward, pressing back the native population with mixed results: the Hottentots became their laborers, the Bushmen became targets of genocide, and the numerous Bantu tribes, such as the Zulu and Matabele, became rivals for control of the land.

When French forces occupied the Netherlands in 1795 the British responded by occupying the Dutch colony at the Cape. Increased British trade with India could not be threatened by French forces in southern Africa, though the British saw no economic value in the colony itself. Still, they took it as their own in 1806 and that ownership was confirmed in the peace process in Europe after Napoleon's defeat. Keeping the colony would not prove nearly as easy as gaining it. As the British began to export settlers to the colony, the Boers resented the intrusion. They had grown used to settling huge ranches and did not want a foreign population robbing them of what they considered their lands. The British could not abide the relationship the Boers had with the Hottentots, which was one of virtual slavery. When the new British administration began to act in favor of native rights, the Boers decided it was time to move. They pushed northeastward, paralleling the coast, into the area known as Natal, recently left empty because of native wars. When the British would not or could not commit sufficient forces to defend the frontiers the Boers were expanding, the Dutch saw it as "kaffir-loving," a policy of favoring "colored" over white. They decided to move again, far enough to get away from British politicians. Thus began the Great Trek.

Starting in 1835 some 14,000 people ultimately migrated into the veld land farther north—lands occupied by native groups who did not want to leave. Here the Zulu and

"The Vet River as Seen by the Boers" (Drawing by S. E. St. Leger)

Ndebele tribes resisted. Their societies, which emphasized military training, were willing to fight the Boers at every turn. Superior fire power finally was the deciding factor, and small Boer republics sprang up wherever they settled to raise their crops and herd their livestock. The Boers became even more conservative in their views: They believed that they were a people chosen by God, the land was theirs to take, and the natives were an inferior race whom it was permissible to use or abuse as they saw fit. When the British annexed Natal in 1842 some Boers stayed while others moved even further north across the Vaal River, establishing the Transvaal Republic.

The two white communities began to tolerate each other. Then, major changes came to the area: In 1867 diamonds were discovered just south of the Vaal River. There was a mining rush, mainly by the British, and the Boers were able to keep few claims. The new wealth created problems. The discoveries were made in territory claimed by both Boertrekkers and British; the British bought out the Dutch claims just south of the Vaal. The main labor force in the mines was composed of natives who, although they worked for much less than white miners, still made plenty of money—money that they spent on firearms to take back to their tribes. The traditional hostility between native and Boer grew sharper, and the British policies were sufficiently irregular to keep the whites hostile to each other as well. The Boers believed the British were too conciliatory to the natives. At the same time, the British occasionally treated the Natal tribes much like the Americans treated their native tribes during the westward expansion, putting them on reservations then persecuting them when the whites wanted the land. As native labor became more in demand, and therefore more expensive, the needs of white businessmen and the fears of black power both grew.

In 1852 the British had recognized the independence of the Transvaal, but the Dutch did not manage their republic well. Owing to expensive campaigns against local tribes and a defaulted foreign loan, the republic was in dire financial straits. In 1877 the British offered to annex the Transvaal, delivering the Boers from their financial problems and providing protection on the frontiers. The local government reluctantly agreed to accept the annexation temporarily while its representatives travelled to London to have it reversed. The reversal did not happen, but the Boers were in no financial or military state to halt the course of events. Britain wanted the Cape Colony to federate all the lands available, much as in Canada, and the Transvaal was necessary for that goal. If the British could establish a united native policy throughout the federation, certainly peace and prosperity would follow. Necessary also was domination over all native lands. The British invaded Zululand in 1878–1879 on trumped-up excuses and established control there. The Pedi were defeated and scattered a few months later and most other tribes saw the futility of resistance. Momentarily at least, the British had made good on their promise to protect the Boers from hostile natives.

Without a native threat, the Boers believed the British presence had become unnecessary and the Transvaal should have its independence restored. When the British refused ("As long as the sun shines over South Africa, the British flag will fly over Pretoria" [Pakenham, 1991]), the Boers began cleaning their rifles. When the British provoked an incident over a Boer who would not pay his taxes, the Boers began organizing. Under the leadership of Paul Kruger (nicknamed "Oom," uncle), who had gone to London to protest the annexation, the Boers declared their independence in November 1880. They raised a force of 7,000 men, three times what the British had in Transvaal, sent men to besiege British garrisons in Transvaal towns and began to fight a guerrilla war. In November and December 1880 and January 1881 they fought three battles and in each defeated a superior British detachment. The embarrassed British government hastily approved negotiations to give the Boers independence. The general on the spot, Sir George Colley, disagreed with the government's offer and decided to press on. He died, with the majority of his force of 400 men, at the battle of Majuba Hill in late January 1881. Kruger accepted the offer to negotiate, and in late March the Transvaal was again independent, although the British did retain the right to direct the Boers' foreign policy. God, "Oom Paul" Kruger, and Mauser rifles had delivered the faithful.

As if to reinforce the belief in divine protection that the Boers enjoyed, gold was soon discovered in the Transvaal. In order to exploit the mines, foreign *(uitlander)* engineers had to be brought in, and these tended to be British. By the late 1890s a large British population had migrated to the Boer republic in order to work the mines. In spite of the wealth they now enjoyed, the Boers remained wary. British expansionists, led by gold and diamond magnate Cecil Rhodes, had acquired land to the north of the Transvaal, effectively seizing the mineral rights, but more importantly denying the Boers any more room to expand. With British territory above and below them, the Boers felt sure that they would soon be obliged to defend their lands. When Rhodes sponsored a raid into the Transvaal, hoping futilely for a British uprising to grab the country and its riches for the empire, the Dutch farmers were confirmed in their fears. They responded by further denying political rights to uitlanders in their country, keeping them in the position of second-class citizens. The native population, of course, remained beyond the hope of even that lofty a status.

This was not a social position the British were prepared to accept. They appealed to the British government to protect them and, desiring not only wealth but the geographic position of Boer lands, the government responded. By controlling Egypt and having a dominant position in countries south of there, a transcontinental, Cape-to-Cairo railroad was possible. This would mean wealth and political power for the British Empire if it could build it. However, to do so the British needed to gain control of the right-of-way through the Boer republics of the Transvaal and the Orange Free State on its southern border. Additionally, some soldiers in the British army still chafed from the defeat the Boers dealt them in 1880-1881 and would truly savor revenge. The British public received a steady diet of anti-Boer propaganda to prepare them for the war that seemed inevitable.

Paul Kruger, now president of the Transvaal, saw the British designs and responded by launching preemptive attacks against British towns in Natal and along the southern and western borders of the Orange Free State. If the Boers could control Natal (which they believed the British stole from them after the Great Trek), the British would have a difficult time bringing in reinforcements. After all, the Cape Colony—even though long under British rule—had a Boer majority among its population.

Britain was again confident that the Boers could be easily overcome and again found themselves shocked. British garrisons were quickly besieged and Boer forces drove 100 miles into the Cape Colony. When the British finally began to arrive in large numbers in November of 1899, the Boers stopped to consolidate. When the British attacked in December, the Boers thrashed them three times in one week. By Christmas, the British had suffered 7,000 casualties. In the face of growing British forces, however, the Boers were ultimately forced to resort to guerrilla tactics. As the British made their way into Boer territory, their enemy melted away into the hills and harassed them with ambushes. The British responded with the one proven method of dealing with a guerrilla movement. As Mao Tse-tung would later write, the population is the sea in which the guerrilla fish swims. Take away the population, and the guerrilla has no one to provide food, information, or refuge. The British rounded up the Boer population of women and children and placed them in concentration camps where they could provide no assistance. They then began a slow, expensive process to literally corral the Boers. They crisscrossed the countryside with barbed wire fencing and regularly placed strongpoints. By building more and more fences, they gradually lessened the area inside which the Boers could operate. Any attempt to break through brought quick responses from the strongpoints. With a smaller and smaller area in which to operate and gather supplies, the Boers were finally starved into submission.

The fighting went on until May 1902 when the exhausted Boers reached the bitter end and signed a peace treaty. They were promised self-government sometime in the future plus immediate financial relief for the losses they suffered—and losses there were. Owing to poor initial management of the concentration camps, huge numbers of civilians died from typhoid, dysentery, and measles—some 28,000 Boer women and children out of a total of just over 111,000, and 14,000 out of almost 44,000 native internees. Seven thousand Boer men were killed in combat. The British lost 20,000 men and spent £200 million, but they had control over the land. The Boers and the British ultimately reached a relatively peaceful coexistence. When World War I came in 1914 the South African contingent helping the British was led by Jan Smuts, who had been one of the primary commanders of Boer forces.

References: Nuttingham, Anthony, *Scramble for Africa: The Great Trek to the Boer War* (London: Constable, 1970); Pakenham, Thomas, *The Scramble for Africa: White Man's Conquest of the Dark Continent* (New York: Random House, 1991); Reitz, Deneys, *Commando: A Boer Journal of the Boer War* (London: Faber & Faber, 1929).

Boxers

An ultranationalist Chinese faction, 1899–1900.

Throughout the nineteenth century, the ruling Manchu dynasty in China grew progressively weaker. This coincided with European colonial efforts in the Far East and resulted in first the British, and then other European powers, forcing concessions from the Chinese government. Not only were trade treaties forced on the Chinese, port cities were virtually assigned to each power as they carved out economic spheres of influence in various parts of China. Britain, France, Russia, Germany, and Japan all had territory in which they held exclusive trade rights. Although the Chinese did profit from this trade, there were serious negative side effects. The traditionally xenophobic Chinese believed that their culture, as the oldest in the world, was therefore the best. Having foreigners dictate policy, profit on their own terms, and introduce alien ideas offended Chinese sensibilities. By the 1890s many Chinese could no longer stand being treated as inferiors and began organizing themselves to do something about it.

Secret societies formed, taking the name *I-ho-ch'üan* (translating as "Righteous and Harmonious Fists"). Many of their banners displayed a fist icon, so the Westerners called them the Boxers. They took an extreme nationalist stance, demanding that everything foreign be destroyed or expelled. As their stance was anti-Christian as well, the Boxers did have some religious overtones, but their aims were primarily political and social. The Chinese government was divided over its attitude toward this society. The Emperor Kuang Hsü wanted to modernize China, taking advantage of Western progress, as had Japan. He, however, was a weak ruler and did not control the government. His mother, Empress Tzu Hsi, responded to the urging of reactionary elements in the government and seized power from her son. Although with no official connection to the Boxers, the empress covertly aided and encouraged their activities. She could thus explain to foreign ambassadors that it was an independent movement over which she had no control.

Unaware of or ignoring any signs of unrest, the Westerners went about their business of engaging in trade and making demands for concessions from the government. In 1899 the United States entered the

Imprisoned Boxers in their compound after the lifting of the blockade by the expeditionary forces. Photograph ca. 1900.

scene. American Secretary of State John Hay, wanting to gain inroads into the Chinese market but excluded because the Europeans controlled the ports, proposed what came to be called the Open Door Policy. Each nation could remain dominant in a single area, but all regions should be open to all foreign trading interests. This would open up markets currently denied to the Europeans because of the sphere-of-interest practice. With an increased customer base and increased access to previously untapped local goods, Hay argued, profits would surely rise. The policy would also, of course, allow America to get in on the China trade as well. The Europeans accepted Hay's proposal, although with varying degrees of enthusiasm.

This economic cooperation agreement was not long in place when the Boxers began direct attacks on Westerners. In Shantung Province, American missionaries were attacked and their converts abused or killed. Appeals to diplomatic personnel in Washington or the Chinese capital of Peking brought little response. In May 1900, Boxers began acting more openly in Peking. Weaponry was produced and purchased throughout the city. Attacks on individuals began in May and the Boxers burned a railway station outside Peking on 24 May. Placards around the city urged the Chinese to destroy the telegraph lines and the railroads as the first step toward ridding the country of the "foreign devils." Had the Boxers immediately followed up on this incident with assaults on the foreign embassies, they almost certainly would have massacred every European there. Instead, they continued to harass people in the streets for several weeks until the Europeans finally began to take seriously the threat to their safety. Chinese diplomats on 19 June ordered the Westerners out of Peking by the following day at 4:00 p.m. When the German ambassador left to register a protest with the Chinese government, he was shot and killed in the streets. Precisely at 4:00 p.m. the shooting started, with a Chinese sniper killing a French sentry.

Throughout the previous days, the Methodist missionaries had been pleading with the diplomats to rescue them and their converts. Just in time they were given permission to gather in the borrowed palace of Prince Su, next door to the British embassy. As all the legations were next to each other, the Europeans had a defensive position they could hold. Some 3,000 people were inside protected by only a few hundred military men with limited weaponry and ammunition. The Chinese attacked almost constantly, and when they were not assaulting the walls around the embassies, they were bombarding them or making noise. Although the Boxers were rarely armed with anything other than swords and knives, they were supported by Chinese imperial troops with modern weapons. How many Chinese were involved in the siege is a matter of speculation, but probably about 20,000 troops were involved, aided by thousands more Boxer volunteers.

Luckily for the defenders, the multinational group inside the embassy enclave rather quickly set aside national rivalries and elected the British ambassador, Sir Claude Macdonald, as their leader. Among the missionaries, diplomats, merchants, and travellers inside the compound were many with practical skills or military experience who could assist in the defense.

The chief Methodist missionary was Frank Gamewell, who before becoming a cleric was educated at Rensselaer Polytechnic in civil engineering. He was the only man in the entire group with any construction knowledge and he was immediately given the task of building and maintaining defensive strongpoints. Embassy guards from France, Germany, Japan, Britain, Russia, and the United States were each given a section of wall to defend.

The Chinese artillery wrought havoc among the people inside the compound, but made little headway against the walls, which Reverend Gamewell kept as stoutly repaired as possible. The Boxers tried to burn out the defenders by setting fire to the Hanlin Library abutting the British Embassy. As this contained a large collection of Chinese art and literary treasures, the Europeans were shocked to see the Chinese set it afire. With men, women, and children working the bucket brigades (and aided certainly by some fortuitous winds), the British Embassy was saved from serious damage, but the fire destroyed the library. Bitter fighting took place along the Tartar Wall, the position held by American marines. The Boxers also mined under the French legation and collapsed part of its walls, but the French defenders occupied the rubble and held on.

Several messengers had been dispatched to the coast, begging for relief. Unknown to the defenders (as the telegraph lines had been cut), the first relief force had been defeated and driven back and the Chinese held the key city of Tientsin. Although throughout the siege, the defenders on the walls looked toward Tientsin and were sure they saw signs of approaching armies, none came for weeks. The economic agreement Hay had negotiated the previous year among the Western powers now became the basis of military cooperation among them. All the interested countries sent troops in the first serious coalition effort since the defeat of Napoleon at Leipzig in 1814. On 13 July 1900 the multinational force attacked Tientsin and captured it after a 15-hour battle. With this in their possession to use as a base, the coalition forces set their sights on Peking, 75 miles away. They arrived on 12 August having fought harassing Boxers the entire way. No one was in supreme command, so the various national forces acted independently. The Russians attacked first and, although they forced an entrance into Peking, they soon found themselves in need of rescue. The individual forces assaulted various gates into the city, but the British found themselves before the one most lightly defended. They broke through on the evening of 13 August and made their way through an undefended sluice gate into the diplomatic compound. The troops, sent over from India, were greeted with hugs and kisses all around. The American forces arrived two hours later.

On 14 August the coalition force captured the outer city and began driving inward. They soon were into the Imperial City, then broke through the final barrier into the Forbidden City. There they found the government had fled, so few prisoners were taken. The invaders were not gentle in their treatment of the inhabitants of Peking and looting was widespread. With the city under firm control, the British general, Gaselee, led his forces into the neighboring provinces to mop up what Boxer resistance he could find. After some weeks, the empress sent emissaries with an offer to negotiate: a return to the *status quo antebellum* in return for the withdrawal of foreign troops.

The negotiations dragged on for months and ultimately the Chinese government was forced to pay an indemnity of $333 million to the offended nations. The United States received $25 million, of which they accepted only half and dedicated the remainder to establishing a fund for Chinese students to study in America. This gesture may have had the longest-lasting effect of the entire incident. High damage claims and looting the Chinese expected from foreigners, but to have one of the invaders invest in the future of China was shocking. From that point, the United States enjoyed a much closer relationship with China than any other Western power—a relationship that lasted through World War II and until the victory of communism in 1949. The Chinese for the most part became no less xenophobic, but the organized resistance to foreign influence that the Boxers symbolized had only a brief life.

References: Lord, Walter, *The Good Years* (New York: Harper & Bros., 1960); McCormick, T. J., *China Market: America's Quest for Informal Empire* (Chicago: Quadrangle Books, 1967); Young, Marilyn, *The Rhetoric of Empire: American China Policy, 1895–1901* (Cambridge: Harvard University Press, 1968).

British East India Company

A trading company with a private army that dominated India in the eighteenth and nineteenth centuries.

In the 1600s after the defeat of the Spanish Armada, the British were able to gain enough freedom of action on the high seas to begin to explore, colonize, and seek international markets. They were already aware of the economic possibilities of India because the Portuguese had established trading posts there during the 1500s that had brought the spices and exotic goods of the East to western Europe. By the time the British began to probe the coasts of India, the Portuguese were a fading power, so setting up their own trading posts and warehouse facilities, or "factories" as they were called, was easy to do. The government in London had sponsored the creation of the East India Company, in which it owned shares and had a presence on the board of directors, but which was primarily a private enterprise. The Company did, however, have the ability to call on the British government for support in times of trouble. In its early years, however, the protection of the factories in India fell not to soldiers of the king but to fighting men privately recruited and directed by the Company.

Three major factories were established in India; at Bengal on the northeastern coast, Madras near the tip of the subcontinent, and Bombay on the western coast. It was the men hired to protect these three trading centers that were to form the basis of the military force operated by "John Company" and that finally became the Indian army. Bengal's first troops were an ensign and 30 men along with a gunner and his crew hired in the late seventeenth century. At Madras, the watchmen and security guards were the basis of the military unit headquartered there. Most of the men recruited into these small units were native Indians who served under the leadership of Englishmen, a practice that remained in effect until Indian independence in 1947. John Company was not the first to hire local men, however, for the French (also trying to establish an economic presence in India) first conceived of the idea. As the ruling Mogul Empire was in its final days and power vacuums existed across India, the French and other Europeans learned that even a small force trained in European tactics, armed with European weapons, and led by European officers could defeat Indian armies vastly superior in number. The first large-scale armies, therefore, were private ones raised by local princes and sultans to protect their territory and expand at the expense of their neighbors. French, as well as English, officers officially and unofficially offered their services to local rulers, not only to profit personally but to give their respective countries a foothold in local politics. This would give them leverage in trade concessions as well as physically challenge other European competitors, like the East India Company.

In 1748 the first regular European force in British service was officially formed from the three fledgling units raised by the three factories. They had now, however, established themselves to such an extent that the British government had set up local administrations under the direction of officials sent from London, and the result were the presidencies of Bombay, Madras, and Bengal. To show their interest in maintaining the strongest presence in India, and certainly to intimidate the French, the British government sent a regiment of the British Army to serve with John Company, the Thirty-ninth Regiment of Foot (infantry).

The outbreak of the Seven Years War in Europe had international repercussions, as British and French forces fought battles around the world: in North America, the Caribbean, and in India. The units raised by European officers now fought each other not just for the local influence of a ruling monarch, but for European influence as well. The key battle in this conflict in India was Plassey in 1757 when British-led forces under Robert Clive defeated French-led forces in an engagement that determined the European dominance of India for almost two centuries. Although this broke French power in India and led to the eventual total withdrawal of the French from the subcontinent, it marked the beginning of serious expansion of the military forces in India. Although foreign competition was banished, local resistance to British expansion was widespread. Even where the Indian rajahs or princes did not actively antagonize the British, the overriding view of John Company was that peace was good for business. That meant that if a prince in a territory adjacent to British-dominated lands was oppressing his people or waging war against his neighbors, then British intervention was necessary to maintain order. By maintaining order from one province to another, the British expanded their influence across most of India. Expansion was never the official policy of the British government: It "just happened." Thus, through the end of the eighteenth century, the armies of the presidencies grew.

By 1795 a general reorganization was needed to set up the Company's army along the same lines as that employed by the British Army. In that year, some 13,000 Europeans lived in India, both civilian and military, while 33,000 Indians served in the Company's armed forces. Three separate commands were retained, but this move established a regular army, although still owned and operated by a private business. In Bengal, the forces consisted of three battalions of artillery, three battalions of British infantry, four regiments of native cavalry, and 12 regiments of native infantry. In Madras, two battalions of British infantry, two battalions of artillery, four regiments of native cavalry, and 11 regiments of native infantry made up the contingent. All the forces accepted recruits from across India, as well as some Afghans. The stigma of fighting against one's own people was no obstacle to these men, for most of them were misfits or exiles. In many cases the recruits were of the lowest castes in Hindu society and viewed the army as the only way out of a hopeless future. Most of the native cavalry units were made up of refugees from the private armies of defeated princes. For all of them, the promise of regular food and pay was something they could not achieve anywhere else. Moreover, as India was so divided among ethnic, religious, and political factions, rarely did one fight "one's own people."

The turn of the nineteenth century incited a new fervor in British administrators in India to grasp a firm hold on the subcontinent, as the rise of Napoleon in Europe threatened European interests worldwide. When Napoleon conquered a country in Europe, he immediately assumed control of all its colonies. This gave him opportunities to harass British colonies around the world. This, in turn, gave the British the excuse to "temporarily" occupy the colonies of other European nations, especially those of the Dutch in Africa and the Far East, in order to deny them to the French. Troops of the Company's army in those years served for the first time outside of India, establishing a precedent that lasted through World War II. Within India, French agents roused independent aristocrats to challenge British power, and they found sympathetic ears in the province of Mysore and among the Mahratta Confederacy in central India. Under the direction of Marquis Wellesley, the Governor-General of the entire colony, British-Indian forces commanded by Wellesley's brother, Arthur (soon to become Duke of Wellington), along with those under Commander-in-Chief General Lord Lake soundly defeated the native forces arrayed against them and established British control in the middle of India in 1803–1804. This experience brought Arthur Wellesely not only valuable command experience but official notice, both of which resulted in his transfer to Spain and victory against Napoleon's armies in Europe. Another war against the Mahrattas in 1817 destroyed the remaining pockets of discontent.

A member of the 17th Regiment Bengal Irregular Calvalry, 1850. (Drawing by A.C. Lovett)

In the period of relative peace that followed, the Company's army was once again reorganized, and the new table of organization showed a vast increase in its size. Of particular interest in this larger, reorganized force was a huge disparity between the numbers of Indian regiments and British regiments, with the Indian infantry regiments outnumbering the British by nearly 24 to 1. In spite of this fact, all the Indian regiments had British officers. Also of note was the introduction of Indians to units of artillery. This had been avoided up until this time, as the British did not wish to share that decisive technology. But the need for artillery had proven so important that Indian units were organized. However, when the Sepoy Rebellion broke out in 1857 the Company had reason to regret their new policy of inclusiveness. In that rebellion, Indian artillery units in the rebel forces caused such great harm to the British and loyal Indian units that one of the first changes made after the rebellion was to ban all Indian artillery forces.

Through the decades of the 1820s through the 1850s the Company's army continued to grow and continued to fight within India, maintaining order. Service in the military now was not just an escape for black sheep but had become a respectable profession. It was the only organization in India, until the opening of the Civil Service to Indian employees, that took recruits from any background and mixed men of all social and religious standing. The only caste system inside the army was that of rank and of the British overlords and the Indian subordinates. As new provinces came under British control or influence, the best soldiers of that region were incorporated into the Company's forces. The army grew to include Mahrattas after the two wars against them, Sikhs after the two wars against them, and Gurkhas after the war against them—all in the four decades prior to 1857. The armies of the three presidencies enlisted men from every region and ethnic group in India. Men recruited from a particular region usually served together, mixing soldiers of ethnic and religious diversity. Furthermore, the Indians were not only trained in European tactics and weaponry, they wore European uniforms. Prior to the Sepoy Rebellion, most of the Indians wore the same red coats and white pants as their British counterparts. Later they adopted a variety of impressive and colorful dress uniforms. It was also in India, among the frontier units, that soldiers first began to wear khaki, a cloth that would come to be part of military dress worldwide.

The army of the East India Company lasted until the Sepoy Rebellion of 1857. By that time it numbered more than 311,000 Indian troops and just under 40,000 British troops, both regular army and Company soldiers. The reasons for the rebellion are not important here, but suffice it to say that in its wake the British government decided that the Company, which had been losing its economic as well as political power for some time, should be dismantled. What had been a semiofficial government became a fully fledged colonial administration. Reforms were instituted in the military, decreasing the ratio of British to Indian troops among other things, and the Indian Army emerged as a very professional and capable force. Its soldiers continued to serve the British Empire in campaigns throughout the world, and the army that an independent India inherited in 1947 was one of the best in Asia.

References: MacMunn, G. F., *The Armies of India* (London: Adam and Charles Black, 1911); Mason, Philip, *A Matter of Honour* (London: Jonathan Cape, 1974); Roberts, P. E., *History of British India* (London: Oxford University Press, 1952).

Buffalo Soldiers

African-American troops serving mainly in the American Southwest during the late nineteenth century.

During the American Civil War, more than 180,000 African-Americans served in the United States Army under white officers in segregated, so-called colored regiments. After the war, with the reduction in size of military forces, these troops were consolidated by Congress into four all-black units: the Ninth and Tenth Cavalry and the Twenty-fourth and Twenty-fifth Infantry Regiments. Although these units would eventually see action in Cuba during the Spanish-American War, in the Philippine Insurrection, and along the Mexican border before and during World War I, their chief fame is for their service on the western frontier in the late nineteenth century. There they earned the name "Buffalo Soldiers," either because Native Americans thought the black troopers' hair resembled that of the buffalo or because their fighting spirit reminded the Indians of the buffalo. Either way, the troopers proudly accepted the name as a sign of respect and honor, and it is still applied today to U.S. Army units that are linear descendants of the original Buffalo Soldiers.

Very high standards of recruitment were set by the regiments' commanders. Because a career in the army usually offered African-Americans better lives than they could achieve as civilians at the time, four or five men applied for every opening in the regiments. Thus, the army had its choice of the best candidates, both physically and intellectually. While white soldiers frequently felt underpaid and ill treated, the Buffalo Soldiers were generally delighted with any pay (recruits received $13 a month, plus room, board, and clothing) and were far more accustomed to hard knocks than their white counterparts. Certainly, once in the army the black troopers found much to their liking. Many of the men availed themselves of after-hours schools established by the regiments and run by their chaplains, so that they might overcome the illiteracy forced on them by slavery. They drank far less than their white counterparts and deserted at a rate of only one tenth that of such "crack" regiments as Custer's Seventh Cavalry or Mackenzie's Fourth Cavalry. Indeed, the Tenth Cavalry posted the lowest desertion rate of any regiment in the U. S. Army in the late nineteenth century.

The Ninth and Tenth Cavalry were among the ten cavalry regiments thinly spread among more than 50 forts in the western states and territories. There they quickly established a reputation for bravery, daring, and incredible endurance. The troopers were constantly in the field, patrolling against hostile Indians over harsh terrain and in every extreme of weather. In over a hundred battles and skirmishes, from the Canadian border to south of the Rio Grande, they distinguished themselves against adversaries such as Geronimo, Sitting Bull, Victorio, Lone Wolf, Satank, and Satanta, not to mention Billy the Kid and Pancho Villa. Although the efforts of the black troopers were often belittled or just ignored by the army administration and the newspapers, professional soldiers understood that the Buffalo Soldiers had developed into the most outstanding fighting units in the army. Toward the end of hostilities in the Sioux outbreak of 1890–1891 four companies of the Ninth Cavalry marched 108 miles through a howling blizzard to rescue twice their number of Seventh Cavalry troopers. Along the way they fought two engagements. For this they earned almost no official recognition.

The Buffalo Soldiers' duties were not limited to fighting. They escorted thousands of civilian contractors' trains and mail stages over the dangerous frontier. They aided local law officers in making arrests, pursued and captured rustlers and horse thieves, and transported criminals to the nearest civilian courts. They protected cattle herds moving west and kept the stage and wagon trails open. They built and maintained many army posts around which future towns and cities sprang to life, strung thousands of miles of telegraph wire, and guarded the United States-Mexican border. Finally, they explored and mapped some of the most rugged and inhospitable country in North America, opening up a large portion of the continent to settlement. For instance, the Tenth Cavalry scouted 34,420 miles of uncharted terrain and opened more than 300 miles of new roads. One patrol alone was out on the Staked Plains of the Texas Panhandle for ten weeks in the fall and winter of 1877 covering over 1,360 miles without losing a single man or horse.

In spite of their abilities, the Buffalo Soldiers suffered frequent injustices, both from within and without the army. Many superior officers discriminated against the black regiments in housing, equipment, mounts, and assignments. Junior officers often refused to accept transfers to the units because they believed the commissions in the regiments to be socially degrading. Despite promises of fast promotion, officers such as George Arm-

"A Scout with the Buffalo Soldiers" (Drawing by Frederic Remington in The Century, *April 1889)*

strong Custer and Frederick Benteen refused commissions with African-American units. Because of such prejudice, the Buffalo Soldiers consistently received some of the worst assignments the army had to offer, but they carried out those assignments without complaint, and without faltering.

Among many civilians the hatreds engendered by the Civil War and Reconstruction were still fresh and in some minds former slaves carrying guns were all-too-painful reminders of Southern defeat and Northern victory. Many Texans saw the stationing of black troopers in their state as a deliberate attempt by the government to further humiliate them. Thus, relationships between troopers and locals were often antagonistic at best, and troopers frequently found themselves in siege-type situations, in danger as much from civilians in the settlements as from hostile native forces on the frontier. However, the Buffalo Soldiers managed to meet this prejudice with a stoic resolve and a devotion to duty that eventually surmounted such mistreatment. As one historian noted: "The protection afforded by the [black] cavalryman's carbines had a marvelous way of transcending the issue of race" (Hamilton, 1987).

With the outbreak of the Spanish-American War, the Buffalo Soldiers were sent to Cuba and, led by John J. Pershing, they participated in the desperate charge that secured San Juan and Kettle Hills, fighting alongside future president Theodore Roosevelt and his outfit, the Rough Riders. After their brilliant performance in Cuba, elements of all four black regiments saw action in the Philippine Insurrection. Scattered among army posts throughout the archipelago, black soldiers participated in military operations from Northern Luzon to Samar, fighting against the hit-and-run guerrilla tactics of the Filipinos.

When the Mexican bandit-general Pancho Villa attacked Columbus, New Mexico, in 1916 a 7,000-man American force got permission from the Mexican government to pursue him. General John Pershing was given command, and he immediately added the Buffalo Soldiers to the expedition. When the United States withdrew from Mexico in 1917 in order to join the Allies fighting World War I, the Ninth and Tenth Cavalry stayed behind on the border to guard against possible Mexican invasion or German subversion. In 1918 they fought a pitched battle with Mexican forces at Nogales that ended any threat of German-inspired Mexican intervention.

In 1941 the Ninth and Tenth regiments were formed into the Fourth Cavalry Brigade, commanded by General Benjamin O. Davis, Sr., at Camp Funston, Kansas. In 1944 all the horse cavalry regiments were disbanded and, with them, the long and proud service of the Buffalo Soldiers ended. With their sweat, blood, ability, and fidelity, the Buffalo Soldiers won the respect that often eluded them in civilian life at that time. In all, six officers and 15 enlisted men of the Buffalo Soldiers won the Congressional Medal of Honor for bravery and gallantry under fire. They were truly the elite soldiers of the late nineteenth-century United States Army.

References: Carroll, John M., *The Black Military Experience in the American West* (New York: Liveright, 1971); Downey, Fairfax, *The Buffalo Soldiers in the Indian Wars* (New York: McGraw-Hill, 1969); Hamilton, Allen, *Sentinel of the Southern Plains* (Fort Worth: TCU Press, 1987).

Byzantines

Dominant military forces of the Middle East between the fourth and fifteenth centuries.

In 330 A.D., Constantine I, Emperor of the Romans, founded a new capital for his empire on the triangular peninsula of land that divided the Bosphorus from the Sea of Marmora, commanding the narrow water passage from the Black Sea to the Mediterranean. He named it Constantinople, and in time it grew to be not only one of the greatest cities of antiquity, but the center of one of the most impressive civilizations the world has ever seen: the Byzantine Empire. Within 200 years the Byzantines (or Eastern Roman Empire, as they styled themselves) had grown to massive proportions, controlling all of Italy, the Balkans, Greece, Asia Minor, Syria, Egypt, North Africa, and Southern Spain. Such an empire could be held together only by a strong and efficient military, and for several centuries the Byzantine army had no equal anywhere in the world.

Although the empire had expanded enormously through conquest, the basic role of the Byzantine army was defensive. Fortifying the long borders was out of the question, and since raiders and invaders could strike anywhere along the empire's frontier, the army needed to be able to move quickly to meet these threats. Like their predecessors, the Roman legions, the Byzantine units formed a professional standing army which was trained to near-perfection as a fighting machine. Unlike the legions, however, the core of the army was cavalry and fast-moving foot archers. Speed and firepower had become the trademarks of the "new Romans."

The stirrup reached the empire from China early in the fifth century, and increased the effectiveness of the cavalry enormously. Therefore, the core of the Byzantine army became the heavy cavalry. A typical heavy cavalryman was armed with a long lance, a short bow, a small axe, a broadsword, a dagger, and a small shield. He wore a steel helmet, a plate mail corselet that reached from neck to thigh, leather gauntlets, and high boots. His horse's head and breast might be protected with light armor as well. By the later empire, armor for both rider and horse became almost complete, especially in the front line units. In a secondary role, unarmored light cavalry horse archers on smaller mounts supported the heavy units with missile fire, while other light cavalry armed with long lance and large shield protected their flanks.

The infantryman that usually accompanied the cavalry in the field was either a lightly armored archer who used a powerful long bow, a small shield, and a light axe or an unarmored skirmisher armed with javelins and shield. Because most Byzantine operations depended on speed, tactically as well as strategically, heavy infantry seldom ventured beyond the camps or fortifications. The heavy infantryman wore a long mail coat and steel helmet and carried a large, round shield. He used a long spear and a short sword. The Varangian Guard, the emperor's

Miniature depicting a battle between the cavalry of the Byzantines and the Arabs

personal bodyguards, were famous for their great two-handed axes which they wielded with great effect. Their armor was almost complete plate and mail from head to foot.

To the Byzantines war was a science, and brains were prized over daring or strength. Military manuals such as the *Strategikon* (ca. 580) and the *Tactica* (ca. 900) laid down the basics of military strategy that really did not vary for almost a thousand years. The army was always small in numbers (field armies almost never exceeded 20,000 men, and the total force of the empire probably was never greater than 100,000) and, because of its training and equipment, very expensive to maintain. Huge losses in combat could be catastrophic, and seldom were great winner-take-all battles fought. The goal of any Byzantine general was to win with the least cost. If by delay, skirmishing, or withdrawing the local population and their goods into forts he could wear out an invading force and cause it to withdraw without a costly pitched battle, so much the better. Bribing an enemy to go away was also quite acceptable.

The warrior emperor Heraclius divided the empire into some thirty *themes,* or military districts, each under a separate military commander. Each *theme* provided and supported its own corps of cavalry and infantry, raised from self-supporting peasant warrior-farmers, enough to provide a small self-contained army that was capable of independent operation. For four centuries this system endured, and Byzantium remained strong. Only in the eleventh century, when the *theme* system and its free peasantry were abandoned, did the empire become weak and vulnerable.

Theme commanders depended on accurate information about enemies and their movements and so maintained a very sophisticated intelligence service. Over time espionage became so important to Byzantine operations that a part of the emperor's bureaucracy, known as the Office of Barbarians, was dedicated solely to gathering military intelligence and disseminating it to the commanders in the field.

Byzantine battlefield tactics, although highly flexible and adaptable, were based invariably on archery first, then shock assault as needed. Since everyone in the army except the heavy infantry carried a bow, an incredible amount of firepower could be directed against the enemy. The highly trained and disciplined cavalry units, supported by the light infantry archers, could pour volley after volley of arrows into enemy units and then, when those units began to lose cohesion, charge with lance and sword, rout them, and pursue them out of Byzantine territory.

Since Constantinople was a major port, surrounded by water on three sides, a strong navy was also necessary for the empire's survival. Byzantine ships were fairly typical oar-driven galleys of the time, but they possessed a great technological advantage over other navies: a weapon known as Greek fire. This was a highly flammable mixture that could be thrown on enemy ships in pots from catapults, or pumped by siphons directly on their decks, breaking into white-hot flames on contact. One of the great secrets of the ancient world is the exact composition of Greek fire, but it probably contained pitch, kerosene, sulfur, resin, naphtha, and quicklime. Whatever the mix, it was a terrifying weapon that was almost impossible to defend against. If water was poured on Greek fire, it burned even hotter. With Greek fire the Byzantine navy reigned supreme for centuries on the Black Sea and the eastern Mediterranean.

The Byzantines were also fortunate in producing many great military leaders over the centuries: emperors such as Justinian I, Heraclius, Basil I, Leo III, Maurice, Leo VI "the Wise," and generals like Narses, Belisarius, and John Kurkuas. Their skills and insights maintained the Eastern Roman Empire for almost a thousand years after the fall of the western branch.

Although the Byzantines fought many peoples over the centuries, in campaigns of either conquest or defense, it was a religious opponent, the Moslems, who became their most intractable, and in the end, lethal, foe.

For seven centuries a succession of Moslem generals led Persian, Arab, and Turkish armies against the armies and walls of Constantinople. Gradually, the empire was eaten away, and its wealth and manpower base eroded. Not only did the Byzantines have to face the Muslim threat, but a growing schism between their church, the Greek Orthodox, and the Roman Catholic Church, isolated them from their fellow Christians. In 1071, the emperor Romanus IV violated one of the mainstays of Byzantine strategy when he concentrated most of his military power in one great battle against Alp Arslan and the Seljuk Turks at Manzikert in Armenia. The result was a devastating defeat, allowing the Turks to overrun most of Asia Minor, the heartland of the empire. Byzantium never really recovered from this debacle. In 1204, Christian crusaders, allied with the city-state of Venice, took advantage of internal Byzantine strife to seize and sack Constantinople. It was not until 1261 that the emperor Michael VIII Palaeologus recaptured Constantinople from the Latins, but the damage had been done. The empire's once great resources, and its ability to maintain itself, were almost gone. On 29 May 1453, Mohammed II, Sultan of the Ottoman Turks, using great cannons (weapons even more fearsome than Greek fire), broke through the seemingly eternal walls of Constantinople and brought the glorious Byzantine Empire to an end.

Certainly, Byzantines made many great contributions to civilization: Greek language and learning were preserved, the Roman imperial system and law was continued, the Greek Orthodox Church spread Christianity among many peoples, and a splendid new religious art form was created. But it is possible that their ideas on military science (mobility and firepower, delay and deception, espionage and statecraft, an emphasis on professionalism over the warrior ethos) might stand as the most significant aspect of their great legacy.

References: Diehl, Charles, *Byzantium: Greatness and Decline* (New Brunswick, NJ: Rutgers University Press, 1957); Griess, Thomas, *Ancient and Medieval Warfare* (West Point: U.S. Military Academy, 1984); Ostrogorsky, George, *History of the Byzantine State* (New Brunswick, NJ: Rutgers University Press, 1957).

C

Cavaliers and Roundheads

Units of the English Civil War, the Roundheads are noted as being the basis of the British Regular Army's "redcoats" for centuries to come.

The English Civil War raged from 1642 to 1646, although fighting sporadically continued for some years afterward. The issue was quite simple, and yet complex at the same time: Who or what was going to rule England, King or Parliament? King Charles I (1625–1648), like his Scottish father James I (1603–1625), believed in the divine right of kings. Unfortunately for them, Parliament had participated in the government of England for centuries, and its right to do so was well established in tradition. Further, Parliament had the power to vote taxes and used this right to defy Charles's attempts at autocratic rule. There were also religious concerns as a strongly Protestant Parliament viewed Charles's Catholic leanings with alarm. Eventually it became clear that the only way to resolve the differences between king and Parliament was through war. Almost everyone in England, lords, aristocrats, clergy, and commoners, fell into one camp or the other. The followers of the king were known as Royalists, or "cavaliers" (after the French word for horsemen), while the supporters of the Parliament were known as Parliamentarians, or "roundheads" (supposedly because their shorter hair cuts gave their heads a round appearance). Parliament had the early advantage of controlling the east and south of England, especially London, while the king's support tended to be strongest in the north and west parts of the country.

The soldiers who fought in the English Civil War were typical of those of the Thirty Years War era. Both sides tried to copy the Swedish army organization of Gustavus Adolphus, but instead ended up with forces distinctly more English than continental. The backbone of each army was the infantry, or foot, which consisted of pikemen and musketeers grouped together in regiments, with an ideal ration of 2 musketeers to 1 pikeman. Typically, pikemen would form the middle of a regiment, with an equal number of musketeers on each flank. The armor of the pikemen would consist of iron helmets, back- and breastplates, with perhaps tassets (thigh guards) suspended from the breastplates, and thick leather gloves. Under this they wore long leather coats known as "buffcoats," thick enough to turn a sword cut. Their main weapon was the 16- to 18-foot English pike, with which they would try to dispatch other infantry and hold cavalry at bay. Obviously, individual pikemen were fairly helpless, only by operating in unison as a block could they be effective. Therefore, it was necessary for them to learn a complex set of maneuvers and drills in order to function as a unit on the battlefield. As in all wars, some regiments were better at this than others.

Musketeers furnished the infantry firepower on the field. Typical firearms for both sides were 13-pound matchlocks or lighter harquebuses, usually supported by a forked rest. Both were slow and tedious to load, but could inflict terrible wounds on enemies at distances ranging up to 200 yards, although to be accurate it was necessary to be much closer, usually inside 40 yards. Aside from firearms, musketeers were equipped with bandoliers from which hung wooden or leather tubes filled with measured gunpowder charges (which often leaked, thus making each musketeer a potential walking bomb), short swords, and sometimes buffcoats. Musketeers trained to fire by ranks, either by "introduction" (advancing) or "extraduction" (retiring), with one rank shooting, then reloading while the next stepped through. As bayonets were not yet invented, musketeers would seek the protection of the pikemen's square when enemy pikes or cavalry came too near.

Infantry regiments were supposed to consist of ten companies, although in practice this number was seldom met. A company could range from 100 to 200 men, so infantry regiments could be quite large.The only units in England that could be called "regulars" when the war broke out were the Trained Bands of London, which went over to Parliament's side; this gave the Roundheads an early and lasting advantage in numbers and quality of infantry during the war.

Cavalry during the English Civil War, more so than on the continent during the Thirty Years War, ruled the battlefield. Equipment was almost never uniform or universal, but most heavy cavalrymen wore a buffcoat with back- and breastplate, a helmet with nasal guard and ear and neck protection, a metal gauntlet on the left hand and forearm to protect the bridle hand, and thick leather boots which extended to the top of the thigh. Some very heavy cavalrymen known as cuirassiers wore an almost complete suite of armor like their predecessor, the heavy knight. Lighter cavalry could wear just a back- and breastplate, or simply a buffcoat.

The lance was seldom used by cavalry at this time, except for some units of light Scottish horse. Most heavy cavalry used the heavy straight broadsword with basket hilt as their shock weapon, and pistols or carbines as their secondary weapons. Firearms were wheel lock or firelock style, since a matchlock would be almost impossible to use or reload on horseback. Some light cavalry were organized as mounted infantry, or dragoons, so called because of the "dragons" or short muskets that they carried. They rode inferior animals to the cavalry horses and were trained to fight on foot as sharpshooters or skirmishers, using their horses to give them greater mobility. Cavalry regiments were organized in six to 12 troops of 70 to 100 men each. Thus a regiment could consist of 1,200 men, but 800 were normal, and some units that had seen hard action were as small as 100 men.

The foremost cavalry regiment among the Roundheads was Oliver Cromwell's famous "Ironsides," whom he raised, trained, and led personally. Said to be twice the size of most cavalry regiments, the Ironsides were certainly the most tightly disciplined horse in the early war and more than a match for any one regiment the Royalists could throw against them. But, since most of the aristocracy preferred to fight on horseback and could afford the necessary horse and armor, the early advantage in horse in quality and quantity lay with the Royalists. Under dashing leaders like Prince Rupert and Prince Maurice, who had both served in the Thirty Years War in Europe, wild Royalist cavalry charges usually swept the fields of Roundhead cavalry early in the war. Unfortunately, Cavalier horse was usually good for only one charge, impetuously chasing off after their fleeting enemies and leaving their infantry vulnerable. This lack of discipline, the inability to rally and charge a second time, became both a hallmark of the Royalist horse and the eventual undoing of the Royalist cause.

Armies of both sides had an artillery train, but the slow rate of fire of cannons of the times (about one round every three minutes) made them truly useful only during sieges. Field pieces weighed between 150 and 6,000 pounds and required 9 to 12 men to serve them. Heavy draught horses or oxen were needed to move these weapons between battles, so once they were set up they tended to remain in place, win or lose.

In 1645, Parliament, at Cromwell's urging, authorized the raising of a "New Model Army," England's first regular standing army. It was to take the place of the militia, trained bands and private regiments of Parliamentary supporters. It was to be some 22,000 men strong, with 14,000 infantry, 6,600 horse, and 1,000 dragoons. Under Commander-in-Chief Thomas Fairfax and General of the Horse Oliver Cromwell, the army was tightly organized, thoroughly and professionally trained, highly disciplined, imbued with an almost religious fervor, and had regular rates of pay. They also adopted regular uniforms, the red coat that would become synonymous with the British Army for the next three centuries.

This New Model Army showed its worth on the field of Naseby on 14 June 1645. Although hard pressed by the more veteran Royalist foot, the Roundhead infantry held their own. Prince Rupert charged with his cavalry and broke the Parliamentary cavalry against him, but as usual they scattered out across the countryside, pursuing the fugitives over two miles back to their baggage train, and leaving his infantry vulnerable and without cavalry support. Meanwhile, Cromwell's horse had charged on the other flank and routed the Royalist cavalry against him. Instead of wildly pursuing, however, the training and discipline of the New Model Army paid off. Cromwell rallied his men, reformed, and charged into the exposed flanks of the Royalist foot and for all purposes won the war. The victorious New Model Army proceeded to roll over one Royalist stronghold after another until, by the summer of 1646, all England was in their hands. Charles I surrendered to the Scots in late 1646, who handed him over to Parliament in 1647. He briefly escaped from captivity, spurring Royalist uprisings all over the country, but these were easily crushed, and he was recaptured in 1648. On 30 January 1649, Charles I, condemned as a "tyrant, traitor, murderer, and public enemy," was beheaded. A Puritan Commonwealth was proclaimed, and Oliver Cromwell came to rule England (with the backing of his New Model Army) as Lord Protector from 1653 until his death in 1658.

References: Ashley, Maurice, *The English Civil War* (London: Thames and Hudson, 1974); Haythornthwait, Philip, *The English Civil War* (London: Blandford Press, 1984); Young, Brigadier Sir Peter, and Wilfrid Emberton, *The Cavalier Army, It's Organization and Everyday Life* (London: George Allen and Unwin, 1974).

Celts

An ancient population dominating northern and western Europe prior to the Roman Empire.

The Celts were prehistoric Europeans, and little else can be said about them as far as unifying characteristics are concerned. A large number of tribes spread from the Atlantic coast to the Black Sea and they collectively came to be called Celts (from the Greek *Keltoi* or Latin *Celtae*) by their more literate, record-keeping southern neighbors. These tribes, described by the Greeks and Romans as barbarians, settled Europe in the ninth to sixth centuries B.C. but were inexplicably overrun about 500 B.C. In the 400s B.C. European barbarian cultures reorganized and came to be called Gauls (from the Latin *Galli* or Greek *Galatae*).

As the numbers of tribes that stretched across Europe under these general headings were as numerous as the Celtic tribes, it is difficult to prove how related they all may have been. Described by archaeologists as the La Tene culture, there are some traces of common speech patterns over a wide span of territory from the British Isles to Asia Minor, as well as some common artistic and religious aspects.

The Celts attacked their Mediterranean neighbors starting around 400 B.C. They invaded past the Alps into Italy, sacking Rome in 390 B.C., but were driven back and settled into the Po River valley in a region that came to be called Cisalpine Gaul. In 279 B.C. Galatians attacked into Greece as far as Delphi. Although driven back after a serious defeat, some Galatians crossed into Asia Minor and established a kingdom around modern Ankara. Traces of Celtic/Gallic culture and language appeared in Iberia in Roman times, but the chief remainder of Celtic heritage is found in the British Isles. Common tribal names and linguistic features connect Celtic populations from northwest Europe and the British Isles, as well as commonalities in defensive works, weaponry, artwork, and religion. The Picts of Scotland and the piratical Scotti of Ireland remained unconquered by the Romans, thus maintaining more of their Celtic languages.

It is from Greek and Roman sources that the first recorded observations of the Celts come, and they focus heavily on the Celtic passion for warfare. The Roman historian Strabo wrote "The whole race...is madly fond of war, high-spirited and quick to battle, but otherwise straightforward and not of evil character. And so when they are stirred up they assemble in their bands for battle, quite openly and without forethought.... [When aroused] they are...ready to face danger even if they have nothing on their side but their own strength and courage" (Cunliffe, 1997). The display of individual valor was most important in Celtic society and was the prerequisite for leadership. The migration of Celtic tribes across Europe is believed to have been based on their ever-increasing need to find enemies to defeat and plunder. A raid of a neighboring village produced loot and status for the Celtic leader. He then held a feast and distributed the booty, attracting the attention of more warriors. He would then lead a second raid to acquire more loot, hold another feast to distribute it, and attract more warriors, and so on. This ever-growing cycle of loot-reward-recruit forced the tribes to range further afield for greater glory and wealth.

Iron swords and a bronze helmet, third to first centuries B.C. (Musée Denon, Chalon-sur-Saone, France)

The Celts were more of a warrior race than a militaristic population, in that they depended more on individual effort and mass attacks than on well-planned strategies. The individual Celt carried a sword and a spear, occasionally bows and arrows, slings, or throwing clubs. The Celts carried shields and often wore metal helmets, but rarely wore body armor in the form of chain mail. Their swords were of iron with blades usually decorated with personal emblems. Spears were used both as thrusting and throwing weapons. The use of bows and arrows was rarely recorded but arrowheads have been recovered in Celtic archaeological sites. In Britain, evidence of slings comes from the stockpiles of rocks discovered at key places in Celtic defensive positions, such as Maiden Castle in Dorset.

In battle, Celtic warriors often wore helmets decorated with attachments, such as animal figures. A helmet discovered in London has large protruding horns, while another unearthed in Romania has a large bird with hinged wings that flapped as the wearer ran.

Although some indication of iron breastplates or chain mail exists, one of the most striking characteristics noted by ancient observers was the propensity of the Celts to go into battle naked, but for a helmet, sword belt, armlets, and a torc (a heavy necklace with religious significance). Contemporary artwork also depicts Celtic warriors fighting in the nude. In northern Britain the Picts were well-known for painting their bodies blue before engaging in combat. Whether these practices were psychological ploys to intimidate foes or whether they held some religious significance is difficult to determine.

Celts usually fought as infantry, engaging in single combat, but have also been depicted in chariots. The two-horse chariot carried a driver and a warrior and was probably used more for transportation to the battle and across the battlefield rather than as a fighting platform. Caesar does not mention any use of chariots by the Gauls, but they are often described in Roman combat against the inhabitants of Britain. The chariot driver was thus an auxiliary to the warrior, keeping close eye on him during combat to race the chariot to his position to move him about the battlefield or rescue him when wounded. When Celtic cavalry is described, a unit of three is most common, the warrior being assisted by two bearers, much as appeared in feudal times with a knight, squire, and page.

Prior to battle, as the armies faced each other, individual Celtic warriors would offer challenges to single combat, usually with much boasting on their part and belittling of the enemy. This resulted in a series of combats that would either convince one side or the other to withdraw or provoke a general melee. As the Celts/Gauls became more accustomed to Mediterranean tactics, the challenges dwindled. Once the battle was to be joined, the Gauls had masses of war trumpets creating an awful din described by Diodorus: "Their trumpets again are of a peculiar barbarian kind; they blow into them and produce a harsh sound which suits the tumult of war" (Cunliffe, 1997). This sounding of the trumpets could have been a combination of psychological warfare and a summoning of the gods of war. Once the battle started, the strength of the Gallic attack was in its ferocity. If the enemy force could withstand the opening shock, the Gauls would often withdraw, having no other plan of battle and having expended their pent-up rage. In some battles, the warriors would continue the attack over the bodies of their fallen comrades, but that was more the exception than the rule.

It was their conflicts with the Romans that spelled the doom of the Gauls. The discipline of the Roman legions proved more than a match for the intensity of the Gallic fighting spirit, and the Gauls lost battle after battle. That, coupled with the arrival of Germanic tribes from the northeast, squeezed the European Gauls out of existence or onto the British Isles. The remoteness of Scotland and Ireland kept them free of Roman influence in society and language, and in Scotland the daunting terrain kept the migrant Scotti free from Scandinavian domination. Ultimately, the English, under Norman and later Tudor rule, conquered the islands and sublimated the Celtic heritage. Only since the eighteenth century with the discoveries of archaeological digs have the Celts come to modern attention. A renewed interest in their culture focusses more on language and society, rather than their vaunted military reputation.

References: Cunliffe, Barry, *The Ancient Celts* (Oxford: Oxford University Press, 1997); Dudley, Donald, *The Romans* (New York: Alfred Knopf, 1970); Jimenez, Ramon, *Caesar against the Celts* (New York: Sarpedon Publishers, 1995).

Charioteers

Specialists in warfare using horse-drawn wheeled vehicles for two millennia prior to the Roman Empire.

The earliest elite or specialized troops in history must have been chariot riders, who first began to appear around 1700 B.C. in the borderlands between the steppes of Asia and the river lands of Mesopotamia. True two-wheeled light chariots developed from Sumerian wooden carts or four-wheeled battle wagons drawn by onagers, as shown in the third millennium B.C. Standard of Ur. However, they differ enormously from their early predecessors, and a great deal of technological advancement, specialization, and expense went into their development.

Before the chariot could become a practical means of conveyance, some method of harnessing the wild horse was necessary. Oxen, onagers, and donkeys all had their drawbacks as draught animals, being either too slow or uncontrollable. Early peoples must have quickly recognized the advantages that the horse offered in both areas. It was necessary, however, to work out a method of controlling the horse with a mouth bit and yoking it to a transport by means of a breast band or padded collar. Even then, horses could not pull heavy loads without these early collars choking them; therefore, chariots had to be developed that were as light as possible, with strong, yet open, frames and bent-wood spoked wheels (eventually the Egyptians built chariots that weighed no more than 75 pounds including harness). Furthermore, the axle that held the wheels had to be designed to pivot so the chariot's maneuverability and turning radius could be improved.

The expertise required to produce good chariots, together with the specialists necessary to maintain them and their horses in combat (grooms, saddlers, wheelwrights, etc.) meant that only wealthy armies could afford them. Moreover, the dominance these vehicles imparted on the battlefield quickly raised charioteers to a position of elite status among warriors of the ancient world.

Although javelins, maces, and swords are shown being used by charioteers in early artistic depictions, the composite bow was their most favored weapon and the one that made them most dangerous. Constructed of laminated wood and horn glued together in a curve, the short composite bow was the perfect weapon with which to rain down death upon masses of infantry and other charioteers as far as 300 yards away.

Archer on a chariot. Fragment of a bronze sheet covering a wooden door from the palace of Shalmanesar III at Yeni-Assur, Mesopotamia (Iraq), ninth century B.C. (Archaeological Museum, Istanbul, Turkey)

True chariots probably originated around 1700 B.C. on the fringes of the agricultural world where the western steppe herdsmen met the settled peoples of the city-states of Mesopotamia. No one knows who built the first chariot, but they almost certainly came from these borderlands. Here the knowledge of producing wheels, draughtpoles, and metal fittings for carts and wagons was pressed into service to meet the needs of nomadic sheep and goat herders for a fast-moving herding and hunting platform: the chariot. The advantages of the new vehicle must rapidly have become apparent. The chariot riders of the steppes discovered that their new weapon allowed them to hunt men as well as animals with equal ease. Around 1500 B.C. nomadic charioteers began to descend upon the civilized lands of the time: the Hyskos invaded Egypt, the Hurrians, Mittians, and Kassites swept into Mesopotamia, Aryans penetrated India, and the Shang overwhelmed northern China. All these invaders faced organized armies, but they were armies composed of infantry with perhaps a few of the clumsy battle wagons mentioned earlier. The chariot riders could circle these herds of men as they circled their herds of sheep on the steppes. One man drove the chariot while the other picked the enemy off with his compound bow, and both easily stayed out of reach of the infantry's short-ranged weapons. The assaulted infantry could not close with the far speedier chariots, nor could they retire. In such fashion charioteers consistently routed larger defending forces and carried off what they wished in food, gold, slaves, and other booty. In time, these aggressive nomads overthrew the very states they were raiding and established their own dynasties, based not on their numbers but on the sheer power of the chariot.

The rule of the invading charioteers was not long, however. All were overthrown or absorbed by the native populations, but their legacy lived on in the adoption of the chariot by the peoples they had conquered. The New Kingdom Egyptians and the Assyrians especially learned from the invaders and put what they had learned into practice: Their states became as aggressive and warlike as the nomads, only now they warred to protect their frontiers and to extend their boundaries in order to forestall new invasions. They made war a form of state policy, and the heart of their new mobile war machines was the two-wheeled chariot.

The New Kingdom Egyptian army had as its nucleus a chariot force, although not a large one. In reliefs and paintings, the pharaoh is always shown in his chariot, in the forefront of the battle, followed by a few nobles in their chariots and the mass of the army on foot. Despite artistic license and the need to portray the pharaoh in the best light, these depictions may be fairly accurate. In the earliest recorded battle in history, at Megiddo in 1469 B.C., the pharaoh Thutmosis III routed the Hyskos and forced their leaders to surrender. Only 83 Hyskos were killed in the battle, and another 340 taken prisoner, hardly the casualties one would expect, had a defeated army been pursued by a large chariot force. Two centuries later in 1294 B.C. Rameses II fought the Hittites at Qadesh to a standstill with an army that, according to Egyptian accounts, numbered only 50 chariots and 5,000 infantry. However, those same accounts claim that the Hittites fielded 2,500 chariots—obviously an exaggeration. Still, the problems and expense inherent in maintaining a standing chariot force ensured that it would never be a large component of any army.

The Assyrians too, as much as the Egyptians, are closely identified with the chariot. But the Assyrian army was far more professional and more organized for war as an imperial task than any of its contemporaries. Assyrian forces included specialized troops, armored infantry, engineers and siege units, and foreign troops who fought with their own unique weapons. However, Assyrian kings rode into battle in their chariots and the nobles, the cream of the Assyrian state, rode with them. At their core, they were charioteers.

The Egyptians, Assyrians, and most of their foes used a two-man crew, a fighter and his driver, in a light chariot pulled by two horses (Assyrians sometimes used four). This seems to have been the ideal compromise between speed, maneuverability, and fire power. After the ninth century B.C. the Assyrians seem to have added a third man, usually a shield bearer, to strengthen defenses. Some carvings and drawings from other ancient Middle Eastern nations depict four-, five-, and even six-man crews being pulled by four horses, although it is difficult to imagine how six men could actually fight from a chariot without constantly getting in each other's way. In these cases the chariot probably was being used as a means of transporting a combat team to the battlefield, rather than as an actual fighting vehicle. Both the Egyptians and the Assyrians moved the axle back from the center toward the rear of the car and allowed the axle a certain degree of movement within its brackets. Both innovations greatly increased the chariot's maneuverability. Assyrian ironsmiths even fitted a studded metal rim to the wheels to give the chariot more traction in turning.

Exactly how the chariot was used in

combat is somewhat unclear. Certainly it acted as a mobile firing platform for archers, but its shock value must have been limited because the horses were unprotected and therefore vulnerable to hand weapons at close quarters. Despite the fact that kings and pharaohs are shown driving their vehicles over dead and dying enemies, anyone trying to fight from a chariot with a mace or sword must have encountered great difficulties. Furthermore, chariots could not maneuver over broken or wooded terrain. Over time combatants would have learned how to counter chariot tactics, forming shoulder to shoulder ranks, using long spears to keep chariots away, protecting themselves with larger and stronger shields, and shooting chariot horses with their bows. Still, for over a thousand years chariots offered the only real mobile fire power and speed in pursuit available, and this made them an indispensable component of the civilized armies of the time.

Eventually, the horse superseded the chariot in battle. The Assyrians had been breeding stronger horses, and by the eighth century B.C. had produced a horse that could be ridden from the forward seat (with the weight over the animal's front shoulders), and thus better controlled. Some Assyrian archers began to ride horses in battle. However, without stirrups, this was still a tenuous platform. On the steppes, some peoples may have already bred riding horses, or the animals may have been traded from Mesopotamia to nomads in the grasslands. Be that as it may, the nomads soon became mounted archers, and the days of the chariot were over. True cavalry simply possessed much more maneuverability than chariots and required far less trouble and expense to maintain. One of the final appearances of chariots in battle seems to have been at Gaugamela in 331 B.C. where the Persian king Darius had a field leveled and prepared so his chariots could charge unimpeded against the Macedonian pike phalanxes of Alexander the Great. The results were disastrous for the Persians and Darius ultimately paid with his life. Some people, like the Bretons, continued to use chariots, but mostly as a sort of "battle taxi" in which to ride to and from combat. Once there they fought on foot. This is the way Homer described their use in the *Iliad,* which was set around the twelfth century B.C. but probably written around the eighth or seventh century B.C. By the time of the Roman empire, chariots had ceased to be weapons of war, or even appear on battlefields, and instead became a quaint means of transport for the wealthy and a source of spectacle for the masses in great chariot races held in the Colosseum.

References: Ferrill, Arthur, *The Origins of War* (London: Thames and Hudson, 1985); Hackett, General Sir John, *Warfare in the Ancient World* (London: Sidgwick & Jackson, 1989); Keegan, John, *A History of Warfare* (New York: Random House, 1993).

Chindits

A special operations unit operating in Burma during World War II.

One of the more overlooked theaters of operations during World War II is the China-Burma-India theater, where Japanese forces ran amok in the early years of the war. After more than four years of combat in China, Japanese forces moved into Southeast Asia during 1940–1942. They were able to occupy Indochina with the assent of the German-directed Vichy French government, but they had to gain the remainder of the area by conquest. That conquest started 8 December 1941 within hours of the Japanese attack on the American naval base at Pearl Harbor, Hawaii. Japanese troops streamed through the jungles of Malaya to capture Singapore, then turned eastward toward the greatest British possession: India. The occupation of Burma not only threatened the eastern frontier of India, but it cut off the overland supply routes from the Indian Ocean to Chiang Kai-shek's nationalist Chinese forces. Extremely engaged in fighting in North Africa, the British could give little support to Indian defense. General Archibald Wavell was given command in India in February 1942 and he called upon the services of Orde Wingate, an eccentric British army officer, to strike at the Japanese.

Wingate was born into army life in India in 1903. Educated by his extremely religious parents, Wingate was a serious but not always successful student when he finally attended school in England. That also characterized his record at the Royal Military Academy at Woolwich. Still, he managed to obtain a commission in 1926 and received his first assignment—to the Sudan. He learned Arabic on his own and was soon in demand for operations in the countryside where his language ability and study of the local customs stood him in good stead. He began to make a name for himself as a capable but erratic soldier. It was his transfer to Palestine in 1936 that marked the turning point in his career.

Palestine was then governed by the British under a League of Nations mandate, the country itself having been set aside as a Jewish homeland by the Versailles Treaty of 1919. The Arabs had little desire to give up the land to Jews, and constant harassment of emigrants took place. Wingate began to embrace Zionism and argued that the Jews should be allowed to organize self-defense forces. Upon being given that task, he created the Special Night Squads to combat Arab terrorist attacks. Wingate developed the tactics used by these irregular forces and became well known in the British Army for this specialty. It is to this early training that many trace the development of the modern Israeli defense forces.

Wingate's success in training these counterterrorist units brought him to the attention of Chaim Weizmann, a leading Zionist, who convinced him to assist in lobbying for Jewish causes in London. This overtly political action was regarded as out of place for a serving officer, and Wingate fell from favor with a number of higher-ranking officials. It was during this activity, though, that Wingate met and favorably impressed Winston Churchill, who would be his greatest supporter in years to come.

When Great Britain went to war in September 1939 Wingate was sent back to Africa to aid in operations against Italian-held Ethiopia. In early 1941 he led his own specially trained "Gideon Force" as part of the British offensive to restore Emperor Haile Selassie. His mission was to disrupt the communications and bases of the Italian army and in this his force was extremely successful. Wingate's force of Ethiopians regularly defeated larger Italian units by bluff and superior maneuvering ability. Wingate escorted the emperor back into Addis Ababa in May 1942. In spite of the recognition he earned for his leadership abilities, he hurt himself by openly criticizing his superiors and theorizing about possible negative actions the British may have planned for Ethiopia. He was reduced in rank and shunned by his peers upon his return to Cairo and in July 1942 attempted suicide while suffering from a bout of malaria.

After his recovery and when in need of friends in high places, Wingate was called on by Wavell. He put Wingate in charge of the Bush Warfare School and soon the talents Wingate developed in Palestine and Ethiopia were transferred and expanded in India. British public opinion was reeling from the loss of Singapore and the Japanese capture of Rangoon, Burma, with the threat that this posed to India. Badly in need of something to stoke morale, Wavell sent Wingate's men into Burma to disrupt Japanese rear areas. The force was composed originally of the Thirteenth King's Liverpool Regiment, the Third Battalion of the Second Regiment of the Gurkha Rifles, the 142d Commando Company, with Royal Air Force support planes. As his troops also contained escaped Burmese and Burma was to be their area of operation, Wingate decided to give his soldiers a name to promote esprit de corps. He decided to name them *chinthe,* after the stone lions placed outside Burmese temples to ward off evil spirits, but this gradually was corrupted into "chindits," the result of a mistake by a newspaper reporter for the London *Daily Express.* Wingate's first operation in Burma was a mixed success. He had no real knowledge of how to operate in the jungle and the dependence on resupply by air was an art in its infancy. Despite suffering from a variety of diseases as well as unfamiliarity with the terrain, the Chindits did indeed create havoc behind enemy lines, but it was more psychological than physical. Wingate returned after a few months in Burma with two thirds of his force, but with valuable knowledge for future operations, including proof that the Japanese were not invincible in the jungles.

The morale boost for Britain was invaluable and upon his return to London, Wingate immediately met with Churchill, now prime minister. Even more impressed with Wingate than previously, Churchill took him to meet with American politicians and military men at a conference in Quebec. Wingate's confidence won over President Roosevelt and some of the generals, and a joint operation was planned with the Chindits, British amphibious forces, and Chinese forces. The target was the central railroad junction of Myitkyina, into which Wingate's men were to be sent by glider to establish a number of strongholds from which to carry out guerrilla operations against the Japanese. What started out as a huge operation began to fall apart because of political concerns. In November 1943 the amphibious attack was canceled. That angered Chinese leader Chiang Kai-shek, who canceled the Chinese attack scheduled to be launched from the province of Yunnan. Other Chinese forces under command of American General Joseph Stilwell remained committed, but the overall operation was severely scaled back. Still, it proved fairly successful, and certainly well timed. The Japanese, in response to Wingate's first operation, decided to take the offensive against the Indian border cities of Imphal and Kohima. The commander of Japanese air forces in Burma warned against this major offensive, citing the British ability to place forces in the rear of the Japanese advance, but he was not heeded. Attacking in mid-March 1944 the Chindits soon secured their positions and harried the surprised Japanese, who had been focussing on their own offensive against India. The Chindit offensive coincided with attacks from the north under Stilwell's command.

Wingate directed the glider-borne landings, but the operations were severely hampered by an irregular supply of aircraft, occasional last-minute changes in forces, and the Japanese capture of one of the proposed landing zones. Still, the forces reached their appointed places and began operations against Japanese supply lines. On 27 March Wingate flew to meet with Colonel Philip Cochran, commander of the air support. The American B-25 bomber carrying him ran into heavy weather and never reached its destination. It was discovered days later buried in a mountainside, although whether it crashed owing to poor visibility or was shot down by Japanese aircraft has never been determined. Wingate's remains were identified and buried, oddly enough, at Arlington National Cemetery in the United States, because it was an American aircraft in which he died. The Chindits operation continued under extremely difficult conditions. The Japanese focussed a large number of men on the Chindits and soon outgunned them at the strongholds they were occupying for resupply by air. The Chindits were in action behind enemy lines from March through July 1944 and fought up to and past the point of endurance. The Chindits came under the command of General Stilwell, who was never a supporter of either the British or special operations. He ordered them to support his offensive even when the men were physically unable to continue. Stilwell's own medical officers told him the Chindits could no longer fight. Every one of them had suffered at least three attacks of malaria, the average loss of weight was 60 pounds per man, and they could no longer carry their supplies—much less continue to fight.

The British official history of the Burma campaign grants but slight credit to Wingate's forces, but the Japanese officers who survived the war told a different story. They were of the opinion that, had the Chindits not been active behind Japanese lines, the additional manpower and air power that the Japanese could have put to use in the planned attack on India would probably have been decisive. Even as it was, their offensive almost succeeded, but the forces diverted by the Chindits proved crucial. Furthermore, because Wingate's first operation inspired the Japanese to switch from a defensive to an offensive posture, their XV Army was almost completely destroyed in its failed offensive and during its subsequent retreat. Had the Japanese remained on the defensive, Stilwell's successful drive from the north would almost certainly have been thwarted and the overland supply route he established into China may not have been built.

References: Bidwell, Shelford, *The Chindit War* (New York: Macmillan, 1980); Rooney, David, *Burma Victory* (London: Arms and Armour Press, 1992); Slim, Field Marshal William, *Defeat into Victory* (London: Cassell and Company, 1956).

Condor Legion

A German air force unit operational during the Spanish Civil War (1936–1939).

In July 1936 conservative Spanish generals began an attempt to overthrow the liberal democratic government recently elected in Spain. The generals, under the leadership of Francisco Franco, faced a serious problem: Much of their army was not in Spain, but in Spanish Morocco. Because the Spanish navy remained loyal to the elected government, as did about half the army, the difficulty for the generals was how the Morocco-based troops could come to the aid of their fellow rebels at home. Representatives of Franco's forces travelled to Berlin to speak with Nazi Chancellor Adolph Hitler. They asked if they could borrow planes from Hitler's air force, the *Luftwaffe.* Hitler hesitated, for failure would not only rob him of aircraft but of status. The convincing argument, however, was political and struck home with Hitler: The elected government was friendly with the Soviet Union. Hitler's hatred for communism almost matched his hatred for Jews, and the chance to strike a blow against international communism was too good to let pass. Hitler lent the Spaniards 20 Junkers, 52 transport aircraft, and six Heinkel 51 fighter escorts.

Thus began Operation Magic Fire. Luftwaffe pilots were "volunteered" to go to Spain and Morocco and train Spanish pilots, as well as to ferry Spanish troops. During the second week in August 1936 the airlift started—the first ever conducted. The Ju-52 was designed as a transport, but was used in Germany mainly as an airliner. Although the plane was designed to carry 17 passengers, the interiors were stripped of their seating and 40 soldiers were stuffed inside. German pilots flew as many as five round trips daily, carrying not only men but equipment and weapons, including 36 artillery pieces and 127 machine guns.

The planes flew without identifying markings at first. However, as the hastily trained Spanish pilots proved incompetent in handling the fighter planes, German pilots soon went into combat and the aircraft began displaying a black "X" on a white field on their rudders. On 25 August two German pilots each shot down a Loyalist aircraft for Franco's nationalist cause. At first these were individual decisions by the Germans, but when the airlift ended in October 1936 (after transporting 13,000 men) Hitler decided to expand his air force's role in Spain. He saw that Spain was not only a place to make a stand against communism, it was also a chance to combat test new aircraft designs, as well as to give newly trained pilots on-the-job training. Thus was born the Condor Legion, so named by Luftwaffe chief Hermann Goering. The original complement was 48 bombers (converted Ju-52s) and 36 fighters. As new designs were manufactured, they were sent to Spain to update equipment. In addition, the Legion operated 12 reconnaissance planes, 14 reconnaissance-bomber float planes, antiaircraft cannon, and maintenance sections. Only the flying personnel were permitted to fight;

army advisors were allowed only to train Franco's troops to use German tanks.

With the Legion fully organized, hundreds more "volunteers" were sent to Spain. They travelled as civilians, running the Loyalist blockade to land in Cadiz, then transferring to the nationalist headquarters of Seville. The strength of the Legion was around 5,000 men, usually rotating through on nine-month tours of duty. The unit was commanded by Hugo Sperrle, with Wolfram von Richthofen (cousin of World War I ace Manfred) as chief of staff. Richthofen was the Luftwaffe research and design chief, and he was able to view new aircraft in combat conditions and report any necessary changes to the factories. In addition to the Condor Legion, Italian dictator Benito Mussolini sent aircraft as well but sent more infantry, ultimately almost 60,000 men.

The Germans faced a mixed group of opponents with a mixed lot of aircraft. Much of the Loyalist air force was provided (at high cost) by the Soviet Union, who also provided manpower, artillery, and tanks. Many of the planes were flown by international volunteers, people from Europe and North America joining the Spanish to fight fascism. The material support from the Soviets provided a great boost in morale as well as combat effectiveness, and the Loyalists beat back Franco's major offensive against Madrid in November 1936. Frustrated by a lack of progress on the ground, Franco ordered the air force to bomb the city, a policy he had scrupulously avoided to that point. For five days German and Italian aircraft with German and Spanish crews bombed indiscriminately day and night, causing more than 1,000 casualties. Madrid continued to hold out. Franco then decided to attack supply lines into the city, and his German-trained tank crews went into battle with Condor Legion air support in the first hint of blitzkrieg tactics that the Germans employed so effectively in later years.

Unable to make headway against Madrid, Franco looked to occupy other Loyalist territory, focussing on the province of Vizcaya. The area was defended by a virtually impregnable series of defenses, and the Condor Legion got the assignment to break them. Newly arrived Heinkel 111s and Dornier 17s, the newest German bomber designs, gave the Germans an edge. The Ju-52s were too slow and had been easy prey for the Soviet I-15 fighter. The new German bombers could outrun the Russian planes. On 31 March 1937 the aerial offensive started, with bombs falling on the forts, nearby towns, and the harbor of Bilbao. Near Bilbao was the small farming town of Guernica. On 26 April the Condor Legion blasted it for three hours, although there was little there of strategic value other than a small arms factory on the edge of town. The bombers attacked everything, including hotels, hospitals, and schools. Low flying fighter planes machine-gunned running civilians. At least 70 percent of the town was destroyed and as many as 1,600 people died. The two structures of military value, the small arms factory and a bridge, were almost untouched. As much as the bombing of civilian areas of Madrid had brought international criticism, it was nothing compared to the loud condemnation from around the globe for the Guernica raid. Publicly, the Germans blamed communist terrorists for the fires that destroyed much of the town. Loyalist resistance in the area did weaken, however. Resistance around Bilbao broke under an armored assault in June in which German tankers fought alongside Spanish crews.

In the summer of 1937 both sides got upgraded aircraft. The Loyalists received Soviet I-16s, which they nicknamed *Moscas* (Spanish for "flies"). The Condor Legion received the latest German machine, the Messerschmitt 109. For a time the two opposing aircraft were well matched, but the engineers in Germany were faster at introducing modifications and in early 1938 the latest Me-109 was almost 50 miles per hour faster than the I-16. The older aircraft, the He-51s were dedicated to strafing missions. The pilots were not happy shooting ground targets, but the Loyalists became such good marksmen that the Germans had to develop new tactics to hit and run before the ground fire inflicted too much damage. Bombing got much more accurate with the introduction of the Junkers 87, the infamous Stuka (short for *Sturmkampfflugzeug*). The dive bomber, although slow in level flight, was pinpoint accurate when bombing and became the most feared aircraft in the German arsenal as far as infantry was concerned.

Throughout 1939, the final year of the Spanish Civil War, the Condor Legion honed its skills. Close air support and rapid armored assaults became common practice, and the development of newer radios made the attacks even more effective as observers on the ground could direct the aircraft to particular targets. The Soviet tanks, heretofore far superior to the German panzers, found their match in the newly introduced German antiaircraft cannon, an 88-mm gun manufactured by the Krupp steel works. Although an extremely effective antiaircraft gun, this cannon also became the most effective tank-killer of World War II. By early 1939 the fighting in Spain was drawing to a close, and Germany had learned a number of valuable lessons. The Germans now had an air force that was not only well trained but combat tested, and the close air support necessary to implement the blitzkrieg was finely tuned. Although Hitler's dream of Franco as an ally never came true, the German dictator had to be thankful for the opportunity the Spanish situation gave to his military to weld itself into a first-class fighting machine, which came close to conquering all of Europe.

References: Mason, Herbert Malloy, *The Rise of the Luftwaffe, 1918–1940* (New York: Dial Press, 1973); Thomas, Hugh, *The Spanish Civil War* (New York: Harper and Row, 1961); Time-Life series, *The Third Reich: Fists of Steel,* (Alexandria, VA: Time-Life, 1988).

Condottieri

Mercenary troops operating in the Italian peninsula from the twelfth through the fourteenth centuries.

The European practice of feudal society made a serf liable for 40 days' military service to his lord per year. The Crusades ended that practice, as troops were needed for years on end. European society of the time also experienced the growing power of the merchant classes, which came to dominate urban life but which had no military experience or inclination.

If the merchants were to protect their wealth and expand their power, they needed troops. In Italy these were "foreign" troops, although not necessarily from outside the peninsula. Anyone from a different city-state in Italy was considered foreign, and the five major powers (Florence, Venice, Milan, Naples, and the Papal states) all hired soldiers from outside their borders. It was considered prudent to hire these outsiders, the argument being that they would have no local ambitions, unlike citizens of the city-state. The city-state offered a *condotta,* or contract, for a soldier to raise the forces necessary, hence the term *condottiere,* or contractor (plural, *condottieri*).

The first mention of these mercenary companies in Italy comes in 1159 with the arrival of the "Company of Death" organized by Alberto di Giussano. These 900 knights fought for Pope Alexander against the Holy Roman Emperor Friedrich Barbarossa. These mercenaries practiced what would come to be the worst characteristic of the condottieri: living off the land and doing so as wantonly and destructively as possible. Profit came not just from the pay from their employers, but from whatever could be acquired along the way.

Most of the condottieri forces were predominantly cavalry, as the makeup of many of the forces were knights without lands or lords, known as free lances. The term "lance" came to designate the smallest unit of the condottieri force, made up of three men. The leader of this lance was the knight, who was supported by his squire, who looked after his armor and weapons, and a young page, who did the dirty work, such as laundry, cooking, and feeding horses. The knight and squire rode good warhorses; the page rode whatever animal was available. Five lances formed a *posta* and five *posta* formed a *bandiera.* A *caporale* commanded five lances, with other ranks commanding larger units through the senior officer, the captain general. Along with the forces went political advisors, or ambassadors, to negotiate with potential employers, and treasurers to handle payment of the troops.

The need for hired armies was so great that soldiering was one of the best methods for personal advancement at that time. Anyone with strength could fight, anyone with intelligence and strength could lead, and both made good money. The vast majority of the condottieri were peasants or the sons of artisans with little hope of fortune. Many rose to great wealth and influence, which they could never otherwise have obtained. The political atmosphere in Italy served the condottieri well, because two major factions struggled for dominance for more than a century. The Guelph and Ghibelline parties represented the forces defending and attacking the power of the Catholic Church. The origins of this struggle came from Germany, where the Welf family fought the Hohenstauffens of Waiblingen over the relative role and power of the church and the Holy Roman Empire. The Catholic Church was constantly trying to extend its power—temporally as well as spiritually—past the bounds of the Papal States it had controlled since the era of Charlemagne at the start of the ninth century. All five city-states jockeyed for position in an ever-changing set of alliances. This meant that a condottieri force fighting *for* the Papal States may, in the next battle, be fighting *against* them, all the while receiving its pay from the same city-state that had just changed sides. Individual condottieri could also just as easily change sides themselves if the price was right, regardless of the political views of their employers.

Condottieri leaders sometimes became nobility and led the city-states themselves, as Francesco Sforza did in Milan. Pay included not just money, but lands and titles, and many times a young bride to seal the bargain. Marriage in the upper classes of Italian society at this time was more often than not a political or economic affair, not an amorous one. Thus did lower class soldiers work their way to the social heights, because marriage into an established family gave one social legitimacy.

In order to reach these heights, of course, one had to be successful on the battlefield. Here is where the condottieri come under much criticism. They were trained soldiers in a population without such, and therefore they were valuable—too valuable to lose, in many cases. This fact meant that fighting between condottieri forces sometime verged on the ridiculous. The condotierri saw to it that sieges were long in order to save the lives of the soldiers as well as to draw more pay. Battles were sometimes negotiated rather than fought. The greatest contemporary critic of the condottieri, Niccolo Machiavelli, wrote disgustedly about the battle of Zagonara: "In this great defeat, famous throughout all Italy, no death occurred except those of Ludovico degli Obizi and two of his people, who, having fallen from their horses, were drowned in the mire" (Trease, 1971). Despite this gibe, the condottieri certainly fought often enough to prove their worth, and men certainly died in real combat, but the condottieri are more remembered for their political maneuvers than their battles. Another mitigating factor for the condottieri is the fact that the condottieri units were dominated by heavy cavalry that needed open ground upon which to fight, precisely the type of terrain that is in short supply in Italy.

For professionals, the condottieri often had surprising difficulty adapting to new weaponry. During the era of the condottieri, gunpowder was introduced and artillery and personal firearms entered the military scene. At first, as knights, the condottieri were horrified at the matchlock muskets because—as the French nobility learned about longbows at Agincourt and Crecy—a peasant could easily take the life of a noble. One condottiere, Paolo Vitelli, put out the eyes and cut off the hands of prisoners who had handled these matchlocks against his forces. Still, one could not allow one's enemies to acquire such a weapon and use it against oneself, so firearm use spread. Artillery also achieved quick acceptance, once it was learned that the stone walls, which resisted catapults, could not stand before cannonballs. Fortress engineering hurried to catch up to, or stay ahead of, cannon development.

The age of the condottieri came to an end around the turn of the sixteenth century when the Italian peninsula was invaded by French troops. A professional force with national, not financial, motivations defeated the mercenaries repeatedly. This was proof that what Machiavelli had called for in his writings—a citizen army—was the wave of the future. Before the demise of the condottieri method, some condottieri had made themselves famous and rich. Francesco Sforza became duke of Milan. The English mercenary John Hawkwood was offered a lifetime contract to fight for Florence. Bartolomeo Colleone retired to become lord of Bergamo and rule his small state in a most enlightened manner. The other side of the coin was equally real: Francesco Carmagnola was beheaded by the Venetian authorities for his failure to win for his employers, and others met similar fates. Although mercenaries remained for centuries a regular source of fighting men, the condottieri were products of their time and quickly faded in the face of the rise of the citizen soldier.

References: Deiss, Joseph Jay, *Captains of Fortune* (New York: Thomas Crowell Company, 1967); Trease, Geoffrey, *The*

Equestrian monument of Colleone by Andrea del Verrochio, Venice

Condottieri (New York: Holt, Rinehart, and Winston, 1971).

Conquistadors

A warrior class of Spain that defeated the Moslems and conquered Latin America during the fifteenth and sixteenth centuries.

In the seventh century A.D. followers of the prophet Mohammed swept out of North Africa and invaded Spain. The Christian Spaniards were quickly overrun and driven into the mountainous provinces of Castile and Leon. Grimly, the Spanish Christians gathered their strength and struck back against the Moslems. This engendered a centuries-long war known as the *Reconquista,* the reconquest. To fight this war, the Spanish kings came to depend more and more on feudal heavy cavalry made up of aristocrats. These men were known as *hidalgos;* over time they also became known as *conquistadors,* or conquerors.

In early 1492 the last Moslem stronghold in Spain, the city of Grenada, fell to King Ferdinand and the Christians, and the Reconquista was at last over. This, however, brought up an old and reoccurring problem: What does a nation do with its military when the wars are over? Thousands of Spaniards knew no other art than war. Their entire lives had been devoted to the enterprise, and to expect them to turn to peaceful pursuits, such as agriculture or business, was naive at best. King Ferdinand found it increasingly difficult to control these bellicose fellows. Bands of unemployed soldiers began to wander the countryside, following popular captains and taking what—until then—had been freely given: the best of everything. Ferdinand had a serious social problem on his hands. Then, in early 1493 one of his admirals, Christopher Columbus, returned from a

A fanciful depiction of the meeting of Cortéz and Montezuma (Engraving by T. Schüyvoet)

voyage of exploration and reported finding a strange new world, which might be India, China, or even Japan. This news was a godsend to Ferdinand, who recognized in it the answer to what to do with his unemployed soldiers.

The New World (despite Columbus's insistence, it was not India, China, or Japan) became a beacon for the Spanish soldiers, for it offered them the chance to serve the mother country, spread the true faith, and possibly get rich in the process. This lure of "Glory, God, and Gold" proved almost irresistible. Soon the New World was teeming with heavily armed professional soldiers who proudly called themselves conquistadors.

Although some of the conquistadors were aristocrats and nobles, most were either young men from noble but poor backgrounds or common soldiers. What they all shared was a thirst for adventure, a dislike of discipline, and a great capacity for greed. Noble or commoner, all conquistadors were passionately individualistic; indeed, they raised individualism almost to a cult status. Their lust for power and wealth made them fierce rivals, and they frequently spent as much time fighting each other as they did the Native Americans. On the other hand, they also saw themselves as "bands of brothers" facing an unknown and hostile world. They were proud, daring, and reckless almost beyond belief, and their capacity for enduring heat, cold, hunger, and pain became legendary. The courage and hubris necessary for a few hundred of these men to march into the midst of hundreds of thousands of native warriors and demand their surrender is almost incomprehensible. Also incomprehensible is the cruelty of which they were capable: They came to the New World with a cross in one hand and a sword in the other, and many of their deeds, committed ostensibly in the name of a benevolent religion, are horrifying in the extreme.

The weapons and training of the conquistadors was typical of late fifteenth-century Europe. Horses were always in short supply because of the difficulties in transporting them across the Atlantic. Consequently, cavalry was usually a minor arm in the conquistador forces, although it was very impressive psychologically to the Native Americans, who were terrified by this new, to them unknown, animal. Most conquistadors were heavy infantry, wearing iron cuirasses (breastplates) and helmets, as well as tassets to protect their thighs. Some wealthier men might have more complete arm and hand protection, and a few even wore suits of plate mail, although this was almost always restricted to cavalry. The conquistadors' weapons were rapiers and two-handed broadswords, pikes and halberds, crossbows and matchlock muskets, and a few cannons. In battle they always tried to seize the initiative, utilizing their superior weapons and defensive armor to shock and demoralize the natives, thus rendering them almost incapable of self-defense. When fighting alongside their own native allies, the conquistadors formed an irresistible spearhead on the attack, easily punching a hole in the enemy's lines through which their allies would pour, exploiting the flanks and rear of the enemy and breaking their formations. These simple tactics proved successful time and again in the conquest of the New World. The conquistadors' success is not surprising: Technologically speaking, the Spanish were almost 2,000 years in advance of any New World civilization. None of the Native American peoples whom the Spanish encountered had developed iron working or the wheel, and without iron and steel weapons and armor, they were doomed.

Disease was also a very important factor in the defeat of the native populations. Native Americans had no immunity to diseases such as measles, smallpox, and the "Black Death" (bubonic plague). These diseases killed millions of them and left the survivors almost powerless to defend themselves from the Spanish onslaught. To many Native Americans it seemed that their very gods had turned against them.

The true conquest of the New World began in 1519 when Hernan Cortés landed on the coast of Mexico with 550 men and 16 horses. He had heard rumors of a powerful tribe known as the Aztecs who ruled a vast and rich empire located to the west of Cuba in the interior Valley of Mexico. From their capital city of Tenochtitlan, which was built in the middle of a lake, the Aztecs, under their emperor Montezuma, controlled perhaps 11 million subject people. However, many of these people resented Aztec rule and, seeing Cortés as a possible savior, they allied with the strange newcomers. Playing on Aztec beliefs that he might be a god, Cortés boldly entered Tenochtitlan and captured Montezuma. Although he was driven from the city by a new emperor, Cortés received reinforcements and in 1520 renewed his assaults.

Cortés's men built a fleet of small galleys on the shores of the lake and, with their Indian allies, instituted a siege of Tenochtitlan. An epidemic of smallpox was raging in the city, and—besieged from within and without—the Aztecs stood little chance. By 1521 Tenochtitlan had fallen, the conquest of the Aztec Empire was complete, and Cortés had literally become a king by his own hand. The surviving Indians found themselves virtual slaves, forced to labor in the silver mines and on the great estates of their new masters.

In 1530 another daring conquistador, Francisco Pizzaro, set off to investigate rumors of another vast empire far south of Mexico. In present-day Peru he discovered the Incas, and used Cortés's methods as a blueprint for his own conquest. Although he had only 150 men, they boldly marched into the heart of the Inca nation to the capital city of Cajamarca. There they demanded an audience with the great Inca Atahualpa. Although Atahualpa was backed by thousands of his professional soldiers, Pizzaro and his 150 men seized the emperor and proceeded to slaughter over 7,000 Inca nobles and retainers without the loss of a single Spaniard. They then offered to ransom Atahualpa for a room full of gold and silver. Although it required several months, the ransom was finally assembled in 1533 at which point Pizzaro ordered Atahualpa strangled. The Inca empire, deprived of its rightful ruler and most of its nobles and administrators, died with Atahualpa. Within two years the Inca people were subjugated, just as the Aztecs had been by their new overlords. Although Pizzaro became rich and was named as governor of Peru by the king, he did not outlive Atahualpa by much. In 1541 he was assassinated in his palace in Lima by rivals.

Other Spanish conquistadors explored the Americas searching for more rich empires to topple. In 1513 Ponce de Leon searched the swamps and everglades of Florida for the Fountain of Youth, a mythical spring reputed to cure ills and rejuvenate those who drank its waters. Hernando De Soto explored the Mississippi River valley in 1539–1542. Francisco Coronado set off to find the Seven Cities of Gold in 1540 and explored and claimed most of present-day Arizona, Colorado, Kansas, and northern Texas. Other conquistadors pushed up the Pacific coast and established settlements in Los Angeles and San Francisco. Although these men failed to find any more Aztecs or Incas, they did help Spain claim an American empire that in time would prove more valuable than the gold of Mexico and Peru. All of this took place in a remarkably short time; within 40 years the great conquest was over. But because of the conquistadors, the world, for good or ill, would never be the same again.

References: Descola, Jean, *The Conquistadors,* trans. Malcolm Barnes (London: George Allen and Unwin, 1957); Fuentes, Patricia de, *The Conquistadors: First Person Accounts of the Conquest of Mexico* (New York: Orion, 1963); Innes, Hammond, *The Conquistadors* (New York: Knopf, 1969).

Cossacks

Horsemen of the west Asian steppes, known for their warlike nature from the sixteenth to the twentieth centuries.

Cossacks are a Russian tribal group that probably originated from the serfs in the

Moscow area during the fourteenth and fifteenth centuries. They fled their peasant lives under the yoke of the aristocratic *boyars* and established farming and stock-raising communities along the Dnieper, Don, Kuban, and Ural Rivers and in Siberia. The name is probably Turkic in origin, *kazak,* translated variously as "freeman" or "wanderer." They first appeared as raiders and pirates in the 1500s and became both soldiers of the czar and pioneers almost by accident. In 1581 they were hired by a merchant family, the Strogonoffs, to drive back Tatars who had been controlling Siberia and raiding into Muscovite lands. Siberia was seen as potentially a source of wealth in furs that the Strogonoffs, with royal support, could exploit. The Strogonoffs also hoped to turn the Cossacks, who had often raided their caravans, into allies or else to see them die at the hands of the Tatars, either of which would suit the Strogonoffs and Russian trade nicely.

Under the leadership of Yermak, their chief (*hetman* or *ataman*), 800 Cossacks entered Siberia in September 1581. Why they launched their campaign with winter coming on is a mystery, for they suffered in the open. In spring of 1582 they pushed deeper into Siberia and met forces of the main Tatar chieftain, Kutchum Khan. At first the Cossacks fared well against superior forces, because they had harquebuses and the Tatars had no experience of gunpowder. With these matchlocks, Yermak defeated Kutchum's forces and captured his capital at Sibir, but the Cossack chief had lost many of his men to disease, cold, and guerrilla action by the Tatars. Although Yermak died a year later (after most of his men), the power of the Tatars was broken and the Russian Czar Ivan IV expanded his country eastward.

The early Cossacks tended to move and raid by river, establishing villages and trading posts at river junctions, engaging in pillage and commerce much as did the early founders of Russia, the Vikings. The Cossacks tamed the frontier for their own purposes but at the same time acted as willing or tacit agents of the czar. By the 1630s Cossacks had reached the Pacific Ocean and a generation later they had traversed the Aleutians into North America. Their wandering also took them southward toward the Caspian and Black Seas, with Russian authority and settlement moving in behind them. In 1650 the Russian Khabarov led a Cossack force across the Amur River in search of sables. They encountered Manchu tax collectors and soon thereafter Chinese troops. Russians sparred with Manchus along the frontier for almost 40 years, and the Cossacks were doing most of the fighting. After signing a treaty in 1689 ceding control of central Asia to the Manchus, the Cossack tradesmen looked toward the Pacific. Cossack fur traders explored and trapped Alaska, western Canada, and even the Rocky Mountains.

Meanwhile, Cossack and Russian interests were not always coinciding in the western lands. Although they served Czar Ivan IV in his campaigns in Astrakhan and the Crimea, with later czars relations ebbed and flowed. During a conflict over the throne between Boris Gudonov and a pretender claiming to be Ivan IV's grandson, the Cossacks seized the opportunity to establish a homeland for themselves along the Don River. In 1648 the Cossacks began their long-standing conflict with Poland after the Poles attempted to acquire territory in the Ukraine populated by Zaporogue Cossacks. The Poles attempted to both impose feudalism on the population and ban the Russian Orthodox faith. Under the leadership of hetman Bogdan Chmielnicki, a mixed Cossack and Moslem Tatar army from the Crimea routed a Polish army at Korsun. Believing that his people alone could not defeat the Poles, Chmielnicki offered his homeland, the Ukraine, to Czar Alexis. Under the Act of Pereyaslav, Russia took over the Ukraine in return for guaranteed local autonomy for the Cossacks. War between Russia and Poland continued until 1667 with the occasional interference of Sweden and the shifting loyalties of various Cossack and Tatar forces. Russia gained most of the Ukraine. When Czar Alexis proved tyrannical, Stenka Razin led a Cossack uprising that temporarily established an independent state around Astrakhan and Tsaritsyn (Stalingrad).

The Cossacks once again fought for the czar when Peter the Great in 1696 captured the Black Sea port of Azov, a battle in which the Don Cossacks played the major role. In 1705 Peter created a new army by drafting a peasant out of every 20 households for lifetime military service, but raised a separate force of 100,000 Cossacks. When Catherine the Great became czarina, she too had mixed relations with the Cossacks. Although she invited 54 Cossacks to be among the 564 representatives from across Russia to assist in drafting a new legal code, her reluctance to emancipate the serfs provoked a Cossack revolt. In 1772 Emelyan Pugachev, a Don Cossack and veteran of service in the Russian army against the Turks and Prussians, proclaimed himself Peter III (who had died some years earlier) and stated he would overthrow the usurper Catherine. With the aid of almost every contingent in southern Russia that had a grudge against Catherine, Pugachev raised 20,000 men and captured a number of cities including Kazan and Saratov, then marched on Moscow. Catherine looked to the nobility for aid and disciplined imperial troops defeated Pugachev's peasants. They surrendered their leader to Catherine, cementing the fate of serfs as well as the relationship between the monarch and the aristocracy.

A Russian Cossack chieftain, ca. 1919 (Photo by the American Red Cross)

Another role in which the Cossacks gained notoriety was in attacks upon Jews. During the war against Poland they had instituted pogroms in the territory they occupied, and when Czar Alexis joined with the Cossacks against Poland his armies killed Jews as well. Again in Catherine the Great's time they slaughtered Jews along the Polish frontier. In 1734, 1750, and 1768 Cossacks ravaged Jewish communities in Kiev and throughout the Ukraine. In the last instance they claimed to have a document from Catherine herself giving them authority "to exterminate the Poles and the Jews, the descecrators of our holy religion" (Durant, 1967). By this time the Cossacks had become master horsemen, and the image of the pogroms against the Jews was to be equated with the Cossack on horseback.

The Cossacks often proved useful to the czars, who in the nineteenth century began to use them not only as part of the army but also for suppressing political dissent. The reputation they had developed in the pogroms was reinforced by the appearance of Cossack cavalry breaking up meetings of whatever groups the government deemed dangerous. When large scale revolt began in 1905 Cossack troops forced it into submission, but when the same happened in 1917 the Cossacks had had enough. Cossack horsemen fought for the czar during World War I, but would not do his bidding in suppressing the Menshevik revolt in March 1917. They did fight against the communists during the Russian Civil War, but were ultimately defeated and forced to submit to the communist system. They were forbidden after the Russian Revolution to serve in the military or even maintain their cavalry traditions, but in 1936 Stalin relented and formed Cossack units that fought against the Germans. Some, however, emulated other Ukrainians who welcomed the Nazis as liberators from the communists, and some Cossack units did serve with the Germans. Whether fighting for or against the invaders, Cossacks went into battle on horseback, probably the last time any large mounted units will ever operate in warfare.

In the wake of the decline and fall of the Soviet Union, the Cossack people have enjoyed something of a resurgence. In all their old territories, but mainly in Kazakhstan, various associations have formed to perpetuate their culture. Such organizations have spread as far northward as Moscow and St. Petersburg. They still seem to fight on both sides of the Russian government, however, by both demanding local autonomy yet protesting Russian cession of territory like the Kuril Islands. In 1992 Boris Yeltsin gave the Cossacks the status of an ethnic group and called for the use of Cossack troops to protect Russia's borders.

References: Durant, Will, and Ariel Durant, *Rousseau and Revolution* (New York: Simon and Schuster, 1967); Longworth, Philip, *The Cossacks* (New York: Holt, Rinehart and Winston, 1970); Seaton, Albert, *The Horsemen of the Steppes* (London: Hippocrene, 1985).

D

Dervishes, or Fuzzy-Wuzzy

A Sudanese tribe led by a radical Islamic leader in the late nineteenth century, best known for their tenacity in battle, especially against the British Army.

In the 1870s Egypt was a semi-autonomous possession of the Ottoman Empire and under the direction of an official known as the *khedive.* Ismail, the khedive, was a particularly corrupt individual who spent the country into such debt that the French and British sent in financial experts to take over the government and straighten out its tax collecting and bill paying. In order to support this action, in 1880 the Europeans sent in troops as well, with the British sending the lion's share. Having foreigners in their government and patrolling their streets did not sit well with the Egyptians, and the British found it necessary to put down a revolt by an Egyptian officer named Arabi. Shortly afterward in the Sudan, the desert countryside south of Egypt, a religious leader rose to power to lead his followers against the infidels. This was Mohammed Ahmed, who called himself the *Mahdi,* or Messiah.

The idea of a Muslim messiah had been foretold for centuries and occasionally a leader arose to gather the faithful against non-Muslim enemies. Thus, Mohammed Ahmed was one in a series of Mahdis who came to power either through self-promotion and exploitation of his followers or true religious fervor. In the Sudan the Mahdi started with a small group of followers and expanded his power through intimidation or by success against the British. The British called his followers dervishes. Technically, this is a term describing collections of Muslim Sufi mystics who often perform amazing feats while in a trance or the throes of religious ecstasy. The term seemed fitting to the British, because the Mahdi's followers fought with a fanatical courage and no fear of death.

The British government, under the direction of Prime Minister William Gladstone, had little interest in the Mahdi until he scored a stunning victory over an Egyptian force commanded by a British officer. In 1883 William Hicks led 10,000 ill-prepared men into the Sudanese desert and was ambushed and massacred at Kashgil south of the major city of Khartoum. This feat convinced many that the Mahdi was genuine and his ranks swelled. One such tribe, the Hadendowa from the hills of eastern Sudan near the Red Sea coast, organized themselves under the leadership of Osman Digna. He had little to recommend him as a soldier and apparently his men had little personal regard for him, but he was an excellent strategist and his raids kept his men in booty.

Digna's men slaughtered two Egyptian forces along the coast near the town of Saukin in late 1883 but Digna scored his most impressive victory on 5 February 1884. Hicks's replacement was Valentine Baker, formerly of both the British and Turkish armies. He commanded a relief force of 3,800, marching to rescue a garrison at the town of

Tokar. Baker's force was a mixed lot: a few European officers, a number of high-quality black troops of southern Sudan who had been slave-soldiers, and a large number of untrained and unmotivated Egyptians. They were ambushed at El Teb by 1,200 Hadendowa tribesmen. The British called these men Fuzzy-Wuzzies, because of their practice of greasing their hair with sheep lard. However, that seemingly innocent name belied the rebels' fighting ability. Although they were armed with nothing but spears and clubs, the Fuzzy-Wuzzy attack was so determined and their reputation so fierce that the Egyptians immediately panicked and ran. The confusion made it difficult for the Sudanese soldiers to fight well and the Europeans who stood to fight were badly mauled. Baker's command lost 2,400 men and 3,000 rifles, along with half a million cartridges, four Krupp cannon, and two Gatling guns.

The British government was finally waking up to the very real threat arising in the Sudan, and Queen Victoria urged Gladstone to send troops. Within weeks a new force of 4,000 men under General Sir Gerald Graham was sailing down the Red Sea to land at Trinkitat, from there to deal with Digna and his Fuzzy-Wuzzy. The Scottish Black Watch regiment distinguished itself in a second battle at El Teb on 28 February, where, with a loss of fewer than 200 dead and wounded, the Scots inflicted more than 800 deaths on the Hadendowa. On 9 March Graham ordered the column to march on Tamai, supposed to be Digna's headquarters. Here the Fuzzy-Wuzzy, well armed with British rifles captured the previous month and with their usual fanaticism, made their mark on military history and literature.

Dervishes of Sudan (Underwood & Underwood stereoview, 1896)

The British advanced in their traditional square formation, which had proven unbreakable for decades. When they engaged the Fuzzy-Wuzzy on 13 March the British had early success. Graham ordered the Scots to advance and in so doing they opened the square. The Fuzzy-Wuzzy immediately swarmed through a narrow gap in the British ranks and proceeded to stab, shoot, and club anyone within reach. Fighting was hand-to-hand and even badly wounded tribesmen continued to hack at British soldiers. The quickly re-formed square kept out any further tribesmen while the inner ranks killed all those who had rushed inside. A trailing square quickly came up in support and drove off the remaining Fuzzy-Wuzzy, who lost some 2,400 men killed that day. Digna retreated to the hills and the British declined to follow him.

This action and these tribesmen were immortalized by the poet laureate of the Victorian British Army, Rudyard Kipling, in his poem "Fuzzy-Wuzzy."

> 'E rushes at the smoke when we let
> drive,
> An', before we know, 'e's 'ackin' at our
> 'ead;
> 'E's all 'ot sand an' ginger when alive,
> An' 'e's generally shammin' when 'e's
> dead.
> 'E's a daisy, 'e's a ducky, 'e's a lamb!
> 'E's a injia-rubber idiot on the spree,
> 'E's the on'y thing that doesn't give a
> damn
> For a Regiment o' British Infantree!
> So 'ere's to you, Fuzzy-Wuzzy, at your
> 'ome in the Soudan;

You're a pore benighted 'eathen, but a
first-class fightin' man;
An' 'ere's *to* you, Fuzzy-Wuzzy, with your
'ayrick 'ead of 'air—
You big black boundin' beggar—for you
broke a British square!

As the Highlanders still point out, the square really was not broken, just temporarily opened in order for them to advance as ordered and the Hadendowa took advantage of the opportunity.

As these actions were taking place near the Red Sea coast, the main drama was unfolding at the Sudanese capital city of Khartoum. Rather than deal with the Mahdi and his followers, Gladstone decided to abandon the region and sent General Charles Gordon to oversee the removal of Europeans from the city. Gordon, who had made a reputation as an independent, charismatic figure when stationed in China, decided that Khartoum should not be abandoned, or perhaps he was slow in implementing his orders. The question is debated concerning his real intentions, but by design or bad luck he found himself surrounded by the Mahdi's forces. News of this siege created much controversy in London, where the government dallied over what to do. After some months public and royal pressure forced Gladstone to send a relief force. The route south to Khartoum, however, is incredibly difficult. The Nile River is the natural route to follow, but a series of cataracts makes transporting supply boats nearly impossible. The expedition's commander, Garnet Wolseley, got off to a late start and then spent weeks constructing boats, bringing boatmen from Canada, training a camel corps—whatever seemed necessary to pass the rapids in the river and the desert beyond.

All the physical obstacles were overcome by January 1885. The advance force had fought the elements as well as the dervishes to be within striking distance of Khartoum, when the force commander, Sir Charles Wilson, stopped for three days to rest and tend his wounded. When ships arrived on the Nile at his camp, he boarded his men and steamed four days to Khartoum, there to find the Mahdi in control, as he had been for the previous two days. Gordon and the city had held back the besiegers with little more than courage for 317 days before being overcome and slaughtered. Many were blamed for his loss, but the brunt of the criticism fell on Gladstone. He finally got the troops withdrawn by deciding an incident in Afghanistan was more threatening.

The Mahdi died not long after his greatest triumph over the British and his followers turned their allegiance to his second-in-command, known as the Khalifa (Caliph). The Sudanese were left undisturbed until 1897 when an expedition under the command of Horatio Kitchener marched south and extracted revenge for Gordon and Khartoum. Kitchener became a national hero, was elevated to Lord Kitchener of Khartoum, commanded the final offensives in South Africa against the Boers, and ultimately rose to the position of Minister of War during World War I. The dervishes and Fuzzy-Wuzzy had for a time, however, humbled the power of the British Empire and joined the Afghans and Zulus as one of the few native forces to do so.

References: Farwell, Byron, *Queen Victoria's Little Wars* (New York: Harper & Row, 1972); Kipling, Rudyard, "Fuzzy Wuzzy," from *The Complete Verses* (London: Kyle Cathie, 1995); Woolman, David, "The Day the Hadendowa Broke the British Square—or Did They?," *Military History,* vol. 11, no. 2. (June 1994).

E

Egyptians

An ancient population dominant in northeastern Africa and the Middle East, establishing a major Middle Eastern empire.

For a nation that had such an effect on the military atmosphere of the Middle East in the first millennium B.C. the Egyptians had a particularly unmilitary background. In the times of the Old Kingdom, more than 2,000 years before Christ, Egypt had virtually no military. This was because it had no need for one. Egypt was an isolated region protected on the north by the Mediterranean Sea, on the west by the Sahara Desert, to the south by the impassable cataracts of the Nile, and on the east by the Sinai desert. With no outside threat, there was no need for an army. The only mention of military activity in the Old Kingdom was during the reign of Pepy, when he commissioned one of his chief subordinates to organize an army to expel some Bedouins. During the Middle Kingdom (2133–1786 B.C.), the Egyptians built fortresses to guard potential invasion routes. These have been discovered along the frontier with Nubia to the south and near the Bitter Lakes at the approaches to the Sinai Peninsula.

Egyptians lived this isolated way for centuries until they learned the harsh lesson of living without an army, a lesson taught them by the Hyksos. These invaders from the east, probably from the neighborhood of Palestine, easily conquered the defenseless Egyptians about 1750 B.C. and ruled until 1576 B.C. It was the Hyksos' chariots more than any other weapon that secured their victory, for until that time the Egyptians had not yet discovered the wheel. Almost two centuries of foreign rule wore thin, and the Egyptians secretly armed themselves and overthrew the Hyksos, who had become soft in the rich Nile Valley. From this point forward, during the time known as the New Kingdom, Egypt was a major power to be reckoned with in the politics of the known world.

With the exception of cavalry, the Egyptians developed every kind of military arm known at the time. The bulk of their forces were infantry, carrying shields and armed with lances or bows. Light infantry carried slings or javelins. For sidearms the infantry usually carried short, double-edged swords. However, some pictures show them with a *khopesh,* which has a wide curved blade vaguely resembling a meat cleaver. Their shields were curved on top and straight or slightly curved along the sides, wooden and covered with leather. A shield was roughly about half the height of a man. Armor was unknown for the common soldier, his protection being little more than a quilted tunic and cap. The higher ranks are depicted in Egyptian artwork as wearing links of metal fastened loosely to permit freedom of movement. The king is usually depicted wearing a metal helmet and often carried a battle-axe or a mace. More than any other weapon, however, the Egyptians depended on the bow. The one they employed was five to six feet long with arrows up to 30 inches long.

The glory of the Egyptian army was the chariot, the weapon they had adopted from the Hyksos. Tomb paintings almost always show the pharaoh in a chariot, usually alone with the reins tied about his midriff as he defeats his enemies. This is probably artistic license, as the two-wheeled vehicles they drove were designed to carry two men, a driver and an archer, and are usually shown with attached quivers of arrows and short spears. The horses were not only decorated with headdresses, but covered at their joints with metal ornaments doubling as protection. The most famous story concerning the use of chariots in Egypt is that of the Exodus, wherein the whole of Pharaoh's force of 600 chariots was employed in chasing the Hebrews. Although the Book of Exodus mentions cavalry, contemporary Egyptian artwork almost never shows men on horseback and those that are depicted are usually foreigners.

Battle scene from a relief in the main temple of Rameses III (1193-1162 B.C.), Medinet Habu, Luxor-Thebes, Egypt

The army of the New Kingdom was a thoroughly professional force, although conscripts were used: one man in 10 was liable for military service. Egyptian units were given names of gods for their titles (for example, Anubis, Phre, Thoth, etc.), which probably reflected the local divinity where the unit was raised. The divisions usually numbered 5,000, subdivided into 250-man companies and 50-man platoons. The artwork of ancient Egypt depicts the soldiers marching in order, but the battles seem to have no structure, just a melee. It is therefore difficult to know what military doctrines may have been developed in Egypt. However, as the point to the artwork was to glorify the pharaoh, the actions of the regular soldiers would not have mattered. In the depictions of attacks on fortifications, no reference exists for any sort of siege engines, like catapults or battering rams. In the pictures only arrows and extremely long pikes are being used in order to clear the walls of defenders, and scaling ladders are then employed. Artwork at Abu Simbel shows how the Egyptians set up camp when on campaign. They did not dig entrenchments, but surrounded the camp with a palisade made of the soldier's shields. The pharaoh's tent is in the center of the camp, surrounded by those of his officers. Separate sections hold the horses, the chariots, the mules, and the pack gear. A hospital section is depicted, as well as another area of camp for drill and punishment. Outside the camp charioteers and infantry are shown exercising. In the center of the camp is a lion, although whether this is literal or the symbol of the pharaoh is disputed.

Once liberated from the Hyksos, the Egyptians apparently understood that the more distant the frontier they could defend, the safer would be the homeland. Thus, Egyptian campaigns began up the east coast of the Mediterranean toward modern Syria. Inscriptions of the time praise war as a high calling, whereas in previous days the main accomplishment of warfare was looting and the acquisition of wealth. (That, of course, remained a goal and the pillage and tribute the Egyptians gathered financed the impressive buildings for which they are justly famous.) The problem they faced was that, unlike the nomads and bandits they had fought in earlier times, they now had to fight trained soldiers of other kings. The Egyptians apparently learned the art of war fairly quickly, however, for the contemporary inscriptions describe the joy the pharaoh felt when he got to go to war. "For the good god exults when he begins the fight, he is joyful when he has to cross the frontier, and is content when he sees blood. He cuts off the heads of his enemies, and an hour of fighting gives him more delight than a day of pleasure" (Erman, 1971).

The Egyptian military maintained a strong presence in the Palestine/Syria region for centuries, sometimes farther away and sometimes closer, depending on the nature of their opponents. They also expanded their borders southward at the expense of the Nubians. However, they found themselves occupied on occasion when they met too strong a foe, most notably the Assyrians. By the time of the Persian Empire in the seventh century B.C. the Egyptians were a fading power, and when they were conquered by Alexander in the fourth century they almost ceased to be important. As late as the first century B.C., however, Julius Caesar, Mark Antony, and Caesar Augustus found Egyptian wealth an important acquisition even if the Egyptian army was of little use as an ally.

References: Erman, Adolf, trans. by H. M. Tirard, *Life in Ancient Egypt* (New York: Dover Publications, 1971 [1894]); Ferrill, Arther, *The Origins of War* (London: Thames and Hudson, 1985); Kenrick, John, *Ancient Egypt under the Pharoahs* New York: John B. Alden, 1883).

Ever Victorious Army

A Chinese army under British command during the Taiping Rebellion of the mid-nineteenth century.

In 1851 China was on the verge of civil war. A religious leader had arisen to unite various factions opposed to the increasingly oppressive rule of the Manchu dynasty. This leader was Hung Hsiu-ch'uan, who took the name Tien Wang, or "Heavenly King." He claimed to have had visions that took him to heaven and inspired the crusade against worldliness and corruption rampant in the Manchu court, especially on the part of the Emperor Hsien Feng. Tien Wang's religious message was a strange amalgam of Christianity and Taoism wherein he played the third part of the Trinity, replacing the Holy Spirit. His "New Christian Testament" appealed to many of China's poor, and Tien Wang also appealed to the established antigovernment Triad societies. Tien Wang's movement was dubbed the Taiping Tien-kuo, or "Heavenly Kingdom of Great Peace." Great slaughter, instead, was the result.

At first the Taiping Rebellion, as it came to be called, remained fairly true to the stated ideals, as the soldiers were bound to remain celibate while in the field and could not loot or pillage after victories. Both cowardice and opium smoking were capital offenses. Under this stringent discipline, the soldiers scored impressive early successes, conquering from their mountainous homeland into the Yangtze Valley. In 1853 the Taipings were in a position to march on the capital at Peking, which almost certainly would have fallen, but instead decided to occupy Nanking as the ancient capital of the Ming dynasty they claimed to want restored. Nanking fell easily because the defenders thought it prudent not to resist, but the Taipings still slaughtered so many inhabitants that their corpses blocked the river when Tien Wang arrived in his barge to take formal possession of the city. The imperial army held on to Peking with a hastily recruited unit that came to be called the Hunan Braves, reinforced with units recalled from Mongolia. The Taipings, however, captured Chinkiang, which put them into a position to threaten the major port city of Shanghai with its large European population.

By 1856 the Taiping movement began to slow. Tien Wang began to emulate the dissolute life of the emperor he was attempting to overthrow. Struggles between him and his generals intensified as some tried to challenge his authority while Tien Wang used others to stave off the threats. The imperial court had its troubles as well. In 1857 the British and French sent in troops and ships in response to threats against their merchants and diplomatic personnel. The Westerners forced a new trade treaty from the emperor, but in 1860 they were back in force again to counter new Manchu demands. When the imperial army did not immediately allow the western force to march to Peking, the British and French shot their way toward the city. When the emperor proposed negotiations with the westerners at his gates, a new treaty was negotiated but the British burned the emperor's summer palace as a warning against future vacillation.

This friction with the Manchu government put British troops in China, and they were there in time to assist with the new Manchu offensive against the Taipings. The Manchus had had some success with an army of mercenaries under the command of an American, Frederick Townshend Ward. They fought fairly well and the Chinese awarded them the nickname the Ever Victorious Army. When Ward was killed, whatever unit cohesion the force may have had fell apart. Because it had been successful, however, the Chinese hoped for a new commander to whip the force back into shape and continue its winning ways. The Manchu government appealed to the British commander in China, General Staveley, to appoint a new leader to restore the Ever Victorious Army to its former glory. Staveley had on his staff a young engineer named Charles Gordon, with whom he had worked in the Crimean War. Gordon was keen to see action, and Staveley rather reluctantly appointed him to the position. Luckily, Gordon had already impressed the regional Manchu commander, General Li Hung-chang, so he proved a good choice and took command in March 1863 at age 30.

Gordon got right to work. While under Staveley's command he had overseen operations that cleared any Taipings out of a 30-mile circumference around Shanghai. He took the Ever Victorious Army, which had just been badly handled in an attack on the city of Taitsan northwest of Shanghai, and imposed his own form of discipline on it. Mainly by example, he created a strongly loyal force. Gordon showed no fear. He personally reconnoitered enemy positions, getting so close he often put himself under fire. When he went into battle he did not carry a weapon, but instead a bamboo walking stick. His force of 4,000 Chinese with western officers were given new uniforms of dark green serge with turbans, a pay raise, and timely payment of their wages.

His first move was to relieve a Taiping siege of Chanzu, where Taiping rebels had given their allegiance to the government and were now under attack by their former comrades. Gordon's army first captured the city of Fushan on the way to Chanzu. Seeing this, the Taipings decided to lift their siege rather than be caught between two forces. The major Taiping fortress of Taitsan fell to Gordon's artillery and a spirited assault through the breach, which the cannon fire produced. At Quinsan, Gordon attacked with a fleet of gunboats along the many canals that surrounded the town. Although Quinsan was a strongly walled city, Gordon's attack was such a surprise that the defenders fled after minimal fighting. Many were drowned in the canals.

The last major Taiping stronghold was Soo Chow, which was surrounded by a 12-mile-long wall. Gordon decided against an assault and laid siege. He also took the city of Woo Kiang upriver in order to cut off any reinforcements or supplies to Soo Chow. The siege lasted from October through December 1863 when the defenders surrendered on condition of clemency for their leaders. Gordon granted it, but the imperial troops supporting his force killed them anyway. Gordon was so upset he considered marching his men against Peking, then decided instead to resign his commission. The Manchus finally were able to convince him to reconsider, but he refused to take any monetary reward from the emperor for his victories.

The Ever Victorious Army was disbanded in June 1864 having lost almost 100 casualties among its officers and 1,440 among the rank and file, more than one third its strength. Imperial troops were given the task of assaulting the final Taiping stronghold of Nanking. They surrounded the city with 80,000 men and the increasingly corrupt Tien Wang committed suicide rather than face capture and execution. The Taiping Rebellion lasted 15 years and estimates of its cost reach as high as 30 million lives. Gordon's performance in China brought him to the attention of the government in London, and he became a popular public figure. He died in the Sudanese capital of Khartoum in 1885 when he was surrounded by the forces of another messianic figure, the Mahdi. Still, his nickname of "Chinese" Gordon, was earned in his first command.

References: Hanson, Lawrence, *Chinese Gordon* (New York: Funk and Wagnalls, 1954); Trench, Charles Chenevix, *The Road to Khartoum* (New York: Norton, 1978); Wilson, Andrew, *The Ever Victorious Army* (Edinburgh: Blackwood, 1868).

F

Flying Circus

An elite German fighter unit in World War I.

World War I was the first time aircraft were used in combat against each other. Before then the United States had used aircraft in scouting roles, and when World War I broke out it was scouting that was the primary job of airmen on both sides. The need to stop aircraft from flying over one's own armies brought about the development of fighter aircraft. By early 1915 some six months after the war's inception, Roland Garros mounted a machine gun on the nose of his Morane airplane and bolted steel plates to the propeller to deflect whatever bullets failed to pass through. He was shot down behind German lines and his idea was improved upon by a Dutch aircraft engineer, Anthony Fokker, who developed the interrupter gear. This allowed bullets to pass through the empty spaces of the propeller while interrupting the flow of bullets when the propeller's blades passed in front of the machine gun. The Fokker E-1 was the first widely used fighter aircraft, and for a while it devastated British and French aircraft.

The life of an airman proved tantalizing to many, especially those who had spent time in the mud of the trenches in northern France. One such soldier who transferred to the air service was a German aristocrat named Manfred von Richthofen, for the cavalry to which he originally was assigned was rapidly becoming obsolete. Richthofen learned to fly reconnaissance planes, with a cameraman in the rear seat to photograph enemy positions. This proved too tame for his temperament, and he learned to fly the Fokker E-1. His early experience in the aircraft was not positive, but he underwent fighter training and quickly improved. In the spring of 1916 he was assigned to a *Jagdstaffel,* a German fighter squadron, which at full strength numbered 16 aircraft.

Like all young fighter pilots in the German air service, he idolized the "aces," men who had shot down at least five enemy aircraft. The leading aces, who rapidly became national heroes, were Oswald Boelcke and Max Immelman, both assigned to No. 62 Squadron. When Immelman was killed, the German government wanted to keep Boelcke alive for morale purposes and so assigned him to behind-the-lines tours. When in August 1916 he returned to command the newly formed *Jasta 2* ("Jasta" being an abbreviation of *Jagdstaffel*) he chose Richthofen as one of his pilots. Boelcke was regarded as the first serious theorist of fighter tactics, and Richthofen learned from the master. The British had been pioneering aggressive fighter tactics, but with the development of newer and faster German aircraft, the Germans took control of the air in the latter part of 1916.

By 1916 the war on the ground had turned into such a stalemate that there was a desperate need for heroes to maintain public morale. It was the fighter pilots who came to fill that role. The French press first invented the concept of the "ace," which the commanders of the Allied air services at first resisted. The British in particular stressed teamwork over individual accomplishments, but the ace concept took on a life of its own. The French were the first to develop an elite squadron, called Le Cignones (the Storks); each aircraft had a stork painted on its fuselage in a different pose. This gave each pilot his individual marking while also promoting unit esprit de corps. The Germans followed suit to an extent: Flight leaders began to paint parts of their aircraft bright colors in order to be better seen by the pilots flying with them.

Jasta 2 underwent a major change after Boelcke was killed in a flying accident in October 1916. In December the unit was renamed Jasta Boelcke. Richthofen was improving his skills and by the end of 1916 had shot down 15 enemy aircraft. In January 1917 he was given command of Jasta 11, and took delivery of the newest of the German fighter aircraft, the Albatross D.III. Jasta 11 had yet to score any victories in air-to-air combat, and Richthofen set about whipping his men into a first-class squadron. As squadron commander, he had followed the general practice of identifying his plane with bright red paint on the wheels and the tail section. Soon, he painted his entire aircraft a bright red. This was to serve a number of purposes. First, he made himself easily identifiable to his own pilots. Second, although he had experimented earlier in his career with camouflage and the German air service was also looking into the idea, his own flamboyance would not allow him to purposely remain inconspicuous. Third, he hoped that his becoming famous as an expert fighter pilot would make the red plane strike fear in his enemies. Soon, his entire squadron painted a portion of their own planes red, and the brightly colored planes came to be called the Flying Circus. Later, all the aircraft in the Jasta were painted solid red.

Baron Manfred von Richthofen (right), known as the Red Baron

Richthofen's Jasta 11 came into its own in April 1917 by which time the Albatross D.III had become the standard aircraft in the German air service. Nothing the British or French had could match the Albatross, and the month came to be called by Allied airmen "Bloody April." In this month, Richthofen became Germany's highest scoring ace, surpassing the mark of 41 kills set by his mentor Boelcke.

Both the Allies and the Germans developed increasingly faster and more maneuverable aircraft as the war progressed, and neither side was able to maintain superiority over the other for long. No matter what planes the Allies introduced, however, Richthofen continued to increase his score. Although wounded in combat and forced at another time by the high command to take leave, he rested only as long as he was required to do so. Combat seemed to have become an addiction with him. He and his squadron grew in notoriety—both inside Germany and out—and he was undoubtedly the best-known soldier in Germany. His younger brother, Lothar, flew with him and took command of the Jasta on Manfred's infrequent departures, and the family tie was one more item for the press to play up.

By April 1918 Manfred von Richthofen was the highest scoring ace of the war, with 80 Allied aircraft confirmed destroyed. He had been promoted to command *Jagdgeschwader 1* (Fighter Group 1). On 21 April, however, he was killed in combat in circumstances argued to this day. Credit for bringing down the Red Baron, as he had come to be called, went at the time to Captain Arthur Royal "Roy" Brown. Brown attacked the scarlet Fokker Dr.1, the triplane Richthofen made famous, as it lined up on a British pilot on his first mission. Richthofen did not bring the enemy plane down quickly as he had become famous for doing, and he was shot down for flying too long in one direction. Richthofen's plane landed behind British lines and the smoothness of the landing seemed to indicate a wounded pilot. Richthofen, however, was dead with a single bullet through his chest. It has since been argued that he was killed in flight by an Australian machine gun crew firing from the Allied lines on the ground. However he died, he was treated to a funeral with full honors by the British Royal Flying Corps.

Jasta 11 continued to operate under the command of Lothar von Richthofen, but he was never the public figure his brother had been. Manfred left behind the Air Combat *Operations Manual,* which described the necessary tactics for handling the larger Fighter Group he commanded at the end of his life. Ironically, it was the final dictum of that manual that he violated when he was shot down: "You should never stay with an opponent whom, through your bad shooting or his skillful turning, you have been unable to shoot down, the combat lasts for a long time and you are alone, outnumbered by adversaries." Manfred von Richthofen also left a legacy of intensity, dedication, and professionalism that fighter pilots ever since have striven to emulate.

References: Bickers, Richard Townshend, *Von Richthofen: The Legend Evaluated* (Annapolis, MD: Naval Institute Press, 1996); Gibbons, Floyd, *The Red Knight of Germany* (London: Cassell, 1932); Richthofen, Baron Manfred von, *Der Rote Kampfflieger* (Berlin: Ullstein, 1933).

Flying Tigers (American Volunteer Group)

An American fighter unit operating in China (1941–1942).

China was the victim of Japanese aggression as early as 1931 when Japanese forces overran and annexed Manchuria, renaming it the "independent" state of Manchukuo. The Chinese could do little to stop the annexation and made few preparations for any continuing conflict with Japan. Chinese Nationalist leader Chiang Kai-shek contracted with foreign air forces for advisors and instructors, but the quality of training Chinese pilots received (mainly from Italian instructors) was extremely poor. Most of the period from 1932 to 1937 was spent, instead, with the Chinese Nationalist faction (Kuomintang) under Chiang fighting a civil war against the Communists under Mao Tse-tung. This internal division certainly encouraged the Japanese to expand their conquests by invading China proper in 1937. The Nationalists and Communists put their conflict on hold for the time being to concentrate on the external threat. Mao's forces fought out of the north of China while Chiang's struggled in the southern part. Chiang appealed to the United States for assistance, which he got after the Panay incident. During the Japanese assault on the city of Nanking, the American gunboat, Panay, was bombed by Japanese aircraft and was sunk with serious loss of life. The Japanese apologized and paid damages. The United States began to pay much more serious attention to the war, although only indirect, under-the-table military aid was forthcoming owing to American neutrality agreements.

By 1940 war in Europe had broken out and American President Franklin Roosevelt was disposed to provide war material to resist aggressors, although the vast majority of the early aid went to Great Britain via Lend-Lease. He did nothing, however, to discourage Chiang Kai-shek from appealing directly to American citizens for assistance. Chiang in 1937 had hired a retired maverick pilot of the United States Army Air Corps, Claire Chennault, to organize and train his air forces. Chennault, whose theories of fighter warfare conflicted with the generally accepted doctrine of the 1930s, jumped at the chance to leave retirement and put his theories to the test. In 1941 Chennault and Chinese General Mow visited the United States to organize a force of American volunteer pilots to come to China and fight the Japanese. Through 1941 Chennault approached pilots he knew well with the idea, but most pilots hesitated to give up their seniority and time toward retirement and promotion to join his group. Once assured that Chennault had the tacit support of the government, however, pilots in the Army Air Corps, Navy, and Marines resigned their positions to join him. The United States government also began to provide aircraft for the budding Chinese air forces.

Chennault recruited 100 pilots and nearly 200 ground crew for what came to be called the American Volunteer Group, or AVG. Acting in the role of modern-day hired gunfighters, the pilots were promised a generous base pay by the Chinese government plus a $500 bonus for each Japanese plane they shot down that was confirmed by direct inspection of the wreckage. The training for the group's combat role was conducted by Chennault, who had spent the last few years fighting the Japanese air forces and learning the capabilities of their planes and pilots. He realized that the new fighter aircraft that the Japanese employed, the Mitsubishi *Zero,* was much faster and more maneuverable than the aircraft he was able to acquire from the United States' government, the Curtis P-40B. Although the most modern American fighter aircraft, it was no match for the *Zero* in one-on-one combat. Chennault therefore developed tactics to exploit the advantages the P-40 possessed, which were fire power, durability, and greater weight. If he could position his planes at a greater altitude than the Japanese, the speed that they would build up in a dive would be greater than that which the *Zero* could achieve. Attack out of the sun, use the greater fire power of the P-40 to inflict damage on enemy aircraft below, and escape with the superior speed developed in the dive: These were the tactics developed to outfight the *Zero* and destroy the Japanese bombers that were wreaking havoc on Chinese cities.

Chennault's men arrived at Rangoon, Burma, in July 1941 and trained through the fall at a base in Burma, Kyedow, well away from Japanese eyes. Because some of the pilots had flown only trainers or bombers, the transition to fighter aircraft was difficult and dangerous. Furthermore, the difficulty in transporting the aircraft, assembling them on site, and trying to acquire spare parts was a massive undertaking. Accidents during training wrecked planes and killed pilots, and the primitive conditions of living and flying from a base carved out of the jungle was harrowing and demoralizing. Some men abandoned the project and returned to the United States in a matter of days after their arrival, but the rest persevered and learned not only how to fly the P-40s but how to fight using Chennault's tactics. They learned that individual action and heroics were to be spurned in favor of close teamwork.

The AVG was divided into three squadrons, deployed at separate air bases to minimize damage from Japanese attacks and to maximize the operational area. First Squadron was based at Kunming; its designation as the First Pursuit Squadron gave rise to their insignia: stick figures of Adam chasing Eve across an apple around which a snake was coiled, upon which was written "the First Pursuit." The Second Squadron, based also at Kunming, called themselves the Panda Bears. The Third Squadron, based at Rangoon, Burma, at a Royal Air Force airfield, designated themselves "Hell's Angels" and used red silhouettes of women with wings, in a variety of

Brigadier General C. L. Chennault and his men of the 23rd Fighter Group, later designation of the Flying Tigers

poses, as their insignia. The one feature all the squadrons had in common took advantage of the large air intake under the propeller of the P-40 aircraft: a full set of snarling teeth painted along the plane's nose up to the intake. This was not original with the AVG. British units operating in North Africa had painted this "shark's mouth" design on the P-40s that they acquired through the Lend-Lease program. It was this feature that gave the "Flying Tigers" their nickname and brought them much more notoriety than similarly painted aircraft elsewhere. This ferocious-looking paint job greatly appealed to the Chinese ground crews and workers at the airfields, who superstitiously believed it increased the fighting capabilities of the plane and pilot.

The Americans saw their first combat on 20 December 1941 well after the Japanese attack on Pearl Harbor brought the United States officially into the war. In action over Kunming the Flying Tigers shot down six of an attacking force of 10 Japanese bombers and returned to base with no losses to themselves. Three days later AVG pilots flying with British airmen at Rangoon intercepted a force of Japanese bombers and fighters with less spectacular results: 10 enemy aircraft destroyed for a loss of five British and four American planes. Fighting continued in Burma and China throughout December, with Christmas Day's action proving especially heartening. Two major raids totaling 108 Japanese aircraft attacked Rangoon, and the defenders shot down 28 of them, losing two planes and no pilots in the process.

In the first six months of 1942 the Flying Tigers fought air-to-air combat against fighters and bombers, escorted British bombers on raids against Japanese targets, and assisted Chinese forces with ground attack. The constant strain wore on machines as well as men, for spare parts were impossible to find, unless cannibalized from damaged aircraft. The damage inflicted during combat seriously affected the performance of the planes and the pilots' confidence began to waver. Finally, they refused to fly ground-support missions as the intense antiaircraft fire was too damaging to their already battered planes. Still, in aerial combat, the pilots excelled. The leading "ace" in the AVG was Bob Neale, who shot down 16 Japanese aircraft; David "Tex" Hill destroyed 12; Bill Reed shot down 11. Six other pilots destroyed 10 Japanese planes each. Numerous pilots became aces by shooting down five or more. By 4 July 1942 the three squadrons had 286 confirmed victories and possibly that many again shot down in locations that Chinese inspectors on the ground could not reach. In the six and one-half months of operations, the American Volunteer Group suffered the loss of nine pilots in combat, four more missing and presumed dead, two killed by Japanese bombs, and nine killed in accidents. In that time they had significantly slowed the Japanese air forces, but could do little to stop the juggernaut of the Japanese army on the ground.

Action in Burma was designed not only to keep the country in British hands but to keep open the Burma Road, the one line of access China had to receive American Lend-Lease supplies. As the Japanese drove deeper into Burma, the Third Squadron withdrew from Rangoon to Magwe, then to Kunming with the rest of the AVG. With never more than 55 planes operational, the American volunteers were just too few.

The Tenth U.S. Army Air Force was created in April 1942. It was designed to replace the volunteers in Asia. Claire Chennault's commission was reactivated and he was given the rank of brigadier general in what came to be called the China Air Task Force. When that was officially activated on 4 July the American Volunteer Group ceased to exist. Only five of the pilots chose to remain in service, the remainder wanting to go home, at least for a while, before reentering the service. This created some bad blood with the incoming personnel, but the difficulty of surviving the primitive base conditions and the stress of combat certainly seems to be sufficient justification for their decisions. Chennault stayed in China and served with the China Air Task Force and later the Fourteenth Air Force through January 1945.

The Flying Tigers were America's first heroes of World War II and, along with James Doolittle's surprise raid on Tokyo in April 1942, did much to raise the spirits of a nation just recovering from the shock of Pearl Harbor and the loss of so many men and possessions in the early days of the Pacific War.

References: Caidin, Martin, *The Ragged, Rugged Warriors* (New York: E.P. Dutton, 1966); Ford, Daniel, *Flying Tigers: Claire Chennault and the American Volunteer Group* (Washington, DC: Smithsonian Institution Press, 1991); Heiferman, Ron, *Flying Tigers: Chennault in China* (New York: Ballantine, 1971).

Franks

A population dominant in western Europe in the fifth to ninth centuries A.D.

The Franks comprised a group of tribes living in the Rhine River area that were first recorded during the latter part of the Roman Empire. The earliest history of the Franks was written by Gregory of Tours, who was a contemporary of Clovis (481–511), one of the Franks' early great chieftains. Prior to Clovis, the history of the Franks is sketchy. The first recorded leader was Chlodio, who led the tribes into northern Gaul in the early fifth century. Chlodio was succeeded by Merovech, who fought alongside the Roman forces against Atilla the Hun at Mauriac Plain in eastern Gaul in 451. It is from Merovech that the first recorded Frankish dynasty, the Merovingians, are named. His son, Childeric, was on the throne by 457 and seemed to remain a friend to the declining Roman Empire; he had perhaps been a captive of the Huns as a child. His Frankish forces again fought alongside Roman soldiers against Visigoths at Orleans in 463 or 464 then kept later Gothic and Saxon invaders away from Roman Gaul.

In 481 Clovis came to be Frankish king, although the sources indicate that he was merely the chief of other Frankish chieftains, a first among equals. He made war against the remaining Roman leadership, under Sygarius, defeating him at Soissons in 486. Clovis soon thereafter defeated rival chieftains and claimed supreme authority among the major Frankish tribes, the Salians. Clovis can thus be considered the first real king of the Franks. He extended his authority to the Seine River with his victory at Soissons and later reached the Loire. A decade later Clovis went to the aid of the Ripaurian Franks around modern-day Bonn and defeated the Allemanni, thus extending Frankish power into Germany.

Clovis converted to Catholicism, possibly owing to the influence of his wife, Clotilda of Burgundy. Some sources suggest that he was a Christian when he won at Soissons, but many claim that he embraced the faith in 496. He chose Catholicism over the Arian version of Christianity, although both were practiced among the Franks. This choice had profound effects, for it started the Franks on the road to becoming protectors of the Church of Rome.

First, however, there were other lands to capture and other enemies to fight. Clovis's expansion to the Loire River brought him into contact with the Visigoths, who controlled southern France and northern Spain. The Ostrogoth king, Theodoric, an Arian and related to Clovis by marriage, had long striven to maintain peace in southern Gaul, but Clovis went to war as the champion of Catholicism. He defeated the Visigothic forces under Alaric at Poitiers in 507 and sent his son to conquer as far as Burgundy. Frankish authority extended over all of France, with the exception of a southern coastal strip and the Breton peninsula. Clovis moved his capital to Paris and established a church to commemorate his victory over Alaric. Rumor has it that, in spite of his Christianity, Clovis plotted to murder the ruling family of the Ripaurian Franks. Whether this is true or not remains conjectural, but he was elected their king after his war against Alaric. With his power solidified, Clovis was recognized as King of the Franks by the Byzantine emperor, Anastasius. He was made a consul under the emperor's authority and treated as if he ruled in the emperor's name, which was hardly the case.

Clovis's four sons inherited parts of his kingdom and regularly made war against their neighbors. Under the leadership of Theudibert, the Germanic tribes were placed under tribute and the Burgunds were destroyed, which gave the Franks control over the Rhone River valley and the port city of Marseilles. Theudibert's expeditions into Italy weakened the Ostrogothic regime there to the extent that Byzantine forces came to control the peninsula.

The next great leader was Dagobert, who defeated the Avars, a Hunnish tribe threatening to expand past the Danube. He also raided into Spain and received tribute (or bribes) from Constantinople. Dagobert's reign also saw an expansion of Frankish trading power and the widespread coinage of gold and silver. He established a mint at the mouth of the Rhine and carried on extensive trade, mainly in the cloth of Frisia, in modern Belgium. He also supported the Church's efforts to convert the Frisians. Dagobert died in 639 the last great king of the Merovingian dynasty. His sons fought among themselves and the eastern (Austrasian) and western (Neustrian) factions of the kingdom struggled for dominance.

In Roman times, Frankish soldiers armed and equipped themselves simply. Tacitus writes, "Only a few use swords or lances. The spears they carry—*framae* is the native word—have short and narrow heads, but are so sharp and easy to handle, that the same weapon serves at need for close or distant fighting. The horseman asks no more than his shield and spear, but the infantry have also javelins to shower, several per man, and can hurl them to a great distance; for they are either naked or only lightly clad in their cloaks. There is nothing ostentatious in their turnout. Only the shields are picked out with carefully selected colors" (Norman, 1971). Tacitus describes few as wearing body armor and only a few with metal or leather headgear. He also says that the king was of noble birth, but the leaders in battle gain their rank through valor. Soldiers also carried an *angon,* a spear used for throwing or stabbing. It featured a barbed head and a long, metal-covered shaft, which proved impossible to remove from a shield once implanted. An enemy soldier thus attacked could not cut the long shaft with his sword because of the metal covering. Thus, the enemy's shield would become unusable and the Frank would close in with a second spear or his axe. When the Franks formed field cavalry units, the horsemen carried spears as much as two meters long with leaf-shaped heads.

Over time, real power in Frankish politics was exercised not by the king, but by the *majordomos* (mayor of the palace) who represented the tribal leaders before the king. It was Pepin II, one of the mayors, who founded the next Frankish ruling clan. He led Austrasian forces to victory over the Neustrians at the battle of Tertry in 687. This made him the dominant figure in Frankish politics and he assumed the role of military leader, the defender of the Frankish lands from outside attack. Pepin's conquest of Frisia brought him into close cooperation with the Irish Catholic monks who were trying to convert the Frisians, and the connection between Pepin's family and the Catholic Church began to solidify. Pepin led campaigns against the Allemanni, Franconians, and Bavarians, and the missionaries followed his conquests. Pepin died in 714 as the most powerful man in Frankish politics, but still mayor of the palace.

Pepin's illegitimate son, Charles Martel, inherited the position of mayor. (His Latin name, Carolus, gave his heirs the title Carolingians.) He led campaigns against the Saxons and Bavarians to secure the northern and eastern frontiers. He, like his father, worked closely with the church to extend Christianity. Charles developed a well-disciplined military based strongly on cavalry, and it was that arm that won for him his most recognizable victory. In 732 the Franks defeated a force of marauding Moslems from Spain at Poitiers in a battle widely regarded as saving Europe from Islamic influence. It was one of a series of battles in which the Franks forced the Moslems to settle south of the Pyrenees. In 737 the last Merovingian king died, but Charles remained mayor of the palace with no king to which he could represent the chieftains. He died in 741 dividing his extensive land holdings between his two sons; Carloman, to whom he granted his eastern holdings, and Pepin III, who inherited land in the west.

Carloman became increasingly interested in affairs of the soul, so much so that in 747 he ceded his lands to his brother and went to Monte Cassino to become a monk. Pepin, with tacit papal approval, removed the last pretenders to the Merovingian throne and made himself king of the Franks. His successful defense of Rome against Lombard invaders endeared him to the Catholic Church, which named Pepin III "King by the Grace of God." The Franks now became the official defenders of the Catholic Church. Pepin spent the 750s challenging the Moslems in Spain and reasserting Frankish claims on southern France. At his death the greatest of the Carolingian monarchs, Charlemagne, came to the throne.

By the time of the majordomos, Frankish society was developing into feudalism and the use of horses became more widespread. Although Charles Martel defeated the Moslems at Poitiers mainly with infantry (described by Isidorus Pacensis as standing "like a wall motionless; they were like a belt of ice frozen together" [Norman, 1971]) he apparently came to appreciate cavalry, for later accounts report his expansion of that arm. It was Charlemagne, however, who brought in the next major changes in the Frankish military. First, he enforced a discipline on his men that had been infamously lacking in previous generations. Fines were imposed for failure to report for duty, desertion, and drunkenness. As for his troops, after warring both against and with the Lombards, Charlemagne seems to have incorporated their cavalry practices. By the time his grandson, Charles the Bald, reined over the Franks, cavalry was the primary arm. By the end of the ninth century, Frankish infantry was almost nonexistent. By royal order, each horseman was to be armed with a spear, a shield, and a bow and arrows and protected by a chain mail shirt. Charlemagne also issued edicts concerning the establishment of supply trains (one of Charlemagne's chief accomplishments was development of logistical support), and he also made naval service obligatory for those living along the coastlines of his Holy Roman Empire.

The Franks dominated western Europe between the fall of the Roman Empire and the rise of the Vikings between the fifth and ninth centuries, and their development of feudalism, which ultimately resulted in the military development of knights on horseback, laid the groundwork for the Normans, who dominated everything from Britain to the Mediterranean until the Renaissance.

References: Gregory of Tours, trans. Ernest Brehaut, *History of the Franks* (New York: Norton, 1969); Lasko, Peter, *The Kingdom of the Franks* (New York: McGraw-Hill, 1971); Norman, A.V.B., *The Medieval Soldier* (New York: Thomas Crowell, 1971).

French Foreign Legion

An elite unit of foreign troops fighting for France since 1831.

In 1830 King Charles X of France, needing an event to divert the population from the ineptitude of his governing, invaded Algeria. The bey of Algiers had insulted a French ambassador, and in the nineteenth century that was almost all that was necessary to start a colonial war. Although 37,000 men quickly captured the city of Algiers and occupied the coastal cities, the hinterland was controlled by Berber tribesmen under the leadership of young and charismatic Abd el-Kader. In order to take the war into the countryside, the French government recruited a new organization on 10 March 1831 made up primarily of foreigners residing in France. It was an organization so desperate for officers that those who had failed in the regular French army had a chance to command in this new unit. Thus, from the beginning, the French Foreign Legion was a haven for any man of any nation to escape his past and serve an adopted country.

The first seven battalions were divided along national lines: First, Swiss; Second and Third, Swiss and German; Fourth, Spanish; Fifth, Italian; Sixth, Belgian and Dutch; and Seventh, Polish. The Legion got off to a particularly inauspicious start. Spurned by the regular army command, the Legionnaires had to scrounge for almost everything. Five thousand men sailed from France for Algeria but they spent more time fighting among themselves than against Berbers. Finally committed to combat, they were sent into the mountains with too heavy wagons and too much ordnance. Abd el-Kader's tribesmen ambushed them in the passes and slaughtered hundreds, while Berber women emasculated and decapitated the wounded.

After this, the Legionnaires were posted to an even worse assignment. The Legion was transferred to Spain to support the child queen, Isabella, against the claims of Don Carlos for the Spanish monarchy. Now reduced to some 4,000 men, the Legion almost did not survive the ordeal, as it was torn apart by infighting and poor command as well as by the better-supplied forces of Don Carlos and the complete lack of logistical support from either France or Spain. The Legion's commander, Joseph Bernelle, was totally cowed by his shrewish wife Tharsile, who became the virtual commander of the French force through her affairs with many of the officers. She was universally despised from the ranks for her capricious ordering of punishment. The dissension this caused did nothing to enhance the Legion's awful tactical situation. Again fighting in mountainous terrain, they were regularly attacked by larger forces under Don Carlos's command. They received no pay or food, so the desertion rate grew as the Legion marched deeper into Spain and fought through a bitter winter. At Huesca, the bloodiest fighting occurred as the deserters fought their former comrades. At day's end, both sides had suffered more than 75 percent casualties. The Legion had virtually destroyed itself. Only 500 men were left when the force was finally given permission to withdraw.

The survivors, however, had finally found the element they needed for unity. Bernelle, for all his shortcomings, had wisely ended the system of segregating the battalions by nationality. From 1835 forward all enlistees had to speak French. The mixing of nationalities ended much of the infighting, and the shared experience of surviving one of the worst campaigns any force ever fought created that spark of esprit de corps the Legion needed. Returned to Algeria, the Legion established itself as a fighting force. It was in the vanguard of an attack on the impregnable mountain fortress of Constantine. There the Legionnaires forced an entrance through the smallest of breaches in the walls created by days of pounding bombardment. Operating under the theory that became a Legion trademark, the men charged headlong into the breach in the belief that the closer to the enemy one gets, the fewer casualties one takes. Within two hours Algeria's strongest fortress was in French hands, thanks to the Legion. From that point forward, the Legion had the army's respect.

Some recruits in training for the French Foreign Legion

The Legion continued to operate in Algeria until that country's complete occupation, then aided the French effort in the Crimean War in 1854–1855. The Legion's next major campaign was in Mexico. The French Emperor Napoleon III occupied Mexico in 1863 after a failed attempt to collect debts. He installed Maximillian as Emperor of Mexico with the hopes of founding an empire in the Western Hemisphere. The Legion was sent to support Maximillian against Mexican resistance. On 30 April 1863 at the village of Camerone, Captain Jean Danjou and 65 men held a hacienda against several hundred Mexican cavalry later reinforced by three battalions of infantry. The battle raged all day until the Legionnaires finally ran out of ammunition. The remaining force, one officer and three men, surrendered. Because of the commitment to fight to the death shown there, the anniversary of the battle at Camerone is one of the Legion's premiere holidays, and Captain Danjou's wooden hand (he lost his left hand in an accident in Algeria) is the Legion's prized relic. After the defense of the hacienda, one of the Mexican officers said, "These are not men, they are demons" (McLeave, 1973).

Perhaps the most famous of all Legion battles was Dien Bien Phu in 1954. The French colonial presence in Southeast Asia had provoked the formation of an underground movement called the Viet Minh, under the leadership of Ho Chi Minh and his chief commander Vo Nguyen Giap. Viet Minh forces had grown steadily after World War II until by 1954 they were a full-fledged army. They occupied the high ground around the French base at Dien Bien Phu in Northern Indochina and pounded the base with artillery for weeks before finally occupying the position. Many of the Legionnaires were Germans, having joined the Legion to escape prosecution as Nazis or to continue as professional soldiers. Like Camerone, Dien Bien Phu was a defeat, but one that showed the Legion's dedication to fight to the end. Four thousand of the original 10,000 defenders survived the battle, which ended when their ammunition ran out. Hundreds more died in the jungle on the 600-kilometer march the Viet Minh forced them to undertake.

The Legion fought in all of France's colonial campaigns, for it violated French law for them to operate within French borders. For most of its existence the headquarters was in Algeria, although now it is in Aubagne near Marseilles. After World War II, the Legion received permission to reside in France, where today about 70 percent of the Legionnaires are based. To join the Legion one must be prepared to commit for five years. Four months of training are given at Castelnaudary, home of the Fourth Regiment, then the volunteer is posted according to his talents: infantry, paratrooper, engineer, diver, etc. After three years of duty French citizenship is available; after the five years, successive enlistments of up to three years are available. After 15 years a pension is granted. The Legion currently has five bases in France, one each in Corsica, Guyana, the island of Mururoa in the Pacific, and Djibouti.

The Legion has become the premiere unit in France for special operations, roughly paralleling the Special Air Service in Britain and the Green Berets in the United States. The paratroops, based in Corsica, are the best of the best and have been used for counterterrorist operations and served with the French contingent in Desert Storm. The Third Regiment in Guyana is trained for jungle operations. The Sixth Regiment, the engineers based at Laudun in France, includes the *Detachment d'Intervention Operationelle Subaquatique* with men experienced in diving and underwater demolition.

The Legion has, of course, always been known as the refuge for men trying to get away from their past. These tend to fall into four broad categories. The first are men who are just looking to get a fresh start after their failures in their previous endeavors. The second are those attempting to avoid a life of poverty and seeing the Legion as an alternative to homelessness and begging. The third category are those young men seeking adventure, while the fourth is made up of those who deserted from other armies but still want to be soldiers. The training emphasizes endurance and practical combat skills, as well as intense esprit de corps. When one wears the traditional white kepi, he must conform to the Legion's code of honor: (1) You are a volunteer serving France faithfully and with honor. (2) Every Legionnaire is your brother-in-arms, irrespective of his nationality, race, or creed. You will demonstrate this by an unwavering and straightforward solidarity which must bind you as members of the same family. (3) Respectful of the Legion's traditions, honoring your superiors, discipline and camaraderie are your strength, courage and loyalty are your virtues. (4) Proud of your status as that of a Legionnaire, you will display this pride by your turnout, always impeccable; your behavior, ever worthy, though modest; your living quarters, always tidy. (5) An elite soldier, you will train vigorously, you will maintain your weapon as if it were your most precious possession, you will keep your body in the peak of condition, always fit. (6) A mission once given to you becomes sacred to you; you will accomplish it to the end at all cost. (7) In combat, you will act without relish of your task, or hatred; you will respect the vanquished enemy and will never abandon either your wounded or your dead, nor will you under any circumstances surrender your arms.

References: Cervens, Thierry de, "The French Foreign Legion," (www.instantweb.com/l/legion); McLeave, Hugh, *The Damned Die Hard* (New York: Saturday Review Press, 1973); Porch, Douglas, *The French Foreign Legion* (New York: HarperCollins, 1991); Young, John Robert, *French Foreign Legion* (New York: Thames & Hudson, 1984).

Goths

A northern European tribe settling in southern Europe during the decline of the Roman Empire, known for their aggressive nature and introduction of cavalry as the primary military arm for the next several centuries.

The Goths were a Teutonic tribe, probably originating in Scandinavia, that arrived in northeastern Europe in the third century A.D. Together with their countrymen, the eastern Goths (Ostrogoths), the western Goths (Visigoths) ravaged the lands of eastern Europe as far as Asia Minor and Greece. The first serious conflict between Goths and Romans came when a number of Gothic mercenaries aided the usurpation attempt of Procopius in Constantinople in 366. After Procopius's failed attempt and subsequent execution, the Roman emperor Valens launched an attack on the Goths across the Danube. After an inconclusive war, the two sides agreed on the Danube River as the boundary between their claims.

Around 370 the two Gothic groups separated, with the Visigoths occupying the land from the Dneister River to the Baltic Sea and the Ostrogoths living east of them to the Black Sea. In 376 the Goths found themselves threatened by the migration of the Huns from central Asia. The Ostrogoths fled westward to pressure the Visigoths, who appealed to Valens for protection and aid. Valens agreed to allow them across the Danube in return for their surrendering their weapons and their male children under military age. The Visigoths, under the leadership of Fritigern and Alavius, agreed and gave up their boys, but resisted giving up their weapons. The Romans abused the Visigoths and provoked their retaliation after killing Alavius during a parley. Fritigern attacked and defeated Roman forces at Marianopolis, in modern Bulgaria, then called on the Ostrogoths for assistance. Emperor Valens, fighting against the Persians, secured a truce there and moved to protect his northeastern frontier. Fritigern's Goths and Valens's Romans fought an indecisive battle at the mouth of the Danube in 377. Then the Goths withdrew after the battle and raised a general barbarian revolt along the frontier. By 378 the Romans finally began to regain control in the province of Thrace, but then met defeat while launching an attack on the Gothic forces near Adrianople. Spurning a request for peace talks, Valens attacked the Goths before reinforcements arrived. The Gothic force of perhaps 200,000 warriors (roughly half Visigothic infantry and half mixed barbarian cavalry) badly defeated Valens, who died in the battle along with some two thirds of his 60,000 troops. The Visigothic king Fritigern was in overall command.

Valens's successor, Theodosius I, learned from his countryman's defeat and, after rebuilding an army and restoring order in Thrace, defeated the Goths and then invited them into his army. The Visigoths served Theodosius, but upon his death in 395 they chose their own leader: Alaric. He had earlier raided Roman lands from across the Danube, but was captured and incorporated into the Roman Army. Upon his election as king, Alaric led the Visigoths through Thrace and Greece. His only serious enemy was Stilicho, a Vandal general in Roman service who had served Theodosius. The Visigoths remained relatively unbothered, however, for the eastern Roman emperor, Arcadius, ordered Stilicho to remain in Italy. Alaric spent the mid-390s ravaging Greece, and then turned toward Italy.

Visigothic forces marched through Pannonia (along the eastern Adriatic coast) and crossed the Alps in October 401. Alaric's forces overran some of the northern provinces but Stilicho's delaying actions kept him in the north. During the winter Stilicho ordered forces from Gaul to Italy and did some personal recruiting among German tribes. The resulting army attacked Alaric's forces, which were besieging Milan. Alaric withdrew and marched south, looking for Stilicho's incompetent emperor, Honorius. After two difficult battles in March and April 402 Alaric asked for negotiations and agreed to leave Italy. Instead, Alaric marched for Gaul, which had been left unprotected. Stilicho learned of this maneuver and blocked him, defeating the Visigoths at Verona. Alaric again withdrew and Honorius moved the imperial capital to Ravenna, behind the marshy outskirts of which he felt safe from attack. Alaric decided to cooperate with Stilicho and was named master-general of Illyricum. When in 408 Honorius ordered Stilicho murdered, the general's followers appealed to Alaric to invade Italy. He did so gladly. After two attacks on Rome were called off (owing to successful Roman bribery), Alaric marched his forces to Rome and on 24 August 410 Rome fell to foreign invaders for the first time in a thousand years. Alaric then marched south to invade Sicily but died on the way.

Under the leadership of Athaulf, the Visigoths invaded Gaul in 412—supposedly to recover it for Honorius. Athaulf accomplished the conquest by 414 and was rewarded with marriage to Honorius's half-sister. He then followed Honorius's direction to reconquer Spain, but died in the process in 415. His successor, Wallia, defeated a number of barbarian tribes in Spain. He was rewarded with a kingdom of his own in southern Gaul. From this point the Visigoths settled into lands ranging from the Rhone River into Spain. The greatest king was Euric, who established a code of law based on a mixture of Roman and Germanic legal traditions. The one thing he could not do, however, was establish a hereditary line, because the nobility forbade it. The monarchy was elective and therefore subject to too much political infighting. The lack of unity laid the Visigothic kingdom open to outside pressure, and in 507 Clovis, the founder of the Merovingian dynasty of the Franks, defeated Alaric II and acquired much of the lands north of the Pyrenees. Although the Visigoths managed to maintain hold of Spain in the face of pressure from the Vandals, they ultimately fell to Moslem invasion. The last Visigothic king, Roderic, was defeated and killed in 711 and the remaining Visigothic tribe was confined to the province of Asturias.

The Visigoths played an important role in the fall of the Roman Empire in the west. They, like many of the barbarians that flooded the Empire, were converted to the Arian view of Christianity and thus often had troubles with the Roman Catholic Church, which viewed them as heretics. As soldiers, they proved themselves so talented that the Roman Army in the east, based in Constantinople, reconfigured itself to adapt to Gothic cavalry. The Goths had little effect on the course of European history after 500 A.D., however, because they spread themselves too thinly—from the Balkans to Spain—and were finally defeated and absorbed by more powerful enemies.

Following their brothers, the Visigoths, through southeastern Europe, the Ostrogoths entered into an uneasy alliance with the Byzantine Empire. They occupied Pannonia in the Danube valley and occasional

A Victorian-era depiction of the Battle of Chalons, where Gothic chieftain Thorismund defeated Attila the Hun

forays took them to the gates of Constantinople. Finally tiring of dealing with them, the Byzantine emperor Leo agreed to pay the Ostrogoths large amounts of tribute in return for a hostage, the heir to the Ostrogothic throne, Theodoric. At age seven Theodoric went to the Byzantine court and became a favorite of Leo, although he did not absorb as much education as his mentor would have liked. He did, however, acquire some culture and the Byzantine lifestyle, which he could put to good use later in life.

Theodoric returned to his people in 471 A.D. after ten years in the imperial Byzantine court. He became king of the Ostrogoths three years later and remained alternately a source of trouble and security on the Byzantine frontier. Finally, Emperor Zeno commissioned Theodoric to invade Italy and defeat the tyrant Odovacer, the self-styled king of that country and leader of a large number of Hunnish troops. The Ostrogothic invasion of Italy numbered the entire tribe of as many as 250,000 people. They entered Italy in August 489 and met Odovacer's forces along the Isonzo River. It was not a one-battle war; the Ostrogoths fought Odovacer's men for four years, finally capturing his capital at Ravenna after a lengthy siege. Theodoric granted Odovacer exceedingly liberal terms of surrender, then killed him at a celebratory feast.

Having removed the leader of a barbarian force, and done so in a barbaric manner, Theodoric became a remarkably gifted and wise leader. He established his capital at Ravenna also, but was unable to get the Byzantine empire to recognize him as anything more than "King of the Goths." In actuality, he was virtually a new emperor in the west. Ostrogoths settled into Italy and Theodoric confiscated the lands of Odovacer's men, plus whatever was necessary to take from the Italians to accommodate the larger Ostrogothic population. Although not at first thrilled with their new overlords, the local population came to appreciate Gothic rule. Theodoric reigned from 493 until 526 and almost all of those 33 years were peaceful. Even the Byzantines had to admit that he was a capable ruler. He treated all citizens equally, whether Roman, Gothic, or foreigner, and all received justice. Although the Goths were practitioners of the Arian sect of Christianity (which denied Christ's equality with God), there was no religious persecution in a country dominated by the Roman Catholic Church. Theodoric authorized reconstruction projects in Rome and encouraged intellectual pursuits.

Theodoric maintained the peace with a strong military, establishing garrisons in Sicily and Dalmatia. He also made good use of political marriages to pacify potential enemies. Theodoric himself married the sister of King Clovis of the Franks, and he married his own sister to the king of the Vandals and a daughter to the Burgundian king. When the Franks attacked the Visigoths in southern Gaul, Theodoric stepped in to save them and extend his own influence into their territory in the Iberian peninsula.

Theodoric's beneficent rule made the Byzantine emperors Justin and Justinian envious. Justinian longed to reestablish a united Roman empire under Eastern rule. His renewed persecution of the Arians in the east provoked Theodoric's wrath, and the final three years of the Ostrogoth king's rule was unpleasant. By threatening and ultimately causing the death of the pope in 526 Theodoric lost most of his public support. His death in that same year left an ambitious wife, Amalasuntha, attempting to rule by placing her and Theodoric's young son on the throne. This only succeeded in provoking the ire of Gothic nobles. A later attempt to rule through a cousin whom she married proved Amalasuntha's undoing, for he soon allowed rivals to murder her. The discontent resulting from these actions encouraged Justinian, who sent his talented general, Belisarius, to remove barbarian rule from Italy. This he succeeded in doing by breaking Gothic power during a siege at Rome and harrying the remaining Gothic forces northward. His capture of Ravenna sealed his victory, but it proved short-lived. When Belisarius returned to Constantinople, the Goths under their new leader Totila went about reconquering the peninsula. Between 541 and 543 most of Italy was once again in Gothic hands. Totila laid siege to Rome in 545 and was finally admitted to the city by disgruntled guards. He was obliged to reconquer it in 549, then fortified it and proceeded to conquer Corsica and Sardinia. By 550 he controlled more territory than had Theodoric.

Justinian had the last word, however. Dispatching a force under the 75-year-old Narses, the Byzantine forces captured Ravenna and defeated the Gothic army. After a mopping-up campaign, the last few hundred Goths were allowed free passage out of Italy across the Alps, never to return. The removal of the "barbarians," however, did not bring better times to the Italian peninsula. The recurring wars had devastated the countryside and had drained Constantinople's finances. There was no money to rebuild, so Italy remained little better than a wasteland in some areas. The Goths provided a short era of stability after the fall of the Roman Empire and under Theodoric the peninsula had the least barbarian of overlords. Enlightened as Theodoric was, the indigenous population nevertheless viewed him and the Ostrogoths as outsiders and, to an extent, heretics. For this reason, little of Gothic rule had any lasting impact on the Italian peninsula other than to put an end to Roman rule. The Lombards soon moved into the power vacuum left by the Ostrogoths and later forced the Byzantines out, but they were defeated in their turn. Italy would not be unified again until the nineteenth century.

References: Burns, Thomas, *A History of the Ostrogoths* (Bloomington: University of Indiana Press, 1984); Heather, Peter, *Goths and Romans* (Oxford: Clarendon, 1991); Wolfram, Herwig, *History of the Goths* (Berkeley: University of California Press, 1988).

Goumiers

North African troops fighting under French command in World War II.

While the French held colonies in North Africa, they recruited local forces both for police work as well as auxiliaries for the French troops. In Morocco, they organized the volunteers into units of approximately 200 men (called *goumiers*) in both infantry and cavalry roles. When World War II broke out, 126 goums were in existence. Some were used against the Italians along the Libyan-Tunisian border before France surrendered. After the Paris government signed surrender terms in June 1940 the local French administrator General Nogues was ordered to disband the goums. Instead, he secretly kept them trained and equipped. When the American forces landed in Morocco in 1942 the French forces, including the goumiers, joined with them against the Axis troops. The goumiers at that time were four regiments strong, organized as the *Groupement de Tabors Marocains*, or GTMs.

More men were recruited after the Axis forces were pushed out of North Africa, and the goums were organized into *tabors* (units of three goums, roughly 1,000 men). Three tabors made up a group. These Moroccan troops served with the American Seventh Army under George Patton in the campaign to capture Sicily in the summer of 1943 then accompanied the Allies into Italy. The First, Third, and Fourth GTMs served in Italy and made their greatest contribution in the final battle for Monte Cassino in central Italy in the spring of 1944. They were part of the French *Corps Expeditionnaire Francais* (CEF) commanded by General Alphonse Juin. On 14 May 1944 a shock force of 12,000 men of the Fourth Moroccan Mountain Division, of which many were goumiers, was placed under the command of General Guillame. They were assigned to infiltrate an extremely rugged section of the German defensive position, known as the Gustav Line. The area was lightly defended because the Germans were convinced that no one could possibly make their way through that difficult terrain. The goumiers, however, were born and raised in such country and could move both quickly and silently. What German soldiers they found they dispatched quickly with their preferred weapons, knives. By 16 May they had captured the Monte Petrella, outflanking the Germans and forcing their withdrawal, easing considerably the advance of the British Eighth Army. That same day they captured Monte Revole and the next day were in possession of Monte Faggeto, which controlled the primary German supply line. To a great extent the actions of the French Moroccans won the battle, for their quick action and appearance in the German rear obliged the Germans, who had held the Allies stalemated for months, to withdraw to other defensive lines further north.

The goumiers made a reputation not only for their skill in mountain fighting but for their ruthlessness. The used their knives more than their rifles and often brought back German body parts as souvenirs. This, of course, had great psychological effects. The goumiers reached the height of their fame in the battle for Monte Cassino, but other Moroccan tabors were involved in the capture of Corsica and Elba. The goumiers also were involved in the secondary landing on French soil in August 1944 along the Mediterranean coast. They fought in France and some went with the American armies into Germany. Other Moroccan troops remained in North Africa on garrison duty through the war.

References: Dear, E.D.S. and M.R.D. Foot, eds., *Oxford Companion to World War II* (Oxford: Oxford University Press, 1995); Ellis, John, *Cassino: The Hollow Victory* (New York: McGraw-Hill, 1984); Majdalany, Fred, *The Battle of Cassino* (New York: Houghton Mifflin, 1957).

Grande Armée

The French army commanded by Napoleon that dominated Europe in the early nineteenth century.

The nature of armies and warfare changed after the French Revolution (1789–1793). After the Peace of Westphalia ended the Thirty Years War in 1648, warfare in Europe was relatively limited in numbers and objectives. Kings fought each other with armies of professionals (often mercenaries) and a balance of power was maintained. No country was allowed to dominate the continent, and an ever-shifting series of alliances reflected the whims of monarchs hoping to gain a piece of land here or there to add to their country. When those European kings joined together in 1793 in an attempt to restore the French monarchy after Louis XVI's execution, they relied on their small professional forces. However, the army that met them was unlike any force that Europe had ever seen. Encouraged by the equality granted them as a result of the Revolution, Frenchmen flocked to the colors to defend their nation and their new system of government. The French government introduced the *levée en masse*, conscription that drew from all classes of society and created a huge, but disorganized and amateur army. It was this disorganization, however, that was the new army's strength, for the French soldiers broke the rules of warfare by not marching in straight lines but by throwing themselves in massive waves over and around stunned and vastly outnumbered adversaries.

The French army beat back the European monarchs and kept the country independent, but internal squabbling, combined with the desire to spread their Revolution, caused political discord at home. As in ancient Rome, so it was in France: When a government is divided, generals can play important political roles. As the hero of campaigns in Italy and Egypt, Napoleon Bonaparte parlayed his military success into political power, overthrowing the weakened revolutionary government and installing himself as emperor of a new France. As a revolutionary himself, Napoleon promoted many of his political predecessors' goals, and many of the social and legal advances he implemented became permanent. But it was the spirit of the large and motivated army, coupled with his own genius and experience, that created the *Grande Armée*, or "Grand Army."

When Napoleon took control of the government in 1799, much of the revolutionary *élan* had faded among both the commissioned and noncommissioned officers. Rivalries arose within the army as the various forces, with different commanders and experiences, believed themselves superior to one another. Napoleon ended the discord in 1804 by combining all of these forces into the Grand Army, with himself as commander. Henceforward, the troops cooperated (for the most part) without petty bickering. Napoleon instead fostered regimental pride, giving each unit its own standard and variety of uniforms. The standard was to be carried into battle and protected at all costs. If a standard-bearer was killed in battle, another soldier would immediately take up the standard, so that the regiment could rally around its colors. The flag was carried in parades and decorated with mementoes of victories, honored in the headquarters, and retired to churches. Rather than petty rivalry, regimental pride created unit pride dedicated to doing the best possible job for emperor and country.

Napoleon's phenomenal victories in the first years of the nineteenth century had made attracting recruits easy. However, after 1809 when he began to suffer setbacks, Napoleon relied more heavily on the draft. Originally, all men who were 20 to 25 years of age were liable for military service (with some exceptions), but by 1812 Napoleon resorted to drafting younger men. He retained, however, the equality of opportunity that had characterized the revolutionary army. Although the Grand Army's top commanders, the marshals, tended to be from the upper classes, it was possible even for recruits from the lowest classes to rise through the ranks. After a battle, dead junior officers were immediately replaced by sergeants promoted almost on the spot.

The army drafted 1,500,000 men between 1800 and 1815. About one fourth of them were from countries occupied by, or allied with, Napoleon. He accepted deserters from other armies into his own and created multinational units. Even his personal Imperial Guard contained soldiers from Italy, Holland, and Hanover. Whether draftee or volunteer, the troops of the Grand Army received little formal training upon enlistment. Instead, they were given small increments of training daily while on the march. This way they picked up valuable insights from veterans and learned what was actually vital for both survival and victory. This method proved inadequate in later years, especially after Napoleon lost almost his entire army in Russia between 1812 and 1813. A new Grand Army, built virtually from scratch in 1813, had veterans drawn from French combat forces in Spain and Italy, stiffening the new force but weakening the donor forces. Still, the recruits performed well, for while they may have lost their revolutionary ardor, Napoleon's charisma was often all they needed. He was liberal in awarding decorations to the troops, knowing that this fostered both loyalty and fighting spirit. Napoleon once commented that it was amazing what someone would do for "a bauble." He also awarded specially inscribed swords or muskets to commemorate outstanding acts of valor. Anyone of any rank or unit could be awarded the Legion of Honor: Of the 40,000 recipients of this award, only 25,000 survived through the Battle of Waterloo in 1815.

Those soldiers that particularly distinguished themselves in combat might be transferred to the Imperial Guard, Napoleon's personal reserve. This force was divided into three sections: The Old Guard was made up of soldiers with at least four years and two campaigns of experience. These were his favorites, and he liked to call them *le grognards*, the "grumblers." The Middle Guard was slightly less selective and contained some foreign units. The Young Guard was made up of the top recruits from each class of conscripts. The Imperial Guard was always better paid and better fed, which led to some envy, but its members often earned their pay. The sight of the Old Guard, always dressed for battle in parade uniforms, at times acted as both a spur to the French troops and an immediate visual threat to the enemy. Napoleon called upon them for the killing blow at battle's end. In his later years, however, he became more and more reluctant to commit the Old Guard, even when necessary. When the Imperial Guard, hastily reformed after Napoleon's escape from Elba, broke at Waterloo, it was the signal for a general French collapse. The Imperial Guard did, however, cover the emperor's retreat. When caught by the British and told to lay down their arms, the Guard commander replied, "The Guard dies, but never surrenders" (Chandler, 1966). At its height, the Imperial Guard numbered 112,000 men.

The Grand Army was organized into a number of corps, each commanded by a marshal. The size of each corps varied, depending on the talent of its commander, the job it was assigned to do, or simply to confuse enemy intelligence gathering. The marshals were appointed for their bravery and loyalty, and those officers that had served with Napoleon in his early campaigns in Italy or Egypt remained his favorites. The marshals, however, were not allowed much independence because Napoleon practiced a highly centralized form of command. He made all the decisions that mattered, and his staff existed not to advise him, but to follow his directives. Although this centralization accomplished its original purpose of uniting the army, it proved deleterious when Napoleon was obliged to detach units or create separate armies to operate in far-flung locales. Thus, his army in Spain, which was almost never under his direct command, suffered by being ignored. It can be said that wherever Napoleon was, success was assured; wherever he was not, it was disaster.

Although regarded as probably the greatest general of modern times, Napoleon had his shortcomings. In particular, his armies—and therefore his campaigns—suffered from inadequate supplies. In Italy his relatively small army was easily able to live off the land, which was a practice Napoleon believed in. When the Grand Army grew, however, and campaigned in countries that were poor, food was often in short supply. Napoleon's strategy depended on speed to catch an enemy unprepared. On the one hand, this made maintaining his army almost impossible with traditional supply lines, which could not keep up. On the other hand, it can be argued that he moved so quickly in order to win and settle in and to allow his supplies to reach him or local supply sources to be tapped. Even when Napoleon took supply problems into account, as in his invasion of Russia in 1812, the bases he established were too far apart and he still lacked sufficient transport to keep them or his troops fed. Thus, when the Russians instituted scorched earth tactics as they retreated, the French were unable to live off the land and suffered accordingly.

Napoleon was able to accomplish a long string of victories not only because of the quality of his army but because of his own brilliance. He developed the *batallion carrée*, whereby his army was divided into four separate corps travelling in an open square. Each corps was sufficiently independent to forage for itself, but close enough to respond quickly when the enemy was located. Once any of the corps engaged the enemy, the other three would respond immediately. For example, if the army were heading east (with corps located at the north, south, east, and west corners of the square) and the east corps met the enemy, they would engage. The north and south corners would come up to outflank the enemy position, while the west corps could draw up behind the east corps to act as a reserve. The Grand Army was therefore quickly in a position to attack the enemy's flanks, move around behind them on one flank or the other, or push the center with the reserve corps.

Napoleon was almost always able to sneak up on his enemies, for he kept the cavalry well in advance of his army to report enemy locations and give himself a screen behind which he could maneuver. Once in battle, Napoleon depended on massed artillery to weaken a section of the enemy line, then exploited that weakness with infantry. Once the line broke, French cavalry immediately turned the retreat into a rout.

Napoleon was almost able to control all of Europe using his Grand Army, but its innate logistical weaknesses and his inability to physically command on all fronts simultaneously seriously weakened it over time. Further, as the Imperial Guard expanded with veterans whom Napoleon increasingly hesitated to commit to battle, the line regiments had to make do with fewer experienced men. When the terrain proved daunting (as in Russia) or his enemies began to learn how to counter his moves (as at Leipzig and Waterloo), Napoleon's star set. When he was exiled to Elba in 1814, the Grand Army ceased to exist. When he escaped exile and reformed his army in 1815, he named it the Army of the North. At its height, however, Le Grande Armée was unbeatable.

References: Chandler, David, *The Campaigns of Napoleon* (New York: Macmillan, 1966); Paret, Peter, "Napoleon and the Revolution in War," in Peter Paret, *Makers of Modern Strategy* (Princeton: Princeton University Press, 1986); Rothenberg, Gunther, *The Art of Warfare in the Age of Napoleon* (Bloomington: University of Indiana Press, 1978).

Green Berets (Special Forces)

An elite unit of modern U.S. Army.

The concept of special forces, units that operate outside the mainstream of the military organization, is not new in American history. From Roger's Rangers in the French and Indian War (1756–1760) through Mosby's Rangers in the Civil War, small guerrilla-type groups have been used to disrupt enemy operations away from a war's main battlefields. In World War II, the United States developed new ranger-type units. In Europe, Darby's Rangers were given special assignments to perform during the Normandy invasion in June 1944. The Devils' Brigade was a joint Canadian-American venture that operated in the Italian theater, then in France. In the Pacific theater of operations, similar organizations were formed. Colonel Frank Merrill's Marauders operated against Japanese forces in Burma, while Lieutenant General Walter Krueger's Alamo Scouts in the Philippines harassed the Japanese in almost miraculous fashion.

Foundations for the Special Forces were laid during World War II. William Donovan's Office of Strategic Services (OSS) operated commando and intelligence-gathering units that penetrated occupied Europe, as well as organized Southeast Asian tribes into guerrilla units to fight the Japanese. These two functions, guerrilla operations and intelligence gathering, split into two separate organizations after the war. President Harry Truman disbanded the OSS but created out of it the Central Intelligence Agency. The Special Forces took up guerrilla operations training, starting in June 1952.

Two men, Colonel Aaron Bank and Colonel Russell Volckman, OSS operatives from World War II, were the driving force in getting Army approval for the creation of the Special Forces. With the advent of the Cold War, secret operations behind enemy lines became an attractive option. Colonel Bank was given facilities at Fort Bragg, North Carolina, for establishing the Special Forces training center. He chose a location on base called Smoke Bomb Hill, and proceeded to fill the 2,300 personnel slots the Army had authorized him. He refused recruits, preferring veterans who had OSS, Ranger, or paratrooper experience, and took only volunteers looking for tough training and a challenge. All had to speak at least two languages and have parachute training, as well as hold at least sergeant's rank. They were also advised that their operations would usually take place behind enemy lines and sometimes in civilian clothes. Because this violated the rules of war, it would leave captured operatives to be tried and executed as spies, not soldiers. The training that Banks initiated was more rigorous than even these men had experienced. Paratroopers and Rangers had been used to acting quickly in advance of major attacks. The Special Forces, however, could be used for long operations in which they would have to sustain themselves in a hostile country with little to no outside support.

After a year and a half in training, the first overseas deployment took place when half the force, designated Tenth Special Forces Group, was sent to Bad Iz, West Germany, in November 1953. The half that stayed in Fort Bragg retained their original unit designation, but the forces in Germany were now assigned the title Seventy-seventh Special Forces Group. Special Forces from this point forward were incorporated into army strategic planning. In April 1956 the first Special Forces troops were sent to Southeast Asia. These were not the first Special Forces in Asia, however, for a small group had operated secretly behind enemy lines in the Korean conflict, an operation that remained classified until the 1980s. The first Special Forces in Southeast Asia, however, were soon joined by other units to create the 8231st Army Special Operational Detachment, which was based on Okinawa. It is here that the Special Forces' basic unit of operation was developed: the A-Team. This 12-man unit contained two officers, two sergeants for operations and intelligence, two weapons sergeants, two communications sergeants, two medics, and two engineers. This organization allowed the team to divide into two six-man units, or Split A-Teams. Each man also had cross-training to take up the slack in case of casualties.

The coming of age of the Special Forces had a political aspect, for it was after recognition by President John Kennedy in 1961 that the organization really began to grow. With increasing tensions between the United States and communist regimes, Kennedy saw the potential for elite guerrilla-style units and he ordered the army to expand the Special Forces. He also directed that the army allow the men to wear the green beret as a symbol of their separation from the regular army. This, he knew, would promote esprit de corps, and the term "Green Berets" came to be interchangeable with "Special Forces."

It was in Southeast Asia that the Special Forces reached the height of their fame, acting as advisors to the South Vietnamese Army in the 1950s and early 1960s. It was a Special Forces soldier, Captain Harry Cramer, Jr., of the Fourteenth Special Forces Operations Detachment, who was the first American killed in that conflict. During that time the Special Forces trained local soldiers and native tribes in guerrilla operations and counterinsurgency. In 1964 the Special Forces established their headquarters at Nha Trang, where it remained until their redeployment to Fort Bragg in 1971. By the end of their service in Vietnam, Special Forces personnel had received a total of 28,311 medals, including 16 Medals of Honor and 2,658 Purple Hearts.

Although Vietnam was their highest-profile mission, during the 1960s the Special Forces also conducted training and operations throughout Latin America, including the capture of Che Guevara. Still, Vietnam remained their major focus. There the Special Forces performed missions beyond just fighting. Some 254 separate posts were set up during the war defended by Green Berets and local personnel that they had trained. Montagnards, Nungs, Cao Dei, and other tribes provided manpower that became the 60,000-strong Civil Irregular Defense Group. Special Forces also provided engineering and medical aid to local villages, along with other noncombat projects designed to establish closer emotional and psychological ties between U.S. forces and the local population. Even though the bulk of the Special Forces were withdrawn in 1971 some remained to carry out missions behind enemy lines, operating out of Thailand into Cambodia and North Vietnam.

After the American involvement in Vietnam ended, the role of the Special Forces diminished rapidly as the army focussed on potential major-force conflict in Europe. The Special Forces commanders convinced the army that the other, less combat-oriented tasks of the organization could be harnessed.

Members of the U.S. military's Special Forces, popularly known as the Green Berets

Under the program called Special Proficiency at Rugged Training and Nation-building (SPARTAN) the men worked on engineering and medical projects in the United States on Indian reservations and in impoverished Appalachian areas, much as they had done with isolated Vietnamese populations. SPARTAN, however, was temporary, as the main goal of Special Forces was combat, and under President Ronald Reagan they got their chance to fight again. Like Kennedy, Reagan saw the need for counterinsurgency operations in hot spots around the world where large forces could not operate. In the early 1980s Special Forces became an entirely separate branch within the army, and the training and entrance qualifications were toughened.

Special Forces troops saw action in Panama during Operation Just Cause, where they engaged the Panamanian Defense Forces attempting to capture a bridge leading to Ranger units. The Green Berets not only defeated the attackers, but suffered no casualties in the action. Such actions brought the Special Forces back into favor and by 1990 five Special Forces groups were on active duty status, based at Fort Bragg, Fort Carson (Colorado), Fort Lewis (Washington), Fort Campbell (Kentucky), and detached units in Germany and Okinawa with reserves in the National Guard. The units continue to train for combat while aiding local populations, in the United States and around the world.

References: Kelly, Ross, *Special Operations and National Purpose* (Lexington, MA: Lexington Books, 1989); Simmons, Anna, *The Company They Keep* (Free Press, 1997); Sullivan, George, *Elite Warriors* (New York: Facts on File, 1995).

Guerrillas

Specialists in nontraditional partisan warfare.

The term *guerrilla* is Spanish for "little war." It came into common usage at the time the Spanish came into conflict with Napoleon's forces in the first decade of the nineteenth century. Although guerrilla war may have obtained its name in this conflict, its concept and practice dates back many centuries, and it is probably impossible to find a record of its first use.

Guerrilla warfare is basically the harassing of a superior force by an inferior one. The key to guerrilla warfare—especially in its beginning stages—is to avoid direct contact with the stronger enemy at all cost. Thus guerrillas seek to attack isolated outposts and units with quick assaults and temporarily superior numbers, then fade into the countryside before a response can be mounted.

One of the first recorded uses of such a type of warfare is in the Bible, in which David organized a small band to harass the incumbent King Saul. His group was regarded by the king as nothing but a band of robbers (which is mostly true, as they had to live off the land and the captured supplies of the king). David based his group in the wilderness where it was easy to hide and difficult for the king's army to surprise him. He also gained the foreign aid of the neighboring Philistines. By aiding the local poor, David's men gained public support. All of these elements have been repeated in guerrilla movements to this day. Later in the Old Testament, Judas Maccabeus led a guerrilla movement against the Greco-Syrian occupiers of Israel. His movement started out in the standard fashion, but as he gained more success his force grew to the point that he could challenge the foreign forces directly. This change from guerrilla war to conventional war is the ultimate goal of most such movements. At this point the guerrilla forces may actually throw off their oppressors and implement their own policies for which they have been fighting, be they political, religious, social, or any combination of those.

This style of warfare seems not to have been utilized much before the Middle Ages, when strong armies attempted to occupy territories that were more technologically backward than they. The English found this type of resistance in Wales, Scotland, and Ireland, where, between the eleventh and fifteenth centuries, the inhabitants fought to maintain their independence. In Eastern Europe, similar struggles were fought, but there the primary goals were social or religious. Peasant uprisings were common and effective temporarily, usually when they were under the leadership of a disaffected noble or someone else with some military experience. But peasant revolts rarely, if ever, reached the point of gaining sufficient strength to defeat the armies of the upper classes. Still, these wars did accomplish much toward the development of ethnic identity in the Balkans, because the hated upper classes tended to be invaders from elsewhere.

In the Western Hemisphere in the colonial period one finds guerrilla conflicts as well. In North America, the native Indian population used their hunting skills to stalk English colonists or (with French support) to ambush columns of unsuspecting British troops. However, their inability to organize along intertribal lines doomed their attempts to failure. Also, the colonists themselves learned Indian methods and fought a counterguerrilla war, which ultimately proved effective. In the Caribbean and South America, escaped slaves occasionally organized and fought guerrilla actions against their former owners. In Brazil, some former slave bands existed independently for years. In Haiti, such forces fought and defeated Napoleonic troops and gained the island's independence in 1803. In the Americas, the terrain proved advantageous to guerrilla movements, because the rugged and heavily wooded countryside allowed for easy ambush and escape.

In the seventeenth and eighteenth centuries, as European armies grew more nationalistic and professional, guerrilla tactics were still employed in some cases. Although the majority of battles were "set-piece," that is, units entering battle in formation, armies often recruited nonprofessional forces, which took the description "irregulars." The irregulars were often used for scouting and harassment of enemy supply lines, and sometimes to demoralize enemy civilians. In Africa and India, British and French colonial armies employed such troops widely where familiarity with local terrain was beyond most European officers' ken. The irregular forces were considered necessary for scouting purposes, but the troops themselves were often distrusted for their "irregular" discipline and loyalty. It was also difficult to control these irregular troops after or away from the battle, and pillaging and looting were common negative aspects of using such forces. Irregulars were also used to infiltrate enemy territory and foment local discontent.

In the American Revolution, the Indian-style fighting the colonists had learned often served them well when fighting the British regular army. The opening day of the conflict, 19 April 1775, proved this: At Lexington a small group of militia stood to face a superior British force and suffered badly. Later that day, as that same British force retreated from Concord to Boston, colonial sniping and hit-and-run attacks inflicted three times as many casualties on the British as the American guerrillas suffered. A month later, a small force of men under the command of Ethan Allen surprised the isolated but strategic Fort Ticonderoga on Lake Champlain and captured it and some 100 cannon without a shot being fired. American commander George Washington spent the war creating a regular Continental Army, but often such commanders as Nathaniel Greene in the Carolinas exhausted the British sufficiently for Washington's regulars to take advantage of them. Greene commanded both regulars and militia, but he employed the standard guerrilla strategy of avoiding major battles while wearing down his enemy with skirmishing and harassment whenever possible.

It was during the Napoleonic Wars (1803–1815) that the strategy not only acquired its name of guerrilla warfare, but also saw some of its methods included in regular warfare. The French Revolution's *levee en masse* drafted huge numbers of peasants into the army. By this time, firearms were relatively common and easy to provide for large numbers of soldiers. However, the traditional fighting method of attacking in lines demanded more discipline than the peasants or their nonaristocratic officers were able to summon in the early days. Therefore, skirmishing and attacking by units rather than in a line became the normal practice. The fact that the peasant draftees were fighting for social and political rights similar to those pursued by peasant uprisings in previous centuries also increased their effectiveness. For a time, "irregular" was becoming "regular." Even these adaptations of guerrilla tactics to regular warfare, however, failed to defeat the traditional guerrilla combat the Spanish peasants engaged in when French forces invaded Iberia. Again, the rugged countryside, the ability of the guerrillas to mass at a single point for temporary numerical advantage and then dissipate quickly, and the constant harassment of supply lines and isolated outposts all proved too much for the French to overcome. In addition to this, the assistance of a foreign power (Great Britain) to provide direction and supplies contributed to the success of guerrilla warfare in Spain.

After the Napoleonic Wars, Europe did not see many guerrillas for the remainder of the century, except in France itself. Urban guerrillas made their appearance during the revolutions of 1830 and 1848, but their limited appeal outside the cities doomed their causes. They made another appearance in 1870–1871 during the Franco-Prussian War with some action against invading Prussian troops. It was here one sees the birth of the term *franc tireur* (French terror), as much terrorist as freedom fighter. Still, the urban guerrilla did provoke government responses. The winding alleyways that were the urban version of the rural wilderness became the target of city planners in the nineteenth century, and wide straight avenues became the popular urban design. This made barricades more difficult to construct and opened up firing lanes for artillery.

Guerrilla warfare appeared more in colonial conflict in the nineteenth century. The French dealt with Muslim guerrillas fighting for their religion as much as independence in Algeria. The British fought the most difficult of guerrilla conflicts in South Africa, while the Spanish put down several revolts in Cuba culminating in serious guerrilla warfare on the part of the Cubans in the later 1890s. In all of these conflicts, the colonial powers were victorious because they had all developed counterguerrilla strategies. The French in Algeria abandoned the fortress-based defense for the aggressive flying column strategy that took the war into the wilderness on the guerrillas' home territory. By using surprise, the French kept the Algerians on the move and thus denied them the ability to plan and gather supplies. The French administration also saw the need to implement political action to pacify the population by granting some of the concessions for which the guerrillas were fighting. Counterinsurgency thus took on as much a political role as a military one.

In the United States, the regular army carried on offensives against Indian warriors in the Great Plains and the desert southwest. As the European powers had done against their guerrilla enemies in Africa and Cuba, the U.S. cavalry also took the war to the Indians, denying them supplies and forcing their surrender. The destruction of the buffalo on the Great Plains destroyed everything the Plains Indians needed for sustenance, and cavalry attacks on villages in the winter to steal their horses robbed the Indians of their only serious method of fighting. On foot they could not feed or fight, and the reservation became the only alternative. This, together with an inability of most tribes to cooperate with each other (a common guerrilla failing) and the overwhelming number of white soldiers and settlers pushing into their territories, meant that the Indians could not possibly win in the long run.

The Boers of South Africa at the end of the nineteenth century proved the most obstinate of guerrilla enemies for the British. Unlike native warriors who lacked modern weaponry, the Boers often had rifles and artillery equal to or better than whatever the British could put in the field. Their ability to live off the land, move about quickly on horseback, and also hold strong defensive positions when necessary made the Boers far superior to any guerrilla forces the British had faced. The British, however, followed the strategy implemented in Cuba by the Spanish: Deny the guerrillas their source of support, the local population. Local populations often provide supplies, information, and shelter to guerrilla armies. To prevent this, the British in South Africa and the Spanish in Cuba rounded up the population and concentrated them in camps, leaving anyone outside the camp by definition a "hostile." Although conditions in the camps at times proved deadly, owing to lack of fresh water, food, medicine, and sanitary facilities, the strategy was effective. With the local population incarcerated in the camps, there was no one to work the farms and the food supply for the guerrilla soldiers dried up. In Cuba, the timely intervention of the United States in the spring of 1898 saved the guerrillas from imminent defeat. The Boers, on the other hand, could look to no outside savior, despite the fact that they received equipment and moral support from other countries. They were forced to sign surrender terms in 1902, although in the long run the Boers' political agenda—local autonomy—was accomplished through legal means.

Guerrilla warfare returned to Europe for a short time in the early twentieth century during the Balkan Wars of 1912–1913. The motivations for these conflicts were nationalistic as well as religious, but—like so many guerrilla movements—the Balkan guerrilla alliances could not withstand their own success. Once the Turks were sent packing by the victorious Balkan fighters, the rivalries within the guerrilla organization guaranteed that peace would not last.

Two very successful guerrilla operations took place during World War I, although not in Europe. In East Africa, Paul Emil von Lettow-Vorbeck used German soldiers and mobilized native troops to make life miserable for the British in one of the most successful campaigns of all time. His activities have come to be the model for irregular warfare. In a completely different climate, T.E. Lawrence mobilized Arab forces to attack the Turks in the Middle East during 1915–1918. Drawing on their Bedouin past, these horse- and camel-borne raiders greatly disrupted Turkish supply lines and outposts. Lawrence kept them supplied from British stores but (except for Lawrence himself) it was virtually a total Arab effort in terms of manpower. Promises of nationhood and freedom from Turkish domination motivated these men. By contrast, Lettow-Vorbeck's operation was conducted almost strictly for military purposes. As could the Boers, the Arabs were able to move quickly as light cavalry. However, owing to the introduction of automobiles and aircraft, this was to be about the last time such operations were feasible.

Guerrilla warfare and revolution came to be almost synonymous in the twentieth century as anticolonial forces grew in strength and popularity, especially after World War I. The great proponent of revolution was Karl Marx, who wrote the *Communist Manifesto* in 1848. Yet his vision of urban warfare of the workers against the owners rarely occurred. The Irish used urban guerrillas in their bid to create an independent Ireland during 1916–1921, but none there ever seriously embraced communism. It took other communist theorists to adapt revolution and guerrilla warfare into a cohesive whole and to seriously integrate the political aspects of revolution into the military strategy of guerrilla conflict. Although Vladimir Lenin in Russia made sure that political officers were in every unit of the Soviet military, it was Mao Tse-tung in China who became the leading theorist of national revolution among the agricultural rather than the industrial proletariat. His *On Guerrilla Warfare* (1937) became a text on national guerrilla uprisings.

Nationalist guerrilla warfare returned in World War II, most notably in the Soviet Union. The partisans that escaped Hitler's executioners were so successful in harassing German supply lines that ultimately almost half the German army was dedicated to rear areas, a fact that seriously affected the fighting at the front. Irregular warfare also showed itself in the formation of commando units that fought in all theaters, especially in North Africa and Southeast Asia.

Anticolonial movements exploded after World War II as imperialism became an ever less popular political theme. Communism, however, became more popular and the United States, which had put down a guerrilla movement in the Philippines at the turn of the century and created special operations forces during World War II, became the primary anticommunist and antiguerrilla combatant. In Latin America, communist guerrillas organized antigovernment movements to remove dictators and implement social and economic reform. By embracing communism and receiving aid from the Soviet Union, these "freedom fighters" became the target of the United States' military attention. No guerrilla movement, however, drew so much attention as that directed by Ho Chi Minh in Vietnam. Although he was an avowed nationalist attempting to free his homeland from French colonial rule, Ho Chi Minh's Soviet training and the supplies he received from both the Soviet Union and Communist China guaranteed American political opposition.

The Vietnamese had fought a very successful guerrilla war against the French after World War II, moving from a purely harassing type of combat to a national army that beat the French on their own terms. When the United States supported a rather repressive but anticommunist regime in the southern part of the country after 1956, Ho Chi Minh returned to his guerrilla tactics. Although the British had recently conducted a successful antiguerrilla operation in Malaya, the Americans apparently did not learn from their example and attempted to defeat the Vietnamese communists by conventional means. Although over time "special operations" forces became more widely used to fight an irregular war, the inability of the United States to offer a seriously attractive alternative political solution to the Vietnamese people almost guaranteed the victory of the communist forces.

As long as weaker forces find themselves unable to face stronger ones in head-to-head competition, guerrilla warfare will exist. However, only those movements that do not fragment, offer and promote a viable program that is acceptable to a majority of the population, and receive some form of outside assistance are likely to be successful, as shown by past experience. As long as the stronger forces have the adaptability to fight a guerrilla war of their own and beat the partisans at their own game, they can win a military victory. However, without having a viable program to offer the population (whether social, economic, political, religious, or any combination necessary), the military victory is likely to be short-lived.

References: Chaliand, Gerald, ed., *Guerrilla Strategies* (Berkeley: University of California Press, 1982); Gann, Lewis H., *Guerrillas in History* (Stanford: Hoover Institution Press, 1971); Mao Tse-tung, *On Guerrilla Warfare*, trans. by Samuel B. Griffith (New York: Praeger, 1961).

Gurkhas

Soldiers of Nepal fighting for the British army.

Gurkhas are the citizens of Nepal, descended from a mixture of Mongoloid races and Rajputs of India. Not surprisingly, they are an extremely hardy people, given the climate and terrain of their country, which features the Himalayas on its northern border. The Gurkhas present an unusual paradox: They are regarded as possibly the best fighters—man for man—of any army in the world, yet away from the battlefield they are also regarded as possibly the most hospitable and friendly people in the world. When in the early 1800s the king of Nepal decided to expand his borders, he pushed westward and southward toward Bengal and Oudh, both territories occupied or protected by the British East India Company. The result had long-term effects on both Nepal and Britain.

In November 1814, four British columns comprising some 34,000 men attacked

Nepal, but only one column met any success. The generals were not prepared for the rough terrain of the country and the peculiar supply needs it entailed. During the second phase of the Gurkha war in 1815 the British fared better and pushed toward the capital of Kathmandu. In December 1815, representatives of the king negotiated a peace, the Treaty of Sagauli. The king, however, rejected the terms of the treaty and the British renewed their invasion. In March 1916 as British forces approached his capital, the king relented and the British decided not to impose more severe terms on him for his delay. By this time, the British were more than happy to stop fighting the Gurkhas because, even with their almost three-to-one advantage, the campaign for them had been a near-run thing.

The two countries emerged from this war with a mutual respect for the other's fighting abilities, and soon the British army was recruiting Gurkha soldiers. Over time, the British recruited ten Gurkha regiments, and the soldiers have proven to be among the best the British army has put in the field. They served in every British campaign in India after they began joining the army of the East India Company in 1816 and remained loyal during the Indian Mutiny of 1857. When the British Indian army began operations outside India, as they did in Burma and elsewhere in the late 1800s, the Gurkhas went with them when some other native troops balked. Even in World War I, Gurkhas joined Force A, which travelled to France, and for a year fought in the trenches against the Germans. There they fought alongside British soldiers of the Leicestershire Regiment and established a long relationship of mutual respect and trust. The Gurkhas adapted to the alien climate of France much sooner than any of the other Indian army serving there and in their 12 months of service earned three Victoria Crosses of the five awarded to Indian troops. The Gurkhas also served in an unfamiliar climate in Mesopotamia, where they fought the Turks in extreme desert heat and excelled in every battle. They also fought the Turks at the failed Gallipoli offensive of 1915. In both campaigns in the East the Gurkhas left behind a memorial. Near the beaches of Gallipoli south of Istanbul is a point of high ground that the Gurkhas held against tremendous Turkish assaults. To this day it is called Gurkha Bluff. in November 1915 while retreating from Ctesiphon, just outside Baghdad, 400 Gurkhas held a small hill against repeated attacks of an entire Turkish division. Gurkha Mound is still its name.

After World War I, the Gurkhas were, through no fault of their own, involved in one of the British Empire's most tragic and stupid events. In Armritsar, India, a large group of Indian nationalists rallied for independence in 1919. Meaning to "make a statement," General Dyer ordered his Gurkha troops to open fire on the crowd in an enclosed area, and they followed orders. Three hundred seventy-nine people were killed and over 1,200 wounded in the massacre, which became a focal point for rallying Indian opposition to British rule. In more traditional operations, Gurkhas also were involved in punitive expeditions against outlaws in Afghanistan and the Northwest Frontier region of India in the interwar years.

When World War II broke out, the Gurkhas were called on once again to aid the British Empire. Gurkha troops served in North Africa where they were able to operate in the hills of Tunisia and aid in driving German troops from well-entrenched positions. In Italy, they also had the chance to operate in mountainous terrain and again proved their worth. They were outstanding in patrolling and reconnaissance in Italy's mountains and often were able to sneak up on German machine gun positions and capture the crews without a shot being fired. In both North Africa and Italy, the Germans came to fear the Gurkhas, for when stealth failed, the Gurkhas were unmatched in hand-to-hand combat. The distinctive Gurkha weapon is the *kukri*, a knife with a blade some 14 inches long, curved slightly about a third of the way from the hilt. The rest of the blade is somewhat leaf-shaped and the blade is sharpened on the concave edge. In the heat of battle many Germans were beheaded by these knives.

Gurkhas also fought in Southeast Asia during World War II. They were stationed in Singapore at the war's outbreak and were still attacking when the British commanders ordered surrender. Some Gurkhas refused and made their way into the jungle, fighting with guerrilla bands against the Japanese. Other Gurkhas fought with Orde Wingate's Chindit forces behind Japanese lines in Burma. When Field Marshall William Slim invaded Burma in 1944 to recover the country from the Japanese, the Gurkhas went with him. Slim made sure of that because he had served with a Gurkha unit since World War I and would not undertake an offensive without them.

Since World War II, the Gurkhas have kept units operating with the British army around the world, including fighting with them in the Falkland Islands in the 1980s. Gurkhas were some of the last British forces to be withdrawn from Hong Kong when the British turned the city over to mainland China in 1997. They are the inheritors of a tradition started in 1815 and the war against Nepal. To serve in the British forces is the height of honor in Nepal. Each year thousands of young men go to recruiting stations to apply for the few hundred positions available. Almost two hundred years of service and bravery keep the British recruiting there. No British officer who served with Gurkhas can help but admire them, and the stories of Gurkhas in combat are countless. For example, in the battle at Singapore before the British surrender in 1942 a Gurkha soldier was wounded in the arm. He asked a comrade to cut the arm off so he could continue fighting. When the comrade refused, the soldier cut off his own arm with his kukri, stuck the stump in creosote to cauterize it, and continued to fight for another fifteen days before capture. Such stories are the rule rather than the exception. Crying *Ayo Gurkhali* ("Here come the Gurkhas"), these troops launched attacks few defenders could withstand. Even the Japanese, for whom surrender is the greatest dishonor, often fled from Gurkha attacks because the Gurkha code of conduct is no less strict than that of the Samurai. Their motto is "Better to die than be a coward," and instances of Gurkha cowardice do not exist.

References: Bishop, Edward, *Better to Die* (London: New English Library, 1976); Farwell, Byron, *The Gurkhas* (New York: Norton, 1984); Tuker, Lt.-Gen. Sir Francis, *Gorkha: The Story of the Gurkhas of Nepal* (London: Constable, 1957).

H

Hessians

Mercenaries from Germanic states, best known for service with the British Army in the eighteenth century.

"Hessian" is the generic term used during the American Revolution to describe German mercenary troops employed by the British. The use of mercenaries in the eighteenth century was quite common because it allowed the employing countries to maintain smaller armies in peacetime while allowing the supplying countries to gain much-needed national income. Mercenaries in Europe first became widely used at the time of the condottieri in Italy in the 1400s. The first well-known mercenary troops came from the Swiss provinces. By the 1700s the German states were the source of most mercenaries. Germany at that time consisted of some 300 individual states of widely varying size, all ruled by a king, duke, prince, or other aristocrat who inherited his position. As many of them felt the need to outdo their neighbors in expenditure, the hiring out of local armies was a ready source of income.

During the American Revolution, the traditionally small British army needed supplementing. King George III was the first British-born monarch of the German house of Hanover, so there were close ties to German states. Six of the German states provided troops to King George, including Brunswick (5,700 men), Anspach-Beyreuth (2,300 men), Waldeck (1,200 men), Anhalt-Zerbst (1,100 men), Hesse-Cassel (17,000 men), and Hesse-Hanau (2,500 men). Owing to the predominance of troops from the last two related states "Hessian" became the common description for any German soldier, although that was not appreciated by the other troops. Britain had hired German troops in the Seven Years War (1756–1763) and other conflicts, so the mixing of Anglo-German forces was hardly new. The employment contracts provided for the lion's share of the purchase price to go to the ruler, while the soldier received the standard low pay of all enlisted men of that era. For a price of some £4.5 million, the British army received the services of almost 30,000 troops.

The troops may have been regarded as mercenaries, but the average soldier probably was not serving for personal gain. Many of the troops were forced into service and many more were not even citizens of the state for which they served, as methods up to and including kidnapping were not uncommon in order to put men in uniform. Traditional tactics, like promising wealth and adventure or taking advantage of drunks, brought in men, as did visits to prisons. Discipline was harsh, but effective enough to train troops that were as good as any at the time. The infantry was obtained in this manner, although the cavalry tended to come from the upper classes.

Officers were aristocrats with little care for the welfare of their men. On the voyage from Europe to America, conditions for the enlisted men often were little better than on slave ships, with cramped accommodations and poor food.

The first action the German troops saw in America was in August 1776 at the Battle of Long Island. There they fought well but gained a bad reputation for slaughtering prisoners. It was in the months following William Howe's capture of New York City, however, that the Hessian troops gained their first serious attention from the Americans. Howe ordered his army into winter quarters after defeating George Washington's army at White Plains in October 1776. Placed in a large arc around New York City, the regiments were ordered to quarter themselves in outlying towns and wait for the spring campaign. A Hessian regiment under Johann Rall was billeted in Trenton, New Jersey. Under the provisions of the Quartering Act passed by Parliament in 1774 the local population was obligated to provide housing and supplies for the occupying troops. This was an odious law to the colonists and one of the "Intolerable Acts" that had provoked the Revolution. Its implementation by mercenaries did nothing to assuage the colonists' ire. Washington, having just suffered three defeats, needed a victory to ensure recruits for the revolutionary army the following spring. He figured that beating the Hessians would rescue the population from a hated occupying force while restoring his flagging reputation for generalship at the same time.

British and Hessian soldiers, from an undated engraving

Washington launched a surprise attack at dawn the day after Christmas 1776, and in a matter of minutes killed, wounded, captured, or scattered almost 1,500 men for a loss of but five of his own. This incident confirmed in the British a condescending attitude toward their allies, the Hessians, whom they thought overpaid and overrated. One British officer wrote to a friend that "these Hessians are the worst troops I ever saw. Government has been Cheated by their sending one half Militia, and the greatest part of the others Recruits, very few Viterons amongst them, they are voted British pay, which their Prince Cheats them out of one half, they are Exceedingly dissatisfied at this, so that to make it up they turn their whole thoughts upon plunder. It was their attention to this Plunder, that made them fall a sacrifice to the Rebels at Trenton" (Lowell, 1884).

Hessian troops seemed to fight quite well when part of a larger force, but the only other time they fought alone was also a disaster. In 1777 as John Burgoyne made his way south from Canada in an attempt to control New York, he sent a force of Hessians to obtain supplies and horses near the town of Bennington, Vermont. They met a force of militia that outnumbered their own 800 troops, locals who used the terrain to its best advantage and outfought and outmaneuvered the Hessians. Once beaten they staged a fighting withdrawal toward Burgoyne's army and met with a 600-man relief force that had arrived too late to assist in the earlier battle. Both Hessian units found themselves swamped by Vermonters. When it was all over the Hessians had lost 900 killed or taken prisoner.

Other than these two defeats, the Hessians acquitted themselves fairly well in every major battle of the Revolution, up to and including the final battle at Yorktown in 1781. They remained in America until the signing of the peace treaty in 1783 but not all of them went home. The years they had spent in America affected many Hessians greatly, for they saw the American farmer working lush fields that were larger than many royal estates at home. The lure of good land, and the discovery of attractive and hard-working American women, convinced many Germans not to go home. The Duke of Brunswick encouraged many to stay in the new United States or in Canada. He could always raise more troops but did not want to pay transport for any more than necessary at that time. There was little reason to go home if one wanted to remain a mercenary, however, for their time was coming to an end. The American Revolution, soon followed by the revolution in France, began the creation of national armies using only citizen soldiers.

References: Hibbert, Christopher, *Redcoats and Rebels* (New York: Norton, 1990); Lowell, E.J., *The Hessians, and the German Auxiliaries of Great Britain in the Revolutionary War* (New York: Harper & Bros. 1884); Smith, Page, *A New Age Now Begins* (New York: McGraw-Hill, 1976).

Highlanders

A Scottish population known for its fighting spirit, both against and with the British army.

Highlanders has become a somewhat generic term for Scots, although such is not the case. The territory that makes up Scotland divides naturally into three parts: the borders, the lowlands, and the highlands. The borders, as the name implies, lie along the southern part of the region along the frontier with England to the south. The lowlands run east to west and then up the eastern coast toward Inverness. The highlands, then, occupy the region running mainly north and south between Loch Lomond and the Pentland Firth.

The Scots enter recorded history when the Romans encountered them in the first century A.D. The Romans called the land Hibernia and nicknamed the inhabitants Picts. The first battle between Romans and Picts took place at Mons Grampius in 83 A.D. The Romans were victorious but ventured no farther northward, instead erecting walls to keep the northerners at bay. The Picts remained between Hadrian's Wall and the Antonine Wall for some 200 years, although it was the Roman army more than the walls themselves that discouraged Pictish aggression.

Near the beginning of the sixth century, the Gaelic Celts in the highland west of Scotland established the first recognizable Scottish kingdom, which they called Dalraida, in the region of Argyll. In 843 the Scots and borderer Picts united under the leadership of Kenneth, the son of Alpin of Dalraida. After this time the term "Pict" disappears into the generic term "Scot." In the eastern part of Scotland the population was of Norse, Danish, and Angle heritage. The Anglo-Roman borderers of the Strathclyde merged with the eastern Angles of Lothian under the rule of King Malcolm II between 1016 and 1018. All of these people were considered foreigners to the highlanders, although the highlanders' ethnic make-up includes all of them. The highlanders were in turn considered barbarians by the others. Unification came in 1034 under Malcolm II's grandson, Duncan, although the relations between highlander and lowlander remained fairly tense.

Society in Scotland at this time was based on the clan, although the number of clans is a matter of some dispute. As the word *clan* is Gaelic, it should therefore designate only highlanders. The number of clans varied somewhere between 35 and 50. The dispute often deals with the way in which the clans were grouped. What some consider clans, other researchers consider subclans of a more powerful chieftain. The basis of the clan was the chief, who was both patriarch and head of government. The chief ruled the clan but could not act without its cooperation, so tyrannic leaders were rare. Even the king had to deal with the possibly contrary nature of his subjects, and no leader would commit young men to war without widespread support within and between clans.

Malcolm III took advantage of the Norman invasion of England in 1066 seeing a golden opportunity to raid southward and extend Scottish dominion. Unfortunately, he did not succeed and ultimately the new Norman king of England, William, forced the Scots to pay homage and deal with the feudal system and its interlocking hierarchy of loyalties. The Scottish king swore fealty, but the commoner in the north may or may not have recognized the king's action. In the twelfth century, Richard the Lionheart sold the Scots their freedom from their oath of fealty in return for funds to mount a crusade to the Holy Land. This suited the Scots well until 1286 when the royal lineage became tangled.

When several men claimed the throne in that year, the Scots went to another king in order to have an impartial judge among the claimants. Edward I of England gladly offered his services, but in exchange for the oath of loyalty necessary for his decision to be binding. He proceeded to name John Balliol as king of Scotland, but Balliol was now technically subservient to Edward. Edward proceeded to provoke Balliol and when rebellion ensued, Edward's victory gave him the Scottish estates, which the disloyal subjects thereby forfeited. Edward's forces occupied southern Scotland for ten years while Balliol languished in the Tower of London. In Balliol's name William Wallace raised a revolt with early success, but eventually he was betrayed and executed.

Throughout all of this the highland Scots remained aloof because their lands were too remote for Edward to occupy. In 1306 Robert Bruce claimed the throne, but his rein was short-lived. He was defeated by rival lowland factions under the Earl of Pembroke and forced to flee. Bruce ended up in the highlands where he promised wealth and power to those clans who would follow him. With the aid of the clan McKinnon, among others, Bruce achieved victory at Bannockburn in 1314. With this success, the highlanders were forever bound into the Scottish political scene. This also set the stage for the Arbroath Declaration in 1320, wherein the Scottish nobility swore that "so long as one hundred remained alive, the Scots would never submit to the English, 'for it is not for glory we fight, for riches or for honours, but for freedom alone, which no good man loses but with his life'" (MacKinnon, 1984). It was supposedly Robert Bruce himself who added a clause whereby any future Scottish king who submitted to England would be immediately dethroned.

Relations between England and Scotland were never cordial, but became closer through necessity in the late 1500s when Elizabeth I died without issue. The nearest relative was James Stuart, and he became at once James VI of Scotland and James I of England. This failed to bring friendlier relations between the two countries, however, for James's Catholic heirs were not popular with England's predominantly Protestant population. As Scotland came to embrace Protestant Calvinism, the northern population often became split in their views of struggles in England. The English throne was contested by both Protestant and Catholic monarchs, as well as by Scottish and English monarchs. It was a Catholic Stuart's attempt to seize the English throne with French aid in 1745 that brought about a major change in Scottish-English relations. Some clans marched with Charles the Pretender, or Bonnie Prince Charlie as he was more popularly known, but many Protestant clans fought against him alongside the English. It was during this conflict in 1739 that the British army commissioned the raising of a Scottish regiment to serve under English command: the famous Black Watch. This regiment got its name from the dark color of its tartan and the fact that it was a unit originally detailed for national defense, that is, to watch the Scottish countryside. Although this unit fought against Charles at the battle of Culloden in 1745 the English government sought to punish those clans that had supported the Pretender. They did so by punishing almost all Scots: The wearing of tartans and the carrying of weapons, as well as the playing of the bagpipe, were all banned—unless one was a member of the army. Hence, those that could not bear to walk the street or countryside unarmed could and did join the British army.

Scottish units were irregularly raised, however, and were often disbanded at war's end. Thus, many highlanders who fought in the regiments raised to serve in North America against the French in the Seven Years War were told that they would be civilians again when the Treaty of Paris was signed in 1763. Rather than face that alternative, the majority of them stayed in America.

William Pitt, the English leader responsible for raising the Scottish regiments to serve in America, praised their fighting ability to Parliament: "These men in the last war were brought to combat on your side; they served with fidelity as they fought with valour, and conquered for you in every part of the world" (MacKinnon, 1984). This was in contrast to his less widely quoted comment at the beginning of the war that sending the highlanders off to war would result in that much less trouble at home. Fifteen years later, more regiments were raised for North America, possibly to fight against their relatives during the American Revolution. After the war in 1783 the majority of these were disbanded. Only three regiments were kept on the permanent rolls: the Black Watch, the Highland Light Infantry, and the Seaforth Highlanders. More regiments were raised again to fight in the Napoleonic Wars (1803–1815). This resulted in a few more permanent regiments: the Gordon Highlanders, the Queen's Own Cameron Highlanders, and the Argyll & Sutherland Highlanders. After the Cardwell Army Reforms in 1881 an alteration from one-battalion regiments to two-battalion regiments brought together other units into the above-named regiments. These, however, broke the tradition of pure Highland units, although the tartans, kilts, and bagpipes remained integral to their heritage.

Scottish units participated in virtually every war the British empire fought in the nineteenth and twentieth centuries. Their bravery, hardiness, and discipline became legendary, but were nothing compared to the legends associated with the kilts and pipes. Enemies called the kilted Scots "Ladies from Hell," but by World War II the kilts were banned during combat, only to be worn on parade. Legends of the bagpipes' wail striking fear in the hearts of opposing troops come from virtually every conflict. One of the more famous comes from the battle at Gallipoli in World War I. British and ANZAC units had had little success against a stout Turkish defense, but at the sound of the pipes from advancing Scots, the Turks fled. Asked why they had fought so well up until that point, Turkish prisoners said any troops that could march, shoot, and slaughter hogs at the same time were too tough to face.

References: Brander, Michael, *The Scottish Highlanders and Their Regiments* (New York: Barnes & Noble, 1996); MacKinnon, Charles, *Scottish Highlanders* (London: Robert Hale, Ltd., 1984).

Hittites

An ancient population that rivaled the Egyptians, dominant in Asia Minor between the nineteenth and twelfth centuries B.C.

Probably originating northeast of the Caucasus, the Hittites migrated into Asia Minor around 1900 B.C. and began establishing a kingdom. They occupied the Anatolian plateau in modern-day Turkey and ultimately extended their influence toward Syria. It is possible that their migration pushed other populations southward, spurring the Hyksos invasion of Egypt. The Hittites probably took their name from the Plain of Hatti that they occupied and upon which they imposed their culture and Indo-European language. Their first conquest was the town of Nesa (near modern Kayseri, Turkey) followed by the capture of Hattusha (near modern Bogazkoy).

Little is known of the Hittites until the seventeenth century B.C. when Labarna (circa 1680–1650 B.C.) established the Old Hittite Kingdom and set up his capital at Hattusha. He was the first major conqueror for the Hittites, spreading their control throughout Anatolia to the coast. Labarna's successors pushed their borders southward to Syria. Mursili (or Mushilish) raided deep into the Old Babylonian Empire, captured Aleppo, and set the kingdom's southern boundary in Syria. This proved to be the extent of the Hittite conquest under Mursili, as they spent the next two centuries quelling internal disturbances and fighting the Mitanni of upper Mesopotamia.

The kingdom returned to some stability under the leadership of Telipinu around 1500 B.C. who laid down strict succession guidelines and possibly established a code of law. Some 50 years later, the New Hittite Kingdom was established. The Hittites had just suffered a defeat at the hands of the Egyptian pharaoh, Thutmosis III, and had begun paying the Egyptians tribute. One of the key figures in the New Kingdom was Suppiluliuma (Shubbiluliu), who seized power around 1380 B.C. and reestablished Hittite authority in Anatolia and defeated the Mitanni. He was unable to defeat the Egyptians, however, and the two powers remained rivals for the next century. During a time of Egyptian weakness under Akhenaton, the Hittites made gains in Lebanon at Egyptian expense. They also spread their power to the Aegean, Armenia, and upper Mesopotamia.

The key battle in the ongoing conflict with Egypt took place in 1294 B.C. at Kadesh on the Orontes River. Pharaoh Rameses II led his army of Numidian mercenaries north to force his will on the Hittites once and for all. When two captured Hittite deserters informed the pharaoh that their army was still many days' march away, Rameses rode ahead of his army to set up camp near Kadesh. The two prisoners turned out to have been planted by the Hittite king, Muwatallis, and the Hittite army attacked the Pharaoh without most of his troops. Rameses fought bravely until his army arrived and their appearance forced a Hittite retreat into the city of Kadesh. Without siege equipment, Rameses could not force their surrender, so he withdrew. Shortly thereafter the two nations signed a peace agreement: The Egyptians recognized Hittite sovereignty in Syria in return for Hittite recognition of Egyptian dominance in Palestine. The alliance was sealed by a dynastic marriage. The two peoples remained at peace until the fall of the Hittite empire, which came at the hands of the "Peoples of the Sea" around 1200 B.C.

Archer on a chariot with charioteer. Late Hittite bas-relief from the entrance block of the city gate at Sinjirli, Turkey, ninth century B.C. (Museum of Oriental Antiquities, Istanbul, Turkey).

The secret of Hittite expansion and superiority lay in the fact that they were the first power to develop the process of smelting iron in large quantities, a method that was probably discovered about 1400 B.C. In a time when everyone used bronze for their weapons, iron weaponry gave its possessors a great advantage. Despite this advantage, however, the bulk of the Hittite army was made up of mounted troops and chariots, from which archers fought. Iron weaponry conferred less of an advantage on these troops, but the Hittite infantry carried iron swords and iron-tipped spears and fought in a phalanx formation. At the battle of Kadesh, the Hittite king was able to muster some 3,500 chariots, each with a driver and two archers. Probably half the Hittite army was in chariots, with between 8,000 and 9,000 infantry and archers recruited from Hittite vassals and allies.

The Hittite kingdom recognized a supreme ruler, but a strong aristocracy made absolute rule difficult. An early form of feudalism was the basic social and governmental structure, with the local lords being responsible for providing troops in time of emergency. The king maintained a standing army, however, especially as the empire expanded and garrisons were necessary to maintain control over subject populations. Further, the king maintained a personal guard of 1,200 (and possibly as many as 12,000) Elamites (from modern-day Iran), talented soldiers available for hire, and other mercenaries were employed as well. All of this lasted until the arrival of the Peoples of the Sea in the thirteenth and twelfth centuries B.C. The Hittite empire collapsed, but Hittite populations survived for several centuries in cities such as Carchemish, on the upper Euphrates, Sam'al (modern Zincirli), and Millid (modern Malatia).

In the Bible, Uriah the Hittite held a major position in King David's army but was unfortunately married to Bathsheba, and David's desire for her resulted in Uriah's being killed. The story illustrates the spread of the Hittite population and the respect for their military abilities throughout the ancient world.

The final blow for the Hittites came in the eighth century B.C. when the power of Assyria absorbed everyone in the Middle East. The Assyrian king, Sargon, however, kept a strong contingent of Hittites in his army after their absorption into the Assyrian empire.

References: Ceram, C.W., *The Secret of the Hittites*, translated by Richard Winston and Clara Winston (New York: Alfred A. Knopf, 1956); Lehman, Johannes, *The Hittites: People of a Thousand Gods,* translated by J.M.Brownjohn (New York: Viking Press, 1977); Macqueen, J.G., *The Hittites and Their Contemporaries in Asia Minor* (London: Thames and Hudson, 1968).

Hood's Texas Brigade

An outstanding unit of the Confederate army during the American Civil War (1861–1865).

When troops of the newly created Confederate States of America fired on Union troops at Fort Sumter in the harbor of Charleston, South Carolina, on the morning of 12 April 1861 the American Civil War began. In southern states, from the Carolinas to Texas, men swarmed to recruiting stations to enlist. Texan enthusiasm matched that of any state in the Confederacy and by the end of 1861 some 25,000 men had joined the Confederate army. Most Texan troops fought in the western theater of war, but a few regiments were ordered east to fight with the Army of Northern Virginia. The First, Fourth, and Fifth Texas Infantry Regiments marched to Virginia, which would be their home for most of the following four years and the site of many of their graves. Collectively, these three regiments, combined with the Third Arkansas made up of both Arkansans and Texans, became the First Texas Infantry Brigade. Their first commander was Louis T. Wigfall, but upon their arrival in Virginia and assignment to Thomas "Stonewall" Jackson's command, they were put under the leadership of a young Kentuckian, John Bell Hood. The Texans became "his" brigade even when he was promoted to divisional command, and they fought in almost every major battle in the eastern theater of war.

The Texans arrived too late to take part in the opening battle of the war at Bull Run, but they were on hand in early summer 1862 when Union troops under the command of George McClellan advanced on Richmond, Virginia, in what came to be called the Peninsular Campaign. The Texas Brigade made its debut at Eltham Landing, when it was assigned to skirmish and delay a Union landing. Whether through enthusiasm or ignorance, the troops overstepped their orders and launched a full assault on the Union lines, attacking so fiercely that the Union forces withdrew. It was a more costly attack than Confederate commander Joseph Johnston had anticipated, but it exceeded his expectations and set a standard for performance that the Texans lived up to for the remainder of the war.

When Johnston was wounded and replaced by Robert E. Lee, the Texans soon came to his attention as well. Well-entrenched Union forces at Gaines' Mill had repelled two Confederate attacks and were about to receive reinforcements. Lee feared that if those reinforcements arrived, the Union troops could turn the tide of battle and possibly regain the initiative toward Richmond. He called on Hood and asked if the Texans could break through the Union lines. Hood replied that they would try. The Texans advanced slowly under heavy fire through Boatswain's Swamp, not firing until they were within ten yards of the Union lines. They then screamed a "rebel yell," fired a volley that cleared the front trenches, and attacked with bayonets. Union troops almost immediately broke, and Lee followed up with supporting attacks that drove McClellan's command back to their starting point at Yorktown. Although suffering heavy losses, the Texans had succeeded where two previous attacks had failed. Lee from this point came to depend on Hood's men.

The Texas Brigade distinguished itself again several weeks later at the second battle at Bull Run, where they first stopped the advance of a larger Union force, then participated in a flanking attack that crushed the Union line and forced its withdrawal from the field. Hood was promoted to command of a division and he gave credit for this to his Texans. On 17 September 1862 at the battle of Antietam Creek near Sharpsburg, Maryland, the Texas Brigade was engaged in the earliest fighting in a cornfield near the Dunker Church. Here the Brigade repulsed a Union corps and then pursued it. However, the Texans were obliged to withdraw, and the battle spread to other quarters, so this was the extent of the Texas Brigade's role in what proved to be the bloodiest day in American history.

The Brigade played little role in the next major battle at Fredericksburg, Virginia, on 13 December 1862 when the Confederates slaughtered Union troops in Ambrose Burnside's poorly conceived attack against strong Confederate entrenchments. The Texans also missed Lee's victory over Union General Joseph Hooker at Chancellorsville in May 1863 because they were detached from the main force on a foraging mission.

General John Hood, leader of the Texas Brigade

Hood's Brigade was in the thick of the fighting in the next battle, however, as Lee attempted to launch a final assault on Union territory. On the second day of the great battle at Gettysburg, Pennsylvania, on 2 July 1863 the Texans were ordered to assault the Union left flank anchored on the small rise called Little Round Top. The ground before the Little Round Top was a massive jumble of boulders called the Devil's Den, in which the Texans fought the most difficult battle of their lives. They once again gained ground against their Union foes, but were ordered to withdraw just as the Twentieth Maine Infantry Regiment launched a bayonet assault off of Little Round Top. The Texans were obliged to withdraw after sustaining heavy losses. Hood was wounded in the arm and so commanded his men during only part of the battle. He lost his arm and spent a few months recovering, months during which the Brigade was transferred west to Tennessee with General James Longstreet's corps. With Longstreet the Texans fought at Chickamauga, where they displayed their vaunted élan in yet another daring charge on 19–20 September 1863. But again, they had to withdraw after more heavy losses in the face of far larger numbers. The following day they attacked again and, after early successes, were attacked in their flank. This produced the only pell-mell retreat the Texans suffered during the war. However, rallied by their newly returned leader Hood, they regained their composure and returned to the battle. Hood was again wounded, this time losing a leg.

Returned to the Army of Northern Virginia, the Texas Brigade served under Lee in the final campaign of the war. In May 1864 General Ulysses Grant took command of Union forces and proceeded to pound Lee's army with a two-to-one numerical superiority. The opening battle in a heavily wooded area in northern Virginia, called the Wilderness, again showed Lee's confidence in the Texans. As Union troops threatened a breakthrough, Lee rode to the Texan position and called for their aid, crying "Hurrah for the Texans! The eyes of General Lee are on you. Texans, charge!" (Foote, 1958–1974). When Lee tried to lead the assault himself, the soldiers would have none of it. They swore not to attack unless Lee withdrew from the line of fire. When a Texan grabbed the reins of Lee's horse and pulled him to the rear, Lee rose in his stirrups, waved his hat and yelled "The Texans always move them!" (Foote, 1958–1974). Move them they did: The Union attack was blunted and Grant soon withdrew.

Grant continued to attempt to outflank Lee. Throughout May and June 1864 some of the most intense fighting of the war took place as the Confederates were slowly forced back to defensive positions around Richmond. At Spotsylvania and Cold Harbor the Texans proved themselves again. The war settled into an extended siege around the city of Petersburg, south of Richmond, from June 1864 through the following April. As supplies grew increasingly difficult to obtain, Lee's forces began to melt away. The Texans vowed they would not dishonor themselves and made a written declaration of their intention to fight on. The Resolutions of the Texas Brigade vowed to "maintain, at all hazards, and to the last extremity, the rights and liberties which a merciful God has been pleased to bestow upon them. We seek a perpetual separation from the hated and despised foe, who have murdered our gray-haired fathers, insulted our women and children, and turned out thousands of helpless families to starve" (Simpson, 1995). When word came to the Texans of Lee's surrender on 9 April 1865 they destroyed their rifles rather than surrender them.

Of the 5,300 men that enlisted and fought in the Texas Brigade, only 617 remained to be paroled after the surrender. They marched home as a unit and received a hero's welcome in Houston on 2 June 1865. They were present when Lee took command in June 1862, gained his favor for their determination in battle, and remained the troops upon which he depended most until the Southern cause was lost.

—Steve Davis

References: Foote, Shelby, *The Civil War*, A Narrative. 3 vols. (New York: Random House, 1958–1974); Simpson, Harold, "Hood's Texas Brigade at Appomattox," in Wooster, Ralph, ed. *Lone Star Blue and Gray: Essays on Texas in the Civil War* (Austin: Texas State Historical Association, 1995).

Hoplites

Infantry troops utilized in ancient Macedonian and Greek warfare between the fifth and third centuries B.C.

The Greek citizen soldiers of Athens, Sparta, and the other Greek city-states were called hoplites (from *hoplon*, meaning "armor"), or heavily armored infantry. Their ancestors, like the heroes in epic poems such as the *Iliad*, fought as individuals, usually from chariots or cavalry. By contrast, the hoplites developed infantry tactics in which they advanced and fought en masse, shoulder to shoulder with shields overlapping to protect each other in the line. These formations were called phalanxes. Phalanxes were compact units of men, usually greater in length than in depth. As Greek colonies spread around the Mediterranean in the first millennium B.C. increased trade brought prosperity to the Greek mainland. This in turn allowed increasing numbers of the yeomen class (landowners not of the aristocracy) to afford the equipment of a hoplite, the bronze helmet, the long spear, the heavy breastplate, iron shield, and greaves (leg armor). Although military service was required for all able-bodied men in Greek city-states at the time, most Greeks agreed that each individual must take responsibility to sustain democracy and the survival of the state. Only citizens of the city-state could take their place in the battle lines.

The Greek phalanx was an ideal formation for a citizen army. It allowed a maximum efficiency of strength with a minimum of training (with the important exception of Sparta, where training was extensive). The strength of the phalanx rested in the mass cooperation of the hoplites, all bunched together, eight to 25 ranks deep, moving irresistibly forward. It was not a permanent formation: Its dimensions and approach to attack varied according to each leader's tactics and the size of the army. As long as the soldiers remained together, their shields interlocking, they had relative safety. However, as a closed tactical formation, the phalanx was incapable of flexibility or operation on broken ground. The Persians never adopted it because archers drawn up in more than six ranks lose their effectiveness. The greatest weakness of the early phalanx was that on open ground heavy cavalry, such as that fielded by the Persians, could drive in its flanks or rear with relative ease. Notably, the Greek victories of Marathon and Plataea both took place on terrain where the flanks of the phalanxes were secured by hills or the sea.

As noted, each Greek provided his own equipment. Not every citizen could afford a horse so, as a result, cavalry played a very minor part in the Greek armies. Because there was always such a small number of Greek cavalry, it would have been foolish for them to try to oppose any enemy who possessed more numerous horsemen—such as the Persians—and apparently they never tried.

Early Greek armies also contained a number of archers, slingers, and javelin-armed skirmishers, called *peltasts*. These men, especially the archers and slingers, required far more training than did the hoplites, in most cases starting in their youth. Many of the Greek archers wore the same body armor as the hoplites, although it appears that a majority were unarmored. It is possible that they were drawn from the less-wealthy nobility, from families who could not afford a war horse but whose wealth could allow their sons sufficient free time to gain proficiency with the bow. It would appear that the best peltasts came from regions that specialized in such troops, such as archers from Crete, slingers from Rhodes, and javelineers from the half-Greek tribes of the Balkans.

In action, the peltasts usually advanced in front of the phalanx showering the enemy with arrows, then falling back to protect the rear or flank of the hoplites once they had engaged. In retreat they could maintain a rear guard. After victories, the peltasts were often left to garrison the conquered lands. Their secondary role in military affairs ran in accordance to their social subordination at home. The phalanx was supreme and the peltasts and cavalry remained very minor arms in the Greek system for many years. As long as the Greek armies retained their citizen-soldier nature, they were bound into a one-dimensional organization.

Citizen soldiers, aside from the men of Sparta, were almost by definition part-time warriors, training only as much as necessary to function adequately. However, with the spread of Greek cities around the Aegean, a new type of soldier appeared. Greek men who owned little or no land began to offer their full-time services for money. These mercenaries, who were constantly in service, could function together as highly skilled units or—dispersed among the ordinary hoplites—could raise the fighting abilities of all the Greek units considerably. Their professionalism allowed the phalanx to become a far more flexible formation. Smaller units of hoplites, along with the cavalry and the peltasts, were organized to protect their flanks from enemy cavalry. Some of these "beefed-up" hoplite units even became capable of dividing themselves into smaller units for special situations.

Another innovation in the use of hoplites is credited to Epaminondas of Thebes, who at the battle of Mantinea overcame the Spartans by strengthening his left flank with extra hoplites, cavalry, and light infantry, and by withholding his right flank from action. Epaminondas had noted that the phalanx had a natural tendency to move to its right in combat, and that two phalanxes locked in melee pinwheeled counterclockwise. His stronger left flank checked the Spartan right flank and his cavalry and light infantry enveloped it on its sides and rear. The Spartan left flank never came into contact, and gave way when the right flank broke. Epaminondas had used the combined talents of the three branches of his army, along with a shrewd observation, to overcome the more traditional (and traditionally stronger) Spartans. This idea of combined arms remained to be developed to its fullest extent by Philip II of Macedonia and his son Alexander III.

The phalanx continued for many centuries to be the tactical master of the battlefield, until it was rendered obsolete by the much more mobile and flexible cohorts of Rome, which were manned by the most professional and perfectionist soldiers in the ancient world.

References: Keegan, John, *A History of Warfare* (New York: Random House, 1993); Parke, H.W., *Greek Mercenary Soldiers* (Chicago: Ares, 1981 [1933]); Sage, Michael, *Warfare in Ancient Greece* (London: Routledge, 1996).

Huns

An Asiatic population that devastated Europe in the fifth century A.D.

The Huns were one of the myriad of tribes that rode out of central Asia, but little can be determined of their origin. Probably they were the Huing-nu, who failed in wars against the Chinese during the late second century B.C. and turned (or were forced) westward. Occasional early sources opine that they were the Nebroi mentioned by Herodotus as a semimythical people living on the fringes of territory controlled by the Scythians. Some of the earliest direct references come from clashes with the Goths around the area north of the Black Sea in the mid-fourth century A.D. The first Hun conquest was of the Alans, who were then used in the vanguard of Hun attacks against the Goths or emigrated into the Roman Empire.

The Huns, like all the steppe peoples, were horsemen. They migrated westward across the Russian plains, constantly searching for new grazing lands. This meant that they were without material resources and, hence, totally reliant on what they could capture, steal, or bargain for. Thus, the metals needed for weaponry, saddlery, or decoration usually came as tribute from people unwilling or unable to resist the huge numbers of Huns. The Huns fought as light cavalry, using bows and arrows almost exclusively. These were compound bows made of horn and hide, as no wood existed on the steppes. Their arrows were also horn-tipped. The Huns used swords for infighting if necessary, although they also carried lassoes in order to immobilize their opponents. They moved as a mass, but subdivided into clans that foraged alone. When time came for battle, they easily formed up and launched mass attacks against outnumbered foes. They had no compunction against retreating or avoiding combat if the enemy seemed too strong, for they did not fight for honor but for plunder. The Huns were completely unable to conduct sieges and the nature of central European terrain, with its forests and mountains, severely limited the ability of their wagon-borne families to maintain the pace set by the horsemen. In the end, it was the nature of the land in Europe that probably contributed to the Huns' defeat as much as any army.

In 376 the Huns began to harass the Caucasus lands controlled by the Ostrogoths. After fighting around the Crimea, the Ostrogoths were pushed back across the Dnieper to the Dniester River, where they began to pressure the Visigoths. The Visigoths had not fared too well against the armies of the Eastern Roman Empire, so their leader, Athanaric, had no wish to see his people defeated by a second enemy. Athanaric established his forces along the Dniester and sent a reconnaissance force east to keep touch with the advancing Huns. This force was easily destroyed and the Huns were on Athanaric's army before his men could finish their defenses. The Visigoths vanished into the countryside and reformed between the Pruth and Danube Rivers, where Athanaric ordered a wall to be built. Again the swift Hun army arrived and surprised the Visigoths, who again scattered and retreated toward the Danube. The refugees, who numbered between 700,000 and 1 million, settled into the forests of Transylvania.

Pressed against the frontiers of the Roman Empire, the Visigoths in 376 begged the Emperor Valens for his protection. The Visigoths were granted land along the Danube in return for military service, which they provided. The Ostrogoths who arrived later also begged imperial protection, but were denied it. They crossed the Danube anyway. Emperor Theodorus I, crowned in Constantinople in 379, led Roman campaigns against the Huns, which were rampaging through the Balkans, but he could not turn them back. The two Gothic peoples combined to fight against the eastern Romans, which left no strong force to oppose the slowly approaching Huns. The Huns settled into Pannonia along the Adriatic coast.

By 432 the Huns were well-established and a force to be reckoned with. Emperor Theodosius II paid tribute to the Hun leader Ruas and gave him a general's commission. Ruas's sons Bleda and Atilla renewed the treaty and fought for Constantinople in campaigns against Persia. Attila grew tired of doing another's fighting and made war against the eastern Romans. Between 441 and 443 he rampaged through the Balkans and defeated a Roman army outside Constantinople, but could not capture the city. He finally stopped upon receiving an increase in tribute. Attila killed his brother, Bleda, and in 447 renewed his war against the Romans. Although turned back from Constantinople again, Attila did manage to gain a threefold increase in tribute and cession of the eastern bank of the Danube. Theodosius's successor stopped paying the tribute in 450 by which time the Huns were looking westward.

Attila hoped to split the attention of the Western Roman Empire between himself and the Vandal leader Gaiseric, who was making trouble in north Africa. In addition, Attila was invited to aid a Frankish chieftain in a succession struggle against the chieftain's brother. Thus, there seemed to be

A woodcut of Attila burning townships during the invasion of Italy

plenty of reason for Attila to march on Gaul. He crossed the Rhine north of modern-day Mainz with between 100,000 and 500,000 warriors, whose families followed, carrying supplies. The Huns, with a variety of auxiliaries, advanced along a 100-mile-wide front, destroying everything in their path but Paris. The Roman general Aetius formed an army of Franks, Germans, and Alans, but could muster no more than half Attila's strength. In mid-June 451 the two armies fought at the site of modern-day Chalons, but Attila could not prevail. He retreated eastward, and western Europe was saved from Asian domination.

Attila turned instead and attacked south into Italy. He had demanded the hand of Honoria, the Western Roman Emperor's sister, and had been refused. The Huns ransacked northern Italy and refugees fled to the marshlands, creating Venice. Aetius returned to face Attila, but the Huns were having problems. One of Attila's commanders had been defeated in Illyricum (northern Greece) and the Italian countryside proved to be disease-ridden and without supplies. Attila met with Pope Leo I outside Rome and, after an unrecorded discussion, turned the Huns northward and left Italy.

Attila died in 453. His sons fought for his throne while subject tribes revolted. The remnants of the Huns retreated northeast of the Danube, leaving the rebellious tribes to their own devices. The last of the Huns, under Irnac, travelled as far as the Volga, but they were defeated and absorbed by the Avars. The Huns proved to be little more than plunderers, travelling from one ripe target to the next, never settling down or building any cities. They accomplished nothing more than mass destruction, gaining a reputation as the "scourge of God" punishing a sinful Roman Empire.

References: Brion, Marcel, *Attila: The Scourge of God* (New York: Robert McBride and Company, 1929); Bury, J.B., *The Invasion of Europe by the Barbarians* (New York: Russell and Russell, 1963); Thompson, E.A., *Romans and Barbarians* (Madison: University of Wisconsin Press, 1982).

Hussites

Protestant religious sect of Reformation Europe which fought for religious freedom and developed the first armored fighting vehicle.

Jan Hus, a rector at the University of Prague, was one of the first figures to speak out against the corrupt practices of the Catholic Church in the early fifteenth century. He was from Bohemia (corresponding roughly to the modern Czech Republic) and was a nationalist as well. He led worship services in Czech rather than Latin, dared to alter the order of worship, and announced that the only source of direction a Christian needed was the Bible: If the pope said something in contradiction of the Bible, then the papal pronouncement could and should be ignored. The Catholic Church was not disposed to let this man go unchallenged, and Hus's presence was demanded at the Council of Constance in 1414. Although guaranteed safe conduct, Hus was taken prisoner, condemned as a heretic, and executed. Many of the common people of Bohemia followed Hus, and they refused to stop following his teachings after his death. Rather than allow this defiance of the church to continue, a papal bull called for a crusade against the heretic Hussites.

These events coincided with political struggles within Bohemia, and between the country and its neighbors. King Wenceslaus IV (of "Good King Wenceslaus" fame) ruled Bohemia but faced opposition from Henry of Rosenburg, who had temporarily imprisoned Wenceslaus in 1395. The nobility and the common people migrated to one camp or the other and for years Bohemia was the scene of guerrilla warfare between supporters of either Wenceslaus or Henry. For a decade roving bands of mercenaries looted the Bohemian countryside, pillaging in the name of their chosen faction. Those that followed Wenceslaus, the more nationalistic of the population, also followed Jan Hus. One soldier who followed both, and came to prominence at this time, was Jan Zizka.

Zizka was an officer in the Wenceslaus's army and a leader of a band of guerrillas, known as *lapkas* ("burglars"). He was well known not only for his military prowess but for the fact that he had but one eye, the left eye having been lost sometime in childhood. He had previously served his king in conflicts against the Order of Teutonic Knights in Poland and took part in the Slavic victory over the Order at Tannenberg, or Grunwald, in 1410. He rose through the ranks to the position of royal gatekeeper and became quite wealthy. He was also an itinerant warrior who fought all over Europe, including service as a volunteer under Henry V's English army at Agincourt. After returning to Bohemia, Zizka joined the Hussite cause and was elected commander of their military forces when Sigismund of Hungary tried to take over the country. At Wenceslaus's death in 1419 Sigismund inherited the Bohemian throne, much to the anger of most of the population, because it had been Sigismund who had guaranteed Hus's safety in Constance.

The Hussites established a headquarters at a town they called Tabor, in honor of the biblical Mount Tabor. Townspeople shared their property equally in a theocratic community. Zizka hoped to harness their religious ardor to military zeal. He instilled a military regimen as stringent as their religious practices, and he forged a disciplined force made up mainly of the lower classes. Zizka drew on both his experience as a guerrilla commander as well as his more formal military experience fighting against the Teutonic Knights. He raided Catholic strongholds for weapons and in order to give his men experience. He also took their farming implements and turned them into weapons. Most notable was the flail, which he had his men reinforce with iron bars and tip with nails. He also made use of the cannon and matchlock firearms that were coming into wide use in Europe.

Zizka's premier weapon, that which made him and the Hussites famous, was the war wagon. The Hussites reinforced ordinary peasant carts with strong planking on one side with gun slits cut into it. Each ten-by-six-foot cart could carry as many as 14 men, armed with matchlocks, pistols, crossbows, halberds, and flails. Some later carried cannon and howitzers. Each also carried equipment for digging and fortification construction. As Zizka could count on but few armored knights early in the Hussites' campaigns, he countered them with this early version of a tank. The war wagons could either draw into a circle and chain themselves together to withstand assaults, or act as mobile gun platforms for attacking the enemy. Each wagon's crew became an independent force, relying on each other to work as a team in combat.

Sigismund invaded Bohemia in 1420 to crush the Hussites and claim his throne. Zizka's forces met them at Sudomer in March with the Bohemians outnumbered 2,000 to 400. Unable to successfully attack the circled wagons while on horseback, the knights dismounted and found themselves at a terrible disadvantage. The Hussites routed the invaders. This victory against five-to-one odds served to give Zizka's forces both experience and confidence. They would need both, for within three months, Zizka was defending the capital city of Prague against Sigismund's army of 80,000. Zizka, with no more than 20,000, defended a prepared position on Vitkov Hill outside Prague. Knowing that capture meant torture and execution, the Hussites fought with a terrible ferocity. The charging knights attacked barricades on the hill that were defended by both men and women. Although the Hungarian attackers managed to capture one watchtower, Zizka's flanking attack drove them back down the hill. Although Sigismund's casualties were relatively light, he decided that taking the hill and the city would be too difficult. He retreated to the city of Hradcany, had himself crowned King of Bohemia, looted the city's treasury, and returned to Hungary.

Zizka continued the fight against Sigismund's allies. He attacked Rosenburg and forced a truce, then campaigned toward Plzen in early 1421. He soon controlled all of west and northwest Bohemia. His forces captured the Catholic stronghold of Kutna Hora, then took Hradcany, then Bor Castle. In the last battle, Zizka was struck by an arrow just below his right eye, which soon led to loss of sight in that eye as well. Even completely blind he was more than a match for his opponents. Riding among his troops carrying a mace shaped like a fist holding a spike, he inspired unquestioning loyalty and confidence.

In 1422 the Hussites offered the throne of Bohemia to Grand Duke Vytautus of Lithuania. This provoked Sigismund to reinvade with a force of 30,000. Zizka with 10,000 men waited for him just outside Kutna Hora. They beat back several Hungarian assaults from the circled wagons, but some horsemen slipped past their camp in darkness and, aided by some Germans inside Kutna Hora, took the city and slaughtered the Hussites inside. Zizka took the offensive the next day and broke the Hungarian lines, but Sigismund was now able to withdraw into the city for the winter. With reinforcements, Zizka attacked surrounding towns garrisoned by the Hungarians. Sigismund decided to abandon Kutna Hora and burn the city behind him, but Zizka's forces were so close behind them that they were quickly able to put out the fires. Without stopping to celebrate, the Hussites charged after Sigismund and caught up to the Hungarians two days later at the village of Habry. There the demoralized Hungarians broke before the onrushing war wagons and fled across partially frozen rivers, where thousands fell through the ice and drowned.

In the wake of this success, Zizka had to deal with factionalism within the Hussite movement. The more religiously moderate Zizka opposed the more radical Taborite sect and withdrew his followers from Tabor to establish his own settlement at Orebovice in eastern Bohemia. His religious views in no way moderated his extremely strict military discipline, however, so he remained in command of an efficient fighting force. He provoked the wrath of the citizens of Prague, who allied themselves with some Catholics and attacked Zizka's camp. Zizka retreated before superior numbers, but made a stand near Kutna Hora, where he once again was victorious. This led to an armistice with the citizens of Prague and a reuniting of the Hussite factions. Zizka led his army to Moravia and along the way fell ill, probably with the plague. He died on 11 October 1424. Legend has it that he requested that his skin be tanned to make a drumhead, so he could lead his troops in battle after his death.

The Hussites remained a formidable force for another decade, beating back successive papist armies. Henry Beaufort of England led 1,000 English archers to Bohemia, where he met 150,000 German anti-Hussite crusaders in full flight. They had been besieging a Hussite stronghold but fled from the relieving force of 18,000; thus was the effectiveness of the war wagon's reputation. A fifth and final crusade was called in 1429 but it never reached Bohemia, instead joining with the English forces engaging the French under Joan of Arc. In the end, it was internal squabbling that destroyed the Hussites. The moderate Hussites and radical Taborites so divided the movement that the Catholics under Sigismund were able to defeat them and temporarily restore Catholic control in 1436.

References: Bartos, Frantisek, *The Hussite Revolution* (Boulder: East European Monographs, 1986); Kaminsky, Howard, *A History of the Hussite Revolution* (Berkeley: University of California Press, 1967); Oman, Charles, *A History of the Art of War in the Middle Ages* (Ithaca, NY: Cornell University Press, 1953 [1885])

Hyksos

An ancient population that conquered and dominated Egypt between the eighteenth and sixteenth centuries B.C.

Power slipped from the pharaohs of Egypt

in the late Middle Kingdom, during the Thirteenth Dynasty (1786–1633 B.C.), when they were conquered in a relatively easy victory by the Hikau-Khoswet people. The name *Hikau-Khoswet* originated from the Egyptian phrase meaning "rulers of foreign lands." An Asiatic group primarily composed of Semites, the Hikau-Khoswet, of Hyksos, reigned over Egypt for well over 100 years, beginning from about 1750–1700 B.C. and ending with the establishment of the New Kingdom in 1567 B.C. The main catalysts that enabled the Hyksos to conquer the Nile delta so easily were the internal dissent among the Egyptians themselves, a counterrevolt of the nobility, and a weakening of the power of the pharaohs.

The Hyksos were said to be well trained and well armed, and were credited with introducing the horse and chariot to Egypt. The Egyptian forces of the time were exclusively infantry armed with copper weapons. Assuming the Hyksos invaded with cavalry and chariots, scale armor, bronze weapons, and composite bows, the Egyptians would have been completely outclassed. Whether the Hyksos entered Egypt in one major invasion or through a gradual buildup of population (both theories are proposed), it is almost unthinkable that the Egyptians could have given them much serious military opposition. Moreover, if the Hyksos forces included Arabs, then camel-borne troops would also have been used, which would have been a complete surprise to the defenders.

During the course of the Hyksos invasion towns and cities were burned, temples were damaged, and the native population was subjected to severe hardships and cruelties. Once the Hyksos gained control, they imposed heavy taxes as well as a strong military dominance on their subjects. Surprisingly, the majority of Egyptians accepted this style of leadership without much resistance.

The origin of the Hyksos is the subject of much debate, although they were probably a Canaanite tribe from the east coast of the Mediterranean, possibly Palestine. The third-century Egyptian historian Manetho describes the dynasties of the Hyksos occupation as Phoenician (XV Dynasty) and Syrian (XVI Dynasty). Most authorities agree that Canaanite culture introduced the chariot into Egypt. The Hyksos could well have been aided in their invasion, at least indirectly, by the Nubians. The Nubians were in conflict with Upper Egypt in the area of the modern Sudan and through the region to the east of the Nile. It has been speculated that the Hyksos were to some extent allied with them. This may explain why the Hyksos remained concentrated in Lower Egypt, perhaps as the result of an agreement with the Nubians to divide the spoils of their conquests.

The Hyksos were not entirely preoccupied with military goals. According to William Hayes, "The Hyksos kings of the Fifteenth Dynasty brought about the construction of temples, production of statues, reliefs, scarabs, and other works of art and craftsmanship" (Hayes, 1959), some of which are regarded as the best examples of Egyptian literary and technical works of that time. Practical and useful inventions such as the well sweep, the vertical loom, and the composite bow, were Hyksos legacies. Egypt until this time was behind other Mediterranean civilizations in technological advancements. Thanks to the Hyksos, they were now able to learn of bronze working, the potter's wheel, and the use of arsenic copper. The Hyksos also introduced hump-backed cattle and fruit crops, as well as teaching the Egyptians new planting and harvesting skills. Evidence suggests that the Hyksos encouraged exercise through dance and expression through new musical instruments.

On the whole, the Hyksos seem to have been a powerful and influential people, but there were only a few rulers able to take credit for the advances. One of the six Hyksos rulers was Prince Salatis, a name that has been interpreted to mean "Sultan." During his rise to power, he banned the contemporary Egyptian rulers from the capital city of Memphis and extended his rule over most of Middle Egypt, eventually taking over

Upper Egypt and Nubia as well. In the meantime, Hyksos rulers had moved the capital to Avaris, the location of which remains a mystery.

Although the Hyksos invaders were eventually overthrown by the Egyptians in the late 1560s B.C. they left behind the tools and knowledge that helped build Egypt's future empire. Even though little information exists on the Hyksos invasion itself, the overall accomplishments of these people were dynamic and paved the way for future Egyptian glory.

References: Baines, J., and J. Malek, *Atlas of Ancient Egypt* (New York: Facts on File, Inc., 1980); Hayes, W., *The Scepter of Egypt* (Cambridge: Harvard University Press, 1959); Van Seeters, J., *The Hyksos* (New Haven: Yale University Press, 1966).

I

Immortals

Elite troops in the Persian army from 559 to 331 B.C.

When Cyrus the Great came to power over Persia in 559 B.C. he established the Achaemenid Dynasty, which would rule the Middle East from the Mediterranean to the Indian frontier for more than two hundred years. He came to rule not long after the collapse of Assyria, which built and maintained its empire through terror. Cyrus proved his ability to conquer in a sufficient number of battles. However, his reputation for ruling with toleration and respect brought the willing support of the countries he placed under his rule, which in the long run may have been more important for winning and maintaining his empire than his military prowess. In spite of this admiration of his subjects, Cyrus had to maintain an army sufficiently potent to protect his frontiers, and the army he built and his descendants wielded had few equals.

All subjects of the Persian empire were liable for military duty, but the people of the Persian homeland, the Persians and Medes, were the core of the military and the forces that the emperor could always count on to be well trained and motivated. Within this core of soldiery Cyrus kept a standing force that acted both as a palace guard and as the elite troops in battle. These were termed the Immortals, for the size of the unit was not allowed to drop below 10,000. In case of sickness or death, there was always another soldier prepared to step in and maintain the unit's constant size. Mostly Medes and Persians served in the Immortals, although there were also some Elamites from the area of modern Iraq.

Reliefs at the palace at Susa (modern-day Shush, Iran) give a glimpse of how the Immortals appeared. In those carvings the troops are Elamites, all dressed and armed alike. Their heads are bare and they wear elaborate robes that reach from neck to ankle, with leather shoes beneath. Each carries a spear with a silver blade and pome-

Two life-size archers from the Palace of Darius the Great, Susa, Iran (Louvre, Départment des Antiquities Orientales, Paris, France)

granate (a metal ball attached to the butt of the spear). Each soldier holds a bow in his left arm with the quiver slung across the left shoulder. The symmetry of the scene breaks down in the personal touches of each soldier's attire. For example, the soldiers' quivers are decorated in different patterns, and their shoes and robes are often of different colors and studded with ornaments of various shapes and colors. Other carved reliefs at Susa of Persian or Medean Immortals show their heads covered with felt caps, and they often wear jackets and trousers rather than robes. Within the depicted unit is an even more elite grouping, the *hazarpat*, 1,000 soldiers whose spear pomegranates are gold.

Although they were the cream of the Persian army, the Immortals are mentioned in historical documents only once in any detail at all: when the Persians under Xerxes launched their invasion of Greece in 480 B.C. The Persian army marched around the edge of the Adriatic Sea with the Persian fleet pacing them. As the Persians marched through Thessaly, the navy was blocked from supporting them by a Greek fleet stationed between the Thessalian coast and the island of Euboea. Thus, when Xerxes's men found themselves blocked in a narrow pass at Thermopylae, the fleet was unavailable to land troops behind the force, which was commanded by Leonidas of Sparta. The Greek force of 7,000 was made up of mixed contingents from around Greece, but the Spartan force of 300 was the only professional unit among them. When Xerxes—who commanded more than 100,000 men—saw the small force, he waited for them to be overawed and flee. When they did not, he attacked.

In the narrow confines of the pass, the Persians could not employ the tactics of maneuver with which they normally fought, and the heavily armed infantry of the Greeks staged a stout defense. The Greek phalanx formation employed long spears with a greater length than anything the Persians carried, so the tightly packed Greek force stood their ground and kept the Persians at bay. Frustrated at the lack of progress, Xerxes ordered his Immortals to attack. They could not break the Greek line either, in spite of the fact that other Persians with whips drove them from behind. Thus, in the only extended description of Immortals in combat, they are defeated. Only by treachery did Xerxes outflank the Greeks and destroy the 300 Spartans who remain to cover the withdrawal of the remainder of their forces.

The Persian army, though defeated in its attempt to invade Greece in the 400s B.C. remained a formidable fighting force that kept control over a huge empire for two centuries. Only with the arrival of Alexander the Great, antiquity's greatest general, did the Persian army meet its match.

References: Ferrill, Arther, *The Origins of War* (London: Thames and Hudson, 1985); Herodotus, trans. by Aubrey de Selincourt, *The Histories* (London: Penguin, 1954); Olmstead, A.T., *History of the Persian Empire* (Chicago: University of Chicago Press, 1948).

Iron Brigade

An outstanding unit of the Union army during the American Civil War (1861–1865).

In the course of American history few events have been as momentous as the Civil War. In 1861 the great experiment in government by the people seemed to be failing and a fledgling United States, not yet a century old, was divided with the inaugural blast at Fort Sumter on 12 April. The call to arms was sounded on both sides and young boys soon became soldiers in great armies. Those boys soon became men as they marched into epic battles with bloodshed and suffering on a scale that staggers the imagination. For the Union army, one brigade was to witness the utmost horror of the Civil War and fight through it while distinguishing itself as the elite force in the Army of the Potomac. Respected by both comrade and enemy, it was known as the Iron Brigade.

The Iron Brigade was organized in the

western states. One of the few completely "western" brigades in the eastern theater of the Civil War, the Iron Brigade took special pride in this distinction. Formed out of the Second, Sixth, and Seventh Wisconsin Infantry Regiments, and the Nineteenth Indiana Infantry, the brigade would later add the Twenty-fourth Michigan Infantry Regiment after the battle at Antietam in September 1862. Although the four initial regiments of the Iron Brigade were all formed at the beginning of the war, only the Second Wisconsin fought in the First Battle of Bull Run in July 1861 taking part in the assault on Henry House Hill. In the months following Bull Run, the Union army underwent drastic changes. The hierarchy of the Army was redesigned, and from this restructuring Gibbon's Wisconsin Brigade was formed. It did not receive the honor of being labeled the Iron Brigade until after its second battle.

Brigadier General John Gibbon was a strict disciplinarian and he trained his green troops constantly. Wishing to instill some esprit de corps in his men, he ordered a distinguishing uniform to set his brigade apart. One piece of this new uniform was the felt "Hardee" hat (the type worn by the regular army) in black rather than the standard blue. The black hat would become the brigade's trademark.

Even with the training and the new uniforms, Gibbon's brigade was still untested in battle. The Brigade's initial baptism of fire did not happen until August 1862 at the Second Battle of Bull Run. While passing a small farm along the road to Manassass, where the rest of the army was massing, Gibbon's brigade was ambushed by veteran Confederate forces under "Stonewall" Jackson. Expecting an easy victory over the smaller and inexperienced Federal force, Jackson's veterans were stunned when the green Union troops turned and charged headlong into the fight, firing organized massed volleys that dropped the front ranks of the Confederates.

The Battle at Brawner Farm had begun—and with it the Iron Brigade's legend. The 2,100 men of the brigade were facing 5,200 enemy troops, which were reinforced as the battle raged. For more than two hours they slammed away at each other, until Gibbon—in the face of overwhelming odds—decided to pull his troops back. After such a difficult battle, the Confederates were only too happy to let them go unmolested, but they would always remember those "damn black hat fellers"—as one Confederate soldier was heard to comment.

In this first fight, Gibbon's Wisconsin Brigade sustained a loss of 33 percent of its active strength while inflicting the same percentage of casualties on the larger enemy force. As impressive as this was, the fight did not end at Brawner Farm, for the next day found the brigade participating in Union General John Pope's ill-conceived attacks on the Confederate line. Throughout those attacks, the soldiers of the brigade fought bravely, once even turning their guns on their own comrades who were trying to run away and forcing them to get back in line to fight. The battle ended with the Confederates controlling the field and the Union Army in full retreat, but Gibbon's brigade had proved itself to the enemy and to its fellow troops.

The brigade got little rest, for less than a month later Confederate General Robert E. Lee launched his first invasion of the North. At South Mountain in Maryland, the brigade was used in a daring assault on the Confederate line on 14 September 1862. While two other Union forces attacked the left and right flanks of the enemy line, Gibbon's brigade was sent up the center to break the Confederate middle. The brigade, assisted only by artillery, fought uphill against an entrenched enemy. From the start of the fighting, it was clear that this would be a terrific contest as each side fired mercilessly into the other. After a back-and-forth struggle, the brigade rallied at a stone wall near the Confederate line. As the Confederates launched an attack on its new position, the brigade met them with fixed bayonets and musket fire. The Confederates paid dearly for their assault. As night fell, the battle began to die down—but not before the two sides had taken grievous casualties. Through it all, the brigade held its line and forced the Confederates to pull back. Union General Joe Hooker witnessed the fight and, in a letter to General McClellan, he commented on the fighting skill of this "Iron Brigade," whose line seemingly could not be broken. The name stuck, and with it the honor of being among the Union army's most prized troops.

The celebration was brief. Lee's army began to concentrate around Sharpsburg, Maryland. McClellan was quick to react and the two armies faced each other along a little stream called Antietam Creek. So fierce was the ensuing battle at Antietam that 17 September 1862—the day of the battle—became the bloodiest single day in American history. The Iron Brigade took part in the opening assault on the Confederate left. Along with the rest of General Hooker's I Corps, the soldiers attacked Confederate forces under Stonewall Jackson. The objective of the Federal assault was the small Dunker Church at the rear of the Confederate line. The battle raged through an open lot and a cornfield with both sides clashing amidst stalks of corn and along rail fences. After two hours of incessant fighting, the Confederate line began to give way and the soldiers of the Iron Brigade and their comrades raced for the Dunker Church with victory on their minds. They were shocked to find, as they approached their objective, a gray line charging out of the fleeing rebels. The expected Union victory was quickly reversed as the famous Confederate force known as the Texas Brigade came roaring into the battle from its reserve position. Tired, wounded, and thrown off guard by the ferocity of this new attack, the members of the Iron Brigade and its companion forces quickly retreated back to their original positions until reinforcements were brought up to push back the Confederate assault. The Iron Brigade stayed on the defensive for the rest of the day. As night fell, it was apparent that Lee and his army had been defeated, but at a severe price.

With the victory came new changes for the Union army and for the Iron Brigade. The Army of the Potomac received a new commander in the form of Major General Ambrose Burnside, and the Iron Brigade received a new regiment in the form of the Twenty-fourth Michigan Infantry. The members of the Twenty-fourth were well aware of their new brigade's fame and they were anxious to prove themselves worthy members and to win their black hats. They did not have to wait long, as General Burnside prepared to launch his famous ill-fated attack at Fredericksburg on 13 December 1862. The Iron Brigade's role in this battle was limited to the far left of the field away from the heaviest fighting, but it did see action. Facing a line of Confederates posted in a wooded area, Gibbon ordered the Twenty-fourth Michigan to clear the woods and, in a manner to make their veteran comrades proud, the Twenty-fourth Michigan broke the enemy line. As the Confederates pulled back, the Iron Brigade was ordered to pursue with the Twenty-fourth Michigan in the lead. The new regiment took severe casualties but did not falter. By the end of the battle, however, the Union Army had suffered its worst defeat and was forced to retreat from Fredericksburg. But the Twenty-fourth Michigan earned something as valuable as a victory: They had earned their black hats and the right to call themselves a part of the Iron Brigade.

After so great a blunder, Burnside was replaced by Major General Joe Hooker as commander. With the arrival of spring, Hooker devised an attack to crush the rebel army. His plan called for a portion of the army to cross upstream of the main rebel force and attack Lee from his rear while the other force crossed at Fredericksburg and attacked his front. In order to cross the river, Hooker needed to secure one of the many river fords that was guarded by Confederate troops. For this task he turned to the Iron Brigade. As Union engineers began to set the bridge, the Iron Brigade, its soldiers lying down in boats to avoid Confederate rifle and cannon fire, surged across the river. Upon reaching the other shore, the troops leaped from their boats and charged the Confederate position. The assault was successful and Hooker had his bridge, but the Iron Brigade had taken heavy losses. Due to its diminished strength, the brigade was held in reserve during the battle of Chancellorsville. At this battle, Lee and his forces decimated Hooker, and the Iron Brigade helped cover the retreat of the Union Army back over the very bridge they had helped secure.

As the Union army suffered yet another humiliating defeat, Lee prepared his army to invade the North for a second time. This time the two armies met at the crossroads town of Gettysburg, Pennsylvania. The first day of the largest battle in the Civil War started with Union cavalry engaging a larger Confederate force. The Iron Brigade was called to reinforce the failing Union line. The Union generals on the scene recognized the need to hold the high ground until the rest of the army could be assembled. This task was left to I Corps with the Iron Brigade in the lead. Here, along McPherson's Ridge and the Chambersburg Pike, just northwest of Gettysburg, the Iron Brigade fought its most difficult battle. The larger Confederate force was slowly surrounding the Union force, but the Iron Brigade did not give an inch, making the Confederates pay for every step they took. The Sixth Wisconsin met the Second Mississippi in a fierce hand-to-hand contest over the regimental colors, with a young Wisconsin private capturing the rebel flag and later presenting it to his commanding general.

As I Corps finally began its withdrawal through Gettysburg and up to Cemetery Ridge, the Iron Brigade was ordered to retreat and headed for the safety of the new Union line. In the presence of a superior force, the Iron Brigade could take pride in the fact that it gave no ground that it was not ordered to give. The Iron Brigade and its companion forces had accomplished their objective: They had saved the high ground and possibly the entire battle—but at an incredible cost. Of the 1,883 men of the Iron Brigade who marched up the Chambersburg Pike that morning, only 671 made it back to the Federal position on Cemetery Ridge that night. The Twenty-fourth Michigan alone lost 80 percent of its regiment. Most of the field officers had been killed, and in some instances entire companies had been reduced to one or two men. The brigade received the dubious honor of having the highest casualty percentage of any unit in the entire Civil War, North or South.

The Iron Brigade never recovered from these losses. After Gettysburg, the brigade was reorganized and supplemented with new regiments that effectively demolished its veteran ranks. The reconstituted Iron Brigade fought in the remaining battles of the Civil War, but the Iron Brigade of legend had fought its last battle at Gettysburg. Nevertheless, history would not overlook the soldiers of the Iron Brigade, and the legacy of the black hats would endure.

—Steve Davis

References: Foote, Shelby. *The Civil War, A Narrative,* vol. 1 (New York: Vintage Books, 1958); Nolan, Alan T. *The Iron Brigade: A Military History* (Indianapolis: Indiana University Press, 1961).

J

Janissaries

Elite slave soldiers of the Ottoman Empire during the fourteenth through the nineteenth centuries.

First organized in the fourteenth century, the Janissaries of the Ottoman Empire became the first regular standing infantry force in medieval Eastern Europe. For four centuries they formed the nucleus of the Ottoman armies that fought the wars of Allah and the Turkish Sultans. On a hundred battlefields they knew only victory or death, and their very presence was frequently enough to send their enemies fleeing in terror. The Janissaries' reputation for bravery and ferocity, coupled with their unmatched discipline and training, made them the most feared fighting unit of their era.

Ironically, in the beginning, none of the individuals who became Janissaries were Turks or even Muslims when they entered the service of the Sultans. The part of eastern Christian Europe under Turkish rule was required every four years to provide a tribute of around 3,000 boys between 12 and 20 years of age. Over the next decade, the boys underwent several stages of training, which involved living and working with farmers and tradesmen in Turkey, and learning the Turkish language and the Muslim religion. At around the age of 25, the best of these recruits were chosen for seven years of training by the Janissaries themselves in Constantinople. By the time a recruit was formally accepted into the corps, his indoctrination was so complete as to assure his total loyalty to the Sultan and to his fellows—unto death. He had become part of the "slave-family."

The clothing of a Janissary usually consisted of a long garment called a *spahi*, frequently made of brightly colored silk, and a cap with a distinctive long sleeve hanging down the back. Horsehair plumes and feather crests adorned this hat, and gave Janissary columns the appearance, said one witness, "of a moving forest." The weapons of a Janissary were the composite bow, later replaced by the harquebus (or matchlock musket), swords, and daggers. A Janissary wore very little armor, perhaps the occasional piece of chain mail, and did not use a shield or pavis. If categorized, he would have to be described as light infantry. The corps was infantry exclusively, although a few hundred might win promotion to the *Spahis of the Porte*, the Sultan's household cavalry. Handpicked archers could be assigned to the *Solaks*, the Sultan's bodyguards. Those 60 Janissaries deemed the finest warriors formed the *Peiks*, the personal guardians of the Sultan. They were distinguished by their caps of beaten gold, and their weapons: a two-handed axe.

After the first century and a half of the Janissaries' existence, the Sultan Suleiman the Magnificent increased the size of the Janissary corps to more than 20,000 men. These were organized in messes of ten men, of which ten messes formed a company. Part of the Janissaries' solidarity was based on the

First attack on Constantinople by the Turks in 1453, depicted in a sixteenth-century oil painting by Jacopo Palma (Palazzo Ducale, Venice)

practice of eating together, and each company's large copper soup cauldron was a symbol of the members' fraternity and unity. The loss of this cauldron to an enemy was equivalent in disgrace to the loss of an eagle standard for Napoleon's troops, while the overturning of cauldrons later in the history of the empire was a sign of dissension and perhaps insurrection against the Sultan.

When not on campaign, those Janissaries not stationed in Constantinople garrisoned large towns throughout the empire. There they functioned as a sort of police force, maintaining law and order, punishing criminals, guarding the frontier, and enforcing the word of the Sultan. In combat, the Janissaries typically formed the center of the Ottoman horde, their flanks covered by wagon laagers chained together, with massed artillery to their front. When opposing other eastern armies, which were composed mostly of cavalry, the Ottomans always stood on the defensive, forcing their enemies into frontal attacks. In this manner, the Janissaries could deliver orderly and well-trained volleys of archery and harquebus fire on the enemy horses, while the Ottoman artillery, which frequently was chained together in large batteries, broke up the cavalry formations and slowed their charge. Against European armies, with their heavily armored knights, the Ottomans adopted deeper formations. Two and sometimes three lines of light and heavy cavalry, usually auxiliaries drawn from conquered provinces, fronted the chained artillery. Their purpose was to slow down the knights and dissipate their charge. Then, close range artillery fire and the Janissaries' musketry would drive the Europeans away before they could close with the Ottoman infantry. Light cavalry waiting on the flanks would then swoop in to pursue and destroy the retreating knights.

Ottoman expansion westward into Europe and the Mediterranean called for attacks on walled cities and castles as much as battles in the fields. It was in siege work that the Janissaries perhaps performed their best. They led the final assaults at Constantinople in 1453 and at Rhodes in 1522. As snipers and sappers they had no equals and, once fortification walls had been breached, their attacks were pushed forward with a fanaticism that ignored danger and death. With trumpets blaring, kettledrums and cymbals banging, they would charge screaming and wailing over their own dead and dying. They boasted that "the body of a Janissary is only a stepping stone for his brethren into the breach." However, their lack of armor and their almost suicidal attacks soon thinned their ranks to an alarming degree. The quantity of training for a Janissary declined from seven years to sometimes as little as 18 months, and the quality of the recruits themselves declined. By the end of the reign of Suleiman the Magnificent, sons of Janissaries had the hereditary right to join the corps, and by 1600 any Turk or Muslim could apply.

Westward expansion brought the Ottomans into battle with pike- and harquebus-armed European armies that were, in many cases, as well trained as the Janissaries. While the Europeans made steady advancements in armor, weapons, and tactics, the Janissaries tended to remain stagnant, rooted in tradition. This lethargy resulted in the Ottoman expansion finally being halted at the great sea battle of Lepanto in 1571. There Christian Europeans, using harquebusses and muskets and protected by steel breastplates and helmets, killed 30,000 of the 60,000 Turks present, signaling the end of Ottoman power in the Mediterranean.

The Janissaries continued as a unique force for another century and a half, clinging to their traditions and privileges. More and more, they assumed a political role in the empire, supporting certain Sultans and bringing down others. In many ways they came to mirror the role that the Praetorian guard played in Imperial Roman politics. Any attempts by the Sultans to replace them with more modern infantry formations resulted in violent Janissary riots. The corps, the force on which the security of the Empire had so long depended, had itself become a threat. Worse, it was a toothless tiger, a worthless military force against its enemies in the nineteenth-century world.

Finally, in 1826 after still another revolt, troops loyal to Sultan Mahmut II surrounded the Janissaries in their barracks and, when they refused to surrender, blasted them into submission with artillery. The survivors were hanged, and their soup caldrons, the symbols of their solidarity, were cast into the Adriatic. Four centuries after beginning in fidelity to religion and ruler, the march of the Janissaries across the history of Eastern Europe and the Middle East ended in mutiny, dishonor, and death.

References: Goodwin, Godfrey, *The Janissaries* (London: Saqi, 1994); Kinross, Patrick, *The Ottoman Centuries* (New York: Morrow, 1977); Shaw, Stanford, *The History of the Ottoman Empire and Modern Turkey*, 2 vols. (Cambridge: Cambridge University Press, 1976–1977).

K

Kamikazes

Suicide pilots of the Japanese air forces during World War II.

Japan's introduction of intentionally planned, government-sponsored suicide tactics in the final year of World War II was virtually unprecedented in all of warfare. Yet, considering the nature of Japanese society over the several centuries preceding the kamikaze, this development seems not only logical, but in some ways inevitable.

In the late 1200s the island nation of Japan was under attack by Mongol forces from mainland China. Early assaults had been met and turned back on the beaches, but the arrival of Mongol reinforcements made the situation look dire for the defending Japanese. They were saved, however, by the timely arrival of a typhoon that destroyed the Mongol invasion fleet. The natural disaster seemed to the Japanese to be heaven sent, so the typhoon that saved Japan was called the *kamikaze*, or "divine wind." It was the recollection of that thirteenth-century salvation that inspired the creation of the twentieth-century kamikaze, to whom many Japanese looked for their salvation from a different foreign invasion almost seven centuries later.

In the intervening centuries, Japan was ruled by a military society under the direction of the *shogun*. He was the titular military advisor to the emperor but was in fact the real power in Japan until 1868. In that year, forced contact with the outside world initiated by the American naval officer Matthew Perry woke the Japanese up to the progress the world had made while they had strictly maintained their own isolation. Within 30 years, under the Meiji emperor, Japan staged a major leap forward to become an industrialized power. Japan army's remained organized along the lines of the *Samurai* warrior class that had dominated the country for hundreds of years. In addition, it created a modern navy that soon destroyed the Russian navy in 1905 and threatened the preeminence of the United States in the Pacific Ocean. Japanese success in wars against China in the 1890s and Russia in 1904–1905, along with its military occupation of Korea, reinforced the martial climate of the new Japan and gave encouragement to the more aggressive nationalists in the military and government. The well-trained and motivated army captured Manchuria in 1931–1932 and took over most of eastern China between 1937 and 1941.

Although this success encouraged many Japanese in positions of power to challenge the United States in the Pacific, some men in key positions counseled restraint. These included Admiral Isoroku Yamamoto, commander of the Imperial Japanese Navy Combined Fleet. He foresaw the potential for destruction latent in American culture, but the other militarists in the government pushed for war. For a war to be dominated by naval operations and their accompanying air maneuvers, the Japanese needed—but did not possess—numeric superiority in ships and aircraft. Thus, they were doomed from the start. But Japanese warriors have never been more prone to extreme actions than when faced with imminent defeat. The virtually inbred creed that no soldier surrenders, that death for one's country and emperor is far preferable to surrender or defeat, almost guaranteed that the Japanese would sooner or later engage in desperate measures.

The United States Marines have had throughout their existence a motto: death before dishonor. It is somewhat fitting, therefore, that they were the first Americans to learn that the Japanese military took that phrase quite literally. In the first offensive ground combat on Guadalcanal, in the Solomons Islands northeast of Australia, Marines faced what came to be called banzai charges. *Banzai* (literally "10,000 years") was the cry that Japanese soldiers raised to their emperor, not only for his long life, but for his soldiers' commitment to die for him. It was screamed by attacking Japanese in assaults that seemed to the Marines like human waves. These charges, coupled with the almost complete lack of captured Japanese prisoners, showed the Americans how determined the typical Japanese soldier was to win—or die trying.

The banzai charges were repeated in almost every battle fought by Japanese soldiers, and the Marines came to almost expect them as battles were winding down and the Japanese defenders were fewer in number. What came to be a common occurrence for Marines to witness was emulated by Japanese pilots starting in 1944. The first recorded intentional suicide attack by a Japanese pilot was in May of that year off the coast of New Guinea. Prime Minister Tojo in the Japanese cabinet had already ordered preparations for "special attack units." The first serious call for self-sacrificial attacks, however, came from lower-ranking officers

A Japanese suicide plane dives on an American ship in World War II.

who felt the personal need to employ special measures to relieve the increasingly desperate straits of the Japanese army and navy, which faced superior American numbers in both aircraft and ships.

By the summer of 1944 when American forces landed in the Marianas Islands and came within bomber range of the home islands, the Japanese army and navy high commands began to listen more closely to the calls for suicide tactics. The Aerial Research Department of Tokyo's Imperial University began designing a rocket-propelled aircraft called *Ohka* ("cherry blossom") with a warhead in the nose. The pilots trained to fly these rocket-bombs were called Thunder Gods. The Ohka were not mass produced (only a few hundred were made), so the vast majority of airborne kamikaze attacks were made by regular aircraft, both bombers and fighters. These made their initial appearance during the American invasion of the Philippines in October 1944. The Special Attack units in the Philippines were commanded by Vice-Admiral Takijiro Onishi. The suicide attacks shocked the American forces, so much so that for six months the public in the United States was not informed of them. Although the attacks were occasionally successful, most of the effect was psychological. It was not enough of a psychological deterrent, however, to force a cancellation of the invasion as the Japanese had hoped.

The pilots who volunteered for kamikaze missions did so from a sense of duty and usually had a lot of time to think about their decision, for almost no one was sent off immediately upon volunteering. In some cases the pilot waited weeks or even months before his assignment came. Before his mission, the pilot donned a white head scarf (*hachimaki*) with the rising sun emblazoned in the center. Many times he also wore a ceremonial waist sash (*senninbari*), called "thousand-stitch belts," in which 1,000 women in Japan had sewn one stitch each in order to show the widespread support for the pilot. They were then served ritual cups of water or rice wine (*sake*). Often the pilots composed death poems, traditional for Samurai warriors prior to suicide.

Survivors of the kamikaze missions did exist. Although some sources tell of pilots who returned with mechanical difficulties being shunned by their compatriots, other sources report that, if no target was found, the pilot was instructed to return to base. This was how Saburo Sakai, Japan's highest-scoring fighter ace, managed to survive the war.

The results of the attacks in the Philippines were encouraging enough for the government to continue pushing the development of the Ohka. Furthermore, in January 1945 the Japanese army and navy chiefs of staff submitted a plan to the emperor to require all the armed forces to engage in suicide tactics. The emperor disagreed. By February, the large number of early volunteers was beginning to dry up, and kamikaze pilots began being drafted. Only a few attacks took place during the Iwo Jima campaign in February and March 1945 but when American forces landed on Okinawa in April, the full force of the Special Attack units was felt. Fifteen ships were sunk and another 59 damaged, with a total loss of more than 48,000 Americans killed and wounded during the Okinawa campaign. The last major assault was in mid-May, after which time the shortage of pilots and aircraft was acute. The last American ship sunk by a kamikaze was on 29 July 1945. The last attack took place on 13 August, only two days before the emperor announced Japan's surrender. Japanese navy pilots who died in the attacks numbered 2,525, with 1,388 army pilots also dying.

Although the aerial kamikazes were the best known of the suicide units, there were also midget submarines fitted out for one-way trips against American shipping. These were called *Kaiten*, or "heaven shifter," in the hopes that they could shift the fate of Japan's forces. Individual soldiers are reported to have laden themselves with explosives and jumped on tanks to disable them. Plans were also under way to encourage the civilian population of Japan to assume a suicidal role when the American invasion came. They were designated the *Ichioku Tokko*, or "hundred million as a special attack force." Many believe that only the shock of the two atomic bombs in August 1945 was sufficient to overcome the duty many of Japan's population were preparing to undertake.

References: Dower, John, *War Without Mercy* (New York: Pantheon, 1986); Inoguchi, Rikihei, Tadashi Nakajima, and Roger Pineau, *The Divine Wind* (Annapolis: United States Naval Institute Press, 1958); Naito, Hatsuho, *Thunder Gods* (New York: Kodansha International USA Ltd., 1989).

Knights

Armored troops dominant in warfare of the Middle Ages.

Of all the warriors of antiquity, none had a longer career or more of a social, cultural, and political influence on his society than did the European knight. For 700 years knights were the supreme projection of military power on whatever battlefields they appeared. Princes and kings attached themselves to the institution, conferred knighthood, and aspired to become knights themselves. Knights frequently were king makers, and sometimes even kings by their own hands. Undeniably, they were the kings of the battlefield, and for much of the Middle Ages most of the world trembled at their thundering approach.

First, foremost, and always, the knight was a soldier: in Latin *milles*, in French *chevalier*, in German *Ritter*, Italian *cavaliere*, Spanish *caballero*, and in Anglo-Saxon *cnicht*. As these terms imply, a knight was usually mounted and because he wore as much armor as possible, he was in the simplest terms an armored cavalryman. The emergence of the medieval knight is clouded in the distant mists of the eighth century, for it was then that the first serious European cavalry arm came into being. In 702 A.D. Muslim invaders came sweeping through Spain and into modern-day France. In order to meet their swift mounted tactics it was necessary that the Frankish rulers Charles Martel and the emperor Charlemagne develop a standing army with an aristocratic, armored, heavy cavalry core. The horses, equipment, and training necessary to support these warriors were very expensive. To meet these expenses, the Frankish emperors tended to seize church lands and either use the proceeds from those lands directly or grant them as estates to the mounted soldiers.

Thus, the knight was born in France as a military necessity to meet the dangers of marauding Muslims. At first, the knight was merely another specialized warrior—very expensive, but necessary. He could serve in the retinue or house of a great lord and receive wages with which he could equip himself, or he could receive land from a lord and use the income from that land to outfit himself for war. Either way, he was the vassal of a lord to whom he owed everything, and the beneficence of that lord (either protection or land) could be withdrawn if the knight's service faltered. As time passed, fewer and fewer knights served directly in the houses of great men, but instead occupied land granted to them for their use and showed up for service when called by their great lord.

Soon, however, especially in England and then other countries, the land granted to a knight became a permanent possession of his family, passed down from father to son, and even to wives and daughters. The knight became a lord in his own small manor, and thus entered the lower ranks of the aristocracy. He could even pay money (called *scutage*, or "shield money") in lieu of actual service.

As a vassal, the knight owed his lord service, avenged his wrongs, protected his power, defended his dignity, and swore allegiance to him unto to death. However, as much as he was a vassal, he was first and foremost a warrior, and war was his profession and his delight. A knight was highly trained and highly dangerous. His ability, equipment, and relationship with the great lords set him apart from the rest of society, and he could do pretty much as he wished, both above and beyond the established laws.

Medieval warfare as depicted in an engraving in the Iconographic Encyclopedia, *1851*

Like most everyone in medieval times, the early knight was illiterate, brutish, and cruel by modern standards, rough in speech and manners, earning his living by violence and unfettered by public justice. He lived by the sword and answered only to greater strength. Unarmed segments of society were bystanders, or worse: victims. Even on a holy crusade or pilgrimage, a knight could, in desperate circumstances, fall upon merchants and peasants and strip them bare, or kill them, with little or no regret. It appears from a distance that society had as much to fear from this warrior as to gain from him.

Then, about the eleventh century, knights and knighthood began to change—to evolve. Part of this change came from the church, which taught forgiveness and gentleness, and tried to restrain these impetuous warriors with the papal pronouncements *Peace of God* (989 A.D.) and the *Truce of God* (1041 A.D.). The *Peace of God* sought to protect the clergy and church lands, and unarmed or poor men, merchants, or men going to or from church. The *Truce of God* restrained violence or the pleasure of war on Sundays and holy days (at that time Thursdays, Fridays, and Saturdays).

Then the church promoted the Crusades, holy wars against the Moslems in the Holy Land. Knights who went were promised forgiveness for their sins, the possibility of estates in the conquered lands, and all the fighting they could stand. In a frenzy composed of equal parts of religious faith, adventure, and greed, thousands accepted the call. By the middle of the twelfth century, knighthood had become the bright sword of Christendom.

How successful these measures were in curbing the more violent natures of the medieval fighting men is debatable, but there is no doubt they did eventually affect the institution of knighthood by forcing knights to realize a responsibility to other segments of society. Eventually, the church broadened this to include a responsibility to protect those oppressed segments of society. Fraternities of knights arose from the Crusades, such as the Knights of the Temple, the Knights of the Hospital, the Knights of St. John, the Teutonic Military Order, and others. These orders achieved a measure of discipline, brotherhood, experience, and sense of duty and service that they managed to pass on to the remainder of knighthood. In all likelihood this was never more than a thin veneer for most, but out of it the code of living known as chivalry was born. With chivalry came the association of the knight with gentle birth, truly a *gentle*man, an aristocrat. Emperors and kings became knights. Excluding women, their entire courts consisted of knights. Their vassals—princes, dukes, and counts—were all knights, and those people in turn surrounded themselves with knights. The only other estate equally represented in medieval society was the clergy. Knighthood soon cut across national lines, forming an international fraternity.

The church then took the final step in gentling these warriors by becoming involved in the Ceremony of Investiture, thus sanctifying the status of knight. This probably began in the eleventh century with a simple ceremony blessing the sword, to dubbing in the twelfth century, to the final elaborate ceremony of knighting complete with fasting, prayer, and a high mass in the thirteenth and fourteenth centuries. In this, the church did as it had often done before: It merely adopted a pagan rite or ritual (the acceptance of a male child into the fraternity of warriors of the tribe or clan) as its own, just as it had adopted so many previous holidays and traditions. In this way, over a few centuries the knight underwent a transformation from ordinary soldier, to kept retainer, to loose cannon, to soldier of Christ.

Originally, knights were no more than well-armed peasants—on the social scale anyway. But the granting of land set them apart, and the time necessary to become proficient with their weapons meant they could not labor like peasants. Soon the idea of a knight as the social equal of a peasant, or of falling to the level of a peasant, became unthinkable. He occupied a position of honor, and his family and the families of other retainers soon grouped around the king or great lord in close knit clans. They intermarried, and continued service to the great lord, and soon their rank became hereditary, as did their lands and their service. They had become lesser nobles.

Theoretically, knighthood was open to all brave or rich men, and any knight could raise a worthy person to membership in the fraternity. However, by the end of the twelfth century this had changed. Only the sons of knights, or those of noble or gentle birth, could aspire to knighthood. The fraternity had become either hereditary or highly exclusive, and both conditions prevented the lower orders from gaining admittance. Knights were now a social and professional class.

A knight's training was imparted individually: A father might train his own son, hire a man at arms to train him, or send his son to serve as a squire in the castle of a great lord where he trained in a group of other squires. Even then, training was as an individual. The candidate for knighthood practiced sword cuts on wooden poles and learned to use a spear on foot or on a wooden horse propelled by his fellows. He hunted stags and wild boars with a spear, either on foot or on horseback, and learned the art of controlling a horse under all conditions. He wrestled with others and fought with wooden weapons, all the while wearing the armor that was to become his second skin. All this training was aimed at making the youngster proficient in horsemanship and the use of arms, and at hardening him to physical pain and the strain of battle.

The chance to show off one's skills and to practice the arts of war came in those great shows called tournaments. The earliest such contests date to 842 A.D. Originally, these were friendly competitions in which the participants used blunted weapons. By the twelfth century, they had become highly dangerous, causing Pope Innocent II to ban tournaments in 1130, 1139, 1148, and 1179. Obviously, these bans were not successful. Tournaments were a means to win glory (under the admiring eyes of young women, who began to attend such affairs toward the end of the twelfth century) without the discomfort and expense of a long campaign. William Marshall, the Earl of Pembroke, gained great wealth from such affairs, acquiring ransoms, horses, and armor from over 500 knights during a lifetime of tournaments in the late twelfth and early thirteenth centuries.

Three technological advances combined to bring the knight into being: the nailed horseshoe, the stirrup, and the high-backed saddle. The nailed shoe transformed a knight's horse into a firm fighting platform that could take him into all but the most heavily wooded terrain. The stirrup traces back to fifth-century Korea. Nomads from the eastern steppes brought the stirrup into the Byzantine Empire, and from there its use spread on into Europe. The stirrup allowed the rider a firmer seat on his mount; he could strike a blow and not unhorse himself. The high-backed saddle allowed the knight to transfer the energy of rider and mount into his weapon, to charge with couched lance and deliver a shattering impact. Without these things, there could be no knights as we know them, and these things were not present in Europe until 850 A.D. at the earliest.

In the tenth and eleventh centuries, the weapons of a knight were the lance and sword. The lance, which was a light spear with a broad leaf-shaped point, could be thrust like a spear or thrown like a javelin. Only at the end of this period did knights begin to charge with *couched* lances, that is, lances lowered to a horizontal position. By the thirteenth century, the lance had become longer, much heavier, and was used couched and only for charging.

The early broad-bladed sword for use in one hand was carried in a leather and wood scabbard. Sometimes a light-weight battle axe with a single fan-shaped edge could be added. On occasion, a mace or iron-tipped club might be carried, especially if the knight had some church affiliation that forbade the shedding of blood. Knights did not use bows or crossbows in battle. By the thirteenth century, swords had increased in weight and length (with blades longer than 38 inches), becoming the "sword of war" with a two-handed grip. Short stabbing daggers became popular, as did heavy chopping swords called falchions. Danish-type axes with six-foot shafts became popular at this time, too.

For defense, a knight depended on his helmet, armor, and shield. The helmet was at first made of solid iron, with a conical or round shape, and an open face. A nasal guard, or bar, was added in the eleventh century. Later helmets were made of two joined pieces of metal, with a moveable visor covering the face. The visors could be decorated with ornate—even wildly grotesque—countenances.

Early armor consisted of a mail hauberk or coat handmade by a time-consuming process of winding metal wire around a rod and cutting the wire entirely down one side of the rod, producing dozens of open rings. These rings were then linked, overlapped, and the ends hammered shut and riveted. Such a mail coat usually reached to the knees, divided in front and back for riding, and had long sleeves. A hood of mail protected neck and chin, mail leggings protected lower extremities, and even mail gloves could be added to complete the ensemble. By the thirteenth and fourteenth centuries, plate armor had replaced mail among the richer knights, and weight became an important consideration. Some plate suits weighed over 90 pounds and required very large and strong (not to mention expensive) horses to carry such loads.

Around 1100, knights began to wear a loose-flowing linen garment or gown over their hauberks. At first these bore no designs, except possibly crosses, and offered little in the way of protection from rain or sun. Over time, these gowns became more elaborate and were emblazoned with the coat of arms of the wearer—an important feature because faces were hidden from view in battle and most knights were illiterate.

The typical tenth- and eleventh-century shield was made of wood covered with leather, concave or teardrop in shape (called kite shaped), round at the top and pointed at the bottom. It hung from around the neck by a strap and was held in the left hand by a shorter strap. Shields were usually painted with geometric designs, fantastic animals, and crosses. Originally, these designs had no purpose other than to indulge personal fancy and identify the bearer in battle or in tournaments. By 1150, a number of shield designs began to be passed on from father to son; thus initiating the system of heraldry. With the advent of plate armor, the shield became unnecessary. It was discarded, except in jousts.

The Hundred Year's War of 1333–1457 spelled the beginning of the end for knights on the battlefield. Dense infantry formations, based on the Swiss style and armed with long spears or pikes, could keep even the most determined knights at bay. Gunpowder weapons meant that even the heaviest armor could no longer protect knights from long-range death. Heavily armored cavalry quickly began to disappear from European warfare, replaced by more agile, and less expensive, horsemen. Knighthood became more an honorary title than a military one. Still, the romantic image of the knight has continued to flourish down through the generations. It lives today in the stories of King Arthur and his Round Table, and even in science fiction visions of the future made popular in films such as the *Star Wars* sagas.

References: Gies, Frances, *The Knight in History* (New York: Harper & Row, 1984); Oman, C.W.G., *The Art of War in the 16th Century* (New York: AMS Press, 1979 [1937]); Turnbull, Stephen, *The Book of the Medieval Knight* (New York: Crown, 1985).

Knights Templar

An organization of religious warriors in the Middle Ages.

The early twelfth century saw two major developments in European society: the Crusades to reclaim the Christian Holy Land from Muslim rule and the armored knight to do the fighting.

The knight was the cream of European feudal society. He swore loyalty to the aristocrat or king above him and received similar loyalty from vassals below him. A man with lands and income, the feudal knight was able to afford the necessary accoutrements for serious warfare and supplied himself with horse, armor, and weapons. These warriors, fighting as heavy cavalry, responded to the call of Pope Urban II in 1097 to march to the Holy Land and liberate it from the possession of the Muslims. The knights succeeded in establishing European control in Jerusalem and the area surrounding it, dominating the eastern Mediterranean coastal region from Turkey to the Red Sea. However, one of the main goals of the Crusades—the protection of Christian pilgrims to holy sites in the Middle East—was not accomplished. The Europeans controlled the major cities, but were too few in number to control the countryside. It was this need for protection of European pilgrims that brought the Knights Templar into existence.

In 1118 a French knight, Hugh de Payans, offered his services to the newly installed king of Jerusalem, Baldwin II, to organize a force to patrol and protect the countryside. Baldwin assigned de Payans quarters at the al-Aqsa Mosque, reputedly the site of Solomon's Temple; hence the name for de Payans's new organization—the Poor Fellow Soldiers of Christ and the Temple of Solomon. At a time when most European nobility were obsessed with gathering wealth any way they could (and many had profited in land and money during the Crusades), the knights who joined the Templars were as ascetic as monks. They wore second-hand clothing and lived by charity. Theirs was a poor existence without worldly diversions. Gambling, fraternizing with women, and hunting were banned. In 1128 the new hierarchy of the Catholic Church, riding a wave of reform, recognized the Templars as a force that could be controlled by them and that would swear no loyalty to king or aristocrat.

The result was basically a force of fighting monks. They trained in and mastered the martial skills of the age, but never had huge numbers. Rarely did Templars fight in groups of more than a few hundred, about 500 being the maximum on duty in the Holy Land with some 2,000 support troops. They established a network of recruiters throughout Europe that maintained a steady supply of men to the ranks. Many of those that joined were not aristocrats, but outlaws or excommunicants. Nevertheless, as long as they swore to fight for

God and their fellow Templars, they were accepted. The Templar's success spawned other similar elite units dedicated to fighting for God's kingdom on earth. These organizations sometimes fought among themselves, but always united in the face of the infidel threat.

The Templars started out fulfilling their role as protectors by building forts, patrolling the roads, and attacking Muslim bands or strongholds. They even forced tribute from the infamous order of the Assassins. All of this construction and military activity required funding, and the recruiting groups in Europe also raised money. In doing so, their order became fabulously wealthy and they became history's first international bankers. In order to pay for recruitment, training, and the needs of the knights in the Holy Land, the Templars had to have sufficient funds to pay for these things no matter where the necessity arose, so a promissory note from one Templar headquarters was payable at any other. Their annual income reached the equivalent of billions of dollars in today's terms. They received vast amounts of land, donated by nobles who did not go to the Holy Land but wanted to contribute or by nobles who joined and pledged their wealth to the order. It is said that by 1250 the Templars controlled 9,000 manors throughout Europe and the Holy Lands.

The Knights Templar were organized into a hierarchy with the Grand Master at the top, followed by the Seneschal, Provincial Marshals, Commander of the Land and Realm of Jerusalem, and the commander of the fleet based at Acre. The Knights wore white mantles with a red cross emblazoned on front and back. Lower ranks had the red cross sewn onto brown or black clothing. The organization's banner was black on top and white beneath; black symbolizing their sternness toward their enemies and the white their devotion to Christianity.

After the end of the Crusades in the late thirteenth century, the Knights Templar were left without a military role. Instead, they turned to banking. Not just their wealth, but also their secretive ways, excited jealousy—even among kings. Eventually, Philip IV of France campaigned against the Knights Templar in an attempt to replenish his own coffers and acquire the Templars' lands. He accused them of a variety of heinous crimes, supported with confessions tortured out of captured Templars. Fifty-four knights were burned at the stake in 1310 and within two years the order was almost completely suppressed. Since that time, however, the Knights Templar have become almost mythical. Persecuted knights fled, taking their wealth and military knowledge to distant lands. The nature of the order's origins, based in what was supposedly Solomon's Temple, led to legendary attributions of mystical powers to the Knights Templar, which they allegedly gained by acquiring religious artifacts found there. Even into the modern day, superstitions about the ultimate fate of the Knights Templar abound: Recent books have claimed that the Templars possessed the Holy Grail and that Christ did not rise to Heaven after his resurrection but moved to France to wed and father children with Mary Magdalene—their descendants being in one way or another involved with a Templar/Masonic conspiracy. The truth is undoubtedly more prosaic: Like most of the orders of their time, the Knights Templar outlived their mission and usefulness with the end of the Crusades.

References: Campbell, George, *The Knights Templar, Their Rise and Fall* (New York: Robert McBride, 1937); Norman, A.V.B., *The Medieval Soldier* (New York: Thomas Y. Crowell, 1971); Partner, Peter, *The Murdered Magicians: The Templars and Their Myth* (New York: Oxford University Press, 1982).

L

Lafayette Escadrille (Escadrille Americaine)

American volunteer pilots fighting for France in World War I.

Well before the United States officially entered the First World War, American volunteers joined the French Air Service. They came to fight against Germany through a number of avenues, including the French Foreign Legion and the American Field Service of ambulance drivers. Some, stranded in France when war broke out, joined other Americans to offer their services. Few were pilots when they joined, but the lure of flying was much greater once they learned, firsthand or through reports, of life in the trenches.

The originator of the unit was the American Norman Prince. He was in France when the Germans invaded, vacationing there as he had done many times before. He wanted to assist France, so he returned home to Marblehead, Massachusetts, entered a flying school, and began looking for other volunteers. He fell in with Frazier Curtis, who also wanted to assist the Allies but thought he would rather join the British Royal Flying Corps. After receiving his pilot's license, Prince returned to France in March 1915 and joined the French army. Because of his flying ability, he was assigned to a French pilot training school, where he learned the rudiments of aerial combat. He also haunted the streets of Paris, seeking out other Americans to join him, and there he met two African-Americans, Bob Scanlon and Eugene Bullard. Bullard joined up, earned his wings, and flew for a while, but later lost interest in flying and ended the war fighting with the French army in the trenches. Scanlon also joined and became an observer, flying in the rear of two-seater scout aircraft.

The French authorities were skeptical of training an entire unit of volunteers, so Prince flew with a French bomber squadron for eight months before he got the opportunity to organize an all-American unit. He was rejoined by Frazier Curtis, who decided against joining the Royal Flying Corps, and together they began to actively seek permission to form an all-American squadron. Curtis worked with an American doctor in Paris, Edmund Gros, who had connections in the French government and with important people in the United States. He gained the financial assistance of William Vanderbilt, a Francophile whose donations supported both the American Field Service and the attempt to organize a flying squadron. Prince and Curtis finally received approval of their plan in July 1915 but the paperwork was not completed and the unit not officially organized until 20 April 1916. Prince had in the meantime collected six more Americans who had fought with the French Army and were looking for a way out of the trenches: Bill Thaw, Victor Chapman, Kiffin Rockwell, James McConnell, Eliot Cowdin, and Bert Hall. Two French officers, Captain Georges Thennault and Lieutenant de Laage de Meux, were assigned to teach them combat flying and tactics and to serve as a liaison with the French government. They were given Nieuport 17s, the standard French fighter plane of the time. Later in the war they would be given SPADs, but the lighter, more maneuverable Nieuport remained their favorite.

Their first combat mission was in May of 1916, but it involved only an unsuccessful attack on three German scout planes and resulted in a number of holes in the Nieuport aircraft from antiaircraft fire. The experience showed the Americans to have more enthusiasm than self-control or discipline. The first victory in the air occurred on 16 May with Kiffin Rockwell receiving credit. In August the squadron, called the Escadrille Americaine, received more pilots. Among them was Raoul Lufbery, a French-born naturalized American who would become the most famous member of the group and the leading ace, with 19 confirmed victories over German aircraft. By late summer, the Escadrille was becoming fairly well known, and the fact that the pilots were Americans brought diplomatic complaints from Germany. The group renamed their squadron the Lafayette Escadrille in an attempt to downplay their nationality, as the United States was still many months away from joining the conflict. In September 1916 the Escadrille suffered its first loss when Kiffin Rockwell was killed in combat. Norman Prince was killed in mid-October.

The Lafayette Escadrille's actual impact on the air war in France was certainly no greater than that of many other squadrons, but its existence provided a morale boost in many ways. The French civilians living near their airfields always went to great lengths to assist the pilots and provide for their needs and wants. The squadron responded by playing on its notoriety and enhancing it. The members followed the already-established practice of creating a squadron insignia to be displayed on their aircraft. The pilots believed that because they were the first American pilots in France, the first Americans, the Indians, should provide the squadron's emblem. A screaming profile painted in bright colors was adapted from the logo of the Savage Arms Company. The pilots also advertised themselves by their choice of squadron mascot. Along with the usual collection of animals that congregate around airfields and military bases, four of the pilots on leave in Paris joined together to buy a four-month-old lion cub, which came to be called Whiskey. A year later they bought Whiskey a mate, which they named Soda. Such actions enhanced their public relations value both in France and the United States, but of course led to exaggerations by the press. There was also some exaggeration concerning the size of the organization. The Lafayette Escadrille, officially designated in the French Air Service as N.124 (later Spa.124), comprised only 38 Americans. Other Americans who flew for the French wanted a special designation in recognition of their status, so all American volunteer pilots were given membership in what came to be called the Lafayette Flying Corps. This semiofficial organization ultimately numbered more than 200 men, including the members of the Lafayette Escadrille.

When the United States declared war in April 1917 many in the Escadrille thought they would be transferred to the American Aviation Service. Colonel Billy Mitchell was sent to command such a service in France, but he was sent alone and without authority to bring Americans under arms from out of British or French service. For several months the French government continued to recruit American volunteers and train them as pilots. Thus, the men stayed under French command until February 1918 when the Lafayette Escadrille was incorporated into the United States Air Service (U.S.A.S.) as the 103d Pursuit Squadron. The pilots received commissions in the United States military, but remained attached to French units and operated from French airfields. Over time, the veterans were assigned to command newly arriving American squadrons in order to share their expertise.

References: Mason, Herbert Malloy, *The Lafayette Escadrille* (New York: Random

House, 1964); Whitehouse, Arch, *Legion of the Lafayette* (New York: Doubleday, 1962); *The Years of the Sky Kings* (New York: Doubleday, 1964).

Lincoln Battalion

A unit of American volunteers that fought in the Spanish Civil War between 1936 and 1938.

In February 1936 the Spanish people elected, by an extremely slim majority, a coalition of representatives from the Popular Front to their government, the Cortes. This was a group of people of mixed political standing, favoring democracy, socialism, communism, and anarchy. Although probably too disorganized to rule effectively, the conservatives in Spain were horrified and convinced that stable government was about to come to an end. This seemed to be confirmed as the government began to make friendly overtures to the Soviet Union. Many members of the army began to plot a coup, and they gathered around the leadership of General Francisco Franco. They came to be referred to as Nationalists. Franco and his supporters were based in Spanish Morocco. However, with the assistance of Adolph Hitler, they were airlifted into Spain and in July 1936 the Spanish Civil War broke out. More than 30,000 soldiers in the regular army remained loyal to the government, but equal that number in Spain, reinforced by another 30,000 from Morocco, gave Franco a potent force. This potency was augmented by Hitler, who provided aircraft, and by Italy's dictator Benito Mussolini, who provided troops, aircraft, and heavy weapons.

Members of the elected Spanish government (who came to be called Republicans) sought aid from other countries, but few were willing to assist. Through the League of Nations, most said that the conflict in Spain was an internal matter and therefore not something with which the international community should become involved. Thus, while Franco received much military assistance, only the Soviet Union offered any aid to the Republicans—and the Soviets offered this at high prices. Any other aid that came to the Republicans came from volunteers, which included young intellectuals from around the world who saw the civil war as the first attempt to stop the spread of fascism. In North America and western Europe volunteers joined Republican recruiters to go to Spain and fight for freedom and democracy. Almost all of the recruiters were communists, but they called for volunteers under a variety of names, mostly popular fronts of one stripe or another. In the United States, the primary recruiting bureau was the North American Committee to Aid Spanish Democracy. Although the organizers were communists, the number of volunteers who actually believed in Marxism is impossible to determine. However, it was almost certainly more than half.

Approximately 3,000 Americans responded to the call, of which about 600 were seamen and 500 were college students. Only about 100 of them had any military training. The oldest was 54, but most were in their 20s. They formed three units: the Washington and Lincoln Battalions and the American-Canadian Mackenzie-Papineau Battalion. Owing to high casualties, the Washington Battalion was absorbed into the Lincoln Battalion fairly early in the conflict. In order to give the impression of a larger American interest, the Spanish always referred to the unit as the Lincoln Brigade, but it was actually part of the Fifteenth International Brigade, made up of the three North American battalions coupled with battalions from Britain, France, and Yugoslavia. The troops were commanded by a Yugoslav, Colonel Vladimir Copic.

Because both British and French governments had officially discouraged volunteers, neither country cared to have Americans pass through on their way to Spain. The French, although they occasionally arrested an American, for the most part turned a blind eye to the volunteers. The volunteers sneaked across the Franco-Spanish border and joined the Republicans at Tarazona, west of the Mediterranean coastal city of Valencia.

There they received—at first, at any rate—only rudimentary training before being thrown into combat in Madrid. There, in February 1937 the International Brigade assisted in beating back a Nationalist attack on the capital.

Although the volunteers gained only slight experience during this battle, their divisional commander ordered the International Brigade to follow the Nationalists and dislodge them from a very strong position on Pingarron Hill in the Jarama River Valley. The Lincoln Battalion was given the key position in the attack, but the entire plan was faulty and the assault doomed. Promised air, armor, and artillery support never materialized, and the Americans (after a protest by their commander) attacked into a hail of Nationalist fire that inflicted 65 percent casualties. The brigade and divisional commanders should never have ordered this attack, but to the American survivors it was their own battalion commander, Robert Merriman, who received the blame for following orders he knew to be suicidal. The Battle of Jarama was the Lincoln Battalion's baptism of fire, and a costly one.

The Americans' second battle took place four months later. Franco's forces had kept up a steady artillery bombardment of Madrid, and the Republicans hoped a diversionary attack would ease the pressure on the capital. They sent 85,000 men, including the Americans, toward the village of Brunete, twenty miles west of Madrid. The Lincoln and Washington Battalions were to bypass the village and secure the high ground, the Mosquito Crest. This time armor was there for support, but it was badly deployed. The tanks sped ahead of the infantry, and the Americans were easy targets for the Nationalists on the hilltop. The result was almost as bad as Jarama had been. The battalion's new commander, Oliver Law, was killed in the battle. Law was an African-American veteran of the U.S. Army. His place was taken by Commissar Steve Nelson, a Croatian-American communist from Pittsburgh. The commissar acted as second-in-command, as well as being the political, morale, and liaison officer. The battle ended in a stalemate, but as Franco diverted large numbers of his men to recapture Brunete, it did ease the Nationalist siege of Madrid.

The Republican cause scored a few successes, but they were always overturned by superior Nationalist fire power in Franco's counteroffensives. Meanwhile, the Republican cause was further harmed by political infighting between rival leaders in the Republican command structure. This went so far as to result in combat between anarchists and communists in Barcelona in May 1937. Political struggles within the American ranks have also been reported. Unconfirmed reports tell of executions not only for desertion, but also for spreading anti-Stalinist propaganda. Even if executions were rare and only for desertion, other reports claim that unpopular political statements often resulted in assignments to the most dangerous areas of the battle. Despite this, the major political arguments took place at the highest levels and the Americans did not seem to have been involved, or even to have taken much notice of them.

The Lincoln Battalion fought in the battles of Aragon and Teurel in late 1937 and early 1938. It performed well in the conquest of Zaragoza, the capital of Aragon, capturing the village of Quito and a thousand Nationalist prisoners. Franco's counterattack, however, forced the Americans out. After Republican forces captured the town of Teurel around Christmas, the Lincoln Battalion was sent into defensive positions there. When Franco launched a massive offensive to retake the town in March 1938 the Lincoln Battalion was virtually wiped out. Pounded by air and artillery, they could do little but cower under what protection they could find. They finally split into two groups to attempt to return to Republican positions. The Americans found themselves behind Nationalist lines and spent weeks roaming the hills in small bands. When they finally returned to Republican lines on the Ebro River, they numbered no more than 100.

Although the few remaining men fought in a last battle along the Ebro in the summer of 1938 they were no longer a real unit. The International Brigade had by this time become predominantly Spanish owing to the large number of replacements brought in over the course of the war. In September 1938 Spanish Prime Minister Juan Negrin announced the withdrawal of all foreign soldiers fighting for the Republican cause. It has been argued that he did this on Stalin's orders, because the Soviet leader then had no more hope of shaming western democracies into action. It is also possible Negrin hoped that a public withdrawal of his foreign troops would pressure Franco to do the same. By that time, the Lincoln Battalion was made up of 200 Spaniards and 80 Americans. They marched through Barcelona in a farewell parade in October. Spanish communist leader Dolores Ibarruri told them: "You can go proudly. You are history. You are the heroic example of democracy's solidarity and universality. We shall not forget you, and, when the olive tree of peace puts forth its leaves again, mingled with the laurels of the Spanish Republic's victory—come back" (Meisler, 1995). Not until Franco died and his dictatorship came to an end in the 1970s were any of these veterans able to return.

The Americans who returned to their country in 1938 were for a time treated as heroes by the public, and many fought for the United States in World War II a few years later. However, in the anticommunist hysteria of the McCarthy era, these veterans were branded as communists. Some of their number were arrested under the Smith Act, which prohibited advocacy of the violent overthrow of the government. One of the arrested veterans, Alvah Bessie, was a member of the famous Hollywood Ten jailed for contempt of Congress in 1954. Many former volunteers in the Spanish Civil War fled the United States to escape political repression. How many of them were communists, either before or after the Spanish Civil War, is difficult to tell, but McCarthy's broad brush tarred them all. Communist or not, the members of the Lincoln Battalion did fight for a cause they believed in: to halt the spread of fascism. It was a cause much of the world was obliged to embrace not long after the members of the Lincoln Battalion did.

References: Eby, Cecil, *Between the Bullet and the Lie* (New York: Holt, Rinehart, & Winston, 1969); Lawson, Don, *The Abraham Lincoln Brigade* (New York: Thomas Crowell, 1989); Meisler, Stanley, "The Lincoln Battalion," in *Military History Quarterly,* vol. 8, no. 1 (Autumn, 1995); Rosenstone, Robert, *Crusade of the Left* (New York: Pegasus, 1969).

Lombards

A tribe from northern Germany that conquered and settled in Italy after the fall of the Roman Empire.

The Lombards first appear in recorded history in the fifth century, during the latter stages of the Roman Empire. The Romans gave them their name, *langobard*, or "long beard." Although known to fight occasionally against either their neighbors or the Romans, the Lombards tended at first to be peaceful pastoral people. Throughout the fourth and fifth centuries they began to migrate southward into the Danube River region known as Pannonia, modern Austria. The Lombards fought for Byzantine Emperor Justinian in his campaigns against the Ostrogoths in the Italian peninsula and received favored status during his rule. His successors, however, favored the Gepids, a hostile tribe neighboring the Lombards. Fearing a war against the Gepids supported by the Byzantines, the Lombards under their king, Alboin, allied themselves with a tribe newly arrived from central Asia, the Avars. Together they were victorious and split the Gepids' lands between them.

In the middle of the sixth century, the Lombards established a new tribal organization based on an aristocratic hierarchy. Dukes and counts commanded clans organized into military units (*farae*), all serving under a king. It was with this new organization that the Lombards, now in fear of their former allies, the Avars, decided in the late 560s to migrate farther into the Italian peninsula. As the long-running war between the Ostrogoths and the Byzantine Empire had left a power vacuum in northern Italy, the Lombards were able to move in and take over fairly easily. By 572 under Alboin's leadership, they had conquered the entire northern peninsula to the Po River, and then occasional districts in southern and eastern Italy.

Alboin was murdered shortly after the Lombards' arrival in Italy, and for the next few decades the tribe struggled internally while they exploited the indigenous people and countryside.

Within Lombard society, military service was required in times of emergency. The nature of the soldiery depended on one's wealth and land possession. The largest landowners were each obliged to provide a horse, some armor, and a lance. The middle-class landowners had to supply a horse and a lance, while the small landowner brought a shield and bows and arrows. As in many earlier cultures, the wealthy, who could afford to raise and maintain horses, served as cavalry. Each man came to the colors as a member of his clan and followed his local lord, with provincial forces gathering under the leadership of a *dux*. Usually the nobility also brought warrior bands called *Gasindii*, full-time soldiers who swore personal loyalty to their lords. Also serving with the Lombards were mercenaries, whose makeup depended on shifting alliances, the relative power of neighbors, or the region of conflict. Magyars, Avars, Normans, Germans, and even Saracens served at one time or another in Lombard armies.

The Lombards established themselves as the dominant force in northern Italy, but they adapted readily to the existing agricultural framework in the area, believing that whatever the Romans had organized was the best format for agricultural production. The tribal dukes exercised the most power, with little or no central control. Only when threatened from outside, by the Franks, did the Lombards again form a united front. In 590 the Lombards elected the duke of Turin, Agiluf, to the kingship and he reconsolidated Lombard power and established a capital at Pavia. King Rothari, who ruled in the mid-seventh century, issued a legal code for his people along the lines of that produced by Justinian in Constantinople. The leading Lombard king was Liutprand (712–744), who further focussed on the internal needs of his kingdom. Later in his reign, he reinstituted the campaign against Byzantine power in Italy.

The Lombard incursion into Italy frightened the pope. At first the Lombards practiced Arian Christianity, which denied the equality of God and Jesus. Their military success, coupled with their heretical views, posed a threat to orthodox Catholicism. Even when they converted to orthodox views in the late seventh century, Lombard power remained a source of concern for the pope. When the Lombards under King Aistulf captured Ravenna in 751 and threatened Rome in 754, Pope Stephen II appealed to the Franks for deliverance. Pepin the Short, first of the Carolingian dynasty, marched to Italy and defeated the Lombards in 754 and 756. Pepin recaptured Ravenna and gave land to the church, creating the Papal States. In return, the pope anointed Pepin as King of the Franks and Defender of Rome.

Aistulf remained as king of the Lombards, but his successor Desiderus was defeated by another Frank, Pepin's grandson Charlemagne, in 773. Charlemagne made himself king of the Lombards and incorporated northern Italy into the Holy Roman Empire, thus bringing to an end the Lombard's independent existence.

Although their rule in Italy was often harsh, the Lombards did contribute to the country's heritage. Much of the legal system of the area descends from Lombard practice. King Rothri, who reigned in the mid-600s, issued a code of law patterned after that compiled by Justinian in Constantinople. One of the most important aspects of Rothri's code was the attempt to end the practice of *vendetta*, or personal revenge. Instead, the personal feud was to be replaced by monetary payment for damages. This was known as *guidrigild*, which appears in later Scandinavian cultures as *weregild*. The Lombards's greatest effect, however, was indirect, in that they removed Byzantine power in Italy once and for all. This ended any chance of Eastern Orthodoxy challenging papal authority in western Europe. In the eleventh century, Lombardy dominated the trade routes from the Mediterranean into the European continent. The resulting wealth gave the Lombards commercial and financial leadership, which later translated into political power. They formed the Lombard League, which resisted the invasion of Frederick Barbarossa of Germany in 1176.

References: Bona, Istvan, *The Dawn of the Dark Ages: The Gepids and the Lombards* (Budapest: Corvina Press, 1976); Hallenbeck, Jan, *Pavia and Rome: The Lombard Monarchy and the Papacy in the Eighth Century* (Philadelphia: American Philosophical Society, 1982); Paul the Deacon, tr. by W.D. Foulke, *History of the Langobards* (Philadelphia: University of Pennsylvania Press, 1974).

Long Range Desert Group

A British commando unit operating in North Africa during World War II.

In 1940 the British forces based in Egypt were isolated and outnumbered, with their primary threat being several divisions of the Italian army based in Libya. If the Italians were to attack the British base at Wadi Halfa on the Nile River, it would effectively sever contact between British forces in Cairo and in the Sudan at Khartoum. This would have been the only supply route available, had the Italian navy controlled the Red Sea. It also would have laid the dams at Aswan open to attack. The Italians could also strike southward toward French Equatorial Africa, dominating it before the French administration there could decide whether to support the Free French under de Gaulle. As the Italian positions were too far from Cairo or Alexandria for British aircraft to patrol, the only way to gain information on Italian actions or plans was on the ground.

In World War I, a small force of British troops had organized the Light Car Patrols, which scouted the deserts fairly successfully with modified Ford Model Ts. Between the wars, a small group of independent British officers had explored the deserts on their own, testing theories about operations in the desert. They learned lessons about food, water, fuel, and navigation. One of those officers was R. A. Bagnold, a major in the Royal Corps of Signals. When World War II broke out, he proposed an updated version of the Light Car Patrols, and in July 1940 British General Archibald Wavell granted him permission to organize such a unit. As everything was in short supply, the newly formed Long Range Desert Group had to scrounge for everything, from weapons to vehicles. The vehicles they appropriated were one-and-a-half ton Chevrolets bought in Cairo or begged from the Egyptian Army. These were modified with extra-strong springs, had the cabs and doors removed, and had condensers fitted to the radiators. The Group's first recruits were from the New Zealand Division, while later volunteers came from the British Brigade of Guards, the Yeomanry, and the Rhodesian army.

The Long Range Desert Group was ultimately organized into columns of five vehicles with one officer and 15 men. Each truck was fitted out with at least two machine guns and often with a 37-mm Bofors antitank gun in the bed or, later, captured Italian Breda 20-mm guns. The men learned to live in the field for weeks at a time on six pints of water a day and with all their meals coming out of tin cans. They also learned to navigate in the desert, which is much like navigating at sea. A sun compass was used, because a magnetic compass often gave false readings from the trucks' magnetic fields. Using a compass and odometer they drove to their targets by dead reckoning with amazing accuracy. They also developed techniques for driving through the Libyan desert, most notably the use of sections of steel track to get out of deep sand.

The Long Range Desert Group went into operation in August 1940. Its first bit of intelligence was that the Italians were planning none of the threatening operations that the British had feared. This meant that the Group could go on the offensive themselves, as well as keep up their primary task of reconnaissance. They began raiding Italian outposts and supply convoys, striking just often enough to keep the enemy unbalanced and looking over his shoulder. In January 1941 the Group sent 75 men in 25 trucks to assault the Italian fort at Murzuq, a journey of 1,500 miles from Cairo. They made the trip to the fort in 17 days, stopping just short of their destination to pick up five members of the Free French forces from Fort Lamy in Equatorial Africa (modern Chad), who had brought extra fuel supplies. The attack was a total surprise and destroyed the fort and three aircraft for the loss of two killed and three wounded. This success encouraged Free French forces under General Leclerc to attack and capture the major Italian post at Kufra on 1 March 1941. The Long Range Desert Group began using Kufra as an advanced base after this time. Over time the Sudan Defense Force began to garrison Kufra and a much steadier flow of supplies began to arrive.

For the remainder of 1941 the Group constantly patrolled the Libyan desert, attacking Italian patrols and supply columns, as well as scouting potential routes for attack for the British army based in Egypt. In November 1941 the major British offensive, code named "Crusader," benefitted from the information that the Group obtained. Also in that month, the unit began operations with the Special Air Service (SAS), a commando organization formed by Major David Sterling. For several month the Long Range Desert Group ferried the SAS troops to a point just short of their target, then evacuated them after their raids. This continued successfully until the SAS began to acquire its own vehicles. The Long Range Desert Group continued to raid and patrol until the final defeat of the German and Italian forces in the North African desert in May 1943. The Group's harassment of their supply lines was a major source of chagrin for Axis commanders and one they were rarely able to effectively combat.

References: Cowles, Virginia, *The Phantom Major* (New York: Harper & Bros., 1958); Kennedy Shaw, Major W.B., "Britain's Private Armies," in *History of the Second World War* (London: BBC Publishing, 1966); Swinson, Arthur, *The Raiders: Desert Strike Force* (New York: Ballantine, 1968)

M

Macedonians

Southeastern European population that dominated Greece and the Middle East. The people of Alexander the Great, they conquered and controlled Greece, Egypt, Persia, and India between the fourth and first centuries B.C.

When Philip II came to power in 359 B.C. Macedonia was basically an agrarian state with very little urban population. A majority of the people were farmers and shepherds and were too poor to afford the equipment of a Greek hoplite, the standard infantryman of the time. Also, owing to the size of the country, the people were unable to gather easily into large groups in a single place. The nobility and landed gentry had developed into a military class that specialized in fighting on horseback, while the common folk fought as unarmored peltasts, or slingers. Together they formed a very weak military organization. Philip increased taxes and used the monies to create a standing army and to pay Greek mercenaries. His army engaged in the intensive training that only the mercenary forces had previously received. Philip merged the natural talents of his people with the accepted tactics of the Greeks, tempered it with necessity, and produced an army of truly combined talents. In essence, he elevated warfare to a new level, and the army he created made his son Alexander a legend.

Though Philip found the money to pay a standing army, he lacked the resources to equip each infantryman with hoplite armor. Instead he opted for offensive reach and mobility. The Greek hoplite spear was about seven feet in length and was intended to be held with the right hand while the left hand held the shield. Philip replaced the spear with a fourteen foot *sarissa* (pike), which doubled the reach of his men, often called *phalangites* ("those fighting in a phalanx"), and allowed them to strike the first blows against hoplites. The sarissa required two hands to wield, so the phalangite's shield was made smaller, and it was attached to the upper left arm with straps. Finally, the entire phalanx was compacted and the formation deepened. The long reach of the sarissa gave an increased number of men the ability to fight on a given frontage. According to ancient accounts, the standard strength of a Macedonian phalanx was 1,500 men. These were probably arrayed in 15 ranks of 100 men each.

The lack of defensive armor allowed the phalangites to attain a degree of mobility that hoplites could never hope to match. They could execute intricate maneuvers at fast speeds and march long distances with little rest. By the second half of Philip's reign he well could have afforded to equip his men with breastplates if he so desired, but by then it had become apparent that armor was no longer necessary to win victories. Alexander must have agreed with this for he appears to have made no attempt to rearmor his phalangites.

Philip created a second group of in-

Battle between Alexander the Great and King Darius, depicted in a mosaic from the House of the Faun, Pompeii (Museo Archeologico Nazionale, Naples)

fantrymen, the foot guards, or *Hypaspists*. It appears that these men had the same equipment as the phalangites, fought in a similar phalanx, and were recruited from the same peasant stock. However, it seems that the Hypaspists were handpicked from the best of the phalangites, and served as a national unit, despite their local origins. In essence, they formed an elite infantry corps about 3,000 strong, which appears to have operated in three phalanxes of 1000 men each. Alexander favored them over his other infantry, and had more confidence in their abilities. Whenever he had to make a long forced march he took along the Hypaspists, and left the phalangites to follow at a slower pace. This is not to say that the phalangites did not fight as well as the Hypaspists but, as the King's personal troops, the guards had a discipline and esprit de corps that the phalangites could never match. Philip's army also included a large number of mercenary infantry, and this continued with Alexander, who reportedly had 5,000 mercenaries with him when he crossed into Asia. In addition, the League of Corinth had placed at his disposal a large force of Greek allied infantry, perhaps 7,000. These men may have assumed the arms of the phalangites or may have retained their hoplite equipment. They were primarily used for garrison and reserve line duties. Darius usually placed his Greek mercenaries in the center of his army, and it is doubtful if Alexander wished to test the loyalty of his hoplites by asking them to fight against brother Greeks. Macedonians, on the other hand, felt no qualms whatsoever about killing Greeks.

In Philip's and Alexander's armies, phalanxes formed the center and left of the main battle line: the unshakable core of the army. Their function was to advance upon the enemy center, pin it in place, and prevent it from reacting to the decisive thrust of the Macedonian heavy cavalry. The phalangites set the tempo of the battle, but never administered the winning blow. The Hypaspists' function was to occupy the right side of the battle line and maintain contact between the phalangites and the cavalry. If need be, each of the phalangite battalions (*taxis*), 1,500 strong, or the Hypaspists, could operate as independent units.

Philip and Alexander recruited the Macedonian cavalry from the nobility and the landed gentry of the country. They formed a body of heavy cavalry known as the *Hetairoi*, or Companions.The Companions wore metal breastplates, greaves, and helmets, and wielded spears, swords, and shields. However, Greeks and Macedonians had no knowledge of saddles or stirrups, and without firm seats it would be impossible to fully utilize the momentum of horses in charges. Spears were almost certainly used in an overhand thrusting manner. About 2,000 strong under Alexander, the Companions fought in tactical units of varying strengths called *ilai*. The strongest ilai became the royal squadron and numbered 300 picked men.The Companions usually attacked in wedge-shaped formations that could penetrate any opposing line of cavalry.

About 2,000 Thessalians reinforced Alexander's Macedonians. They also fought as heavy cavalry in small units and made use of the rhomboid or diamond formation, which functioned the same as the wedge. When forced to stand on the defensive, the Thessalians adopted a looser linear formation, more conducive to skirmishing.

In addition to the Thessalians, Alexander had the services of groups of Greek mercenary cavalry; Macedonian *Prodromo* (scouts); and Paeonian, Odrysian, and Greek allied cavalry, about 3,000 in all. They functioned as light cavalry. The Prodromoi and Paeonians carried the cavalry sarissa, and were known as *sarissaophorai*(lancers). The remainder of the light cavalry fought with javelin and shield.

Cavalry was the single most significant element in the Macedonian system. From a nonexistent force in the Greek armies it grew to represent 20 percent of Alexander's total manpower, and its importance far outweighed its numbers. The Companions became the major offensive weapon of the Macedonian army. Their charge decided all of Alexander's battles against the Persians, and he always personally led them into combat. The Companions' position was on the right side of the battle line and the Thessalians' on the left. Alexander stationed the other cavalry units wherever they might be needed, but mostly they ended up on the right flank, to keep pressure off the Companions and allow them to make their climactic charges unimpeded.

The majority of the light infantry had to be recruited from outside Macedonia, one unit of archers being the only native troops of this type. The Agrianians, Triballians, Odysians, and Illyrians furnished men who were skilled in the use of the javelin. For generations Crete had provided units of archers to the Greek world. They were valued for their ability, if not for their tenacity. In all, Alexander had about 9,000 light infantry. These men did not resemble the peltasts of the Greek armies. They wore no armor and carried only light shields. They cushioned the flanks of the phalanx, fanned out in front of the army, and intercepted charging light cavalry, chariots, or elephants. They harassed the enemy and supported friendly charges with archery fire, and they diverted any pressure from the Companions. Finally, they operated in broken or wooded terrain where the phalangites or cavalry could not go.

The strength of the Macedonians lay in the combined use of all their armies' branches: phalanx, cavalry, and light troops. As the army moved into action, the phalanx advanced to engage the main strength of the enemy. The archers opened fire, usually on the enemy cavalry. The javelineers would move forward, just in advance of the main line, covering them from accurate enemy archery and seeking to disrupt enemy charges.The left flank under Alexander's subordinate Parmenion usually adopted a defensive posture, inclining back from the main battle line or pressing ahead, as the situation warranted. Parmenion fed units into the battle as needed to maintain his flank. The light cavalry units on the right would move out to intercept enemy flanking movements as the Hypaspists sought to maintain contact between the Companions and the phalanxes and ensure an unbroken line. The second line of infantry would stand ready to move up to reinforce faltering front-line units, to intercept any breakthroughs and reform the line, or to face about if the army became encircled. While this transpired, the Companions—with Alexander at their head—waited for a gap to appear in the enemy ranks. The javelineers sought to ward off any units that might impede their charge. Finally, at the decisive moment, Alexander would launch the Companions. Their wedges would pierce the enemy forces like arrows and explode laterally, rolling up the ranks in both directions. The following Companions would drive through the widening gap into the rear of the enemy army. The enemy center, attacked on its front, flank and rear would give way and the battle would be over. This same pattern was repeated in each of Alexander's three great victories over the Persians, the battles of Granicus, Issus, and Gaugamela, and in his other engagements for which accounts exist.

Each Macedonian unit knew what was expected of it. The objective of the entire army was to set up the enemy for the decisive thrust to be delivered by Alexander and the Companions. The divisions of the army did not have to win their particular engagements; rather, they had only to pin the enemy and prevent him from overwhelming them. Thus, in a rather selfless manner, the entire army existed to provide Alexander's 2,000 elite horsemen the opportunity to repeatedly cover themselves with glory. Of course, the alternative was defeat and quite possibly death, which also had to affect not only the soldiers' outlook but their performance as well.

The question might be raised as to what the Macedonians would have done if one of Alexander's charges had been repulsed. Quite simply, the task of achieving victory would fall to the Thessalians, or the phalangites, or the Hypaspists. Just because these units never won any of Alexander's large battles does not mean they were not capable of doing so. Each was a formidable fighting unit, as they proved time and again in independent actions, and each could, if necessary, deliver the telling strike themselves.

Further proof of this can be seen in the wars of Alexander's successors. The Macedonian system lived on with these men and the empires they founded. However, two armies of a similar nature knew what to expect from each other, and the chances for a decisive blow to be delivered by the heavy cavalry declined markedly. By 217 B.C. at the Battle of Raphia between the heirs of Ptolemy and Seleucus, 115,000 men took the field on both sides; only 11,000 were cavalry. This heralded the era of the Romans when tactical mobility was further extended to the infantry while the horsemen entered a 400 year eclipse.

References: Adcock, Frank, *Greek and Macedonian Art of War* (Berkeley: University of California Press, 1974); Ashley, James, *The Macedonian Empire* (McFarland & Co., 1997); Ginouves, Rene, and Giannes Akamates, *Macedonia: From Philip II to the Roman Conquest* (Princeton: Princeton University Press, 1994).

Magyars

Asian peoples related to the Huns who invaded Europe in the ninth century, establishing the Hungarian population.

A fanciful legend traces the origins of the Magyars to Nimrod, a descendant of Noah's son Japheth, who left Babel after the ill-fated attempt to construct there the tower of biblical fame. Nimrod had two sons, Hunor and Magyar, who in turn begot the two great tribes of the Huns and the Magyars.The myth has it that the tribes followed a magical elk to the Caucasus where they lived in peace. As time passed and the tribes grew, the Magyars remained in the Caucasus and the Huns began a nomadic life, which ultimately took them past the Volga into Europe. There, under the leadership of Attila, the Huns waged a campaign of terror and conquest. After Attila's defeat and death, his sons returned to the Caucasus and pleaded with the Magyars to return with them to Europe where they could find new lands and opportunity.

Though the legend is compelling, in reality the Magyars seem to have had Finno-Ugric origins with traces of Turco-Tartar elements. They had long practiced a nomadic lifestyle in central Asia and finally migrated westward past the Ural, Volga, Don, Dnieper, and at last, the Danube Rivers. In this movement, they successively fought and defeated other nomadic tribes, such as the Khazarsand Petchenegs. The pressure of the Petchenegs and Bulgars finally drove them into Europe. As the Magyars entered eastern Europe, they encountered the power of the Byzantine Empire, which hired them as mercenaries and introduced them to Christianity. Likewise, Germanic kings hired them to aid in fighting the Slavs.

By the ninth century A.D. the Magyars had moved into central Europe under leadership of Arpad. Under his direction, they entered the Hungarian plain with some 150,000 men. They defeated the Slavs and Alans and settled in, using their new home as a base for further raids into German and Italian lands. The Magyars became the permanent occupants of this region and became known as Hungarians. Magyar soldiers under Arpad ranged successfully into the Italian peninsula as far as Milan and Pavia in 899 leaving only upon receiving sufficient bribes.

The Magyars fought in much the same style as the Huns and were precursors to the Mongol invasion of Europe. Employing mostly light cavalry and archers, they avoided close contact with their enemies, harassing them into exhaustion and then exploiting any openings. The heavy cavalry developed in Europe at this time did not at first succeed against the Magyars, but over time the European defenders adopted some of the eastern tactics and began to have more success.

By 907 Magyar interest in German lands forced the Germanic rules into cooperation with each other. Luitpold of Bavaria allied with Ditmar, the Archbishop of Salzburg. Nevertheless, their efforts proved futile and the Magyars defeated them at Presburg. In the 920s the Magyars raided as far as the Champagne region of France, into northern Italy again, and as far as the Pyrenees. The Magyars created as much terror in their campaigns as the Vikings, who were pressing from the north, but the Germanic nobles soon began to prevail against them. Henry the Fowler defeated them in 933 at Merseburg, inflicting 36,000 Magyar casualties. He and his successors began fortifying the frontier, which lessened the frequency of the Magyar raids, while the Bavarians turned the tables and began to raid Magyar lands. Nevertheless, in 954 up to 100,000 Magyars attacked deep into Germany and France, taking advantage of the revolt of Lorraine against Otto the Great, Henry's son. They again made a huge pillaging sweep through France and into northern Italy and back to the Danube valley. Otto finally defeated them the following year at Lechfeld, after which the Magyars were on the decline.

At home in Hungary, they settled down to a more stable and civilized lifestyle under the leadership of Duke Geyza in the 970s. Christianity replaced their Asiatic animistic and totemic beliefs and they began showing a toleration and acceptance of other cultures. King Stephen (997–1038) defended his homeland from takeover by the Holy Roman Empire and acquired authority from the pope over a national church. Stephen oversaw the construction of monasteries and cathedrals and, for his efforts and example, was later canonized. The Magyar language became and remains the official language of Hungary: But for the battle at Lechfeld, it may have been the language of much of western Europe. For all their terrorism of the west, it was the Hungarians who ultimately defended western Europe from the Ottoman Turks as they fought to bring down the Byzantine Empire and expand the

Moslem faith into Europe in the mid-fifteenth century.

References: Bartha, Antal, *Hungarian Society in the 9th and 10th Centuries*, translated by K. Baazs (Budapest: Akademiai Kiado, 1975); Macartney, C.A., *The Magyars in the Ninth Century* (Cambridge: University Press, 1968); Vambery, Arminius, *Hungary in Ancient, Medieval, and Modern Times* (Hallandale, FL: New World Books, 1972).

Mamluks

Moslem slave-soldiers who rose to power in Egypt during the Middle Ages.

The Koran states that the only legitimate sources of slaves are the children of slaves and prisoners of war. It was through the second route that most of the slaves that lived under early Islam came to their condition. Because slaves were used for every conceivable purpose, perhaps it is not surprising that the rulers of Egypt used them as soldiers, or *ghulams*. The Fatimid (909–1171) and Ayyubid (1171–1250) dynasties of Egypt built armies of slave-soldiers. As happened in other slave-holding societies, those most talented rose in power and influence, despite their official status as slaves. Just as trustworthy eunuchs rose to positions of political power as advisors to royalty, so did slave-soldiers rise to command armies under the caliphs and viziers.

The *mamluks* (from the Arabic word for "owned") were white slaves, acquired in raids conducted into Turkey and the Caucasus. Other slave-soldiers were called *Abid al-Shira* ("purchased slaves"), and they tended to be of Sudanese or Berber descent. A Mamluk was usually purchased and trained by his master, which in theory would ensure the slave's loyalty to the master. When they became trustworthy, they were often freed and awarded a piece of land called an *iqta'*. Ownership of the iqta' provided the Mamluk not only with produce from farming, but with enough of an estate to control his own slaves or peasant tenants. Thus, the iqta' roughly corresponded with the feudal system developing in Europe, whereby the master could call on his subordinates to provide troops for him when campaigning was necessary. The master who could provide Mamluks for war became known as the amir, and his rank varied according to the number of Mamluks he controlled. Thus, there were amirs of five, amirs of 10, and so forth—up to amirs of 100, although the actual number of Mamluks under an amir's command might vary wildly. Still, five was the minimum number in order to be given the title of amir. Under the control of the caliph, the core troops of the Fatimid dynasty were the Royal Mamluks, an organization that usually numbered 5,000 men (although it varied widely in later times). The Mamluks fought as fully armed cavalry, while the troops they procured from their own estates, as well as other auxiliaries recruited by the government, operated as infantry armed with spears or bows.

The Mamluks fought well and bravely under their Moslem masters, but in the mid-thirteenth century, they took power for themselves. The final Ayyubid sultan, al-Salih, died in 1249 but his wife Shajar-al-Durr kept his death secret for a time and gave orders in his name. When she was discovered, rather than remove her, the Moslem leaders in Cairo paired her with the Mamluk general Aybak. After they married, Shajar-al-Durr continued to rule and had Aybak assassinated, but he is regarded as the first of the Mamluk dynasty. The dynasty lasted more than 265 years and saw occasionally brilliant leaders as well as a renaissance in the arts.

The first Mamluk leader to distinguish himself was al-Malik Baybars (ruled 1260–1277). He was born a slave rather than captured, and his training as well as innate talents took him to the heights of command in the Ayyubid army. He commanded the forces that defeated and captured French King Louis IX in 1250 at the battle of Masura, during Saint Louis's abortive crusade. He was second-in-command to Qutuz ten years later at the battle of Ain-Julut, where the Mamluks defeated the Mongols and turned back the Asian tide flowing into the Middle East. During the army's return to Cairo after the great victory, Baybars killed Qutuz and named himself sultan. He spent his reign repeatedly defeating European Crusaders, a feat that gained him the highest respect in Moslem eyes. When not fighting, he was a judicious ruler who showed remarkable religious tolerance in his domain. The government organization he established served the Mamluk dynasty through to its end in 1517. He also oversaw the construction of numerous public works and built both a strong navy as well as a strong standing army.

The Mamluk army was divided into three main divisions: the Royal Mamluks, the Mamluks of the amirs, and the al-Halqa. Under Baybars the Royal Mamluks increased to as many as 16,000 men. From the ranks of the Royal Mamluks came the amirs. The amirs continued to provide and command other Mamluks, but they also commanded the al-Halqa, which first were organized in 1174 and served as cavalry. The soldiers serving in these units were Egyptians or the sons of freed Mamluks. Although by this time the term "Mamluk" was more historical than descriptive of soldier slaves, native Egyptians and Arabs still could not become Mamluks. Thus, they were relegated to serving in the al-Halqa contingents. Even the sons of Mamluks were segregated into this third contingent and treated as second class because they had not been born Turkish or raised as slaves. This is almost certainly the only time in history that one could attain a higher social and professional status by having been born or raised a slave than having been born free.

After 1381 a second ruling family rose to power from Mamluk descendants: the Burjis. The Burji dynasty, although it lasted another 136 years, was rocked by almost constant palace intrigue and assassinations. During this time the sultans spent lavishly and Cairo became the richest city in the Mediterranean world. However, the instability of the succession to power spelled the dynasty's doom. Selim I of the Ottoman Empire defeated the Mamluk armies in 1517 after which Egypt became a vassal state ruled by a Turkish governor. Still, the Mamluks retained some influence in government, serving under the Turkish pasha and still holding command positions in the army. When in 1798 Napoleon Bonaparte arrived to attempt the conquest of Egypt, a Mamluk army fought him. The Mamluks were defeated at the Battle of the Pyramids in 1798, but after the French withdrew, the Mamluks tried to regain the throne. The Turks defeated them in 1805 and again in 1811, breaking Mamluk power for good.

References: Glubb, John Bagot, *Soldiers of Fortune: The Story of the Mamlukes* (London: Stein & Day, 1957) Irwin, Robert, *The Middle East in the Middle Ages* (Carbondale: Southern Illinois University Press, 1986); Muir, William, *Mameluke, or Slave Dynasty of Egypt* (New York: AMS, 1973).

Marathas

An Indian ethnic group that resisted the British occupation of India.

The homeland of the Marathas, another of the martial races of India, is the Deccan, the plateau of central India south of the Narbudda River stretching to the west coast. This region was one of the final acquisitions of the Aryans in prehistoric times, and the inhabitants are descendants of both those invaders and the aboriginal tribes that lived there prior to conquest. The Marathas first displayed their warlike tendencies with the arrival of the Moslems in India. As Hindus, the Marathas fiercely resisted the imposition of Islam, especially under the Mogul dynasty. Their leader was Sivaji, called "the mountain rat," and his successes against the Moguls, including the kidnaping of an emperor, laid the groundwork for what became the Mahratta Confederacy. Prior to the arrival of the British in the 1700s, the only serious military opponents the Marathas had faced were the Afghans, who had defeated them along the border at Panipat in 1761. That defeat laid the foundation for internal disputes that brought about the two Maratha wars.

As long as Sivaji lived, the Marathas were united, but after his death the population broke into factions under rival princes who swore only nominal fealty to a central government under the rajah of Satara. The chief minister of the rajah was the *peshwa*, a hereditary position that exercised great influence. The princes collectively formed the Maratha Confederation, and for all their independent stances stood together when faced with outside threats. The confederation consisted of the princes Scindia, Holkar, and Bhonsla, along with the peshwa, and the European military advisors they employed at the opening of the nineteenth century, who were predominantly French refugees from the court of the recently deposed Tipoo Sultan of Mysore.

The Marathas staged two campaigns against the British. The first started in 1804 as the British were embroiled in European problems with Napoleon. Always on the alert to find some way to divert the British, Napoleon sent agents to India (where the French presence was coming to an end) to stir up trouble. Indian princes had long hired Europeans to train and command their armies, and the Marathas accepted the offer of French assistance against the growing power of Britain along the western coast of India. The forces comprising the Maratha army were neither citizen-soldiers nor patriots, but mercenaries and outlaws fighting for pay and to practice their chosen profession. Long a haven for raiders and bandits, British possessions around Bombay had suffered from decades-long harassment. As it was the British East India Company's view that law and order promoted profits, conflict between them and the Marathas would certainly have broken out even without French aid.

It was the British defeat of Tipoo Sultan in 1798 that precipitated the conflict. The British had viewed Tipoo Sultan as a particularly despicable character who needed deposing, so they replaced him with a more cooperative ruler, who became the Nizam of Mysore. Upon disbanding the French forces, the Nizam was urged to accept a garrison of East India Company soldiers: four battalions from Madras and some artillery to defend the capital city of Hyderabad. These troops were necessary to defend Mysore from the bandit raids emanating from Maratha territory, while the British at the same time opened negotiations with the Marathas to end the banditry and cooperate against the threat of Afghan pressure. These negotiations, coupled with the death of Peshwa Madho Rao, led to internecine fighting among the Marathas. The new peshwa, Bajee Rao, broke ranks and allied himself with the British in return for East India Company troops and artillery. The Marathas responded by naming Bajee's brother, Amrut, to be peshwa, which led to an inevitable conflict between the confederacy on one side and the British, forces loyal to Bajee Rao, and the forces of the Nizam of Mysore on the other.

The army that took the field against the Maratha Confederacy was led by Arthur Wellesley in his first major combat command. In total, some 50,000 men were under his command, operating in a number of smaller columns. He quickly captured the supposedly impregnable fortress at Ahmadnagar, then found himself facing a huge challenge at the village of Assaye at the Jua and Kelna Rivers. On 23 September 1803 with only 4,500 men, Wellesley charged a force of 55,000 led by a number of French officers. In a few hours Wellesley drove them from the field at a cost of almost half the British force killed or wounded. He followed these successes with victories at Argaon in November and Gawilarh in December, while one of his subordinates captured the fort at Aseergurh.

While Wellesley consolidated his hold in the southern region of Maratha territory, a second army under General Lord Lake operated farther north in the vicinity of Delhi, where he rescued the Mogul emperor, Shah Alam, from his Mahratta captors. Lake's army operated against Holkar, one of the Maratha

INDIA IN 1765

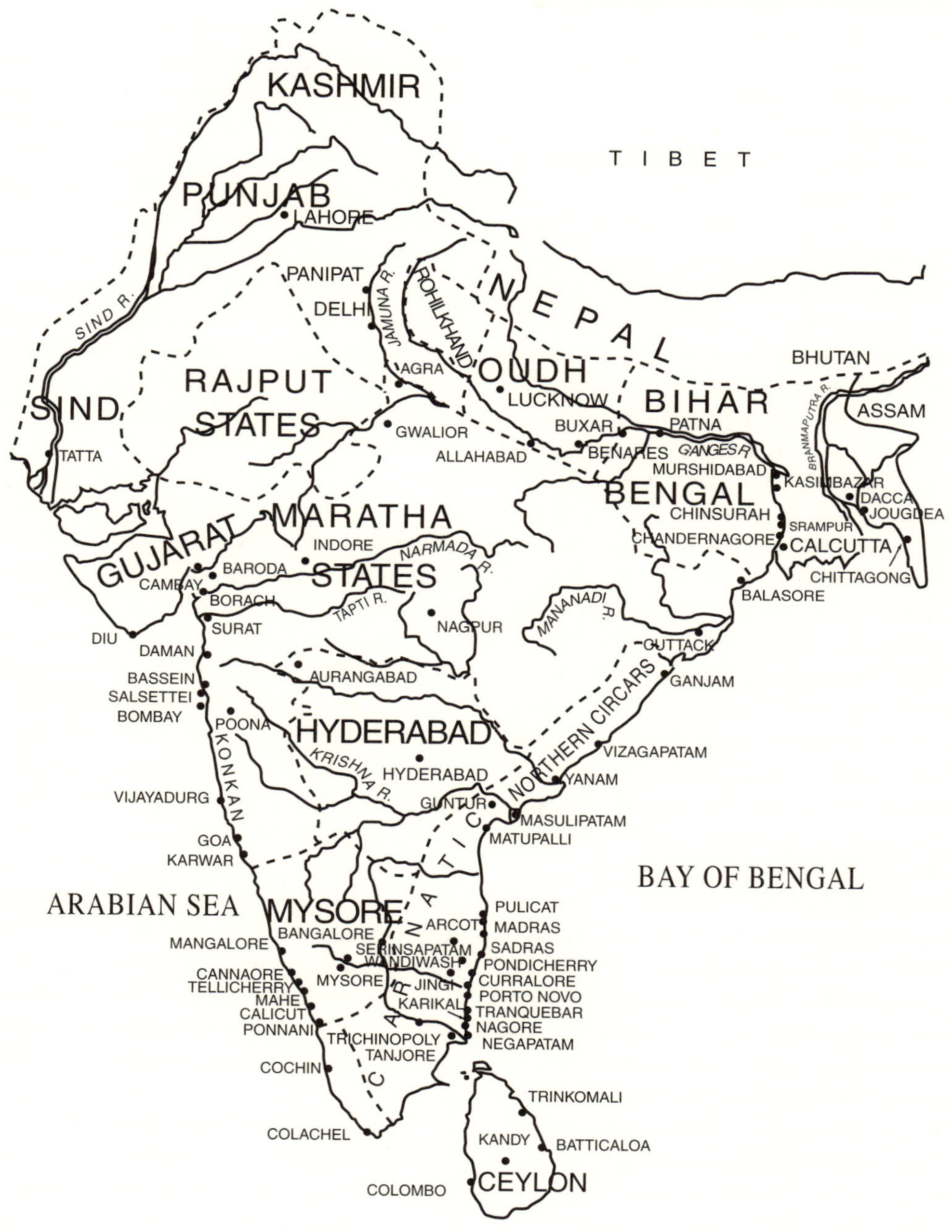

princes, while Wellesley had fought against princes Scindia and Bhonsla. Lake soon captured Agra and sent forces in pursuit of fleeing Marathas, but was obliged to defend Delhi from a major counterattack. Throughout 1805 Lake campaigned in the Punjab, ferreting out Holkar's forces and those of his allies. Lake's ultimate defeat of Holkar at Armritsar led to the war being ended in 1806. Lake remained in India, but Wellesley was transferred to Europe to lead British forces in Spain against Napoleon's army there, for which he was ultimately given the title of Duke of Wellington.

Peace between the British and Marathas was kept for more than a decade, but in 1817 the confederacy started hostilities again, owing to the activity of mercenary outlaws called *Pindaris*. The Pindaris, remnants of old Mogul armies, were raiding and pillaging so extensively that the British had to respond. They called on the Marathas for aid under the terms of the 1806 agreement, but received little assistance. The British forces thus had to campaign against the Pindaris while keeping an eye on the always restless Marathas. The erstwhile British ally Bajee Rao now chafed under British control and, under the guise of raising troops to aid the British, actually organized an army totalling 86,500 cavalry and 66,000 infantry to add to the 16,500 cavalry and infantry of the Pindaris. The combined number never operated together, but threatened the British from a variety of directions.

The opening of the conflict came in November 1817 when Mahratta troops attacked the British garrison stationed at Bajee Rao's capital of Poona. British forces under Sir Thomas Hyslop and Lord General Francis Rawdon-Hastings made fairly short work of the Second Maratha War. The Pindaris were successful only against defenseless villages, while the Marathas, though numerous, had lost most of their quality soldiers in the previous war. When Bajee Rao surrendered in early June 1818 Maratha power was broken for good and the East India Company attained dominance in the subcontinent. The British were obliged to interfere in a succession dispute in 1825–1826 but, as was their practice, the British began to incorporate the best Maratha soldiers into the Indian Army. The wars against the Marathas were the most difficult that the East Indian Company fought prior to the Sikh War of the 1840s and 1850s. When the Sepoy Rebellion broke out in 1857 the Maratha troops remained loyal to the British in spite of the fact that some of the Rebellion's leaders claimed to be fighting to restore Maratha power. Marathas also proved themselves to be quality troops when they fought alongside British forces in Mesopotamia in World War I.

References: MacMunn, G.F., *The Armies of India* (London: Adam and Charles Black, 1911); Mason, Philip, *A Matter of Honour* (London: Jonathan Cape, 1974); Roberts, P.E., *History of British India* (London: Oxford University Press, 1952).

Merrill's Marauders

An American special forces unit operating in Burma during World War II.

Operating from French Indochina, which Japanese forces had occupied in September 1940 thanks to help from the German-controlled Vichy French Government, the Japanese struck with amazing speed into Southeast Asia on 8 December 1941. They drove through Thailand and southern Burma to capture the British stronghold at Singapore and also drove west to occupy most of Burma. This put them in a position to threaten British India and allowed them to shut down the overland supply route into China, the so-called Burma Road, which the United States had been using to supply its ally, Chiang Kai-shek. In order to reopen a supply line, American General Joseph Stilwell planned a joint effort from India and China. British and Indian forces would operate out of the northeastern Indian province of Assam from the city of Ledo, while Chinese forces would attack out of Hunan toward the town of Bhamo, to which a road from Ledo would be built. The British found themselves quite busy dealing with Japanese offensives against India, but their long-range penetration group, Orde Wingate's Chindits, successfully harassed Japanese rear areas and tied down a large number of Japanese troops. To accomplish that same end, Stilwell used an American group, the 5307th Composite Unit (Provisional).

The 5307th was made up of volunteers who had had experience training or fighting in the jungle. Veterans of the Guadalcanal battle, as well as those who had fought the Japanese on New Guinea, formed two thirds of the 3,000-man force. The remainder came from forces stationed and trained in the Caribbean jungles. In late 1943 they organized in India, where they absorbed some of Wingate's theories on jungle warfare and behind-the-lines operations. Command of the unit went to Brigadier General Frank Merrill, although the unit did not gain its nickname, "the Marauders," until newspapers coined it later. During training, Merrill's men were told that the optimum duration for action such as they were undertaking (according to Wingate) was no more than three months. The men of the 5307th came to assume that after that time they would be withdrawn from combat.

The 5307th was the only American combat unit in Burma, although Stilwell was in command of the entire theater from Burma to China. Thus, Stilwell expected the unit to perform to the highest standard in order to motivate the Chinese divisions. It was a successful stratagem. The Chinese carried out most of the direct assaults, while Merrill's men carried on enveloping movements to harass the Japanese rear and supply lines. The Americans left Ledo in February 1944 and linked with the Chinese operating from Hunan, then worked southward. The two-pronged attacks proved successful: The Japanese XVIII Division was defeated and forced to withdraw from Maingkwan in the first week of March, then was dislodged from Shaduzup at the end of the month. Both times the Japanese were forced to withdraw hastily and under fire. The Marauders were supplied by air in this stage of the operation, but Stilwell wanted to acquire an airfield from which to provide close air support and establish a supply depot. He chose the town of Myitkyina (pronounced "Mitchinah").

Myitkyina possessed the only all-weather airfield in northern Burma, and it was the northern terminus of the Rangoon to Mandalay railroad. Holding this town would both aid the Allies and hamper the Japanese supply situation. Working with local Kachin tribesmen, Merrill's men and elements of the Chinese Thirtieth Division (totaling some 7,000 men) arrived secretly at Myitkyina and quickly seized the airfield on 17 May 1944. The Japanese, however, managed to maintain a strong hold on the town itself, in spite of repeated attacks. The Marauders' mission was to hold the airfield while the remainder of the Chinese drove through Japanese positions at Kamaing. The Chinese took the town with a bayonet charge in a downpour on 16 June but the Japanese withdrew in an orderly fashion to the village of Mogaung. Chindit attacks, combined with a major Chinese assault, captured Mogaung on 26 June. From this point, the Chinese were poised to strike directly toward Myitkyina to link up with the Marauders.

The Japanese stubbornly held out in Myitkyina, even maintaining a steady stream of supplies and reinforcements. The Sino-American force attacking the town had been in constant action since they captured the airfield in May and were on the verge of collapse. Furthermore, the three-month period of operations that the Americans assumed they were in for had expired and they were ready to be withdrawn. However, neither Stilwell nor his area commander, Hayden Boatner, acknowledged such a promise and they needed men to attack. However, as the Chindits experienced in their early operations, men in the jungle under the constant strain of combat and the elements have a limit. Merrill's men had reached it. The rate of

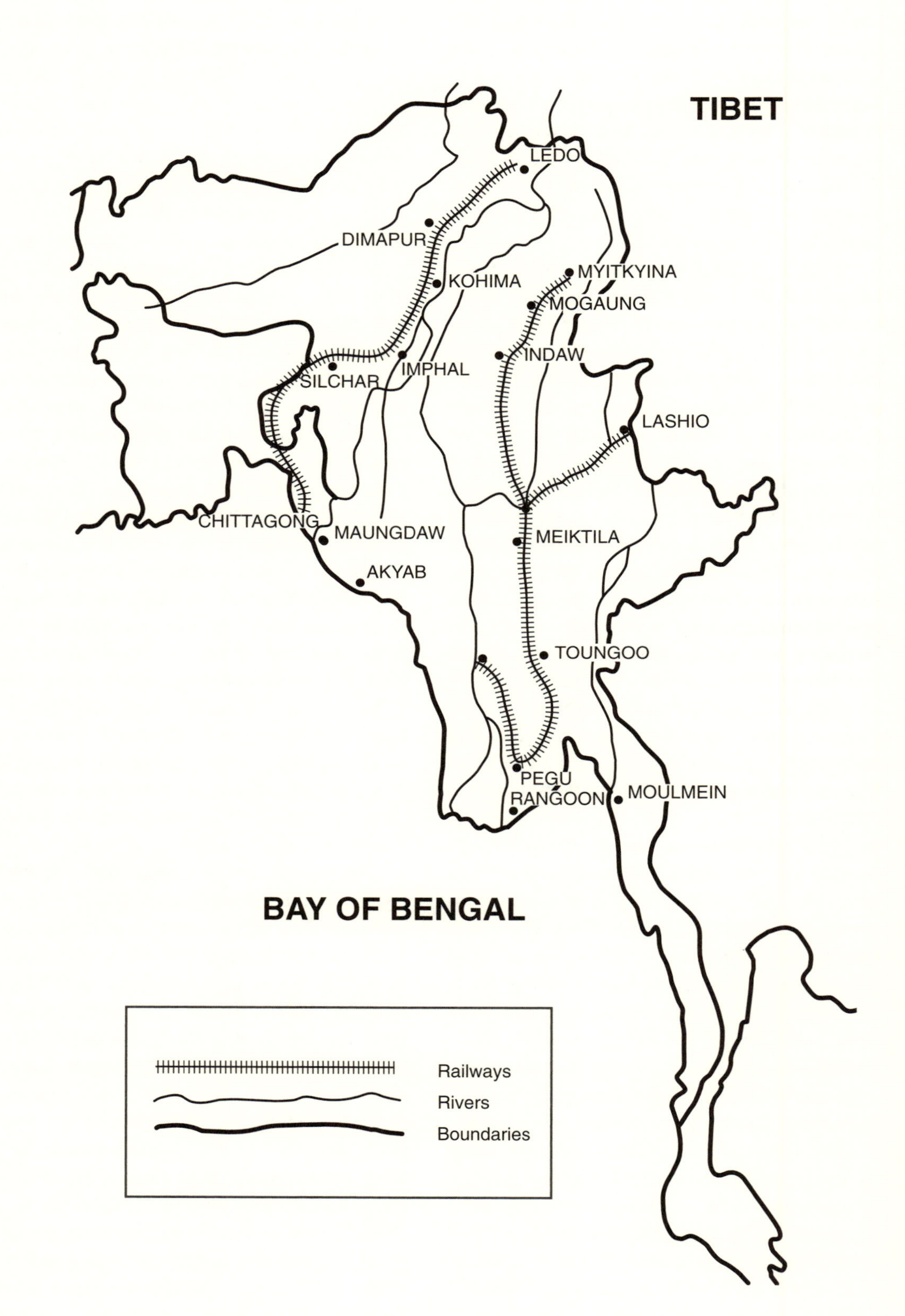
TIBET
LEDO
DIMAPUR
KOHIMA
MYITKYINA
MOGAUNG
INDAW
IMPHAL
SILCHAR
LASHIO
CHITTAGONG
MAUNGDAW
MEIKTILA
AKYAB
TOUNGOO
PEGU
RANGOON
MOULMEIN
BAY OF BENGAL
Railways
Rivers
Boundaries

sickness swelled and men often fell asleep while fighting. The morale of the unit collapsed. Stilwell wanted them to stay because they were the only American unit operating. The Chinese were still fighting well, but their organization and supply system was much stronger than Merrill's.

The siege of Myitkyina ended on 3 August when a new Japanese commander deemed the delay to the American plans sufficient. He withdrew his men after an 11-week battle and the loss of approximately 3,000 dead. The Americans also suffered heavy losses. The 5307th consisted of 1,310 men out of the original 3,000 when they first arrived at Myitkyina. Half that number were evacuated to hospitals between their arrival on 17 May and 1 June. When the last of the unit was pulled out on 3 August it consisted of only 200 Marauders. For their time in combat, the 5307th Composite Unit (Provisional) earned a Distinguished Unit Citation, summarized thus: "After a series of successful engagements in the Hukawng and Mogaung Valleys of North Burma, in March and April 1944 the unit was called on to lead a march over jungle trails through extremely difficult mountain terrain against stubborn resistance in a surprise attack on Myitkyina. The unit proved equal to the task and after a brilliant operation on 17 May 1944 seized the airfield at Myitkyina, an objective of great tactical importance in the campaign, and assisted in the capture of the town of Myitkyina on 3 August 1944" (Dupuy, 1966). Fifty-five men received the Bronze Star, 40 received the Silver Star, six were awarded the Distinguished Service Cross, and four received the Legion of Merit.

References: Bjorge, Gary, "Merrill's Marauders: Combined Operations in Northern Burma in 1944," in *Army History*, Spring/Summer 1995; Center of Military History, *Merrill's Marauders* (Washington, D.C.: Historical Division, War Department, 1945); Dupuy, Trevor N., "Burma: The Drive from the North," in *History of the Second World War*, vol. 71 (London: BBC Publications, 1966); Stilwell, Joseph W., *The Stilwell Papers*, ed. Theodore H. White (New York: William Sloane Associates, 1948)

Minutemen

Special militia units operating at the outbreak of the American Revolution.

The Minutemen of the American Revolution were formed some months before the outbreak of hostilities. In early September 1774, delegates from 12 of the 13 colonies assembled in Philadelphia to discuss a response to the Coercive (or Intolerable) Acts recently passed in London by Parliament. These were designed to punish the American colonies in general—and Massachusetts in particular—for the infamous Boston Tea Party, as well as other mischief and troublemaking that the colonists had perpetrated since the Boston Massacre of March 1770. The representatives in Philadelphia decided to implement an embargo on British goods, a tactic that had proved successful in the past, in order to pressure the British government. It was the adoption of the Suffolk resolves, however, that really made war inevitable.

The Suffolk Resolves were introduced by a delegation from Suffolk County, Massachusetts, where Boston is located. Adopted by the First Continental Congress toward the end of its September 1774 gathering, the Resolves called for Americans to ignore the Coercive Acts, to arrest a British officer in return for any American arrested, and to attack British facilities if the British moved troops to enforce order. The final resolves called for the removal of any militia officer not 100 percent trustworthy and for the inhabitants of every town to "use their utmost diligence to acquaint themselves with the art of war as soon as possible, and to, for that purpose, appear under arms at least once a week." These resolves, and the threat to attack the British directly unless the Coercive Acts were repealed, was made by an unauthorized body acting with only the limited support of the people, who had not elected them to speak for the country as a whole. When word of the Suffolk Resolves reached London, the British government had no choice in how to respond. In 1774, as today, governments could not negotiate with what they perceived as terrorists, and King George ordered the dispatch of trained troops.

The colonies were racked with local political conflict. The colonies had a royally appointed governor who, along with the popularly elected legislatures, had control over the militia. In Massachusetts particularly, and other colonies to a lesser extent, provincial congresses and committees of safety were forming that acted like governments and in many cases came to control the militias. "Disloyal" officers were removed and more "patriotic" officers appointed. The traditional militia organization consisted of the volunteer militia and the common militia: the first traditionally more ready to respond while the second organized and prepared for duty. Militia units across the country (again, more commonly in Massachusetts where most of the revolutionary sentiment was centered) were told to appoint one man in three, or one in four, to be prepared for a quick response to back up the threat made through the Suffolk Resolves. These men quickly came to be regarded as "Minutemen," for their supposedly instant readiness.

Throughout the autumn and winter of 1774–1775, the Minutemen trained much more often than normal. Prior to this, the common militia had often gathered no more than once a year and then often more for socializing than training. Still, the quality of the Minuteman units varied according to their leaders and the motivation of the rank and file. In those months after the Continental Congress met, tensions between British troops and colonials intensified, with incidents sometimes resulting in minor bloodshed. With the promised reinforcements on the way, however, British commander General Thomas Gage laid plans for seizing the rebel supplies of munitions stored at Concord, some 20 miles outside his headquarters of Boston. Although he strove for secrecy in his planning, the colonials kept a constant vigil on British troop activities. When he ordered his men into action on the night of 18 April 1775 his troops were no sooner forming up than rebel messengers were already riding the countryside to alert the Minutemen. The most famous of these was Paul

On 19 April 1775, British troops were met by American Minutemen at Lexington, Massachusetts, where the first shots of the American Revolution were fired.

Revere, but he was hardly the only one to be spreading the word.

The first unit to gather on the night of April 18 met at Lexington, a town roughly halfway between Boston and Concord that was the site of their weekly drills. The men drifted in from their farms in the area and gathered inside a tavern to await the British arrival. The British appeared as the sun was coming up on 19 April. Colonel John Parker assembled his 75 to 100 Minutemen on Lexington Green. When some 700 British troops came marching into view, the Minutemen, who were mainly young farmers without combat experience, must have been having second thoughts about having volunteered. When ordered by a British officer, John Pitcairn, to disperse, Parker decided that would be the better part of valor and ordered his men to do so. As they were leaving, a shot was fired. Pitcairn reported later that some colonists, having jumped over a wall, fired four or five shots at his men, who had been ordered not to fire but to disarm the rebels. Although just who fired the first shot has been a source of debate since that morning, it was most likely one of the Minutemen. Hours of anxious waiting and the appearance of well-ordered troops by comparison with what the Minutemen could muster, almost certainly conspired to produce an itchy trigger finger or a nervous accidental firing.

When the smoke cleared, eight Americans were dead and ten were wounded. Although all the Americans were familiar with their weapons and had as a target a mass of soldiers in formation silhouetted against the rising sun, the Minutemen managed to wound only one British trooper and hit Pitcairn's horse. Brushing aside this feeble resistance, the British marched on to Concord, reaching the town late in the morning. Most of the rebels' stockpile of weapons had been removed by this time, so the British destroyed what they could find and turned to march back to Boston. As they approached the Sudbury River on the outskirts of Concord, they found another Minuteman force. After the experience at Lexington, they could not have been worried. However, these soldiers stood their ground and their firing was much more effective. The British regrouped and forced the Minutemen back across the Old North Bridge, but from that point on the British force was in serious trouble.

Word spread quickly about the dawn encounter, and angry colonists grabbed their muskets and made for the Concord-Boston road. Here the heritage of fighting Indians in North America proved itself valuable, for hundreds of colonists lined the road and, from the cover of trees and farmhouses, began to snipe at the British column. Hit-and-run guerrilla warfare, which was the common form of fighting in the colonies, proved deadly to the British. Although met by a relieving force of 1,200 at Lexington in midafternoon, the British had no better luck in fighting the harassing enemy. By the time the British returned to Boston, they had suffered some 270 dead and wounded, while the colonists had only 95 casualties.

Within a matter of weeks, 20,000 colonists were besieging Boston. The Revolution had begun in earnest, and many more than just the Minutemen were now bearing arms. Indeed, the need for Minutemen, a rapid response force, was no longer necessary. The volunteers who went to Boston to stand up for their rights or to avenge the deaths at Lexington included men who ultimately formed the core of the Continental Army under George Washington, but the militia would prove to be both the bane and boon of the war effort. They always outnumbered the force that Washington tried to mold into a regular army, but their training, discipline, and morale were always directly proportional to their success on the battlefield. The Minutemen, the cream of the militia units prior to the outbreak of the fighting, lost their special status after the first day of the Revolution.

References: Alden, John, *The American Revolution* (New York: Harper & Row, 1954); Fischer, David Hackett, *Paul Revere's Ride* (New York: Oxford University Press, 1995); Smith, Page, *A New Age Now Begins* (New York: McGraw-Hill, 1976).

Mongols

An Asiatic population that conquered from China to Europe between the thirteenth and fifteenth centuries.

The Mongols, one of the most feared of all warrior populations, were horsemen from the steppes of central Asia. Their reputation is almost completely attributable to one man, Genghis Khan. Born in the middle 1100s and named Temujin, this son of a dispossessed tribal leader endured captivity as a child to avenge his father's murder and reclaim leadership of his tribe in young manhood. From that point he built a nation, absorbing conquered peoples and incorporating them into his greater Mongol horde. Although without formal education, Genghis Khan showed an innate intelligence in psychology, strategy and tactics, and statecraft. Without his vision there almost certainly would never have been a great Mongol people.

A handful of Mongol tribes named Temujin *Genghis Khan* (roughly translated "all-encompassing leader" or "universal ruler") in 1206. He quickly set about expanding his domain by superior leadership and organization. Upon defeating an enemy tribe, he would force the survivors to swear personal loyalty to him, thus making the resulting society his own. Although ruthless in battle, he was open-minded in peace. He absorbed the technology and learning of conquered peoples and forced no one to practice any particular religion. He oversaw the compilation of the Great Yasa, a code of laws that covered every part of Mongol life. Once the conquests came to an end, the resulting *Pax Mongolica* allowed for increased trade and a freer flow of ideas as people and goods began to pass back and forth from East to West. Upon his death in 1227 Genghis Khan had established such an effective organization that the expansion continued almost without hesitation after his funeral.

The Emperor Kublai, Grand Khan of the Mongols and Tartars, commanding in a battle fought between Peking and Siberia (Lithograph by M. Gauci, 1826)

The innate toughness of the Mongol people, developed over generations of surviving on the relatively barren steppes, served them well in training, travel, and battle. The nomadic Mongols had always been horsemen, traveling in search of pasture for their animals and food for themselves. Genghis Khan took advantage of these traits and molded some of the finest light cavalry the world has ever known. Each man carried his own supplies, on his back and on two spare horses. The spares were used as fresh mounts and one of them was a mare to provide milk, which was often fermented into a drink the Mongols called *kumiss*. The soldiers carried two kinds of bows and three kinds of arrows, using different combinations for different types of targets. They also carried a lance, javelin, or scimitar.

The Mongols were organized into graduated groupings, starting at units of ten men, then 100 men, 1,000 men, and finally 10,000-man units called *tumans*, the basic divisional structure. Twelve tumans comprised an army. The armies stayed in close contact through riders and signal flags, a system so effective that it provided for incredible coordination in attacks. In open battle the Mongols would converge on an enemy from all sides and pelt them with arrows from long range, then close on the disorganized and outnumbered foe with lance and sword. Genghis adopted siege weaponry from conquered populations and used it effectively. Cities that opened their gates on demand were spared, those that resisted were put to the sword and torch. The reputation for brutality thus accomplished was often sufficient to cow city dwellers into surrender. Working with spies and turncoats also allowed the Mongols to bring about a swift end to most sieges.

Genghis Khan led his forces eastward past the Great Wall into China and westward almost to the Caspian Sea. His son Ogatai, teamed with Genghis's most talented general Subotai, extended the Mongol dominions as far as the northern edge of Arabia, northern India, Russia, and all of China as far as modern Vietnam and achieved great victories over European forces in Poland and Hungary. Only the recall of men to attend Ogatai's funeral stopped their attempted spread into Europe.

Genghis's grandson Batu Khan led the Golden Horde that established Mongol control over Russia, an occupation that lasted until the 1400s. Another grandson, Kubilai, occupied China and absorbed much of Chinese culture and learning. His only defeats came in two failed attempts to invade Japan in the 1270s and 1280s. Yet another grandson, Hulagu, invaded the Middle East and controlled territory as far as the borders of Egypt. In the latter part of the fourteenth century, the destructive invader Tamurlane claimed descent from Genghis Khan and raided deep into India. The Mongols controlled the vast part of Asia for almost two centuries, but ultimately fell to the twin vices of greed and laziness. The good life of the civilizations they conquered seduced the warriors and they lost their edge; it is a story repeated often in history.

References: Chambers, James, *The Devil's Horsemen* (New York: Atheneum, 1979); Curtin, Jeremiah, *The Mongols: A History* (Westport, CT: Greenwood Press, 1972); Kwanten, Luc, *Imperial Nomads* (Philadelphia: University of Pennsylvania Press, 1979).

Mosby's Rangers

A partisan cavalry unit of the Confederate army during the American Civil War.

John Singleton Mosby was a lawyer practicing in far western Virginia in the years immediately preceding the Civil War. He was a staunch Unionist and made no attempt to hide his feelings, openly supporting Democrat Stephen A. Douglas for the presidency in 1860 against the wishes of the Southern wing of the party. He also spoke against secession when South Carolina started that process in December 1860. Like the most famous Virginian of the war, Robert E. Lee, Mosby found that when Virginia seceded from the Union he had to remain loyal to his home state. Nothing in his first months as a soldier distinguished him—other than his quick temper—which had landed him in trouble and even in jail in his earlier life.

About the time of the opening battle of the war at Bull Run in July 1861 Mosby came to the attention of the man destined to command the Confederate cavalry arm, J. E. B. Stuart. Stuart saw in Mosby a man with enough intelligence to avoid recklessness but enough dash to act while others talked. Mosby served under Stuart and was active in Stuart's famous ride around the Union army prior to the Seven Days battles in the summer of 1862. Soon afterward, Mosby was given command of his own unit, although he was obliged to raise his own recruits. Mosby was captured while on a trip to visit Confederate General Thomas "Stonewall" Jackson to confer about recruiting. He was held only ten days before being exchanged, but in that time he learned of the Union plans to abandon the thrust toward Richmond under George McClellan and focus on a second attack from the north under John Pope. This information convinced Lee to turn his back on McClellan and face the new threat, defeating Pope at the second battle at Bull Run in August 1862.

His ability to gather intelligence beyond doubt, Mosby acquired men and enhanced his reputation. He was ordered to operate behind Union lines in the neighborhood of Washington, D.C. He was eminently successful, stealing supplies, attacking camps, capturing enemy troops, and even kidnaping Union Brigadier General Edwin Stoughton out of his bed. Mosby received a promotion to major and was given command of the newly formed Company A of the Forty-third Battalion Partisan Rangers in June 1863. He soon proved his worth once again by slipping, with some of his officers, into the camp of Joseph Hooker's Army of the Potomac. The spies captured documents relating to Hooker's intentions, then made their way back through camp undiscovered.

After the Confederate setbacks at Gettysburg and Vicksburg in July 1863 the need to harass Union forces and tie them down was much greater. Mosby's Rangers spent the summer and fall of 1864 in the Shenandoah Valley looting the countryside and tying down General Philip Sheridan's command so completely that they were unable to aid Grant's siege of Petersburg. It was during this time that Mosby's enemies dubbed him the Gray Ghost. In October 1864 his men damaged a rail line near Martinsburg, West Virginia, and waited for the train to pass. When it derailed, the Rangers entered the wrecked train and looted Sheridan's payroll of $170,000. Although Mosby unknowingly missed an opportunity to stop a train upon which General Grant was traveling unescorted, he still was such a thorn in the Union side that a price was put on his head. The reward was still unclaimed (and still offered) when the war came to an end 9 April 1865. Indeed, Mosby's last raid took place the day after the surrender had been signed. Unwilling to give himself up for execution, he waited until the "Wanted Dead or Alive" order was rescinded more than two months after the war's end. He was therefore able to claim the status of being the last Confederate officer to surrender.

After the war Mosby remained in the public eye, not as a war hero but for his almost immediate return to the Unionist stance he had held prior to the conflict. Mosby supported candidates often unpopular in the South, including Grant. When Grant ran for the presidency in 1868 Mosby saw in him an honest man who would work for reconciliation between the two regions. Mosby spoke with Grant, and the two became good friends. He became Grant's main advisor on southern issues after the election, and Mosby in return lobbied for an increase in federal jobs in the southern states. Mosby served as U.S. consul in Hong Kong and as an assistant attorney in the Justice Department. His popularity in the South suffered for his political activity, but as the immediate fervor of the war passed, Mosby was once again embraced by his state. Before his death in 1916 at the age of 82, he received a medal from his alma mater, the University of Virginia.

References: Jones, Virgil Carrington, *Gray Ghosts and Confederate Raiders* (New York: Henry Holt & Co., 1956); Siepel, Kevin, *Rebel: The Life and Times of John Singleton Mosby* (New York: St. Martin's Press, 1983).

Normans

A northeastern European population that conquered Great Britain and areas of the Mediterranean during the eleventh and twelfth centuries.

In the century after the first millennium, a remarkable people appeared on the European stage, a people of purposeful drive and indomitable will. Their attitudes and practices changed their world and helped to shape ours. Feared, reviled, and ultimately rehabilitated in modern history, the Normans were a catalyst for change in Europe. Like the comet that marked William the Conqueror's impending invasion of England in 1066, the Normans swept across the story of medieval Europe—a firebrand omen of a new order. The tale of their passage through this era illuminates the faults and failures of other peoples and throws a light on nations, kingdoms, and cultures to come.

The early years of the tenth century witnessed the last gasp of Viking expansion in Europe, an invasion of northern France by Hrolf the Ganger (also known as Rollo). Although successful in general terms, Hrolf found the exertions of his undertaking so debilitating—and the resistance of the degenerating Franks so effective—that a conciliatory offer from Charles the Simple proved irresistible. Viking opportunism and practicality could not pass up a deal like the Treaty of St. Clair-Sur-Epte: Rollo (as he was known to his new liege) received the area around Rouen (and a royal daughter) to have and to hold in exchange for an agreement to be a faithful vassal and to keep friend and foe alike from pillaging the territory. While these particular Northmen (that's the origin of the name "Norman") assimilated into Frankish culture and military practice with some speed, they were still only a generation or so removed from a Viking tradition that practiced peaceful trade and coexistence only with those who looked as though they could put up a good fight. Others were slain and sacked as a matter of regularity. Only one Norman relapse to these old raiding ways is reported: Shortly after the death of Charles the Simple, the Normans made an unsuccessful foray through western France and were defeated along with the Aquitanians by Rudolph at Limoges in 929. Thereafter, with increasing adaptation to Frankish culture, the Normans became boisterous yet faithful adherents to the French throne.

Duke Robert of Normandy demonstrated his support for the French king Henry I's cause by assisting in campaigns on Henry's behalf against rebellious nobles in northern France, including Champagne and Blois (about 1033). Henry returned the favor by helping Robert's illegitimate heir, William, in a fight against his own rebellious nobles, notably at Val-Les-Dunes (1047) where the rebellion was finally suppressed. Some Norman lords had objected to the circumstances of William's birth. Others simply used the excuse to make a grab for land and power. The Conqueror of 1066 was previously known as

The Norman army prepares to fight King Harold, as depicted on the Bayeux Tapestry, 1066. (Musée de la Tapisserie, Bayeux)

The Bastard, and at a tender age had to leave home at night in his socks when news of Duke Robert's death became common knowledge. Two years after Val-Les-Dunes, William and Henry were at war with one another, William successfully repulsing a French invasion in 1049 and fighting the prolonged and inconclusive war (1053–1058) that was typical of the era. Once firmly in control, William looked to his own interests and prerogatives.

The Normans had adopted the Frankish military system, which reflected the efforts of Charlemagne and his successors to emulate what fragments of Roman organization, tactics, and strategy remained extant. Javelin-armed heavy cavalry formed the core of the Frankish army, including mounted nobles and their retainers in an irregular approximation of late Roman *equites*. These horsemen, in their scale and chain mail armor (but still lacking stirrups), saw themselves as heirs to the Roman tradition and consciously imitated what they perceived to be the dress and style of their great precursors. True Roman drills, formations, and evolutions were unknown, but devotion and sufficient practice of established moves enabled the army to remain quite effective against the Franks' more barbarous enemies.

Frankish infantry retained the shield-wall, shoulder-to-shoulder tactics of other Dark Age armies. In battle, they seem to have been effective enough, and in straitened circumstances would have been strengthened by dismounted cavalry—a practice unthinkable a hundred years later, when the lofty concepts of chivalry had taken hold. Auxiliary troops included archers (reintroduced to western Europe by Charlemagne, but allowed to languish under later kings), javelin skirmishers, light cavalry from Gascony and Brittany (possibly descendants of Alans resettled by the Romans), and lighter infantry and cavalry recruited from defeated Slavs, Magyars, Vikings, and others. The wisdom and willingness to use a greater variety of troop types to cope with different battlefield situations originated with Charlemagne. It differentiated his armies from the monolithic masses of his enemies. However, the effectiveness of his system was not lost on Norman leaders in France, England, or in the Mediterranean.

Charlemagne bequeathed the Frankish armies a somewhat improved supply system that utilized frontier fortresses as advanced depots for operations along the frontiers. He also seems to have begun the rudiments of intelligence and staff work, including the study of opponents' strengths and weaknesses and the considerations of more esoteric factors in the field of strategy than simply finding the enemy and having at him. To what degree these practices survived when Norman armies took the field in the eleventh century no one can say with certainty, but William's preparations for the invasion of England and his apparent awareness of Anglo-Saxon moves and situations certainly support a tradition of attention to such details.

Norman armies evolved their own distinctions from their Frankish models. Missile troops were used more extensively, including archers, slingers, and the first documented use of the crossbow at the Battle of Hastings. Norman mercenaries fighting in Italy brought the stirrup and lance to western Europe (the partial transition from javelin thrust overhand to couched lance can be seen on the Bayeux Tapestry) and the result was a vastly improved cavalry charge. Stirrups allowed the mass and velocity of charging horse and rider to be concentrated on the point of the couched lance, a lesson learned from Byzantine cataphracts at Cannae in 1018. Stirrupless javelin cavalry could not withstand such a charge, nor could any but the most determined infantry. The lesson was not lost on practical Norman warriors, and by the 1070s the change to charging, lance-carrying cavalry seems to have been complete.

Breton allies and mercenaries retained the javelin throughout the period however, and preferred skirmishing with thrown javelins until an opportunity to charge in with swords and sidearms was presented. A Breton tactic, the feigned flight, was possibly a throwback to those Alans settled in Armorica (Brittany) by Romans in the chaotic fifth century. The tactic is recorded, by the chronicler William of Poitiers, as having been used successfully at Hastings, another instance of Norman willingness to adapt and innovate their style of warfare.

Another innovation of the time was the appearance of bodies of professional warriors, formed by enterprising nobles to hire out to other nobles, kings, and aspiring kings in order to flesh out, support, or supplant their regular standing forces. A substantial part of The Conqueror's army at Hastings consisted of such troops. The practice of forming these professional troops also points, albeit distantly, to the permanent companies and ultimately regiments formed in this manner by contractors in the 1500s through 1700s.

When William of Normandy landed at Pevensey in the fall of 1066 he and the army that accompanied him had a number of distinct advantages working for them. In less than a month, the English/Saxon army had already dealt with a raid by Tostig Godwinson (English King Harold's renegade brother) and a more serious full-scale invasion by King Harald Hardraada of Norway (an authentic hero and man of the world who was single-minded and ruthless in a manner reminiscent of William of Normandy). The Battles of Gate Fulford and Stamford Bridge had depleted the northern English levies, and although King Harold surprised and destroyed the Norse army at Stamford Bridge, killing Tostig and Hardraada as well, the victory was a bloody one and cost Harold losses he could ill afford in the ranks of his housecarls. These household troops, or bodyguards, were first-rate warriors. Clad in mail and using large axes that required both hands to wield, the housecarls were the only professional troops available to King Harold. The loss of a third or more of their number was a far more serious blow to English fortunes (Harold's fortunes) than the decimation of the northern feudal levy.

One is moved to pity King Harold: Prodigious feats of organization, marching, and tough fighting had availed him little. As he rested his foot-sore and wounded army at York, word reached him of William's arrival in the south. Less than a week had passed since the victory at Stamford Bridge. It is a measure of Harold's resolve and abilities that he would cobble together an army and fight again, over 200 miles away, in less than two weeks.

That William of Normandy profited from the works of Tostig and Harald Hardraada is without question. He seems to have communicated with Tostig when the latter was in Flanders a year earlier. Any suggestion of collaboration or alliance with the renegade Godwinson or Hardraada, beyond obviously wishing them well, is a matter that is very hard to determine with the facts at hand. Indeed, this aspect of the events of 1066 may remain a mystery for all time.

In the south, William had moved from Pevensey along the coast to establish a base at the more defensible port of Hastings. Aware of what had transpired in the north, the duke no doubt played down Harold's victory and broadcast the more comforting truth: Harold's army was tired, bloodied, and far away. Norman morale was also surely bolstered by the knowledge that Pope Alexander II had sanctioned what amounted to a "holy" crusade to regain what was rightfully William's: the throne of England. It is beyond the scope of this account to explain the near-Byzantine maneuvers to position this or that person to inherit the English crown that were undertaken in the latter days of Kind Edward the Confessor—or to discuss the merits of each of their claims. Suffice it to say that William the Bastard of Normandy and a sufficient number of nobles and mercenaries (and a pope) believed that he had a valid claim.

King Harold Godwinson defeated the Norse invasion of his country at Stamford Bridge on 25 September 1066. On 1 October he heard of the Norman landing in the south; in the middle of the night of 13 October King Harold encamped his exhausted army about seven miles north of Hastings. Prodigious marching and the housecarls' endurance had again succeeded in placing the English army in position to strike its foes. But the army that deployed on Senlac Hill the morning of 14 October was not the force that had prevailed at Stamford Bridge. The remaining housecarls formed the front rank of a massive phalanx-like formation. Supporting ranks were filled first by "Select Fyrd," fairly well-equipped landowners and freemen, and then by men of the "Great Fyrd": peasants, townspeople, and tenant farmers with a random assortment of simple, often ad hoc weapons. Except for the housecarls, the English army consisted of part-time troops with little training or organization. We know that the housecarls had few bowmen, and the southern feudal levies also seem to have contained fewer as well—a fact that, in the end, may have proved crucial. Certainly the command and control structure of this force was primitive. Harold seems to have believed he was outnumbered; he was certainly outclassed by the enemy army. He chose a defensive position that blocked the London road. On the slope of a hill, with both flanks anchored and the dependable housecarls in the front rank, King Harold prepared for the attack, which he thought would not be long in coming.

The Norman army has already been described in general terms. The force that took the field at what we call the Battle of Hastings consisted of three divisions: a Breton force on the left, Normans in the center, and French and Flemish on the right. Each division deployed a line of light infantry archers in front, supported by a line of infantry men-at-arms and followed by heavy cavalry. Estimates of numbers vary greatly. Based on what is known—that a hard and even struggle took place here for more than eight hours—it can be assumed that any advantage in efficiency on the Norman part was offset by the strength of the English position. It is thus possible to say that the two armies were evenly matched.

The Battle of Hastings was an all-day affair during which William attempted to break the English shield wall with almost no success. He finally was able to break the English line by feigning retreat and drawing some of the less disciplined of Harold's troops down the hill after him. There, on open ground, his cavalry could operate. William continued a rotation of archery harassment and infantry and cavalry assaults on the English throughout the afternoon. He ordered his archers, unopposed by a like force on the English side, to utilize high-angle fire so that their projectiles would plunge down onto the defenders from above. The English, given no relief from continued Norman assaults and missile fire, were approaching the limit of their endurance. At about this time, a chance arrow struck King Harold in the eye and wounded him mortally.

Taking heart from this development, William and his army renewed their attacks with vigor. The English army began to come apart. The Fyrd fled from Senlac Hill. Harold's housecarls stood firmly by their dying king. Now completely surrounded, they did not break so much as they simply reached a point where they could not hold together any more. A few diehards fought on in retreat through the dark, but by nightfall the Normans held Senlac Hill. Shortly after the battle, William seized Dover, then marched on London. Christmas Day of 1066 he was crowned William I, King of England.

The campaign to put William in that seat had amounted to a "national" effort by the Normans in planning, preparation, and ultimate conquest. A curious footnote to these endeavors is the unusual conquest of southern Italy and Sicily late in the eleventh century that can only be described as a triumph of individual initiatives and small cooperative ventures. Again the superiority of even small bodies of Norman troops, combined with resolute Norman leadership paid big dividends for those sufficiently daring.

Normans appear in the Mediterranean almost accidentally. Norman pilgrims returning from the Holy Land are recorded as having helped to defend Salerno against a Moslem attack. Fighting Moslems evidently seemed no harder than scrambling for inheritance and rewards back home, so before too long second (and subsequent) sons and a host of adventurers began showing up in Italy. The pilgrim route seems to have lost some appeal as well: Normans are subsequently mentioned in Italy as mercenaries for hire, and none too picky about who their employers were, either. A small Norman settlement appeared in Aversa under Rainulf in 1027 followed by expansion in Apulia and Calabria through the 1030s and 1050s.

George Maniakes's Byzantine army that invaded Sicily in 1038 included many Normans, as did many papal armies of the era. It is emblematic of the Norman experience in Italy that they fought for and against both the major players in the peninsula until their own position improved sufficiently to challenge their previous employers. These ruffians would soon prove to be a problem, as was illustrated in the Civitella campaign. A papal army of Pope Leo IX was trying to relieve the region of Apulia from Norman depredations (depredations were how Normans made themselves at home in those days). The brothers Humphrey and Robert Guiscard, with 3,000 men totally routed the papal army's mixed bag of Italians and Germans, of whom only the Germans put up a fight and were cut down to a man. The pope was handed over to the victorious Normans by the citizens of the town, who had witnessed the battle and could see which way the wind was blowing. It is surmised that Leo IX caused no more trouble.

A successor of Leo, Pope Nicholas II, was given time to form a better assessment of these Normans and wound up making a deal with Robert Guiscard: In exchange for help against German Emperor Henry IV, Robert was appointed Duke of Calabria and Apulia and authorized to conquer Sicily. Sicily was being held by the Moslems at the time and Nicholas wasn't too concerned with offending them. Dynasty-building seemed a Norman pastime. While conquering Sicily from the Moslems, Robert Guiscard and his associates also managed to pinch off Byzantine holdings in Italy—the last was Bari, taken in 1071. Not content with beating the Byzantines in Italy, Robert carried the fight to Greece in 1081. He won handily against Alexius Comnenus at Durazzo in 1082 and may have grabbed a large slice of Greece itself had he not been called back to Rome by the pope.

Pope Gregory VII had refused to recognize Henry IV as emperor. Henry, in a snit, besieged Rome in 1083. Hearing the pope's call for aid, Robert Guiscard collected an army of Normans, Moslems, and Lombards and marched north. Refusing to risk a battle, Henry withdrew. Robert's army then sacked Rome—whether as a warning to the pope or out of frustration is not really clear. A note of interest is the continued Norman use of foreign specialists and auxiliary troops in their armies. Lombard lancers, Moslem archers, and Italian infantry made up sizeable portions of the Norman armies in Italy and Sicily.

After squabbling with the papacy, the Byzantines, the Moslems, and one another, the Normans carved something like a kingdom out of southern Italy and Sicily from 1060 to 1300. As the Kingdom of the Two Sicilies, it would last for centuries, much longer than the Normans themselves. But history will not forget the vitality and skills—albeit often violent—of this great people.

—Michael Forbes

References: Davis, Ralph H. C., *The Normans and Their Myth* (London: Thames and Hudson, 1976); Lindsay, Jack, *The Normans and Their World* (New York: St. Martin's Press, 1975); Loyn, H. R., *Anglo-Saxon England and the Norman Conquest* (New York: Longman, 1991).

P

Paratroopers

Specialized troops trained to enter battle by parachute.

The concept of transporting soldiers by air behind enemy lines is as old as piloted flight, which began with the Montgolfier brothers' balloon in the 1700s. Napoleon considered using balloons to transport soldiers across the English Channel. In World War I observers in balloons were supplied with parachutes for emergencies, and visionary American General Billy Mitchell proposed dropping parachute troops behind German lines in 1919—had the war gone on that long. In 1922 the Russians began promoting private trials with parachutes and gliders. The first serious government paratrooper training began with the Italians, inspired by the air power theories of Giulio Douhet. In 1927 the best method of deploying the parachute was considered. The Italians chose the static cord method: A line connecting the parachute pack and the aircraft would pull the pack open and jerk the parachute out. Complete battalions were training by 1930 and the Italians organized two airborne divisions, but they never made a combat drop.

The United States Army toyed with parachuting in 1928 preferring the individual rip cord for deploying the chute. The use of paratroopers for sabotage was considered, but the army dropped any further development with the coming of the Great Depression. It was Germany that first realized the idea of airborne warfare. Hitler's government supported glider clubs as a method of training airplane pilots in contravention of the Treaty of Versailles. When he began to openly violate the treaty in 1935 gliders and pilots were developed and available. Because Germany was surrounded by countries with strong natural or man-made defenses, the concept of delivering troops behind those defenses appealed to Germany's military planners. In 1936 a paratrooper school was established at Stendal in Bavaria and, following Italian doctrine, the instructors chose the static line method of deployment. Command of the school fell to Major-General Oswalt Bassenge. No one knew exactly for what the paratroopers would be used or even which branch of the military would command the forces, but training went forward. These parachute forces were called in German *Fallschirmjaeger*.

Bassenge's school trained troops from the army, the Luftwaffe (air force), and the elite troops, Schutzstaffeln (SS), but there was no command coordination or organization. In 1938 when he was told to prepare for possible operations in Czechoslovakia, Bassenge informed the government and military that he could not possibly command a unit mixed with soldiers from various branches of the military and that some organization had to be created—both for training and combat operations. In response, the Luftwaffe commander-in-chief, Hermann Goering, appointed Major-General Kurt Student, commander of a Luftwaffe division, to command the paratroops. Student at this point really became the father of the German airborne forces. He organized the Seventh Flieger (Flyer) Division of both parachute and glider troops made up of troops from the SA (*Sturmabteilung*, the paramilitary wing of the Nazi party), the army's Sixteenth Infantry Regiment, and the Luftwaffe's Hermann Goering Division. His division consisted of two parachute and seven glider battalions. The Seventh Flieger Division saw no combat in Czechoslovakia because diplomats did the work in September 1938. However, Student did stage an exercise in Moravia after Germany occupied the Czech Sudetenland. It was an impressive drop, but soon afterward his men were dispersed back to their original organizations and Student was left with only a skeleton force. He was given permission to build up the Seventh Flieger Division and by the outbreak of war in September 1939 he had the parachutists trained. The army had guaranteed the Twenty-second Infantry Division to be available for transport to the battlefield by glider or transport aircraft.

The paratroopers were not used in combat when Germany invaded Poland in 1939, but Student was instructed to prepare for operations in Western Europe for the spring of 1940. Finally, in April of that year the airborne forces saw action. The operation was to be in support of the Nazi invasions of Denmark and Norway. The paratroopers were to seize airfields and hold them undamaged for German aircraft to bring in manpower and supplies. The two Danish targets were captured with no trouble, but bad weather and alert enemy troops made operations in Norway more difficult. Still, in spite of incurring casualties, the paratroopers secured their targets and proved the viability of the concept. In Holland in May 1940 gliderborne troops were used more widely in seizing Dutch forts and bridges in the area around Rotterdam. The Dutch were more prepared for airborne operations, having learned from the Norwegian experience, but the Germans still had some notable successes. Although some of their landings around Rotterdam were disasters, others went off without a hitch. The most successful of these came near Maastricht and the Albert Canal. Bridges across the canal had to be captured if the Germans were to easily invade Belgium, but their construction, preset demolition charges, and the extremely strong Eban-Emael Fort defied conventional attack. Glider troops aided by paratroopers, however, seized two of the three bridges intact and quickly captured the surprised garrison in Eban-Emael.

A U.S. soldier of the 82nd ABN Division.

Even more successful for the new airborne arm was the German invasion of Crete. The British army held strong positions on the island in the eastern Mediterranean and the Germans had no serious ability to mount an amphibious landing. Again, parachute and glider troops seized key airfields and allowed the Germans to funnel in troops and equipment. What was considered a virtually impregnable island fell in a matter of days with the help of these airborne forces. Successful as these operations were, however, they were the final major airborne operations Germany conducted. Although used again for airfield seizure in North Africa after the American landings, the paratrooper landing there was a small operation with limited effect. In the future, the paratroopers that had become elite forces were used strictly as infantry, fighting mostly in Italy.

British and American army commands were quick to grasp the potential of paratroopers, but only after the Germans proved the concept workable. The British committed a hastily trained battalion to combat in North Africa near the Algerian-Tunisian border. They were dropped in coordination with the American landings on the North African coast on 8 November 1942 and seized airfields held by the French colonial forces. British and American airborne forces took part in the Allied invasion of Sicily in summer 1943, and the results were tragic. Most of the Allied shipping lying off the coast had not been forewarned of the parachute drop and began firing at their own aircraft as the transports flew toward the drop zones. In addition, poor weather and an unnecessarily long and complicated flight plan caused some 60 percent of the gliders to crash into the sea rather than reach the island. In spite of the fiasco, those paratroopers and glider forces that did land did good work. British paratroopers seized a key bridge and held it long enough for amphibiously landed forces to link up to them. American paratroopers, although scattered over 65 miles, still managed to collect enough men to hold the key position of Gela Ridge against two German armored and several infantry assaults. A second landing a few days later fared little better when these paratroopers too were recipients of deadly "friendly" fire.

The best airborne operation the Americans conducted was on the night of 5–6 June 1944 as Allied forces invaded the Normandy coast in the famous D-Day landings. The American Eighty-second and 101st Airborne Divisions landed behind German lines in order to capture bridges and control road junctions to delay any German reinforcements sent to the beachhead. Although hampered by bad weather, the two divisions dropped by parachute and glider accomplished almost all of their objectives. Their next major operation, however, was not so successful. In the autumn of 1944 British General Bernard Montgomery designed a three-stage airborne operation to seize a set of bridges across rivers and canals in Holland. Once the bridges were in paratrooper possession, they were to hold them until armored columns linked up and relieved them. Poor planning and command decisions resulted in a fiasco, especially for the British First Airborne Division. That division held on to the bridge in Arnhem until overrun by a German counterattack, and the soldiers had to make their way individually and in small groups back to Allied lines. The American target bridges were captured and held, but as was observed after the operation, Arnhem was a bridge too far. For the remainder of the war, American airborne troops, like their German counterparts, for the most part fought as infantry. The 101st Airborne Division gained its greatest fame in this role by being one of the units holding the road junction of Bastogne, Belgium, during the Germans' last major offensive through the Ardennes Forest in December 1944: the famous Battle of the Bulge.

Paratroopers fought in the Pacific theater of operations as well. A small Japanese force was successful in capturing its objectives in Indonesia in January 1942. American paratroopers landed in New Guinea, where the jungle terrain made flanking operations difficult for conventional ground forces. When American forces returned to the Philippines in 1944 American paratroopers saw action on the islands of Leyte and Luzon and were involved in the recapture of the stronghold on Corregidor. World War II also saw the first use of paratroopers for commando operations, the role for which they are most used today. British General Orde Wingate jumped with his "Chindit" guerrillas into Burma to harass Japanese rear areas with some success.

After World War II, airborne training altered a bit. The soldier who was trained to jump out of airplanes with a parachute was still considered a member of the elite forces. Warfare in underdeveloped countries with poor road networks, however, made the need for large-scale airborne operations necessary. The introduction of the helicopter revolutionized airborne warfare. Starting initially with the American experience in Vietnam in 1965, large-scale, helicopter-borne assaults almost came to be considered conventional warfare. For small-unit actions, long-range reconnaissance, and commando operations, helicopters became the primary method of delivery.

In modern armies some airborne divisions still primarily depend on developing skills in parachute training, and special forces around the world (such as the Green Berets, French Foreign Legion, and the British Special Air Service) all have jump-trained soldiers. Paratrooper landings are still the preferred method of quiet insertion behind enemy lines, and for sabotage and other guerrilla operations, dropping by parachute will probably remain a necessary military skill.

References: Barker, Geoffrey, *A Concise History of the United States Airborne* (Brandon, FL: Anglo-American Publishing, 1989); Hickey, Michael, *Out of the Sky* (New York: Scribner, 1979); Weeks, John, *Assault from the Sky* (New York: Putnam, 1978).

Peoples of the Sea

A mysterious ancient population that brought about a Dark Age in ancient times, during the thirteenth and twelfth centuries B.C.

In the late thirteenth century B.C. the known world of the Middle East was fairly peaceful. The two major powers in the region, Egypt and the Hittites, had settled into spheres of influence, and the entire area was engaged in widespread trade. All of this was upset by the arrival of the Peoples of the Sea, or simply Sea Peoples. Whence they came has been the subject of debate since their first arrival more than 3,000 years ago. The primary contemporary accounts of these peoples are in Egyptian, with some few others from the eastern Mediterranean city-state of Ugarit. The Sea Peoples first appeared as invaders in 1218 or 1208 B.C., allied with the Libyan king Meryre. Meryre seems to have organized a coalition force of northern soldiers of fortune, but "northern" is an all-encompassing word in this case. The various peoples recruited included men of the Ekwesh, Lukka, Sherden, Shekelesh, and Teresh tribes. The Teresh have been identified (possibly) as Etruscan, the Shekelesh with the Sikels of Sicily, and the Ekwesh as Achaean Greeks. The Lukkans have been identified as pirates operating out of southwestern Anatolia, and the Sherdens seem to have given their name to Sardinia, although that may have been a later conquest. The Sherdens, however, were the first of the northerners to appear and, having been defeated by the Egyptians, began to fight with them, probably as mercenaries.

The introduction of the Sherdens to the Egyptian army could possibly signify a major change in military thinking at the time. For a few centuries, the dominant arm of the Middle Eastern armies were the chariots, so much so that by the late thirteenth century B.C. they were practically the sole arm, with infantry being used merely for policing, guard duty, and the occasional punitive expedition into rugged terrain where chariots could not go. Because chariots and the horses needed to pull them were expensive, the social elite became the military elite, while the masses remained unarmed and untrained for the most part. The Sherdens, however, introduced a new element to chariot warfare. Prior to this time, a support group of infantry, called runners, followed after the chariots in battle in order to finish off

Warriors fighting on board ships, in a naval battle with the Sea Peoples. A relief from the north wall of the main temple of Rameses III, Medinet Habu, Luxor-Thebes, Egypt.

wounded enemy soldiers and gather loot. The Sherdens, using newly introduced long swords and hunting javelins, became light infantry that moved quickly through the battlefields, disabling enemy horses and attacking enemy charioteers and archers. This proved extremely effective, so much so that the era of the chariot as a fighting machine was about to come to an end.

When Meryre invaded Egypt with his Sea People allies in 1218 or 1208 B.C., they came on foot and with few chariots. The allies were dressed in light body armor with horned helmets, long swords, and round shields. They invaded in the early years of the reign of Rameses II's son, Merneptah. At that time, the chariots of Egypt prevailed and the Libyans lost 6,000 dead, the Ekwesh 2,200, and other northerners significant numbers as well. Nine thousand swords were captured, but only 12 Libyan chariots, indicating Meryre's determination to fight with infantry.

This was just the beginning of the Sea Peoples' invasion, however. They had probably already overtaken mainland Greece (possibly identified with the Dorians who brought about the Greek Dark Ages) and also destroyed Troy in an action that may have been mentioned in the *Iliad*. In Homer's story of the siege, the foot soldiers of the invaders overcame the chariot forces of the Trojans. The Hittite Empire was overcome at this time (the early twelfth century B.C.) and invaders worked their way down the eastern Mediterranean coast, sacking Ugarit. As they approached the Egyptian frontier, Pharaoh Rameses III rallied his army to meet them. The two battles that ensued are memorialized on Rameses III's tomb at Medinet Habu. The inscription describes the successes of the invaders as they approached: "They laid their hands upon lands as far as the circuit of the earth, their hearts confident and trusting."

Apparently, Rameses III had learned from the failures of his neighbors, for when his army fought the Sea People invaders in 1175 B.C. he had abandoned most of his chariots and fought the first battle primarily with infantry; the second battle was a naval conflict. In both, the Egyptians were victorious, but the battles ultimately proved negatively decisive for Rameses and his descendants. With the development of trained infantry as the new dominant arm of the military, the era of the social and military elite was doomed. Masses of infantry, well trained and armed, were vital for the new armies, and the social repercussions were immense. Egypt began a downward slide from this point onward, and was never again a major power.

The Sea Peoples, while unable to conquer Egypt, did not leave the region. Many of the populations along the eastern Mediterranean coast are believed to be their descendants, particularly the Philistines. Indeed, the settlement of the Middle East in the wake of the invasion casts a dark age over much of the area, for no major power arose again until the Assyrians almost three hundred years later, between 1000 and 612 B.C. Whether the Sea Peoples were little more than professional soldiers of fortune who inflicted new weaponry and tactics on late Bronze Age societies, or whether they were mass populations engaged in migration more than conquest, is a question that may never be answered completely.

References: Drews, Robert, *The End of the Bronze Age* (Princeton, NJ: Princeton University Press, 1996); Sandars, N. K., "The Sea Peoples," in Cotterell, Arthur, *The Encyclopedia of Ancient Civilizations* (London: Rainbird Publishing, 1980); Silberman, Neil Asher, "The Coming of the Sea Peoples," in *Military History Quarterly*, vol. 10, no. 2 (Winter 1998).

Persians

Little is known of the military practices of the early Achmaenid Persians (559–331 B.C.) before Xerxes's invasion of Greece in 480 B.C. The early Persians must have possessed a sophisticated concept of war, for they managed to conquer and hold quite a large empire. They were probably drawing upon the military traditions of the Assyrians and the Medes, whose empires they assimilated, and combining them with the tribal methods of warfare of the eastern nomads. Regardless of how they acquired their military expertise, the army that Xerxes led into Europe was definitely an efficient fighting machine.

The heart of Xerxes's army was his heavy cavalry and an elite corps of infantry, the 10,000 Immortals (so-called because when one was killed another was supposedly waiting to take his place, thus maintaining their number). Around this unshakable core revolved the full panoply of the Persian horde: fighting men drawn from the far reaches of the empire, each contributing their own unique martial talents. Infantry composed the majority of the army and this more than likely was by design. Xerxes knew he would be fighting in hilly and broken country, besieging cities, and maneuvering in conjunction with his fleet. It is understandable that in such circumstances he would recruit more foot than horse soldiers. He could just as easily have fielded a force predominantly composed of cavalry.

Three features of the Persian army of this time are worth noting. The first is a heavy dependence upon the bow. It would appear that a majority of Persian troops carried bows, sometimes in addition to their other weapons. Persian tactics revolved around showering the enemy army with arrows until it became disorganized, then closing with the Immortals and the heavy cavalry for the *coup de grace*. It is fairly safe to assume that all the Asian peoples against whom the Persians fought used basically these same tactics. As a result, the Persian army evolved into a force skilled in skirmish and maneuver, able to withstand only short periods of hand-to-hand melee.

The second notable feature of the Persian army was a lack of body armor, aside from light chain mail for the Immortals and heavy cavalry. Because the troops stressed the skills of skirmish and maneuver, they had little need of personal body armor. A wicker shield and light mail provided about as much protection from an arrow as would a metal cuirass. One of the favorite tactics of the Immortals, for instance, was to form "mantelets" by standing their shields up with an attached prop, usually their rounded-end spear, and using this shield wall for cover while firing their bows. Also, because the Persian army bore the responsibility for the protection and control of the entire empire, troops were required to be able to march to any part of the country to repel invaders or put down rebellions. Mobility was vital to such a force, and the kings built military highways for that purpose. In an empire of such vast distances and often extreme temperatures, the disadvantages of armor, namely weight and heat, would not be offset by its protective advantages. Finally, armor was expensive and (aside from the Immortals and heavy cavalry) it appears there was no standing army. Troops levied from the subject races of the empire were responsible for their own equipment, and probably very few could afford costly chain mail.

The third important feature of the Persian army was its polyglot nature. Whenever the king assembled an army it would be slightly different. At least 20 different peoples fought alongside the Persians at one time or another. If this collection engendered no other problem than a language barrier, that alone would have been sufficient to cause great difficulties. But other problems can readily be imagined, such as racial and tribal hatred, differing dietary requirements, and differing customs and traditions. The fact that the early Achmaenid rulers managed to mold such divergent groups into an effective fighting force, capable of defending the empire, capturing Athens, and nearly conquering Greece, is a credit to their expertise and efficiency. It has been suggested by some historians that religion, in this case the Revelation of Zarathustra, also may have exerted a unifying influence on the Persians hordes.

However, in the century and a half between Xerxes's invasion of Europe and Alexander's invasion of Asia Minor, the Persian military system changed. Xerxes's

Persian warriors. Staircase of the Audience Hall of Darius I. Achmaenid period, Persepolis, Iran.

dreams ended with the Greek victory at Plataea in 479 B.C. in what the poet Aeschylus labeled the "triumph of the spear over the bow." Though simply stated, this sums up the situation. The Persian infantry, even the Immortals, could not stand up to the bronze-encased phalanx of the Greeks. The Persian rulers were immensely impressed by the fighting qualities of the hoplite. The Peloponnesian Wars had produced a large number of Greeks who had no trade except war, and they were more than willing to hire out to anyone who could pay. Rather than begin to train their own hoplites, the Persians found it easier and cheaper to hire large numbers of these Greek mercenaries.

The sheer power of the hoplite was demonstrated for all to see in 401 B.C. when 13,000 Greeks hired themselves to Cyrus the Younger for a war against his brother Artaxerxes. At the Battle of Cunaxa outside Babylon, the Greek phalanx was unstoppable and Cyrus was well on his way to becoming king. Unfortunately he had the ill-luck to get himself killed, and the remainder of his army melted away, leaving only the Greeks as a viable unit. Despite treachery and all Artaxerxes and his satraps could do to stop them, the Greeks stalked majestically 1,500 miles back to Greece with the majority of their force intact. This deed, known to history as the *Anabasis*, or "March of the 10,000," clearly illustrated that nothing in the Persian empire could stand up to the hoplites.

Before too long, most satraps in the western empire had forces of mercenary Greeks. By the time of Darius III, the Persian heavy infantry had disappeared, and the main infantry force was made up of the mercenaries, perhaps as many as 20,000. The demise of the Immortals may be attributed first to expenses. Throughout history, elite troops have been costly to maintain, and the Immortals were no exception. The Persian kings found they could not afford to pay both the Immortals and the Greek mercenaries, and since the hoplites consistently outperformed the Persian heavy infantry in combat, they seemed to represent a better investment. They were supplemented by native levies, half-armed peasants of questionable enthusiasm, and hill tribesmen, who were brave but undisciplined warriors. The majority of these levies were light infantry who fought with the javelin or bow. At Issus a force of young Persian recruits called *Cardaces* were put up against the Macedonians with disastrous results. The Cardaces probably represented an attempt by Darius to reconstitute an elite Persian unit, but they were squandered before their training was complete.

Another reason for the eclipse of the Persian infantry could have been the Persian land system. Aside from the Greek city-states along the coast, the entire empire was the king's land. He ruled it through satraps or through grants to large landowners. It was the duty of these men to provide fighting troops in return for their offices. By the time of Darius III, this had come to mean units of cavalry retainers instead of infantry. Horsemen were far more useful in governing the large Persian holdings. In this area at least, the quality of the local forces had not declined. However, Persian cavalry were still armed with the bow and javelin.

The armies of Darius, like those of Xerxes, were polyglot in nature, but there the resemblances end. The emphasis had shifted from fire power and maneuver to shock and melee. The proportion of cavalry was much higher in Darius's armies (by the time of Alexander the Great's victory at Gaugamela they probably constituted 40 percent of the total manpower), and the number of archers and bow-armed troops was lower. The Greek mercenaries had replaced native soldiers as the backbone of the Persian forces, and the hoplites' sole function was melee combat.

More importantly, the Persian army had lost the ability to work together in a combined fashion. The mercenaries were the only truly professional force left in the empire. The cavalry retainers and the subject tribes undoubtedly fought well at times, but they lacked the cohesion and tactical coordination that only a standing army could achieve. The entire thrust of Persian military thought had changed, partly as a result of their own neglect, and partly through exposure to the Greek world. Persian power became but a memory, and the Immortals marched only in the fading wall murals of crumbling palaces.

References: Aeschylus, *Persians*, trans. Edith Hall (Warminster: Aris & Phillips, 1996); Delbruck, Hans, *History of the Art of War* (Lincoln: University of Nebraska Press, 1991); Fuller, J. F. C., *The Generalship of Alexander* (Westport, CT: Greenwood, 1981).

Plains Indians

A native population of central North America. There were numerous tribes; the most notable were the Sioux, Cheyenne, Crow, Kiowa, and Comanche.

Included among the greatest light cavalry the world has ever seen must be the native people of the North American plains. They hunted mastodons and caribou, and later the great herds of buffalo that covered the plains. Although game was abundant, these early Indians faced severe logistical problems because they hunted and traveled on foot. New World horses had become extinct, probably due to overhunting by the Indians themselves. Since the buffalo herds moved constantly, the Indians had to follow and could keep only those possessions that they could carry themselves. The old, sick, or injured would frequently have to be abandoned as the hunting band moved on. Their existence must have been very poor in terms of material wealth. Native Americans simply did not have the opportunity to transform their cultures and their lives the way the Mongols, Huns, and other great steppe horse peoples of Asia did.

In 1540 the Spanish conquistador Francisco Coronado explored north from Mexico City in search of the Seven Cities of Gold. He took with him more than 1,200 horses and mules. When the Plains Indians saw these Spanish ride by, their world changed in an instant. They proceeded to steal every Spanish horse available and within a half century the horse had transformed the culture of the tribes living on the southern Great Plains and through them eventually all the Plains tribes. No longer were they earthbound hunter-gathers, but now they entered into history as the mounted and fearsome "Lords of the Plains."

From the northern to the southern Great Plains, an area stretching from modern-day Canada to Texas, the major Indian tribes were the Sioux, the Cheyenne, the Pawnee, the Crow, the Arapaho, the Kiowa, and the Comanche. Although each tribe had its own language and customs, they all had one overriding thing in common: their culture, their very way of life itself, was completely adapted to and dependent on the horse. The buffalo herds supplied the Indians with the necessities of life, such as food, shelter, and tools, but it was the horse that transformed that life. Mobility lent to them by the horse made the Plains Indians formidable foes, both strategically and tactically.

Strategically, the Indians presented no fixed targets at which their enemies could strike. Because they practiced no agriculture, they were not tied to the land, and they roamed freely over thousands of square miles of open prairie. Although they belonged to distinct tribes, the Indians actually lived most of their lives in small individual hunting bands of anywhere from 50 to 400 people. These hunting bands would congregate as tribal units once every one or two years for a great celebration or religious festival (sometimes known as a sun dance), but would quickly break up again as their food supplies dwindled. Every man, woman, and child in the band was mounted, and all the accouterments of their lives from tipis on down were designed to be easily transportable. A hunting band could easily travel 80 miles in a day, but if necessary could cover 200 miles in a 24-hour period. This mobility, combined with the vastness and emptiness of the land over which they roamed, made it almost impossible for slower-moving, European-influenced cavalry forces to even find the Indians, much less bring them to battle on favorable terms.

On a tactical level, the Indians held most of the advantages, too. All true Plains Indians fought only from horseback, armed with a short compound bow, long lance, and shield. Some Indians adopted firearms—especially repeating rifles—as they became available, but most tribesmen were indifferent marksmen at best. It was with the bow that they were most dangerous. At close range this powerful weapon could propel an arrow completely through a buffalo. A typical plains warrior could fire an arrow more than 200 yards, renock and fire three or four more missiles before the first had reached its mark, and do all this while riding his horse at full speed, controlling it only with knee pressure. Not only did Indians ride excellent horses, but every warrior took the warpath with several horses in tow, as opposed to the single animals organized cavalry or civilian militia forces rode. This tremendous advantage in quality and number of mounts allowed the Indians to pick and choose their fights, to fall back in the face of superior odds, to ride down inferior forces, and to easily escape when battle went against them. They always fought on their own terms, and almost never allowed their enemies, primarily the United States Cavalry, to bring superior weight in numbers or fire power to bear on them. For more than three centuries these warriors blocked the advances of Spain, then Mexico, and then the United States into their hunting grounds. Even the famous Texas Rangers did no better than to hold their own against these warrior peoples.

Every Plains Indian tribe possessed an in-

Sioux Indians charge Colonel Royall's detachment of cavalry, 17 June 1876.

tensely militaristic culture in which advancement in rank and prestige was based almost solely upon deeds in war and the hunt. Warriors sought to exceed each other in daring reckless exploits. For them, the greater the danger, the greater the honor gained. Among these peoples, warfare became as ritualized as among medieval knights, and warrior societies abounded. Every tribe had its elite fraternity, the best of the best. Among the Cheyenne, it was the Dog Soldiers, and among the Kiowas it was the *Koietsenko*, the Principal Dogs, both so-called to honor their faithful companions. Usually no more than ten members would be allowed, and each had to earn his place by numerous recognized acts of bravery, called "counting coup," which could include being the first to touch an enemy in combat, or stealing a horse, or taking a scalp. Election to these societies brought not only great prestige and political power, but also great responsibility. Each member had to be ready to lay down his life to protect the hunting band or tribe. Some wore a cloth or leather sash around their bodies, and in times of great danger would pin this sash to the ground with a knife or arrow, and there they would stay, in the path of the enemy, covering the retreat of their people until death. Only another member of their society could release them by unpinning the sash. These warrior elites set examples for all others to emulate, a pinnacle for which to strive.

At the end of the American Civil War, new U.S. Army leaders emerged, foremost among them William Tecumseh Sherman. During the Civil War, Sherman had been the leading proponent and practitioner of the concept known as "total war"—the idea that in war there are no noncombatants and no rules. In 1864 he had led an army across Confederate Georgia, burning everything in his path, and in the process had destroyed the will of Southerners to resist. By 1871 Sherman had become General of the Army, the highest ranking officer in the U.S. military, and he resolved to do the same thing to the Plains Indians that he had done to the Confederacy: Break the will of the enemy people to resist.

The first step in this process was to destroy the Indian's supply system. The buffalo herds appeared to be limitless, but they were not. At the urging of the U.S. government, tanning companies hired small armies of buffalo hunters (composed of men such as Buffalo Bill Cody) to harvest the buffalo for their hides. From 1872 to 1882 an estimated 20 million buffalo were slaughtered. Fewer than 1,200 animals were left by the end of the killing. This massive butchery shocked many, but General Philip Sheridan summed up the government's position when he said "Let them kill, skin, and exterminate the buffalo, as it is the only way for civilization to advance." Thus the Plains Indians' supply system, their principal means of sustaining life, was destroyed.

The second step in Sherman's plan was to strike directly at the Indians themselves. Sherman noted that the Indians' mobility was not complete. The horses they rode ate prairie grass, and during the dead of the winter there was no fodder for them. All the plains tribes passed the cold months in winter encampments, and during those months the Indians were nearly as immobile as the Confederate cities had been. The U.S. Army rode grain-fed horses and could carry fodder with their columns in wagons; they could even move infantry in wagons. In truth, the U.S. Army was not much slower in winter than they were in summer, but at least they could operate, so Sherman laid plans for a winter campaign on the southern plains in the fall and winter of 1874–1875. The purpose of this campaign was to sweep the plains with columns of cavalry and infantry, searching for the Indian encampments and, when discovered, to attack them. The intention was not so much to kill Indians, although Indians certainly were killed. Instead, the intention was to destroy everything that supported the Indians' way of life. This operation, known as the Red River War, was grimly effective. The army maintained a relentless pressure on the Indians, attacking them at every opportunity, destroying their homes and food supplies, and pursuing the survivors across the frigid plains. One by one, the exhausted southern tribes came into the reservations the government had established in order to surrender. Their horses and weapons were seized, and their chiefs were arrested and sent to far-off prisons. In this manner, the power of the tribes of the southern plains was broken.

On the northern plains, the U.S. Army did not fare as well. In June 1876 Lt. Colonel George Armstrong Custer and more than 260 men of the Seventh Cavalry were wiped out at the Battle of the Little Big Horn River by Sioux and Cheyenne warriors led by chiefs Crazy Horse and Sitting Bull. The Indian advantage was brief. Subjected to the full power of the U.S. Army, which utilized the same winter war tactics that had broken the southern tribes, the northern Indians were hounded from encampment to encampment, driven across the plains and even into Canada, before they too came to the reservations to surrender. By 1881 the last of the great nomadic warrior peoples in North America had finally submitted to overwhelming numbers and the power of modern civilization.

References: Hamilton, Allen, *Sentinel of the Southern Plains* (Fort Worth: TCU Press, 1987); Secoy, Frank, *Changing Military Patterns of the Great Plains Indians* (Lincoln: University of Nebraska Press, 1992); Utley, Robert, *Frontiersmen in Blue* (New York: Macmillan, 1967).

Polish Winged Hussars

An elite cavalry unit in Poland in the seventeenth century.

Traditionally, the term *hussar* is used to describe light cavalry. However, in Poland in the sixteenth and seventeenth centuries, special units of heavy cavalry dominated by Poland's nobility took the name hussar for their heavy cavalry units. The origin of the word probably derives from the Slavic word *gussar*, meaning "bandit," a term that described the harassing form of combat in which they engaged. In a time of heavily armored knights, lightly armored hussars were used mainly for scouting and pursuit. Large numbers of foreign volunteers swelled the ranks of Poland's army in what was that country's heyday as a European power.

The hussars who were accepted from other countries brought with them their traditional uniforms, which were among the most aggressively fashionable cavalry attire ever worn. The Polish nobility saw a chance to flaunt their wealth and position while serving their king and country, so the flashy hussar uniform drew them in large numbers. The nobility, however, had been the armored knights and preferred the role of attacking to scouting, so they blended their traditional role with the more fashionable name and uniforms.

The uniform that they adopted started with the traditional tight-fitting pants, fur-lined jackets with braiding, and round fur hats with flat tops. For protection, the hussar wore a metal breastplate and a skirt of chain mail or heavy cloth. In battle the fur hat was replaced by a metal bowl-shaped helmet. In keeping with his need for expression, the hussar often wore a cape made of leopard skin and lined with silk. The horses were decorated as well, the rider painting them with dye, fitting the harness and livery with brass, and festooning the horse with feathered plumes. For dress parade, the traditional wing-shaped shield would sometimes be topped with stuffed animals, such as eagles.

The most distinctive accoutrement, however, was the addition of tall feathered wings attached to the saddle or the hussar's back. There is some debate as to the function of these wings: some authorities say they were purely decorative; some say they were to foul lassoes used by steppe horsemen; some say that the feathers emitted a loud whistle when the horseman was at a gallop that enhanced the already fearsome visage of the onrushing cavalryman.

For weaponry, the Polish hussar had both a collection of personal arms and his steed itself. The type of horse necessary to bear an armored rider had long been bred in Europe, and the Poles mixed these with Arabian horses stolen or received as tribute from the Ottoman Empire. The strength, size, and endurance of the mixed breed made these horses among Europe's finest and only the wealthiest could afford them. Each hussar charged the enemy with a lance that measured as long as 24 feet, easily outreaching the pikes held by the defending infantry. Not surprisingly, the lance was also brightly decorated and strung with a pennant designating the rider's unit. The hussar operated in a time when firearms were making their first major appearance in Europe, and he often carried wheel-lock pistols himself. His primary weapon, however, was a sword, either a straight-bladed sword for stabbing or the standard curved sabre for slashing. Some also carried a six-pound sledgehammer for throwing; it was tied to a lanyard fastened to the saddle for easier retrieval.

The hussars rode into battle organized in a unit called a *poczet* ("post"), consisting of a nobleman and two to five retainers, depending on how many the nobleman could afford to equip. Multiple poczets were organized into a *choragiew* ("banner") numbering up to 200 men. This was the basic operational formation, and could be joined to as many as 40 more into a *pulk*, which operated as an independent division. Their main tactic was relatively simple: Mass into a wedge formation and break the enemy line. The hole would then be exploited by following infantry or light cavalry units while the hussars wrought havoc in the enemy rear.

The first major victory in which the hussars fought was in September 1605 at Kircholm near the Lithuanian border. Seven hundred of the winged hussars attacked a formation of 8,300 of Charles IX's Swedish infantry and broke them. They also distinguished themselves against the Russians at the battle of Klushino in 1610 where 3,800 horsemen and 200 infantry defeated a force of 30,000, killing 15,000. Against the Swedes at the battle of Sztum in 1629 the hussars stood out in what was an inconclusive battle except for the serious wounding of the great Swedish king and general Gustavus Adolphus. Perhaps the hussars' greatest glory was achieved among the later victories. Serving in the army of the great Polish leader, Jan Sobieski, they fought against the Turks and proved decisive in the battle of Chocim, where 30,000 Turkish soldiers were defeated and Poland was cleared of Turkish forces. The hussars were also prominent in Sobieski's 30,000-man force that defeated the Turks at Vienna in September 1683. There, on the right wing of the Polish-German force, they pierced the Turkish lines, found themselves surrounded and hacked their way out. They then reformed and charged again, breaking the Turkish line.

After the victory at Vienna, the hussars' days were numbered. By this time, armies were becoming increasingly dependent on firearms and the heavy cavalry was a dying breed. The Poles turned increasingly to the more traditional light cavalry for scouting and pursuit roles and the winged hussars faded away. They did, however, go out on a winning note, for they were never beaten in battle. Time and technology, not defeat, forced their demise.

Reference: Guttman, John, "Poland's Winged Warriors," *Military History*, vol. 10, no. 5 (December 1993).

Prussians

A population of a German state important in eighteenth- and nineteenth-century Europe, known for their military-dominated society.

The Treaty of Westphalia in 1648 ended the Thirty Years War. Perhaps in revulsion of the widespread devastation, warfare for the next one and a half centuries was more sedate. Professional armies fought only among themselves. Civilians were for the most part left out of the fighting, as governments now grasped the need for taxpayers and suppliers of food and material. European warfare settled almost into a great game, with alliances constantly shifting and no one country being allowed to dominate all others. In this atmosphere of increasing military professionalism, the most professional of European armies was born, created by Frederick William Hohenzollern, the great elector of Brandenburg (ruled 1640–1688).

In the seventeenth century, north central Europe was still a collection of duchies and principalities somewhat generically described as German. When Frederick William died, he left behind a powerful, though medium-sized Germanic state with a population of 1.5 million people and an army of some 28,000 men. In 1701 the Kingdom of Prussia was created from Frederick William's territories. The army he created was enlarged and polished by two successors, Frederick William I (ruled 1713–1749) and his son Frederick II (ruled 1740–1786). Frederick I took Prussia, which looked politically and socially like almost every other small European state, and turned it into a war machine the like of which had not been seen in Europe since Sparta in the sixth to fourth centuries B.C. He did it not so much with national pride as with iron discipline, forcing men into the ranks and keeping them there by brute force. The lash was a constant form of punishment and hanging (even for minor infractions) was used only slightly less often. Frederick did, however, create an army that was obedient to the will of its officers and its king, and it set the standard for armies in Europe until the French revolutionary army under Napoleon. By the end of Frederick I's reign, the army numbered 80,000 men, the fourth largest in Europe, and one that had one soldier for each 25 civilians.

However, it was under the rule of his son, Frederick II, that the Prussian army rose to its height in size and ability. Frederick II came to be called "the Great" for his military ability as well as his cultured court. Frederick the Great took his army into the War of the Austrian Succession in 1740 and soundly defeated the larger armies of his neighbors. In the Seven Years War (1756–1763) he successfully beat back almost continual invasions of Prussia by Austria, Russia, and France in possibly the most masterful use of interior lines ever seen. Although still a relatively small state in terms of overall population, Frederick's army was in 1763 the second largest in Europe at 162,000 men. He was also masterful in administering his government, keeping his country financially stable in spite of regular warfare, while larger states like France went bankrupt.

After Frederick the Great's death, however, the guiding hand was missing and sorely missed. The command structure, made up of Prussian aristocrats called Junkers, began to rest on its laurels. Although the previous monarchs had been innovators, the Prussian army at the end of the eighteenth century was secure in its traditional iron discipline and tested methods. It, like every other army in Europe, was completely unprepared for the French Revolution and the military transformation it brought about. With the overthrow of the aristocracy (the traditional breeding ground of officers throughout Europe), the French called on all equal citizens to defend their rights and their country. This led to the *levee en masse*, the conscription of huge numbers of soldiers. They were almost completely untrained, and for a time that was their advantage. Rather than march in lines, they swarmed the battlefield, and invading generals were at a loss about how to respond. Smaller professional armies were swamped by vast numbers of Frenchmen, who quickly became veterans. When a professional harnessed the size and enthusiasm of the French army, it became a virtual juggernaut. Napoleon Bonaparte was that professional, a military mind that appears in history only occasionally. He proceeded to dominate all of Europe, and the professional soldiers of other countries were no match.

In 1806 Napoleon invaded Prussia and the proud Junkers, secure in their traditional power, marched to destruction. At Jena and Auerstadt they were virtually slaughtered and Prussia was humbled. But Napoleon's

Prussian guards in Brussels, 25 November 1914

conquests took with them the seeds of his destruction. Nationalism became the motivating factor in military service, and citizens of other countries rallied to their nation as had the French. In Prussia a further modification took place, for here the army learned military as well as political and social lessons, and the result was the formation of the general staff concept. Prussians developed the concept of specializing various command necessities, such as planning, supply, intelligence gathering, recruiting, etc. They also developed a command for studying history and the military developments of other nations. After Napoleon's defeat, Prussian officers observed every war fought anywhere in order to learn from others' mistakes and advances. Observations were scrutinized and fine-tuned for inclusion in the Prussian army. Never again would an enemy's new strategies, tactics, or weaponry catch them unaware. Also in this time, military philosophy came into its own, and the Prussian Karl von Clausewitz's work *On War* became a bible for future soldiers and commanders.

In the 1860s the next major figure in Prussian history, Otto von Bismarck, began to exercise control. Bismarck was chancellor of the Prussian government under Kaiser Wilhelm I, and his dream of Prussian power took the state to its next level. Using the revitalized Prussian military, he embodied the Clausewitzian dictum that "war is an instrument of foreign policy by other means." He played his neighbors against each other and forged a shifting set of coalitions to consolidate Prussian political power in Shleswig-Holstein, south of Denmark. In 1866 he quickly crushed his recent ally Austria, then bound that country to him by means of a moderate peace treaty. In 1870 he trumped up an excuse to go to war with France and scored his greatest triumph. The French army, the largest of the time, was beaten in a rapid series of battles that not only destroyed the army but resulted in the capture of the French leader, Napoleon III. Paris held out for several months before finally surrendering in 1871. In the meantime, Bismarck had consolidated the remaining Germanic principalities into the nation of Germany.

Thus, after 1871 Prussia was the dominant state in a German nation. The general staff system that the Prussians had pioneered began to be copied by other nations. The military, which was born in the 1600s, had created the state of Germany more than two centuries later. However, the ambition of the German rulers, Wilhelm II in 1914 and Adolph Hitler in 1939, perverted that accomplishment by seeking not a stake in European politics, but world power.

References: Crankshaw, Edward, *Bismarck* (New York: Viking, 1981); Dupuy, Colonel Trevor N., *A Genius for War* (New York: Prentice-Hall, 1977).

R

Rangers

Elite commando units of the American colonial and United States armies.

The concept of rangers, or ranging units, developed during the wars between the colonists and the Indians in North America. They were first organized in 1670 and saw action in King Philip's War in Massachusetts from 1675 to 1676. They proved successful enough that when French colonists and their Indian allies began harassing the English colonial frontier in the 1750s new units were organized. The best known of these was Rogers's Rangers, organized by Robert Rogers of New Hampshire, who founded nine such companies to fight with the British regular army that was dispatched to North America in the ensuing French and Indian War. They fought using Indian tactics and proved quite successful—so much so that the British army began training some of their own troops in ranger tactics. Rogers is regarded somewhat as the father of the ranger concept, for he developed and implemented a training program for this style of fighting during the war. Much of their success, however, was tempered by a lack of discipline, which sometimes worked against them.

When the colonies rebelled against England in 1776 Rogers formed a company of rangers to fight on the side of the British against the colonists in New York and Connecticut. The Americans, of course, had plenty of men with experience fighting Indians, so it was little trouble to form ranger units of their own. The Continental Congress called for ten companies of expert riflemen to be raised. The accuracy of their rifles, in contrast to the commonly used musket of the time, proved valuable in many instances. Colonel Daniel Morgan's Riflemen played a key role in slowing General John Burgoyne's advance into New York by inflicting heavy losses at Freeman's Farm near Saratoga. In the south, Francis Marion's Partisans were all expert riflemen and horsemen who carried out numerous attacks on British supply bases in the Carolinas during Cornwallis's campaign in 1780–1781. Known as the Swamp Fox, Marion also intimidated area loyalists to ensure a lack of local intelligence for the British. Although Rogers fought for the British, his training and orders from the previous war were followed by Americans in the Revolution. The British again adopted ranger units themselves, as they had in the French and Indian War, mainly manned by American loyalists.

After the war, the American regular army shrunk to almost nothing, and the primary fighting units in the new United States were militia raised by each state. They often fought Indians and thus maintained the necessary skills to implement ranger tactics when necessary. Twelve ranger companies were on the active rolls during the War of 1812. One of the most famous of all ranger units, the Texas Rangers, was informally created in the Mexican province of Texas in the 1820s to fight Indians, then formalized as a unit in 1835

Conclave between Pontiac and Rogers's Rangers, ca. 1766 (Reproduction of a ca. 1912 painting)

during the war for Texas independence. The Texas Rangers proved most effective in scouting and guerrilla operations during the ensuing Mexican-American War of 1846–1848.

In the American Civil War, partisan ranger units were employed by both sides, though more often by the Confederacy. Colonel John Mosby was probably the premiere ranger commander of this war, although units under the command of John Hunt Morgan and Turner Ashby were also effective in behind-the-lines attacks to interdict Union supply lines. Morgan's Rangers carried out the deepest penetration of the Union by any Confederate unit when they attacked through Kentucky into Indiana and almost to Lake Erie before they were caught and captured near East Liverpool, Ohio, in 1863. This incursion so frightened Union commanders that men assigned to Tennessee for the upcoming battle at Chickamauga were withdrawn to protect rear areas.

After the Civil War, there were no formal ranger units, although some cavalry commanders employed Indian-style tactics in fighting the tribes of the Great Plains. Not until 1942 was a unit organized and again given the name "Rangers." At that time, 2,000 Americans were trained in Ireland by British commandos. The 500 that completed the training came to be the First Ranger Battalion under the command of Colonel William Darby. Some of these men took place in the abortive Dieppe raid on the coast of northern France in August 1942. They fought in Algeria when American forces landed there in November 1942 and received a presidential unit citation for their service in the battle of El Guettar in March 1943. Darby organized two more battalions of rangers in North Africa and all three together became the Ranger Force, better known as Darby's Rangers. They served in the invasion of Sicily in the summer of 1943 and then took part in major operations in Italy, including holding the Chunzi Pass against eight German attacks in 18 days. They also played a key role in neutralizing beach defenses at Anzio on 22 January 1944. On 1 February 1944 the unit was destroyed almost to the last man while attempting to infiltrate the Italian town of Cisterna; the six survivors went back to the United States to join the Canadian-American Special Service Force, the so-called Devil's Brigade.

Colonel James Rudder commanded a new ranger unit formed at Camp Forrest in Tennessee in 1943. These men landed at Omaha Beach on the Normandy coast early in the morning of D-Day on 6 June 1944 and scaled cliffs at the heavily defended Pont du Hoc where German artillery was causing extreme casualties. As the Americans were pinned down by heavy German fire, Twenty-ninth Infantry Division commander Norman Cota ordered the Fifth Ranger Battalion, "Rangers, lead the way off this beach." The motto "Rangers lead the way" was born here.

Ranger units also operated in the Pacific theater, where they were known as Raider Battalions among the marines. One of the chief army units was under the command of Lieutenant Colonel Henry Mace. His Sixth Ranger Battalion went into the Philippines in September 1944 and carried out many missions behind Japanese lines. In January 1945 they liberated a prison camp at Cabanatuan, defeating 200 Japanese defenders for the loss of two killed and ten wounded while freeing 500 American and Filipino prisoners.

The ranger units were once again disbanded at war's end but were reborn in 1950 at Fort Benning, Georgia, under Colonel John Gibson van Houton. He was ordered to create a ranger headquarters and four airborne ranger companies. Most of the volunteers for the ranger school came from the Eighty-second Airborne Division. The men were taught infiltration techniques, sabotage, demolition and familiarization with U.S. and foreign weapons. The first class was composed of eight companies, each of which was assigned to an infantry division. They saw their first action in Korea where they carried out scouting missions, ambushes, and long-range patrolling. One of their major successes was the destruction of the Twelfth North Korean Division Headquarters nine miles behind enemy lines. One of the companies, the Sixth, was transferred to Europe in the face of increasing communist activity. The final ranger company graduated from Fort Benning in October 1951.

U.S. Army Rangers check the movement of a military convoy behind a wall near the Kuwaiti border, 20 January 1991.

In Vietnam, ranger tactics were once again introduced in the form of Long Range Reconnaissance Patrols (LRRPs). Thirteen LRRP companies assigned to various brigades and divisions maintained the ranger tradition of deep patrolling, ambush, and intelligence gathering. As the original rangers had done, the Vietnam-era soldiers fought in the style of the enemy and usually beat them at their own game. On 1 June 1969 the companies were banded together to create the Seventy-fifth Infantry Regiment (Ranger). It was deactivated after the war, as all previous ranger units had been. This pattern of creation during wartime and recreation during the next war came to an end in 1973 when Army Chief of Staff Creighton Abrams called for a permanent ranger establishment. The First Ranger Battalion was stationed at Fort Stewart, Georgia, and the Second Ranger Battalion at Fort Lewis, Washington. A small detachment of rangers operated as security forces for the abortive Iran hostage rescue mission in 1980. The rangers were also among the first troops into Grenada on 25 October 1983 securing the airfield at Salines as well as the medical school campus where American students were located. The operation was marked by confusion, mainly on the part of the aircraft carrying the ranger units, which had little training in night flying operations. On 27 October they captured the Cuban barracks at Calivigny. The barracks were undefended, but a number of casualties were suffered in helicopter accidents.

A year later, the army activated the Third Ranger Battalion, followed by the formation of the Seventy-fifth Ranger Regimental Headquarters at Fort Benning in 1986. The unit strength was nearly 2,000 men, and all of them took part in the 1989 Operation Just Cause, the invasion of Panama. Again, their assignment was to capture and hold the main airfields. They also assisted in the capture of the headquarters of the Panamanian Defense Forces and guarded the Vatican embassy, where President Manuel Noriega took refuge before his surrender. Rangers also conducted raids during Desert Storm in 1991 and were deployed in Somalia in 1993. Here they engaged in a serious fire fight with the supporters of local warlord Mohammed Aidid and lost six dead and several wounded—more losses than they suffered in the Desert Storm and Panama operations combined.

The ranger tradition established in the days of the American colonies remains active in today's rangers, who continue to train to fight by stealth and surprise in order to inflict as much psychological as physical damage on their enemies.

References: King, Michael, *Rangers* (Ft. Leavenworth: Combat Studies Institute, 1985); Payne, Chuck, "'Rangers Lead the Way': The History of the U.S. Army Rangers" (http://users.aol.com/armysof1/Ranger.html).

Red Shirts

Volunteer troops who followed Italian revolutionary Giuseppi Garibaldi, 1834–1867.

The Italian peninsula in the mid-nineteenth century was a hotbed of political intrigue. Ever since 1820, Italian nationalists inspired by French revolutionary ideals had attempted to unite the peninsula, but they had consistently been defeated by Austrian armies. In 1848–1849 Italian forces had better luck and succeeded in forcing some Austrian retreats, but they were unable to prevail over the talented Austrian General Radetzky. Radetzky, with French reinforcements, besieged Rome from April to June 1849. When the city fell, Austria was once again master of most of Italy. But despite the variety of independent kingdoms within the peninsula and the direct or indirect control of Austria, a movement toward Italian unification persisted. The most likely leader of a unified Italy was Victor Emmanuel of the house of Savoy, king of the Piedmont. His able and Machiavellian prime minister was Count Camillo di Cavour, who wheeled and dealed with all the players in the Italian drama.

In 1859 Piedmont, aided by Emperor Napoleon III of France, fought a short war against Austria for control of the northern provinces. Although Austria lost all its battles, it kept its army intact and in Italy. Austrian Emperor Franz Josef and Napoleon negotiated a settlement without consulting Cavour or any other Italian, leaving an even more unsettled situation as Piedmont, the Papal States of central Italy, Austria, and France saw the war end with no final settlement distributing territory. In 1860 Cavour once again negotiated with Napoleon III, secretly promising him the provinces of Nice and Savoy along the French border in return for a free hand and French support in Piedmont's acquisition of central Italy. That deal, made public in March 1860, infuriated Italy's premiere revolutionary, Giuseppi Garibaldi.

Garibaldi, as a young Sardinian sailor, had been fighting for Italian unification and independence since 1834. Fleeing Austrian captivity that year, he moved to South America where he helped defend Montevideo, Uruguay, from Argentine aggression. His followers there, in need of uniforms, acquired the only consistent outfits they could: surplus red tunics manufactured for slaughterhouse workers. For the remainder of his career, Garibaldi's followers would be identified by their red shirts. He led a contingent of 5,000 in the defense of Rome in 1849 and made the French pay dearly for their capture of the city; he then fled to America. He spent a number of years in the United States and even became a citizen, but he could not stay away from his troubled homeland. When he learned of Cavour's arrangement with Napoleon III, Garibaldi returned to action. He gave lip service to Victor Emmanuel and by doing so gained covert aid from Cavour's government. With Peidmontese weapons and financial aid, Garibaldi in 1860 went back to war.

Garibaldi, at heart a republican, seemed willing to accept a monarchy under Victor Emmanuel if it would unite Italy. As unification needed to start somewhere, Garibaldi took advantage of political strife in the southern Kingdom of the Two Sicilies. When the harsh government based in the capital city of Naples moved to suppress popular uprisings on the island of Sicily, Garibaldi and his nationalist followers invaded. "Garibaldi's Thousand" landed on 4 April 1860 at Marsala and rallied the Sicilian population. They defeated the Neapolitan forces at Calatafimi in mid-May and captured Palermo on 27 May, then defeated another Neapolitan force near Messina on 20 July. With the aid of British naval vessels, Garibaldi's men crossed the Straits of Messina and marched on Naples, capturing the city against only slight opposition on 7 September. The Neapolitan king, Francis II, withdrew the bulk of his force northward to the fortress of Gaeta, which Garibaldi soon besieged.

As Garibaldi was overthrowing the tyrannical Neapolitan government, Cavour maneuvered. While supplying Garibaldi with equipment and trained men, Cavour was obliged to publicly criticize the invasion in order to keep his involvement secret. He also directed his own General Manfredo Fanti to invade the Papal States in order to support "popular risings," which Cavour had secretly instigated. Napoleon III, who had a Catholic population to keep happy, guaranteed Pope Pius IX's safety. He had, of course, already ceded to Cavour the occupation of central Italy when he received Nice and Savoy earlier in the year. So, like Cavour's public/private dichotomy over Garibaldi's offensive, Napoleon III had to play the same game concerning the Piedmontese advance toward Rome. As long as the city was not occupied, the pope was not harmed, and no French possessions were attacked, Cavour had Napoleon III's private permission to do what he liked. Napoleon also urged Cavour to protect Rome and the pope from Garibaldi.

The Red Shirts besieged Gaeta from 3 November 1860 through 13 February 1861. Garibaldi realized that, while his forces had plenty of revolutionary ardor, they did not have the patience to maintain a long siege. He therefore was obliged to request Cavour's assistance in capturing the fortress. Piedmontese ships bombarded Gaeta and forced its surrender. Shortly thereafter, an all-Italian parliament declared Victor Emmanuel king of all Italy. Cavour died shortly thereafter, but Garibaldi was intent on finishing the job of unification by including Rome and Venice, both of which remained independent. Victor Emmanuel covertly supported occasional attempts at besieging Rome, but the French had made a public promise to protect the pope and they stood by it. When Garibaldi returned from Sicily in late summer 1862 to march on Rome, the new Italian government could not allow this idealist to upset their close relations with Napoleon III's France. At the battle of Aspromonte Italian forces defeated Garibaldi's army on 29 August 1862. Garibaldi was taken prisoner, but was released with all of his men shortly afterward.

Garibaldi was not yet finished. In May 1866 Italy concluded a mutual defense treaty with Prussia, and a month later declared war on Austria to coincide with Prussia's attack on that country. Garibaldi's charisma was such that 30,000 men flocked to his banner when he called for volunteers. Garibaldi hoped that an Austrian defeat would mean liberation of Venice from Austrian control and Italian annexation of the city. Garibaldi's force gained some small successes in the Alps, but the poor performance of the Italian regular army, as well as the short duration of the war, kept him from gaining any territory for his country. However, the Austrians did give up Venice to France in return for French aid in negotiating with Prussia and Napoleon III gave the city to Italy. All that was left to make a completely unified nation was to acquire the traditional capital city, Rome.

Garibaldi took it upon himself to wrest political control of Rome away from the pope. Victor Emmanuel again tacitly supported him. France, which had evacuated its defensive forces from Rome in December 1866, seemed to be abdicating its responsibility to Pope Pius. Garibaldi therefore organized yet another force of volunteers to annex Rome and invaded what was left of papal territory in January 1867. Napoleon III had to respond. Recently expelled from Mexico and fearful of the rising influence of Prussia, the French leader believed that France could not appear weak. In October 1867 Napoleon III sent 2,000 men to Rome. Combined with 3,000 papal troops, the French General de Failly met Garibaldi's 4,000 at Mentana, near Rome, on 3 November. The French, armed with the new, rapid-firing *chassepot* rifle, mauled the Red Shirts in their final battle. Italian authorities arrested Garibaldi and his men, but again released them quickly. Garibaldi was forced to remain on the sidelines when in 1870 Italian forces finally captured Rome.

In spite of his long war against the French, Garibaldi and his two sons went to France in 1870 and fought against the Prussian invasion there. Afterward he returned to his home on the island of Caprera. His fighting days done, he was elected to the Italian parliament in 1874, and he died in 1882.

References: Coppa, Frank, *The Origin of the Italian Wars of Independence* (New York: Longman, 1992); DePolnay, Peter, *Garibaldi, the Man and the Legend* (New York: T. Nelson, 1961); Hibbert, Christopher, *Garibaldi and His Enemies* (London: Longman, 1965).

Redcoats

British army soldiers from the seventeenth through nineteenth centuries.

Although the British army of the eighteenth and nineteenth centuries was one of the smallest European regular armies, it developed a reputation as one of the best. The soldiers were recognizable by the red coats of their uniforms, a bright color that seems incongruous for combat—considering the dull camouflage uniforms of modern armies. This was not mere affectation, for all the armies of the time wore distinctive colored uniforms. The color was not chosen just because it looked good while the troops marched and drilled, but because of the nature of the battles of the time. Massed musket fire at close range was necessary then because of the lack of range and accuracy of the weapon, and the smoke created by the black powder created a hazy view. The nearness of the forces at the time of firing meant that the troops, having fired, closed on each other quickly with bayonets. In the resulting melee, the chaos of the struggling bodies obscured by the massive amounts of smoke made it necessary for soldiers to immediately recognize who was on their side and who was an enemy. Brightly colored uniforms were helpful in making this crucial determination.

The men recruited into the British army were hardly the elite, despite the high quality of the army in battle. Although most of the officer corps were of the upper classes, because commissions were available for purchase, the foot soldier was an English, Irish, or Scottish peasant. Usually they were recruited young, when the urge for adventure and an escape from the monotony of the farm was greatest. They were also recruited from the jails, especially in time of war when men were needed quickly. Young men on the run from a bad home life, an unexpectedly pregnant girlfriend, or through peer pressure joined the ranks, described at the time as "taking the King's shilling," the first payment upon joining.

Pay for the soldiers was small, and what they received was required for the purchase of daily rations. Money was held back from their wage to pay for the new uniforms they were to receive annually, as well as to pay for the replacement of sundries like socks, shirts, hats, etc. As the pay was distributed to the regimental commander for disbursement, anything he could save by issuing lower quality goods meant extra money in his own pocket. All this meant that, while food, shelter, and clothing were provided more regularly in the army than some were used to as civilians, joining the army was no way for a young man to put money aside for his future. Moreover, when that future arrived was somewhat problematic. Usually recruits (especially the criminal types) were discharged after six months or at the end of the conflict. Because the British populace traditionally feared a large standing army as a potential

British soldiers surround General Wolfe, killed at the Siege of Quebec, 1759.

tool of abuse by the king, regiments brought to full strength for wartime were cut to cadre strength or disbanded when the fighting stopped. If a soldier found that he liked the army life or had no reason to return to civilian life, opportunity for reenlistment in another unit was high.

For the first year of his enlistment (if in peacetime), the British recruit learned to march in close order drill and to handle his musket. Musket firing was rare, although the practice of loading and reloading was repeated over and over. Unless the country was at war, the government was hesitant to pay for large numbers of musket balls, so actual live firing may have been done once or twice a year, hardly enough to gain proficiency at marksmanship. Marksmanship was one talent with limited usefulness in armies of the day, for the musket was a highly inaccurate weapon. Therefore, the need to load, aim, and fire by the numbers—that is, to volley fire—became more important than accuracy. The British platoons went into battle in three ranks: the first knelt, the second crouched, and the rear line stood, all according to directions laid out in the regulations written in 1728 which were taken almost directly from Humphrey Bland's 1727 *Treatise of Military Discipline*. In later modifications, the ranks also staggered themselves so that they shot between as well as over the soldiers in front of them. The ability of the redcoats to exercise discipline in firing volleys in combat was one of the factors that made them superior to most continental armies of the time. The soldiers also received slight instruction in the aggressive use of the bayonet, it being primarily viewed as a defensive weapon.

Incessant marching and countermarching drilled into the soldier the instant and unthinking response to orders. After several months or a year the unit began weekly or semiweekly drill with other units, learning how brigades and ultimately armies moved in coordination on the battlefield. This drill proved vital to the performance of the soldiers in battle. Just as important to performance was the discipline a redcoat recruit received—not just the ability to follow orders—but the punishment that came from not doing so. In the British army punishment was detailed for a large variety of offenses, with the most common penalty being flogging. Up to 1,200 lashes could be imposed as a sentence, although they were usually not given all at once. Lesser offenses brought extra duty, while more serious offenses warranted execution. As the sentence was usually imposed and carried out by the sergeant, and only occasionally by officers, the soldiers came to fear their sergeant even more than the enemy. This also proved valuable on the battlefield.

The British proved themselves steady and disciplined in the series of continental wars fought through the first half of the eighteenth century. When they fought in North America, however, they began to adapt some of the frontier tactics of the colonists to their own forces. The rough terrain and guerrilla tactics employed by the Indians and their French allies in the American colonies obliged the British to respond in kind. Not only did they use colonial militia but they began organizing separate platoons and companies to fight in a more open style. Grenadier units served on the flanks of the regular battalions and regiments, and in the French and Indian War (1755–1760) light infantry units also were created to act as skirmishers and provide rapid response for flank protection or following up a retreating enemy. Independent ranger units were created as well, operating away from the regular troops in scouting and ambush roles.

A new training manual was introduced in 1792, adapted from Colonel David Dundas's 1788 *Principles of Military Movements*. (A 1778 manual, introduced in the midst of the American Revolution, was never really used.) Having learned in North America that a few shots followed by a bayonet charge incurred fewer casualties, Dundas introduced this new method of combat in his work. The soldiers now formed two ranks when firing rather than three, but both ranks stood and locked themselves into a tightly packed mass with (theoretically) each man taking up 22 inches of space but in reality being jammed up against each other. This created a solid mass of fire, and the new regulations called for firing not by platoons but by battalions as a whole. This type of fire would create a massive hole in the enemy ranks, which hopefully a determined bayonet charge would then exploit. Dundas did not widely incorporate the use of light infantry tactics developed in America, however, although he did recognize them as an accepted part of every regiment. The light infantry again served as scouts and skirmishers, and more importantly (in the long run) were equipped not with muskets, but with rifles. With more accuracy, the riflemen were charged with sniping and harassment, something difficult to do with short-range muskets. Muskets, however, being easier and quicker to load, remained the primary weapon for the majority of the soldiers.

The redcoats did not fight the French directly for much of the Napoleonic Wars, but did engage them extensively in Spain between 1808 and 1814. Napoleon established authority over Spain early in his tenure as emperor of France and later installed his brother on the throne. England provided the army to assist the Spanish monarchy. Under the able command of Arthur Wellesley and with the assistance of Portuguese and Spanish troops and guerrillas, Spain became a major thorn in Napoleon's side. When Napoleon escaped his exile on the island of Elba in 1815 it was the British army (supported by the Prussians) that dealt him his final defeat. Wellesley, now the duke of Wellington, and his redcoats defeated Napoleon at Waterloo and gained both the duke's and the army's greatest fame.

The British army had no more continental fighting for 40 years, but fought regularly against colonial forces around the world. The redcoats fought in Africa, India, Canada—anywhere the British Empire held sway. As long as the musket was the primary weapon, the "thin red line of heroes," as Kipling called them, were the mainstay of British land power. Over time, however, two things worked to change that. One was the increasing number of campaigns fought in rough terrain against guerrilla enemies, wherein red uniforms were easy targets for snipers. The second was the introduction of the rifle as the main weapon of almost every army in the world. With increased range and accuracy, close ranks of men were now too easy to hit from great distances, so more open formations and more subtle uniform coloration became a necessity. The last major conflict in which the redcoats were prominent was the Crimean War of 1854–1856 but that was also the last major war with muskets. The American Civil War was fought primarily with rifles and rifled muskets, and the close formation (while still used) proved itself to be a recipe for disaster as defensive positions and massed artillery became primary tactics. The last time the British went into combat with redcoats was in the first Boer War, in 1881. The Dutch South African farmers, however, were not only equipped with modern rifles, they were experienced with them. Although the red-coated troops had fought against the Zulus just a few years earlier, against modern weaponry this practice had become suicide. After this time, red uniforms were relegated strictly to the parade ground.

References: Chandler, David, and I. F. W. Beckett, *Oxford Illustrated History of the British Army* (London: Oxford University Press, 1994); Reid, Stuart, *British Redcoat, 1740–1793* (London: Reed International, 1996); Reid, Stuart, *British Redcoat, 1793–1815* (London: Reed International, 1997).

Romans

A population centered in present-day Italy that built the dominant empire of the European and Mediterranean world from the sixth century B.C. to the fifth century A.D.

The soldiers that laid the groundwork for the Roman Empire and the Pax Romana were the Bronze Age warriors of the Etruscan civilization. These men fought primarily with spears, or swords if they were wealthy enough. Those even wealthier who could afford horses fought as cavalry. They followed a king and fought, as did most of the ancient world, in the phalanx formation. The basic unit of the early army was the *century*, made up—not surprisingly—of 100 men. These centuries were grouped together as legions, probably numbering at full strength 4,000 men. When the century and legion were created, the ancient warriors became soldiers, fighting as a team rather than as individuals. The Etruscans of central Italy, the people who ultimately became Romans, were governed by monarchs until 509 B.C., the traditional date of the founding of the Roman Republic.

As Rome became a more organized society and expanded its borders, its increasing wealth meant that the army was better supplied and armed. Rome depended on citizen soldiers who spent the majority of their time farming but responded to the government's call in time of emergency. The aristocracy provided the officer corps and, as before, the better-armed soldiers. Because the independent farmers formed the bulk of the army, however, they could often influence—if not control—the military and its decision making. From the fifth through the third century B.C. the upper class patricians and the lower class plebians struggled for both military and political control in what was called the Struggle of the Orders. In this time Rome was regularly at war, so the patricians needed to keep the plebians content in order to ensure the necessary numbers on the battlefield. As the wars began to range further afield, necessitating longer time away from the farm that provided the farmers' sole means of support, the government in the fifth century began appropriating money to pay its soldiers and to provide for more standardized equipment. Longer service began to be rewarded by rank and pay, and midlevel command gradually went to experienced veterans rather than well-born aristocrats. However, the wealthy dominated the government after the third century and only the chief executives, known as consuls, had the authority to assume the top command.

As long as the Romans fought along the coastal plains, the phalanx formation served them well. However, when they fought enemies in the rugged terrain of central Italy, they found it necessary to alter their organization and tactics. The legion was the primary unit, although now expanded slightly to 4,200 at full strength. The new unit was the *maniple*, consisting of two centuries, although that term now designated a unit type rather than exactly 100 men. The army began to go into battle, not in the squares of the phalanx, but in lines. The first line was made up of 1,200 men, the youngest and least experienced soldiers, with gaps between the maniples. The second line, staggered so that its maniples matched the gaps in the first line, was made up of 1,200 men with greater age and experience. The third line, again staggered to match the gaps in the second line (thereby creating a checkerboard pattern) was comprised of 600 of the most experienced veterans. The remaining 1,200 men of the legion were used as light infantry, skirmishers, and scouts. Ten 80-man cavalry squadrons fought on the flanks. The infantry in the three lines were armored with helmet, chestplate, and greaves, and carried a large oval shield. The younger front-line soldiers carried the traditional thrusting spear but the men in the second and third lines now carried a throwing spear, called a *pilum*. All the men carried a *gladius*, a short double-edged thrusting sword.

Praetorian soldiers, from a Hadrianic relief (Louvre, Paris)

This improved weaponry called for better training, especially with the gladius. This in turn required more time spent away from the farm in order to master the weapons, and hence a greater need for longer-term soldiers. When war was frequent and close by, combat itself provided sufficient training for the soldiers. Campaigns began to take place farther and farther away, however, again pointing up the need for long-term professionals. So long as the government required some property ownership for membership in the army, farmers could not grow the necessary crops to feed the nation and fight foreign wars at the same time. As Rome and other cities grew, fewer people were left as farming property owners. After the destruction of much of the Italian countryside during 17 years of Carthaginian campaigning in the Second Punic War, even fewer farms existed. The urban population had to be included in the military. That meant soldiering would no longer be a civic duty, but a profession.

The leader that brought about this change was Marius. In the Roman wars against the African leader Jugurtha (111–106 B.C.), Marius began recruiting the poverty-stricken city dwellers to his army. To pay them, he promised loot and pillage after battle plus a cash bonus or a land grant at war's end. This solved the problem of manpower, but it also created what was, in effect, a private army raised by Marius, not the government. Although he was a consul and therefore the legal commander in chief, the army was still his personal organization. Marius also reformed the legion in light of experience in northern campaigns against Germanic tribes. The legion was expanded to include 5,000 to 6,000 men, and the maniple was replaced by the *cohort*, a unit of six centuries. Marius also did away with the light infantry. He introduced rigorous training procedures that developed not only skill with weapons but overall physical fitness as well. He made the army more mobile when he reduced its baggage train by loading up each soldier with 80 to 100 pounds of equipment. The legion was given a silver or gold eagle for its standard, promoting esprit de corps.

All this worked well, and Marius was successful in a number of foreign campaigns and in defending the Italian peninsula from invasion. However, when he began to use his army for political influence, the nature of Roman government and society began to change. For a long time, the average soldier remained loyal to the government, but when his commander provided his pay and bonuses, a soldier's loyalty could easily shift. In the early decades of the first century B.C. garnering an army command and its soldiers' loyalty became the most important path to political power. By midcentury, Julius Caesar had invaded Italy from Gaul, defeated other consular armies, and made himself consul for life. This violated the long-standing law of year-long terms for consuls and provoked Caesar's assassination. By that time, however, generals held the political power, and Caesar's nephew and successor, Octavian, became Rome's first emperor, forever abolishing the Republic.

Once in power, Octavian (who took the name Augustus) worked to remove the army from the political realm. He divided Rome's foreign holdings into imperial and senatorial provinces, with the army based in the imperial provinces. The senate controlled the nearer provinces, while Augustus appointed legates to command the legions along the frontiers. Thus, the commanders (and therefore their legions) remained loyal to Augustus. The officers were political appointees, as were the tribunes that made up their staffs. The army was in reality run by the centurions, who were experienced noncommissioned officers: the actual administrators of any decent military force in any time or place. Time of service was set at 20 years for citizens, 25 years for foreign auxiliaries, and the retirement bonus was guaranteed. For foreigners, Roman citizenship was also thrown in as a retirement perk. As more distant provinces ever farther from the capital became part of the empire, more and more people became Roman citizens. This kept the citizenship requirement from limiting the number of men in the army. It also—by the second century A.D.—meant that about 1 percent of the army was actually Roman. The legionaries remained heavy infantry while the foreigners provided light infantry and cavalry. Also, part of the legions were made up of engineers and technicians to build and operate catapults.

Augustus also reestablished the Praetorian Guard. Previous commanders had kept personal guards for their security, and Augustus created a force of 4,500 German infantry organized into nine cohorts along with 90 cavalry. This was an elite unit that had a shorter enlistment (16 years) and triple the pay of other units. It was not a crack combat unit, but was always kept in or near the capital and was first on the scene in case of any political trouble.

Most importantly, Augustus for the first time created an official standing army. Garrisons were needed to protect distant provinces from border raids and to maintain order. The army stood at 28 legions, roughly 150,000 men, with an equal number of auxiliaries. The garrisons were on the frontiers to act as staging points for offensives designed to beat back any invading forces. These garrisons became permanent, and in order to supply the soldiers' needs, towns grew up around them. Many of modern-day Europe's major cities started as Roman garrisons. Augustus's army was large enough to meet military attacks from any quarter, but because it was greatly reduced in size from the army that existed when he took power, it seemed a much smaller political threat. Still, the army remained the tool of the caesar more than of the government, and even when Augustus's heirs proved incompetent or evil, the army for the most part remained loyal to them. When Augustus's line died out, the resulting struggle for power took Rome back to the days of commanders with private armies jockeying for power.

The second century A.D. saw some good caesars and the army remained loyal to them, but with the rise and then the assassination of Commodus (ruled 180–192) the legions began pushing their own commanders as caesars. As the military became less Roman and more provincial, the caesars themselves began to come from the provinces. After Commodus, Severus rose to power and openly courted army support. Because the Praetorian Guard had become increasingly political, he disbanded it and then immediately recreated his own version, opening it to non-Romans that were loyal to him more than to the position of the caesar. He stationed a legion in Italy for the first time, breaking tradition but keeping more military power on hand in case of political emergency. He also gave the soldiers a major raise, the first in a century. He allowed the soldiers to marry and opened civil service positions to veterans, which made the army more attractive as a path to a life-long career. Although the army remained effective, it began to attract employees rather than fighters.

After Severus and his line ended in 235 A.D. a half century of anarchy rocked the empire. Almost any military commander with any legion support at all could and did make a run at political power. The army organization began to change as well. Not only was it becoming more political, it altered its form. Heavy infantry began to give way to cavalry in response to the Parthian and Sassanid Persian armies that the Romans faced in the Middle East. Also, more barbarian raids occurred in northern Europe and cavalry was necessary to provide a more rapid response, especially because the army was so busy engaging in politics. The Praetorian Guard also began to take on more cavalry as the emperor needed quicker response time in the ever-shifting political arena. The infantry arm grew smaller and smaller as fewer recruits joined and the government spent more money on domestic needs. The quality of training dropped off dramatically, and the frontier forces became more defensive in nature and more local in composition. The Germans became more aggressive and the frontier receded in the north. With a less effective army it was more difficult to maintain order in the provinces or carry on effective diplomacy with enemies. The period of anarchy took from the provinces the civilizing presence of Romans, which had always been the empire's strength.

The anarchy came to an end with the rise of Diocletian in 285. He divided the empire in eastern and western halves and created the tetrarchy, whereby the eastern and western caesars each had a junior colleague to aid in administration and to take over upon the caesar's death or retirement. That system lasted until Diocletian retired in 305 at which time the empire was once again rocked by civil wars. The army was now almost half a million strong, and divided into three types of soldiers. First were the *limitanei*, locally recruited and haphazardly trained defensive forces on the frontiers. The limitanei were primarily farmers who defended fortresses when foreigners attacked, a job that required much less training and competence with weapons. These were backed by the *comitatenses*, better trained and more mobile reserve forces that responded to attacks. Finally, there were the *palatini*, the elite units within the mobile forces. Although the primary unit was still called a legion, it was now comprised of about 1,000 men on the frontier and 3,000 for the reserves. The discipline that had made the Roman army virtually unbreakable on the battlefield was gone, and combat was once again a free-for-all as it had been in the time of the Etruscans.

The Roman army was increasingly made up of "barbarians" as more and more men were recruited along the frontiers, especially the German frontier. The warlike Germanic tribes had always been worthy opponents, and by the fourth century they became worthy allies and soldiers. Constantine disbanded the Praetorian Guard during this time and replaced it with the *scholae palatinae*, an elite unit of Germans. Other circumstances forced the use of Germanic troops, like the major migrations from northern Europe in the fourth century. Goths, Vandals, and other populations spread south and west, pressuring the Roman frontiers and often breaking through. When the Goths defeated the eastern Roman army at Adrianople in 378 the Emperor Theodosius gave them land and titles in return for their becoming his army. In 395 the empire was formally divided into independent halves, and "Roman" became more descriptive of a political, rather than a geographical, entity.

The eastern Roman Empire based in Byzantium focussed on Middle Eastern affairs for the most part and established itself as a major power for another thousand years. The western Roman Empire became little more than home for a succession of occupying populations until 800 when Charlemagne finally restored some political order, albeit in France rather than Italy. Thus, the Roman army came to an end, replaced by Byzantine armies in the east and multiple ethnic armies in the west. For a thousand years it had successively dominated central Italy, the entire peninsula, the western Mediterranean, then everything from Britain almost to Persia. The legionary was both soldier and civilizer, and the culture that spread with those armies affects Europe to this day.

References: Grant, Michael, *The Army of the Caesars* (New York: Scribner, 1974); Luttwak, E. N., *The Grand Strategy of the Roman Empire* (Baltimore: Johns Hopkins University Press, 1977); Watson, G. R., *The Roman Soldier* (Ithaca: Cornell University Press, 1969).

Rough Riders

Volunteer cavalry serving with the United States Army during the Spanish-American War in 1898.

When the United States went to war against Spain in 1898 the U.S. Army was small. This was in keeping with the traditional American view against a large standing army, an attitude held since colonial times. Therefore, when war broke out in April it was necessary to raise an army as quickly as possible. Americans did so in the same fashion they had always done, not through conscription but by raising volunteer units.

Although most of the units raised were infantry, some cavalry units were also formed. What came to be designated the First Volunteer Cavalry was officially under the command of Regular Army Colonel Leonard Wood. However, its highest profile member and the one responsible for its character was Theodore Roosevelt. Roosevelt had long advocated action against the Spanish over their actions in the Cuban Revolution, and now that war had come he was not about to let others do all the fighting. Roosevelt believed that one should participate in the actions one advocates, so he quickly resigned his position as assistant secretary of the navy in order to join his friend Leonard Wood in San Antonio, Texas, where the First Volunteer Cavalry was forming in early May. Friends of Roosevelt flocked from across the country to join their comrade, and he attracted a mixed lot of recruits. Fellow polo players from Ivy League universities joined cowboys from the Dakotas with whom Roosevelt had worked in his younger days.

The unit's training in San Antonio was fairly informal. An unnamed Rough Rider described them as "twelve hundred as separate, varied, mixed, distinct, grotesque, and peculiar types of men as perhaps were ever assembled in one bunch in all the history of man...and one—possibly two—Democrats" (Millis, 1931). Roosevelt's extroverted character and almost childlike enthusiasm dominated their short tenure in San Antonio. After just two weeks of training, the unit was ordered to Tampa, Florida, for transport to Cuba.

The scene in Tampa was one of utter chaos. Supplies piled up near the docks as men arrived from all over the country, with most of the infantry arriving from their training experience in Alabama. The U.S. Navy possessed virtually no transport vessels, for it had not conducted operations outside the United States since the invasion of Mexico in 1847. Thus, transport ships had to be leased and those readily available had just returned from South Africa, where they had delivered horses for the British army. The still uncleaned ships sat in the Florida heat as increasing numbers of men and material arrived at the harbor, yet no one was in command to order any movement. Finally, when orders did arrive from Washington, the men scrambled aboard any handy ship and staked out what space was available for their unit—leaving all the supplies ashore. When the supplies were finally placed aboard ship, it was completely haphazard, for the science of loading was still far in the future. At this point, the number of ships available was sufficient only for men and material, which meant only essential animals could be taken along. Mules for hauling supply wagons and artillery, as well as officers' mounts, were taken aboard while the remainder were left behind. Thus, the First Volunteer Cavalry found itself without horses when the convoy sailed for Cuba.

Disorganized as the operation had been so far, it became worse when the force reached the south Cuban coast. Unable to land at the Spanish stronghold of Santiago, the convoy anchored offshore some five miles east of the city at the town of Daiquiri. As this town did not possess a harbor, the soldiers, supplies, and animals had to go ashore the best way they could. For the army and its supplies that was by longboat; for the horses and mules, it was by swimming. Horses and mules were jumped overboard and then expected to swim for the beach, but hundreds drowned in the process. Only the total lack of resistance on the part of the Spaniards kept this landing from becoming a disaster.

Once ashore, the army faced toward Santiago. Between their position and the city lay a number of hills upon which the Spaniards had constructed defensive positions. It was in the assault on these hills that Roosevelt and the Rough Riders would enter American folklore. With their horses drowned, the Rough Riders were obliged to walk into combat. Roosevelt, who had two horses brought to Cuba on his yacht, was the only Rough Rider mounted. The other famous misconception about the Rough Riders' combat experience concerns the location of their attack. They did not charge up San Juan Hill, but rather Kettle Hill, next to it. The blockhouses on San Juan Hill were assaulted and captured by infantry units. Roosevelt led his men up Kettle Hill, so named because of a large vat on the top used for sugar refining. According to Roosevelt's account of the charge, there was a lot of shooting but not many casualties, at least not among the Americans. The Spanish artillery was more effective than their infantry, but a mixed formation of Rough Riders, the Tenth Cavalry, and regular army troops captured Kettle Hill and the one just past it, from which they could look down on the city of Santiago.

There was no real Battle of Santiago. Spanish troops stayed inside their defenses awaiting an American attack that never came, owing to the hesitation to assault strong entrenchments. The destruction of the Spanish fleet attempting to escape Santiago harbor, coupled with the realization that no aid was coming, convinced the Spanish authorities to surrender their forces in Cuba without major fighting. The besieging American force suffered greatly from disease, and many more Americans died from that enemy than from combat with the Spanish. Shortly after the Spanish surrender, diplomats in Paris began work on a peace treaty.

What made the Rough Riders so famous was not really their actions, but their publicity. Almost as soon as Roosevelt returned to the United States after the war, he began writing a book on his experience in Cuba, and *The Rough Riders* was an instant best-seller. It was during his campaign for national office (vice-president in 1900, president in 1904) that Roosevelt called on his comrades from Cuba to speak for his cause. The press constantly asked him about the charge up San Juan Hill, and he finally got tired of correcting them and accepted the misinformation without contradiction. Thus, the highest profile unit in the war that brought the United States to international power became famous for something it never did: mount a cavalry charge up San Juan Hill.

References: Freidel, Frank, *The Splendid Little War* (Boston: Little, Brown and Company, 1958); Millis, Walter, *Martial Spirit* (New York: Houghton, Mifflin, 1931); Roosevelt, Theodore, *The Rough Riders* (New York: Charles Scribner's Sons, 1924 [1899]).

Royal Air Force (Battle of Britain)

Air force that defended Great Britain in 1940.

Few organizations in the twentieth century have garnered so much attention as "the few" immortalized by Winston Churchill during the Battle of Britain in the summer of 1940. With Adolph Hitler's Germany in control of almost all of continental Europe, Great Britain was the single nation able to hold out against the Nazi aggression. If Hitler had had his way, an invasion of Britain would have removed this last obstacle to European domination, and the Royal Air Force was the lone fighting group that could halt the proposed invasion. Hitler needed control of the skies for his air force to effectively keep the British navy at bay while his army crossed the English Channel. If the Royal Air Force (RAF) could be neutralized, nothing—it seemed—could halt Germany's conquest.

Hitler's *Luftwaffe* (air force) was twice the size of Britain's RAF, with some 2,000 fighter and bomber aircraft. The Battle of Britain was mainly a fighter's battle, and the two air forces were able to employ some of the finest fighter aircraft available anywhere. The *Luftwaffe*'s main fighters were the Messerschmidt Bf-109 and Focke-Wulf FW-190, both fast and agile single-engine aircraft, but both with limited range. The Messerschmidt Bf-110 was a twin-engine aircraft in which the Germans held high hopes, but it proved much inferior to the two primary British fighter planes and so was relegated to primarily escort and fighter-bomber roles. The RAF employed mainly the Hawker Hurricane and the Supermarine Spitfire, the former in greater numbers but the latter a superior fighter. When possible, the British attempted to employ the Hurricane to attack German bomber aircraft while the Spitfire was the preferred machine for dogfighting, as air-to-air combat was called.

Britain's major weapon, however, was more scientific than mechanical. Within the previous few months British scientists had invented radar, which effectively precluded the Germans from launching surprise attacks. With advance knowledge of approaching German planes, the RAF could respond to particular threats and avoid the fuel- and time-consuming practice of constant patrols. Radar allowed the RAF to concentrate forces at the point of attack and, by conserving fuel, to give them more time in the air than the short-range German fighter aircraft had. Once the Germans learned this, the logical response was to focus their attacks on the radar sites. The construction of the radar antennae, however, made destroying them difficult. They looked like nothing more than radio antennae, tall towers made up of structural steel; thus, there was more open space in the construction than steel, making bomb fragments of little effect. The Germans possessed a dive bomber, the Junkers Ju-87 *Stuka*, which was incredibly accurate and capable of dropping bombs directly on the antennae, but the *Stuka* was quite slow and easy for British fighters to destroy. Extremely high dive-bomber losses suffered in late June and early July 1940 forced the Germans to formulate another strategy.

Spitfires during the Battle of Britain

If the RAF had no airfields from which to operate, they reasoned, then the British aircraft could be destroyed on the ground. The Germans proceeded to implement this plan with their force of medium bombers, made up of three different aircraft: the Junkers Ju-88, the Dornier Do-17, and the Heinkel He-111. All three of these were twin-engine bombers with independently manned machine guns for defensive armament. They were effective and accurate and the aircrews were highly trained, with experience gained in earlier campaigns against Poland, Denmark, Norway, and France, as well as (in some cases) combat experience gained during the Spanish Civil War. The German attacks on the airfields were effective in damaging or destroying British hangar and repair facilities, but the airstrips themselves were, for the most part, dirt fields that were easily repaired. The German campaign limited, but did not eliminate, the RAF's ability to put fighters in the air and defend themselves.

By August the Germans came to the realization that this second strategy was not working well enough. German strategy shifted to destroying British aircraft factories, reasoning that the RAF would then not be able to replace its losses, while German factories could continue to produce replacements for their aircraft lost in combat. This new strategy, coupled with the continued bombing of facilities at the airfields, began to bear fruit. Further, it was difficult for the RAF to replace their lost pilots in a timely fashion. By late August 1940 the Royal Air Force was rapidly dwindling as daily aerial duels took their toll. By mid-September the crisis was critical. Only an emotional decision by Adolph Hitler saved the RAF and Great Britain.

As the *Luftwaffe* was bombing British targets by day, RAF bombers attacked targets on the continent at night. In late August, a small British force attacked Germany's capital city, Berlin. Although the raid did little damage physically, it was a severe blow to German morale. Hitler was infuriated that Churchill would allow his air force to attack targets that had no military value but were strictly civilian centers. If that was Churchill's choice, Hitler reasoned, then he could and would respond in kind. He ordered his air force to stop bombing factories and start bombing cities. This reprieve for the aircraft factories allowed them to begin replacing the aircraft they had been unable to build during the German raids, and the immediate crisis passed. Most importantly, the RAF was still operational, though at the limits of its strength, when Hitler decided on 15 September to postpone his invasion of the British Isles until better weather the following spring. The postponement turned out to be permanent, however, when Hitler redirected his attention eastward and began preparations for an attack on the Soviet Union.

The Royal Air Force, by maintaining air superiority, thwarted Nazi invasion plans. The men who flew in the summer of 1940 were mainly young British pilots with only marginal experience. Among the pilots who became famous during this battle were Douglas Bader, equally well known for his aggressiveness and the fact that he lost one leg above and one leg below the knee in an accident before the war; Johnny Johnson, who went on to become the RAF's highest scoring ace, credited with shooting down 38 enemy aircraft; and Alan Deere, a South African who answered the call for volunteers from across the British Empire. Also flying for the RAF were units incorporating Australian, New Zealand, and Canadian pilots; two squadrons of Polish pilots who escaped the conquest of their country by the Nazis; and the Eagle Squadron made up of volunteer American pilots.

References: Hough, Richard, and Denis Richards, *The Battle of Britain* (New York: Norton, 1989); Macksey, Kenneth, *Invasion* (New York: Macmillan, 1969); Wood, Derek, and Derek Dempster, *The Narrow Margin* (New York: Coronet, 1969).

S

Sacred Band of Thebes

An elite fighting unit of ancient Greece in the fourth century B.C.

The Sacred Band of Thebes was founded in ancient Greece by the Theban leader Gorgidas. It was probably first formed as a guard for the city-state's citadel. It contained 300 men for whom Thebes provided training facilities and barracks. At first the Sacred Band did not distinguish itself in combat, possibly because Gorgidas placed its soldiers in the front ranks of the central Theban phalanx, where it was integrated with other soldiers. This did not allow the special training of the Band to be demonstrated, for other less-talented soldiers "diluted" the Band's strength. The army therefore did not benefit from the striking power that the Band was supposed to provide.

Under the later leadership of Pelopidas, however, the Sacred Band came into its own. Pelopidas commanded the Sacred Band at the Battle of Leuctra in 371 B.C. in which the Thebans fought the Spartan army, generally regarded as the best army in Greece. Epaminodas commanded the Theban army, and he placed the Sacred Band in the key position on the left flank. Epaminodas's strategy was to form an oblique angle with his army in order to divide the Spartan army and isolate its right wing, the strongest part. The Spartans reacted quickly to the attack by turning their forces and attempting to encircle the Thebans. As their turning movement was just starting, the Sacred Band struck. The shock of the assault broke the Spartan ranks, resulting in "a rout and slaughter of the Spartans such as had never before been seen," according to Plutarch.

The Theban victory at Leuctra proved decisive, for it led to the decline of Sparta as the premiere military power in Greece. The Thebans followed up the victory by expelling the Spartan government, which had been imposed on Thebes, then creating an army made up almost entirely of Theban citizens with very few mercenaries. Within the Theban army, the Sacred Band's decisive role in the Leuctra victory took its members to elite status and ensured that in the future no dilution of their strength would be allowed; they would always fight as a separate unit. Patriotism soared not only in Thebes but throughout Greece as the power of Sparta waned.

The Sacred Band derived its reputation for outstanding fighting ability not only from its training but from the makeup of the unit. The 300 soldiers were 150 homosexual couples. Homosexuality was not uncommon in ancient Greece and attracted no negative comment. The theory within this organization was that the desire to protect and impress one's lover would bring out the best fighting spirit in each soldier. No one would dishonor himself or his partner by fleeing battle and bringing shame upon them both. Therefore, the unit would remain close-knit as each soldier acted not only for himself but also for his partner, as well as for the unit and army as a whole.

The Band remained the elite of the Theban army until both unit and army were defeated in 338 B.C. Thebes and Athens that year formed an alliance against the rising power of Macedon under Philip II. They marched to meet the Macedonians at Cheronea but could not withstand the power of the Macedonian army and the brilliance of its leader. The Macedonian victory brought Philip to power in Greece while destroying the power of the city-states. After the battle, Philip walked the field. When he came to the area where the Sacred Band had fought and died to the last man, he is reported to have commented, "Perish any man who suspects that these men did or suffered anything that was base" (Plutarch, 1986).

The Sacred Band achieved its reputation by defeating the premiere army of ancient Greece, the Spartans, but they could not match the new organization and tactics introduced by Philip, whose army—led by Philip's son Alexander—would conquer most of the known world. The Sacred Band existed for only a few decades and was never revived after its annihilation at Cheronea.

References: Plutarch, trans. by Ian Scott-Kilvert, *The Age of Alexander* (Middlesex: Penguin Books, 1986); Warry, John, *Warfare in the Classical World* (London: Salamander Books, 1980).

Samurai

The warrior class of feudal Japan between the thirteenth and nineteenth centuries.

The Samurai, the warrior class of ancient Japan, dominated that country's political and social structure for centuries. The Samurai came into existence in the early thirteenth century with the establishment of a feudal society in Japan. As in medieval Europe, the large landowners dominated the economy in an agricultural society and therefore had sufficient monetary resources to pay for the best in military supplies. Thus, as in Europe, the ability to own armor, horses, and superior weaponry brought one an exalted social status to be carefully maintained. These military trappings became symbols of social position, as well the ability to use this weaponry, and to live in a manner in which martial talent and attitude were paramount. The Samurai thus were dedicated to perfecting their martial skills and living by a strict code of honor that supported the feudal system. At the height of the Samurai's preeminence, loyalty to one's overlord and the ability to defend his property and status, even to the detriment of one's own property and status, became the pinnacle of honor.

The original soldiers of Japan were called *bushi* ("warrior"), from the Japanese pronunciation of a Chinese character signifying a man of letters and/or arms. The rise of these warriors to the status of a special class began with an interclan struggle in the late 1100s. The Genji and Heike clans were maneuvering for influence in the imperial court and the Heike managed to obtain the upper hand. In the fighting that ensued, the Genji clan was almost completely destroyed, but two sons managed to escape northward from the area of the capital city, Kyoto. When the elder son, Yoritomo, reached his majority, he rallied his remaining supporters and allied with the clans of northern Honshu that looked down on the imperial clans, which they considered weak and effete. Yoritomo's return renewed the fighting and in the second struggle it was the Heike that were defeated.

In 1192 Yoritomo was named *shogun* (roughly "barbarian-defeating generalissimo"), the supreme military position as personal protector of the emperor. However, as the emperor had more figurative than literal power, the position of shogun came to wield real authority in Japan. What national unity Japan had ever attained, though, came through the population's belief in the emperor as the descendent of the gods that created the world. Therefore, the shogun could not seize the throne without alienating the people. The emperor could not rule, however, without the military power of the shogun to protect him and enforce the gov-

A Samurai warrior, from a Japanese woodblock print

ernment's will. Thus, the shogun became the power behind the throne in a mutually dependent relationship.

Yoritomo and his descendants enjoyed a relatively brief ascendancy, but by the middle 1300s factional struggles broke out. For a time there were two rival emperors, each with his warrior supporters. In the latter half of the 1400s the Ashikaga clan went through an internal power struggle before it took control of the country, though that control was often merely nominal during the century that they ruled. As the emperor and the central government exercised less control over time, the local landed gentry, or *daimyo*, came to prominence and wielded real power in the countryside. By alliances and conquests, these feudal lords enhanced their economic, political, and military positions until by the late 1500s there was serious fighting among these leaders and the emperor had no shogun to protect him or display his authority. It was in the 1500s that the Samurai came to be a true warrior class of professional, full-time soldiers, sworn to their daimyo overlords.

The Samurai tended to dominate the command positions as heavy cavalry, while the mass of soldiers became pikemen. All soldiers, no matter their status or function, carried a sword. For the Samurai warrior, the sword became a symbol of his position, and the Samurai were the only soldiers allowed by law to carry two swords. Anyone not of the Samurai class who carried two swords was liable to be executed. The two swords were the *katana*, or long sword (averaging about a three-foot blade), and the *wakizashi*, or short sword (with the blade normally 16–20 inches long). The finest swords became the property of the richest warriors, and being a sword smith was the most highly respected craft. Both swords were slightly curved with one sharpened edge and a point; they were mainly slashing weapons although they could be used for stabbing. The short sword in particular was a close-quarters stabbing weapon and also used in *seppuku*, the Samurai's ritual suicide. The blades were both strong and flexible, being crafted by hammering the steel thin, folding it over, and rehammering it, sometimes thousands of times. The sword and its expert use attained spiritual importance in the Samurai's life. The other main weapon in Japanese armies of the time was the *naginata*, a long-handled halberd used by the infantrymen. It consisted of a wide, curved blade sharpened on one edge and mounted on a long pole. By 1600 this had been largely replaced by the *yari*, more of a spear. Occasionally, unusual weapons were developed, like folding fans with razor-sharp edges.

Japanese armies also had bowmen, although most archery was practiced from horseback and therefore in the province of the Samurai. By the end of the sixteenth century, however, Oda Nobunaga became the first of the daimyo to effectively adopt firearms. European harquebuses had been introduced to Japan in the 1540s by shipwrecked Portuguese, and Japanese artisans began to copy the design. Nobunaga fielded 3,000 musketeers in a battle in 1575 with such positive effect that the other daimyo rushed to acquire as many of the weapons as possible. The technology advanced little in the following generations, however, owing to Japan's self-imposed exile from the rest of the world.

The Samurai also wore elaborate suits of armor, mainly made of strips of metal laced with leather. The finished product was lacquered and decorated to such an extent that it not only was weatherproof and resistant to cutting weapons, it became almost as much a work of art as a fine sword. Armor proved unable to stop musket balls, however, and became mainly ceremonial after 1600. In the latter 1500s the struggles between the daimyo came to a head with the emergence of Oda Nobunaga (1534–1582). Starting with a relatively small landholding in central Japan, he schemed and fought his way to become the strongest of the lords. In this time the daimyo built huge castle/fortresses, equal to or better than anything built in Europe at the time. Nobunaga defeated many of the military religious sects on his way to dominance, but not surprisingly created a number of enemies, which allied and attacked his palace in 1582 burning it to the ground with him inside. Nobunaga was succeeded by Toyotomi Hideyoshi (1536-1598), one of his commanders, who almost succeeded in accomplishing Nobunaga's dream of unifying Japan under his rule. At his death in 1598 one of his vassals, Tokugawa Ieyasu, took control of half of Hideyoshi's forces and won the battle of Sekigahara. He was named shogun in 1603—the first to hold that position in years—and finished consolidating his power in 1615 with the capture of Osaka castle, where the last remnants of the defeated Hideyoshi faction held out.

The Tokugawa shogunate lasted until the middle 1800s when it was dismantled during the Meiji Restoration. This movement returned real power to the emperor and abandoned the traditional feudal state that had kept Japan isolated and technologically backward for more than two and a half centuries. During the Tokugawa period, however, the Samurai both experienced their golden age and sowed the seeds of their own downfall. The Samurai came to hold the ruling administrative positions as well as exercising military functions. The Samurai warrior, which had over time blended the hardiness of the country warrior with the culture of the court warrior, was the pinnacle of culture, learning, and power. The problem was that Tokugawa had succeeded too well, establishing a peace that lasted 250 years. Without the almost constant warfare that had preceded the Tokugawa era, the Samurai warrior had fewer and fewer chances to exercise his profession of arms. He became more of a bureaucrat and therefore he could not be rewarded in combat nor expand his holdings through warfare. The Samurai class increased in numbers, but not through "natural selection" in combat, and their increased numbers in an increasingly bloated bureaucracy brought about their economic slide. The merchant class became increasingly wealthy, while the samurai upper class became increasingly impoverished. The tax burden required to operate the government fell increasingly on the peasants, who turned to shopkeeping rather than follow an increasingly unprofitable agricultural life. By the time the American Matthew Perry sailed into Tokyo Bay in 1854 and "opened" Japan to the outside world, the artisans and merchants were the only ones in a position to deal with the new reality and the Samurai's status in society quickly dropped.

In spite of this setback, the martial attitude engendered by centuries of military rule never completely left the Japanese national psyche. The military became modernized with European weaponry, but the dedication to a martial spirit and professionalism remained strong in the new warrior class. In the 1920s and 1930s the military came back into power and dominated the government, laying the groundwork for national expansionism to obtain the raw materials necessary to maintain and expand their military and industrial base. The cult of the Samurai, *bushido* (the "Way of the Warrior") enjoyed a resurgence in the Japanese military. It showed itself in the brutal actions of the Japanese in their dealings with defeated enemies in China, Southeast Asia, and the Pacific, and in their dedication to death before dishonor in serving their emperor. The world saw firsthand the twentieth-century version of the Samurai in the extremely difficult fighting against Japanese soldiers during World War II and in the Japanese use of suicide tactics late in the war in an attempt to save their country from invasion and defeat. Japanese texts on Samurai philosophy and lifestyle, such as *Hagakure* and *The Five Rings*, still influence the views of the modern Japanese in their business practices.

References: King, Winston, *Zen and the Way of the Sword* (New York: Oxford University Press, 1993); Turnbull, Stephen, *Samurai Warriors* (New York: Sterling Publishing, 1991); Turnbull, Stephen, *The Samurai: A Military History* (New York: Macmillan, 1977).

SEALs

An elite unit in the U.S. Navy.

World War II was the first conflict in which amphibious landings took place with regularity, and the doctrine for such operations to a great extent developed during the landings themselves. From 7 August 1942 when American forces invaded the island of Guadalcanal in the Solomon Island chain northeast of Australia, the United States dominated amphibious warfare. Although used at first primarily by the United States Marines, over time the U.S. Army and other countries adopted the use of amphibious tactics. Early difficulties with natural and enemy-built obstacles led to the formation of navy combat demolition units in May 1943 which were designed to locate and neutralize anything in the way of the landing craft. They operated not only as the immediate vanguards of landing forces, but also as scouting units far in advance of any major landing.

As the fighting in the Pacific progressed, more specialized units were formed to handle newly discovered aspects of amphibious operations. Combat swimmer reconnaissance units were formed to explore potential landing sites, and underwater demolition teams (UDTs) took part in landings on the islands of Kwajalein, Roi-namur, Pelelieu, and Okinawa, opening holes in beach and offshore defenses through which troops could advance. Commander John Koehler led the development of UDT methods, creating courses in long-range and night reconnaissance, special weaponry, and small-unit tactics. This training continued after World War II, and when fighting broke out in Korea in the summer of 1950 UDTs were back in action. An early setback in a failed mission to destroy a bridge behind North Korean lines led to more fine tuning of UDT training and doctrine. Leadership of this training during the Korean conflict was under the direction of Marine Corps Major Edward Dupras, who had served in guerrilla and raider units during World War II. He oversaw the short-lived Special Operations Group that secretly scouted the planned invasion route into the harbor of Inch'on in September 1950. UDTs continued to operate during the fighting in Korea, training Korean personnel and acting at times under the command of the newly created Central Intelligence Agency (CIA). During this time it was discovered that once ashore, these units could and should be able to operate further inland, thus expanding the role of the UDTs. Therefore, the navy created special operations teams to do just that, laying the groundwork for the SEAL teams, so named because of their ability to operate by sea, air, and land. They were officially designated as such in January 1962 upon the directive of President John Kennedy, whose interest in covert operations also created the Green Berets. The SEALs from the start were a separate organization from the UDTs, which kept their operations limited to coastal and offshore demolition.

The mission statement developed for the SEALs contained five points: (1) carry out clandestine or covert operations against selected enemy targets, especially in harbors and along rivers; (2) serve as guides for agents operating behind enemy lines and facilitate their entry and removal from their missions; (3) perform short-range and long-range reconnaissance missions; (4) conduct counterinsurgency operations; and (5) act as advisors and trainers for U.S. allies. The first major operation in which the new organization found itself was Vietnam, where SEALs both saw action and trained South Vietnamese units in SEAL tactics. By 1966 the SEALs were active in two major areas in Vietnam, the Mekong Delta and the Rung Sat Special Zone, operating with the "Brown Water Navy," light river craft patrolling Vietnamese waterways. They also continued to be used in occasional CIA operations. Vietnam proved to be the primary training ground for SEALs and their implementation of new tactics and ideas. The concept of teamwork was finely honed here and remains the basis of SEAL training. Although SEALs are expected to be able to operate and survive independently if necessary, the sublimation of the individual to the team is paramount.

Members of Naval Special Warfare Group Two conduct ship-to-ship boarding procedures in 1996.

In order to become a SEAL, one has to go through Basic Underwater Demolition/SEAL training (BUD/S) at the Naval Special Warfare Center at Coronado, California, a 35-week course divided into three phases. In Phase One, the recruit has two weeks of physical and mental testing to determine his basic fitness for the course. He then spends three weeks learning first aid, lifesaving, and handling small boats. At the end of his fifth week, the true test of the SEAL takes place, five days called Hell Week. Placed in a six- or seven-man team, the recruit is pushed to and past his physical limits and constantly challenged mentally and psychologically. Here, those unable to cooperate in teams are weeded out, as well as those physically or mentally unable to continue. There are also those that fail to finish owing to injury, but they are given second chances later. Having survived Hell Week, the recruit then can catch his breath while learning how to chart beaches.

In Phase Two, the recruit learns to handle weapons and explosives, as well as receives training in intelligence gathering, handling prisoners, navigation on land and sea, and marksmanship. SEALs learn to handle a variety of firearms, as well as hand grenades and mines. Mock operations are conducted during this phase to implement the information just learned. The seven weeks of Phase Three of the training is focussed on dive training. Once this is complete, BUD/S is over. However, SEAL Tactical Training continues for the six months after BUD/S, which is a probationary period. During this time the SEAL also undergoes parachute training at the Army's Fort Benning, Georgia, jump school. At the end of that time, a review board is conducted and SEALs who meet the standards are awarded badges marking their acceptance into the organization. In the 1980s only 15–30 percent of those entering BUD/S graduated the course.

In the wake of the Vietnam conflict, special operations in the military suffered a reduction in emphasis and recruits, but the SEALs managed to maintain a high enlistment rate. The Navy Special Warfare Center continued to develop doctrine for covert amphibious operations. The SEAL teams came under the direction of the fleet commanders in chief, with Teams One, Three, and Five based at Coronado under the C-in-C (commander in chief) Pacific while Teams Two, Four, and Six were based at Little Creek, Virginia, under the command of the C-in-C Atlantic. In addition, a special warfare unit was based in Europe and one in the Pacific, where they trained with similar units in allied military forces. Special delivery vehicle units and special boat unit teams support the SEALs as the transportation that delivers them to their mission site. All these teams are dedicated to the tasks of counterinsurgency, intelligence gathering, counterterrorism, deception missions, as well as the traditional coastal and beach reconnaissance missions.

In 1983 the UDTs were deactivated and incorporated into the SEAL command. By 1987 the size of the organization was expanded from 17 to more than 60 platoons, with a directive in place to expand a further 60 percent by 1991. In order to do so, a higher graduation rate (approximately 55 percent) from BUD/S is required, a requirement that older SEALs believe could decrease the quality of the graduate. The view of the navy, however, is that with the increased need for technical training that the earlier SEALs did not need, the higher number is necessary if the mission is to be fulfilled. Even with a higher graduation rate, the SEALs remain the elite unit of the United States Navy. They resent the motion-picture portrayal of the SEALs as mercenaries or loose cannons. One of its members described them thus: "A SEAL is a motivated, proud, highly skilled individual who can make split-second decisions that count. He's a military professional charged with the responsibility of carrying out his missions with success. SEALs are people who are special, and once you've become one, there's nothing else you can't do" (Walker, 1989).

References: Hoyt, Edwin, *SEALs at War* (New York: Bantam Doubleday Dell, 1993); Kelly, Orr, *Brave Men, Dark Waters* (Novato, CA: Presidio Press, 1992); Walker, Greg, "Elite SEAL Units," in *International Combat Arms*, vol. 7, no. 6 (November 1989).

Seminoles

An American Indian tribe which fought for homeland in Florida, defeating the United

States Army and maintaining their independence.

The Seminole Indians of Florida have a heritage of independence that is reflected in their tribal name, which translates as "those who live apart." Although originally they were probably part of the Creek Indian Confederation, the Seminoles became a conglomeration of tribal mixtures that ultimately spoke a wide variety of dialects, called *Mikasuki*, derived from the Lower Creek Hitchiti language. By the early nineteenth century they inhabited a number of villages scattered throughout Florida, each organized along the lines of an independent city-state after the Seminoles rejected the authority of the Creek Confederation. The Seminoles included in their society almost anyone who chose to live among them, including escaped slaves from the United States or Spanish holdings in Florida. They kept slaves themselves, after a fashion. Slaves given to them became more like tenant farmers, paying a portion of their crops or livestock to their "owners." It was their acceptance of escaped slaves, however, that brought them into conflict with American Southerners.

When parties of Southerners ventured into Spanish Florida to recover their slaves, they often brought back anyone with whom the slave happened to be. This sometimes included Seminole wives whom the slaves may have married and the children they had produced. The tribe resented this kidnapping of its members. Hence, they attacked slave catchers in their territory and mounted attacks into Georgia on plantations there. In 1817 the federal government looked the other way when Andrew Jackson, hero of the War of 1812, invaded Florida on punitive expeditions against the Seminoles. When foreign citizens were killed and the Spanish government protested, the American response was to buy Florida in 1819. The Spanish, who had little real interest in the land, realized they could either sell the territory or have it taken away. They chose to sell for $5 million. The new American administration assigned the Seminoles to a reservation in the central part of the peninsula, ending what was termed the First Seminole War (1816–1823). They also promised the Indians food, farming equipment, and money, none of which was forthcoming. When the Seminoles complained, the U.S. government in 1835 offered to pay them to leave Florida and relocate west of the Mississippi.

Upon receiving this offer, a Seminole chief showed the American negotiators at Payne's Landing what he thought of it. He drove his knife into the agreement, initiating the Second Seminole War. The chief at that time was Osceola, and he came to symbolize the fiercely independent nature of the Seminoles. He was to his tribe what Geronimo would later be to the Apache, and Sitting Bull or Crazy Horse, to the Sioux. Osceola was originally a Creek but was driven from the Mississippi Territory during the War of 1812. During the Second Seminole War, he mounted an extremely effective guerrilla campaign against the American army, beginning in December 1835 when his men ambushed a 112-man company of the Fourth Infantry Regiment. Only two soldiers escaped

Osceola, from a painting by George Catlin, 1838

to tell the story of the massacre. Using the swamps as cover and refuge, the Seminoles attacked the soldiers sent into the region to capture them and sent them and their leaders back to the states in disgrace.

This guerrilla warfare was natural for the Seminoles, but the U.S. army had become lax in these tactics. The invading U.S. soldiers had no experience with swamps and were as afraid of the natural predators found there as of the Indians. Disease and heatstroke felled the majority of casualties. Still, the army's constant raids on Seminole villages and the destruction of the Seminoles' crops began to have some effect. In 1837 some of the tribe surrendered to General Thomas Jesup. He fed them and arranged for their transport to Tampa, from whence they were to be transported west. While awaiting this move, Osceola sneaked into the camp and convinced his comrades to go with him. When he learned of the flight of his prisoners, Jesup asked Osceola for a parley. When Osceola appeared under a white flag, Jesup arrested him. Osceola, already sick with malaria, died after a short imprisonment in South Carolina in January 1838. Other leaders, including Abiaka, a prominent medicine man, kept up the fight.

Taylor was known as a "soldier's general," ready to undergo the same hardships as his men. He marched into Florida with 1,000 men, artillery, pack mules, and wagons. He ran into Chief Alligator near Lake Okeechobee on Christmas Day of 1837. Alligator placed his men on a rise almost surrounded by swamps, forcing Taylor to attack him head-on. The mire sucked under men and horses alike, making outflanking operations impossible. Seminole sharpshooters picked off officers and non-commissioned officers during the assault, but Taylor kept up the pressure and Alligator finally ordered his men to fade into the swamps, leaving behind their 13 dead and nine wounded. It was a victory, but a Pyrrhic one. Seminoles continued to harass soldiers and civilians alike. But by 1841 the continued destruction of their villages and farms forced many Seminoles to surrender. Chiefs came in one by one to give up their followers and be transported west. Some 4,000 had surrendered by 1842. However, several hundred never surrendered and continued to live deep in the Everglades where U.S. soldiers would not or could not go. The American government ultimately spent almost $20 million, the services of 30,000 men, and the deaths of almost 1,500, but no peace treaty was ever signed with the Seminoles. To this day the Florida Seminoles point with pride to the fact that they were the only undefeated tribe in the wars that the United States waged against the Native Americans.

References: Heidler, David Stephen, *Old Hickory's War* (Mechanicsburg, PA: Stackpole, 1996); Mulroy, Kevin, *Freedom on the Border* (Lubbock: Texas Tech University Press, 1993); Wright, J. Leitch, *Creeks and Seminoles* (Lincoln: University of Nebraska Press, 1996).

Shaolin Priests

Warrior priests in China who developed specialized martial arts from the fifth to nineteenth centuries.

Information on the Shaolin temple where the development of martial arts training began is sketchy and at times contradictory. The main Shaolin temple was located just outside the city of Zhengzhou, in Henan Province, in the Central Plains of China near the Songshan Mountains. One source states that the Shaolin order was founded in 497 A.D. by Ba Tuo, a Buddhist monk from India. Ba Tuo was interested in the Chinese martial art known as *wushu* and his followers perfected their skills in this form of training. Other sources state that Bodhidharma (or Tamo in Chinese), another Buddhist monk from India, was the founder of the Shaolin religion in the mid-sixth century. He supposedly visited the Chinese emperor, who had sponsored a widespread translation of Indian Buddhists texts from Sanskrit to Chinese, in the hopes of making the faith more accessible to the public. Apparently the emperor believed that undertaking this worthy project would lead him to Nirvana. Tamo disagreed, believing no one could achieve that exalted state through the work of others. Hence, the two parted company.

Tamo then traveled to a Buddhist monastery nearby, but was refused entrance because he was a foreigner. He withdrew to a nearby cave and engaged in intense meditation, a practice that convinced the nearby monks that he was, indeed, serious about entering their company. Once there, Tamo observed that the priests, engaged in translation all day, were in poor physical condition. Tamo believed that in order to perfect oneself, meditation was necessary, and intense meditation was physically challenging. He thus developed a series of exercises for his fellow monks to develop their physical strength and stamina and to enhance the flow of *chi*—the life force. Drawing on hatha and raja yoga, both developed in India in the second century B.C., Tamo developed movement exercises based on 18 animals from Indo-Chinese iconography. These exercises were not originally intended as a martial art, but nevertheless became the foundation of *kung fu* (or *gung fu*). It is possible that Tamo refined the practice of martial arts already existing since the time of Ba Tuo. Or, perhaps he was more instrumental in altering the teachings at the temple, for it is reported he developed what came to be the Chan Sect.

It was the particular blend of Buddhism and Taoism that became the basis of Shaolin, named after the temple where Tamo lived. The temple was constructed in a wooded area that had been deforested and only recently replanted. It was named *Shaolin*, which means "new forest" in Mandarin Chinese. Apparently, during the Sui dynasty (589-618) the Shaolin found favor with the emperor, who granted them 1,648 acres of land upon which they built extensive buildings and employed a large staff of attendants. The wealth of the temple attracted the attention of bandits, further motivating the monks to train for self-defense. The exercises they practiced blended into the Buddhist/Taoist creed of nonviolence by being strictly defensive, and in levels of intensity and lethality designed to reflect the aggressiveness of the attacker. Thus, the Shaolin priest was not to attack, only defend himself in direct relation to the intent of his attacker. This means, however, that an attacker intent on killing the priest would be met with equal force and intent.

The practice of kung fu that the priests developed was a variation on wushu martial arts and Luohan boxing. During the Song (or Sung) dynasty (960–1279), the Shaolin abbot Fu Ju invited wushu experts from around China to visit the temple to exchange knowledge and training techniques. After three years, a Shaolin boxing manual was created describing 280 exercise routines. The monks also developed techniques using a variety of weapons, most notably the cudgel. This choice was consistent with the original Buddhist teaching against the use of sharp or pointed weapons, although over time the Shaolin monks developed skill with those weapons as well. The four major weapons of the Shaolin priests came to be the cudgel, spear, sword, and broadsword, although small weapons hidden about the monk's person were also used.

Because of its relatively central location and the less restrictive rules (compared with other orders) laid down by the Chan Sect, the temple attracted retired generals, malcontents, and refugees from the law. The spreading fame of the Shaolin priests impressed the government, which alternately used their skills in wars against rebel peasants such as the Red Turbans or in conflicts with Japanese pirates, or persecuted them and attacked their temples. Occasionally, a priest would decide to support one political faction or another, bringing kung fu even more into public notice. These few politically or militarily active monks ultimately brought the wrath of the government down on the sect as a whole.

In the 1600s China came under the rule of the Manchu dynasty, who were invaders from the north. Elements supporting a return of the deposed Ming dynasty organized the Hung Society, which probably grew out of another secret society called the White Lotus. Although unsuccessful in their attempts to restore the Ming dynasty, members of the Hung Society inspired a similar rebel movement based at a Shaolin temple in Fukien. These monks answered the emperor's call for troops in 1672 to put down an invasion from western tribes, and succeeded in doing so. However, the government discovered that the Shaolin were merely positioning themselves for a rebellion. Their temple was destroyed. In what came to be famous in Chinese folklore, five escapees of that destruction hid under a bridge, where they were rescued by five brave men. They were soon joined by five more monks. These earned the titles of the Five Early Founding Fathers, Five Middle Founding Fathers, and Five Later Founding Fathers, and these 15 organized continued revolts against the Manchus. In 1674 these men swore to be fraternal brothers and fight to overthrow the Manchus, and their band came to be called the Heaven and Earth Society. How much of this story is true is debatable, but the burning of the temple has often been eulogized in Chinese literature and drama. As a movement, the Heaven and Earth Society spread to southern China and across to Formosa then back to cover the whole of China, and the Heaven and Earth Society played a key role in later uprisings such as the Taiping Rebellion in the mid-1800s.

References: de Bary, William Theodore, et al., eds., *Sources of Chinese Tradition* (New York: Columbia University Press, 1960); Winderbaum, Larry, *The Martial Arts Encyclopedia* (Washington: Inscape Corp., 1977).

Sikhs

A religious sect that resisted the British occupation of India in the nineteenth century.

The Sikhs are one of what are called the martial races in India, in this case originating in the northwestern province of the Punjab. Sikhs are not truly a race, but rather a religious sect, so the title in their case is something of a misnomer. They are one of the groups upon which the British administration drew for soldiers in India during the nineteenth and twentieth centuries.

The term *Sikh* means "disciple." Sikhism is a form of Islam with Hindu aspects. The first Sikh *guru* was Baba Nanak, born in 1469. He developed the sect with a reformed Hinduism, including the principles of simplicity, purity, and brotherhood. The sect grew under the oppression of the ruling Moghul dynasty. Baba Nanak was succeeded by nine gurus. The tenth, named Govind, radically altered the nature of the faith. Apparently unwilling to passively accept persecution, he turned the Sikh faith into a powerful military sect that attracted lower caste Hindus who had little or no earthly future in their own social system. Some two thirds of the Sikh converts came from the martial race of Jats, although many of that race retained their Moslem faith and thus split the Sikh community. Probably in order to instill some fighting spirit, Govind added the term *Singh*, or "lion," to the title of Sikh.

A person entering the Sikh faith does so not by birth but by baptism, initiated by the sprinkling of water from a two-edged dagger. Joining the faith requires a certain austerity and thus many young men postpone the baptism. The British Indian Army, when recruiting from Sikh society in the Punjab, took those baptized and used to a tougher life. The holy life ordained originally by Nanak became a zealous one under Govind, dedicated to religious fervor. The hardiness of the Sikh soldiers comes also from their profession (mainly farming) and their heritage, for the Jats who make up so many of the Sikh faith are reputed to be descended from the Aryans, who conquered India from the north at the start of historic time. The military brotherhood established among the Sikhs, called the *Khalsa*, was the core of their army. Another branch of the Sikhs recruited by the British into the Indian army were inducted into the Pioneer, or engineer/construction regiments. Those Hindus of lower caste, obliged to sweep for a living, gained status by joining the Sikh faith as well as the Indian army. The engineer/construction units, along with Sikh fighting units, served with distinction in the Indian army. However, before this distinguished service for the Crown could come about, the British first had to defeat the Sikhs in two wars.

The First Sikh War was fought in 1845–1846. The Sikhs had been molded into a first-rate fighting force by their leader, Ranjit Singh, in the first decades of the nineteenth century. As an ally of the British, he learned his training methods from the army of the British East India Company and by hiring European mercenaries. The war was actually started by a Sikh leader, Tej Singh, who was unable to gain the support of the army in his bid to replace Ranjit Singh after his death. Tej Singh provoked a war with the British hoping that victory would unite the nation behind him. The British found the Sikh army the most difficult force they had yet faced in India. In four battles between December 1845 and February 1846, the Sikhs showed their ability to prepare strong defensive positions and to use their artillery extremely well. The British won all four battles but took heavy losses in the process. The peace treaty forced on the Sikhs obliged them to cede the territory of Kashmir along with an indemnity of £1 million. They were also forced to reduce the size of their army. The British did not annex the Sikh homeland, fearing the cost and manpower it would take to hold it, but did assign a resident to oversee Anglo-Sikh relations.

H.H. Raja Sir Hira Singh Bahadur of Nabha, Hon. Colonel 14th Sikhs, from a drawing by A. C. Lovett

In late 1848 Sikh nationalists masterminded an uprising against the British presence in their country. The uprising centered around the city of Multan. The capture of this city in early 1849 after a number of hard-fought battles marked the end of the Second Sikh War. In the wake of this conflict, Governor-General Dalhousie annexed all of the Punjab, expanding the borders of British-held India to the mountains of Afghanistan. The quality of the Sikh army had made a great impression on the British, and the British administration began to consider the incorporation of Sikh troops into the India army now that their country had been incorporated into British India. Indeed, two regiments had been formed after the First Sikh War and had served under British officers between conflicts. The leader of one of those units, Herbert Edwardes, was instrumental in building up the trust and mutual respect between soldiers of the two armies. Moreover, the reforms that the British instituted in the Punjab after they annexed the province did much to alleviate the oppression of many of the locals and earn their respect. When much of the Indian army mutinied in 1857 the Sikhs remained loyal and proved to be as fierce in combat alongside the British as they had been against them.

Sikhs served in the Indian army and incorporated into their ranks both Hindu and Moslem compatriots. They buried their differences and fought together alongside the British in campaigns up through World War II, but were unable to survive the independence of India in 1947. When India became free, and when Pakistan seceded to its own independence, regiments from the northwest had to go with one country or the other. Moslems went to Pakistan, Hindus and Sikhs went to India, and strong bonds built up over decades were destroyed in a matter of months.

References: Mason, Philip, *A Matter of Honour* (London: Jonathan Cape, 1974); Roberts, P.E., *History of British India* (London: Oxford University Press, 1952); Singh, Khushwant, *A History of the Sikhs*, 2 vols. (Princeton, NJ: Princeton University Press, 1963–1966).

Spartans

A Greek population known for its militaristic society between the sixth and fourth centuries B.C.

Of all the warrior populations of the ancient world, few are as well known as the Spartans. Unlike the Assyrians, who made aggressive warfare a national pastime, the Spartans built a society geared more toward martial training and values rather than pure aggression. They were probably the first society that dedicated itself to a martial lifestyle, much like the Mongols, Zulus, or Gurkhas in later centuries.

The country of Sparta lay on the Peloponnese, the peninsula extending southward from the main body of Greece. Like the rest of the region, Sparta was defeated by the Dorians, who invaded and occupied Greece around 1200 B.C. It seems, however, that the inhabitants of the Peloponnese had a more positive, relatively cooperative relationship with the invaders. The town of Sparta was founded around 900 B.C. and by the middle 800s B.C. its inhabitants had conquered the surrounding area and established a *polis*, or city-state. The city-state was ruled by two kings, which were under the direction of a council of elders.

The traditional story of the establishment of the Spartan military society holds that the statesman Lycurgus laid the groundwork by establishing the nation's constitution in the ninth century B.C. In reality, the constitution was probably developed over time and in a manner that differed from most of Sparta's contemporary city-states. While other Greek polises reacted against the power of the aristocracy by revolution and the establishment of individual rulers, the Spartans developed a society in which there was no real aristocracy. All citizens, called Equals, trained and fought together in the same fashion. All citizens held land worked by helots, or serfs, which supported the Equals, all of which were soldiers. A merchant and artisan class held rights somewhere between the two.

Toughness of mind and body were cultivated from birth, when a newborn male was subjected to inspection by the elders and a decision made as to its fitness for life. Those who failed were abandoned to nature. Those who passed were treated little better, for they were often forced to sleep outside. At age seven, the boy was taken from his home to start his education and training. In the barracks he was given his earliest training by the teenagers who had graduated from this first stage. The youth was often given short rations and told to steal if he wanted more. Those successful were praised; those caught were punished. This taught them to forage and prepared them for likely deprivations during campaigning. The boys were also given but one cloak, and were denied sandals in order to toughen their feet. As they grew older, certain boys were chosen to become assassins, practicing on helots that may have strayed from their dwellings.

Upon reaching adulthood, the young Spartan was expected to marry; indeed, bachelorhood was a crime punished by public taunting or beatings by groups of women. If unattached men or women reached an age at which it was unseemly for them to be single, they would be placed in a darkened room and pair off by touch. Many thought that mating in such a way was about as successful as arranged marriages or love matches. Once married, however, the man was obliged to live in his barracks with the group of comrades with which he had grown up and trained. He could visit his wife but had to return to the barracks to spend the night. Only at age 30 could he start his own household. At this age, the Spartan male was accepted as an Equal and allowed voting rights.

The weaponry the Spartans employed was little different than that used by other Greek armies. Each infantryman was termed a *hoplite*, from the *hoplon*, or shield that each one carried. The hoplon was originally a wooden circle edged with brass, but the Spartans covered the entire shield, with brass. It was large enough to give protection to the bearer and to overlap with the soldier next to him, making a shield wall. Each man had body armor and a helmet, with additional armor, such as greaves or arm protection, as his wealth allowed. The hoplites marched and fought in the phalanx formation. This was a square of men several ranks deep and wide. In combat, the soldiers would tighten their ranks to create the shield wall, then advance with lowered spears. The spears were originally six to eight feet long and when deployed created a hedgehog effect. The phalanx was a shock formation that took little talent to employ and the typical battle ended when one of the phalanxes broke and the soldiers fled. The Spartans, by creating a disciplined army, had a distinct advantage over those armies made up of conscripts or short-term volunteers. Ancillary forces of archers, cavalry, or lightly armed infantry rounded out the army, but these were mainly used in pursuit once the phalanx had done its job.

Sparta established its dominion over the southern Peloponnese by the middle 400s B.C. then extended its influence over most of the remainder of the peninsula through alliances. This Spartan-dominated group came to be called the Peloponnesian League, and the members allowed Sparta to dictate their foreign policy and draw on their manpower in time of war. Nevertheless, Spartan policy did not advocate conquering for conquest's sake. Instead, the Spartans preferred staying in their own region to keep control over their land and their helots. When they did venture outside their own borders, they at first did so not for conquest but for defense.

In the 490s B.C. Persian King Darius crushed a revolt along the coast of Asia Minor by cities that had been supported by Greeks. He resolved to invade Greece to punish them for interfering in his affairs and to add the region to his empire. In 490 B.C. the Persian army marched around the Aegean Sea into Greece. Darius' forces were defeated at Marathon by a Greek army dominated by Athenians; the Spartans were observing religious festivals and did not arrive at the battlefield until after the Athenian victory. The Spartans did get into the war ten years later when Darius' successor, Xerxes, again attempted to impose Persia's will on Greece. This time the first troops Xerxes' army met were part of a Spartan-led force at the coastal pass of Thermopylae. After repelling repeated Persian attacks with an army of 6,000, the Greeks under Spartan King Leonidas were outflanked by a Persian unit taking a mountain path. Leonidas had committed 1,000 men to protect that path but they failed to do so, for reasons unclear. About to be surrounded, Leonidas sent most of his troops away, forming a rear guard with his 300 Spartans, some Thespians, and 400 Thebans. The unit was slaughtered to the last man by Persian archers. It was the Spartans that brought the world the concept of "death before dishonor."

Spartan seamen participated a decade later in 480 B.C. in the Greek naval victory over the Persian fleet at Salamis, then capped their performance with a leadership role in the victory over the Persians at Plataea in 479 B.C. These successes established Sparta as the preeminent military power in Greece, although Athens was the economic and naval power. Ultimately, the two city-states clashed in a decades-long conflict, the Peloponnesian War, lasting from 459 to 404 B.C. The war was fought in three phases. In the first, the Spartan army dominated the land warfare and bottled up the city of Athens. The Athenians dominated the seas and harassed the Spartan coastline, raising helot revolts. It has been described as the battle between the elephant and the whale: each the best in its element but unable to come to grips with each other. The opening phase ended in a draw.

Phase two was fought mainly in Sicily, site of Athenian colonial interests. There, a Spartan general commanded troops for the city of Syracuse, which the Athenians besieged. Conflicting goals and orders brought about an Athenian defeat that cost them huge numbers of men and ships, weakening their naval power and prestige. This led to the third phase of the war, in which the Spartans enlarged their navy with assistance from Persia. Although the Athenian admirals managed to win victories, each successive battle further weakened their fleet. It could not be rebuilt as quickly as the Spartans received new ships from the Persians, and finally, in 405 B.C., the Athenian fleet was lost to the Spartans in the Dardanelles. Without the ability to supply their city by sea, the Athenians slowly starved under the Spartan siege. By 404 B.C. the Athenians surrendered, ending a conflict begun in 459.

This proved to be the apogee of Spartan power, for Sparta proved unprepared and unable to rule all of Greece. The society Sparta had developed over the centuries was suited to a limited population and could not be forced on a large one. Sparta had spent too many citizens in too many wars to be able to impose its will on all of Greece. The Spartans began fighting their erstwhile allies, the Persians, who sent agents into Greece to sow dissension among the city-states. Spread too thin, the Spartans could not maintain their position. They could uphold their independence and dominance in the Peloponnese but in few other places. Sparta ultimately fell, as did all of Greece, to the rising power of Macedon in the mid-fourth century B.C.

References: Ferrill, Arther, *The Origins of War* (London: Thames and Hudson, 1985); Forrest, W. G., *A History of Sparta, 950–192 B.C.* (New York: Hutchinson, 1968); Warry, John, *Warfare in the Classical World* (London: Salamander Books, 1980).

Special Air Service

Elite unit of the British army.

During Great Britain's war against Italian and German forces in North Africa in World War II, special operations forces were active in harassing Axis supply lines and creating confusion in their rear areas. The Long Range Desert Group was the first of these organizations, but the Special Air Service (SAS) came to be not only the more famous, but the longer-lasting, unit. The SAS was created in the summer of 1941 and was commanded by Major David Stirling. Stirling had formerly served in the Scots Guards and No. 8 Commando and was given the task of organizing the SAS by General Sir Claude Auchinleck, then in command of British forces in Egypt. The unit and its mission were Stirling's idea, but the possibility of inflicting serious damage on the Germans for the cost of training and equipping but a handful of men was attractive to the British high command. Stirling was ordered to recruit six officers and 60 men, to be designated "L" Detachment, Special Air Service.

Stirling's idea was to use small groups of men rather than the 200-man minimum advocated by most commando theorists. Stirling argued that because most commandos operated by sea, too many men were wasted in protecting the boats. Better, he argued, to insert half a dozen men who were all active and able to get in and out quickly without discovery. In November 1941 Stirling's men were in action with the Long Range Desert Group (LRDG). The LRDG had been mapping and raiding across the Libyan desert and was assigned to provide the transport for the SAS. The SAS commandos parachuted into action on the night of 16 November against Gazala, but the weather so dispersed the aircraft and paratroopers that the operation was a complete failure. After that, the LRDG was the delivery team that took the SAS commandos to within walking distance of their target. From there, the SAS would slip into an enemy position, set explosives, and withdraw before the excitement started.

The SAS operated with increasing success

for 15 months in 1941–1942, destroying German and Italian aircraft, vehicles, ammunition, and fuel depots, in addition to mining roads and attacking supply columns. This forced the German commander, Erwin Rommel, to divert badly needed troops from the front to cover his supply lines. Stirling, however, was captured early in 1943. He managed to escape from Italian prison camps four times, but was finally transferred to the high-security German prison at Colditz. The SAS, which was Stirling's brainchild, had grown by the time of his capture to include French and Greek squadrons. By the time of the Normandy invasion in June 1944 the SAS had grown to brigade-size, with two British and two French regiments and a Belgian squadron. Stirling designed the unit's insignia, a winged sword with a banner bearing the motto: "Who Dares, Wins." Paddy Mayne commanded the unit for the remainder of the war.

The SAS was disbanded after World War II, but when Winston Churchill was again elected prime minister in 1951, he ordered its revival. Like the American Special Forces, the SAS developed doctrine for guerrilla fighting in the light of Cold War combat necessities. The SAS operated in all the British postcolonial actions, in Malaya (1948–1960) and Africa (1952–1955) particularly. Its role grew from sabotage to intelligence gathering and reconnaissance, then to counterinsurgency and antiterrorist operations.

The SAS evolved into Great Britain's elite unit, and inclusion in its ranks is as difficult to obtain as it is desirable. As part of NATO, British forces could be called upon to fight in a number of different climates, and those men accepted for SAS membership undergo the most rigorous training. The training includes action in desert, tropical, mountain, and arctic conditions, extensive training with a large number of British and foreign weapons, amphibious and airborne operations, language training, as well as intense physical conditioning. In the past few years, the commandos have included in their repertoire high-technology weaponry and equipment as it is developed.

The SAS has received public notice in recent history for two high-profile operations. The first was in May 1980 when terrorists took over the Iranian embassy in London. The SAS entered the building surreptitiously then, using stun, flash, and gas grenades, rescued the hostages, killing four of the five terrorists with no losses to themselves. This was an impressive deed, considering that the British government had only a few months prior expanded the SAS role to include antiterrorist operations. The SAS returned to its usual role of deep penetration and sabotage during the British war with Argentina over the Falkland Islands in the South Atlantic in 1982. Operating with the equally elite Special Boat Service, the SAS placed men secretly on the Falkland Islands prior to the main British assault. They observed Argentine troop movements, observed and directed naval gunfire, captured (with 75 men) a 140-man Argentine garrison on San Carlos Island, destroyed an Argentine air base on Pebble Island, and cleared obstructions barring the landing of British regular forces.

The Special Air Service is kept small, maintaining only three 256-man regiments. The Twenty-second SAS Regiment is full-time, based at Hereford in England and operating the SAS training facilities. The Twenty-first and Twenty-third Regiments are territorial and reserve units. Each is made up of four squadrons of four troops, each troop containing 16 men, usually operating in four-man teams. There is some specialization within the Twenty-second, but for the most part all the men are trained in almost all specialties, to be prepared for action anywhere at any time, no matter which unit is currently on call. The commandos not only engage in constant training, they have been used regularly in Northern Ireland operating against the Irish Republican Army. They also are regularly called upon to travel to other countries to assist in organizing and training similar type units for other governments. They assisted the Dutch in a hostage situation aboard a train in May 1977 and the Germans on a mission to rescue hostages aboard a

Lufthansa airliner held in Somalia later that same year, among other similar events. The British government is determined to keep the complement of the SAS small, which means the few who enter its ranks should be kept busy.

References: Cowles, Virginia, *The Phantom Major* (New York: Harper and Bros., 1958); Kelly, Ross, *Special Operations and National Purpose* (Lexington, MA: Lexington Books, 1989).

Spetznaz

Special forces units in the Soviet Union since the 1920s.

Just as the United States has special forces organizations like the Green Berets and the Rangers and the British have the Special Air Service, so the Soviet Union's counterpart was the *Spetznaz*, a contraction of the Russian words for "special-purpose troops." These troops were expected to do a wide variety of jobs, which included spreading disinformation and training guerrillas, as well as fighting. They trace their heritage to similar units formed in the wake of the Russian Revolution of 1917 that performed in the Russian Civil War and against anticommunist guerrillas in the Ukraine and Central Asia during the 1920s and 1930s. During World War II Spetznaz commandos trained the partisans that wrought havoc on the Nazi rear areas, then served in the postwar era in operations in Czechoslovakia and Afghanistan.

At the height of Soviet military strength in the 1980s the Spetznaz forces numbered between 29,000 and 37,000. These were divided into 24 brigades, 41 long-range recon-

A soldier from the Spetznaz special forces unit guards the Russian Interior Ministry headquarters in Moscow, 1996.

naissance companies, three diversionary regiments, and 27 or more agent detachments. They also had detachments operating with the Soviet fleet and the GRU, the Soviet military intelligence organization. The three diversionary regiments served at theater-of-operations level where they were detailed for long-range reconnaissance and sabotage. Those serving with the navy had training in scuba and midget submarine operations. All units required parachute training.

The primary difference between the Soviet special forces and those of the United States or Great Britain was that the bulk of the troops were conscripts serving only the required two-year tour of duty. Actually, the troops themselves were only rarely aware that they were members of a special unit. Most were aware only that they were receiving specialized training. Unlike the Green Berets, in which each man is required to have multiple specialties, the Spetznaz troops had only one per man because the two-year enlistment would not allow for any more varied training. The only training the Spetznaz troops had in common with their Western counterparts was an increased emphasis on unarmed combat, parachute qualification, and airborne/heliborne operations. The officers, being soldiers with longer tenure, received more specialized training, including instruction from the GRU Academy for senior officers.

As the Spetznaz training was only a more intense version of normal Soviet instruction, so were the commandos' weapons only slightly different from normal military issue. Weapons equipped with silencers were one such option, although the quality of that equipment tended to be inferior to Western counterparts. The Spetznaz forces were issued the best semiautomatic weapons, the AK-74 and AKSU, along with PKM general-purpose machine guns, RPG-7 and RPG-18 for antitank use, 30-mm and 40-mm grenade launchers, and occasionally Strela hand-held surface-to-air missiles. There are reports of small Spetznaz units operating in the early 1970s in Vietnam testing Dragunov sniper rifles. In Afghanistan it was reported that some Spetznaz were equipped with a spring-powered knife and most of the troops wore body armor. Their communications equipment was always the best available.

The Spetznaz forces in post–World War II Soviet doctrine were designed to neutralize critical targets behind enemy lines, such as nuclear launch sites, headquarters, or communications centers. Such deep penetration ability was proven in Czechoslovakia in 1968 and Afghanistan in 1979 as Spetznaz troops seized key locations that paralyzed enemy reactions. Indeed, Soviet assassins killed Afghan leader Amin to facilitate the pro-Soviet coup. Reconnaissance troops (*Razvedchiki*) were contained within all Soviet army divisions. All these parachute-trained troops would have been used for deep penetration operations, although mainly in a scouting rather than a combat role. Raiders (*Raydoviki*) operated in company- and battalion-sized units for sabotage and guerrilla training, along the same lines as operations assigned to U.S. Army Ranger units. The *Vysotniki* troops acted like American Green Beret units. Operating in small units, their missions would be more specialized, secretive, and dangerous. These would have been trained in HALO (high altitude, low opening) parachute jumping.

More specialized units appeared during the Soviet operations in Afghanistan. Mountain troops were observed there in greater numbers than Western analysts predicted, with the special training and equipment such operations entail. Training facilities were also reported to have been planned in Afghanistan for mobile desert warfare operations that potentially could have been used farther south in Iran. The GRU-trained troops had even more specialized training for covert operations. These soldiers learned to act individually, in civilian clothes or enemy uniforms, for intelligence gathering, sabotage, and even assassination. All the Spetznaz units, especially those with the most delicate missions, would have been committed immediately upon commencement of hostilities, rather than beforehand, in order to try to make impossible any early warning of the enemy.

The fear of Spetznaz operations to commence at the outbreak of any hostilities was sufficient at the height of the Cold War for Western armies to hold large-scale exercises dealing with the threat. Special operations forces, such as the SAS or Green Berets, at the "aggressor" military bases in the United States, Great Britain, and throughout Europe practiced identification procedures and base defense training. Spetznaz success in places like Afghanistan was sufficient rationale for such exercises. With the end of the Cold War, however, many such training operations have been downgraded. However, with terrorism still a problem overseas, base defense for American troops is still vital. Although the Spetznaz have officially been severely cut back since the collapse of the Soviet Union (as have all Soviet forces), their skills will almost certainly become available in Third World military markets just as other Soviet specialists and weaponry are.

References: Isby, David, *Ten Million Bayonets* (London: Arms and Armour Press, 1988); Kelly, Ross, *Special Operations and National Purpose* (Lexington, MA: Lexington Books, 1989).

Storm Troops

Specialized soldiers operating with the German army in France in World War I.

World War I in France was fought in what was certainly the most futile way possible. The Industrial Revolution had produced weapons of mass destruction like the machine gun, tank, and poison gas, yet the generals throughout most of the war sent their troops into combat in the same fashion soldiers had attacked for more than one hundred years: mass infantry assaults with soldiers rushing forward line abreast over open ground. The trench system that was developed soon after the war started made such attacks suicide, yet the generals continued to send their men forward like this from 1914 through 1918. The "no man's land" between the trenches became a killing ground, while the trenches themselves became underground living quarters that only occasionally were lost or gained by combat. The only change in tactics was to precede each assault with massive amounts of artillery. This, however, gave the defenders plenty of warning when and where the infantry assault would be coming. As soon as the artillery stopped, the defenders came out of their underground shelters and mowed down the advancing troops. Millions of men died.

In 1918 with the war going badly for them, the Germans developed a new method of fighting in an attempt to break the stalemate of trench warfare. They learned a lesson from the Eastern front, where Russian general Brusilov had surprised an Austrian army after attacking with only minimal artillery fire. The Germans took this idea and honed it into the *Sturmtruppen*, the Storm Troops. Instead of attacking in mass waves, they reasoned, send in smaller units on the heels of shorter preliminary barrages. Give them objectives to reach behind the enemy lines, which would paralyze communications and reinforcement while sowing seeds of panic. Move quickly and do not worry about rear or flanks, for the main offensive would follow and clear those up. These rubrics did not represent a particularly new concept, for small parties of men had throughout the war infiltrated enemy positions in order to reconnoiter the lines or bring back prisoners. The Storm Troops, however, would do this on a much larger scale, operating from squad to battalion-sized units.

The effectiveness of this new tactic was enhanced by the talents of two German officers. General Oskar von Hutier, commander of the German Eighteenth Army, had been the man who developed the new tactics and tested them against the Russians on the Eastern front. He commanded the forces that launched the new style of attack against the British in France. The other key figure was Colonel Georg Bruchmüller, who developed a new type of artillery barrage to assist in the

Storm Troops' assaults. Instead of tearing up the ground with large amounts of high explosive, as had been done for the previous three years, he used more poison gas shells. Mustard gas was used on the flank areas of the assault, as its slow diffusion rate would hinder reinforcement from neighboring trench lines. Phosgene gas, which dissipated much more quickly, would be used on the areas of immediate attack to immobilize the troops defending them as well as into the rear areas to neutralize British artillery positions.

Operation Michael was the code name for the first attempted use of Storm Troops tactics in France on 21 March 1918. It succeeded brilliantly. The British Fifth Army in the region around St. Quentin and Albert was caught unawares and soon fled in panic as Storm Troopers, using hand grenades and flame throwers, captured hundreds of prisoners and quickly made their way to rear areas. Here they found evidence of such hurried withdrawal that mess halls still had food cooking with no one in sight. The Germans fed themselves and pushed on toward their objectives of road junctions and British artillery positions. By the end of the day they had accomplished what had been dreamed of by every general since the war started: a hole in the enemy's lines that could be exploited, putting Germans in the Allied rear areas to start the long-hoped-for war of maneuver.

It was fortunate for the British, however, that they had fled so quickly, because the Germans were unable to keep pace. The British managed to establish another defensive position along the Somme River. This is not what stopped the Germans, however. Instead, they succumbed to exhaustion and looting. The Germans had been on short rations and supplies for some months and, to them, the British rear areas were a paradise of food and equipment. In three days they had created a massive bulge in the Allied lines, capturing more territory in less time with fewer casualties than almost any operation of the war. However, three days of constant moving and fighting had worn the Storm Troops out, and the burden of their accumulated loot further slowed them down. German Commander Field Marshall Ludendorff called the offensive a success and canceled further assaults for the time being.

Ludendorff followed up Operation Michael with Operation Georgette, a similar offensive against the British positions further north around Armentieres. This was launched on 9 April 1918 and was just as successful for the Germans, although they failed to reach their intended goal of the rail junction at Hazebrouch. Had that fallen, it would have severed the supply line to the British army from the ports along the English Channel. Still, Operation Georgette caused another massive bulge in British lines as they were again mauled and pushed back. Again, exhaustion on the part of the Storm Troops slowed their advance as time went by.

Buoyed by the huge gains made during these two offensives, Ludendorff prepared for a similar attack to the south in the area called the Chemin des Dames along the Aisne River. It was a quiet sector held by French units and British divisions that had been sent there for rest and refitting. It was more rugged than the area of Operation Michael, so the Germans added some mountain troops to the Storm Troop units. On 28 May 1918 the Germans once again threw the Allies into a panic. The French troops, already demoralized from earlier slaughter, broke and ran. Reinforcements found themselves overwhelmed by the rapid German advance. The Germans captured undamaged virtually every bridge across the Aisne River. The offensive moved inexorably toward Paris as reinforcements were pushed forward. At this point a new player emerged: the United States. Although America had declared war on Germany more than a year earlier, it was still drafting and training men, most of whom were still at home. Some 120,000 Americans were in France, but they were half-trained and untested. They were also the only troops available. American General John Pershing temporarily lent the American Second, Third, and Forty-second Divisions to the French, and they stemmed the German tide.

From 30 May to 17 June 1918, American marines and infantry halted the Germans, at enormous cost, at Belleau Wood south of Soissons. The German advance stalled at what came to be called the Second Battle of the Marne River, but Ludendorff ordered more men into the push for Paris. Had he followed his original intent and attacked in Flanders far to the north, he may have collapsed the entire Allied line. Instead, the lure of Paris was too great—but the Allies were now reinforced and waiting. This time it was Allied artillery that did the most damage, and the follow-up attacks by American and French troops at Soissons and Chateau-Thierry marked the beginning of the end for the German war effort.

Through the summer and fall of 1918 the Allies pushed a broken and undersupplied German army out of France and to the borders of Germany itself before an armistice was signed in November. The German Storm Troops had succeeded in their tasks, but the introduction of their tactics was a case of too little, too late. The lesson learned by the Storm Troops was not forgotten, however. The Germans between the wars focussed on the idea of mission-oriented attacks that did not worry about flanks. The problem of exhaustion was solved by the development between the wars of German armored forces. The theory of quick penetration and disruption of rear areas was reborn in 1939 in Poland with the blitzkrieg that almost took Adolph Hitler's armies to European domination.

References: Barnett, Correlli, *The Swordbearers* (New York: Morrow, 1964); Pitt, Barrie, *1918: The Last Act* (New York: Ballantine, 1963); Toland, John, *No Man's Land* (New York: Doubleday, 1980).

Submariners

Specialized sailors operating in underwater craft.

Going underwater is not a recent phenomenon. Aristotle reported that Alexander the Great's men used a type of diving barrel at the siege of Tyre in 332 B.C. English sailors used crude diving bells to recover valuable cannons after the British fleet defeated the Spanish Armada in 1588. Cornelis Drebble, a Dutch engineer, attempted to travel under water about 1620. Drebble built a wooden-framed submarine covered in leather and waterproofed with grease. Twelve oarsmen powered the craft that could submerge to 12 feet. Submarine designs became abundant by the 1700s, and England had 14 patents by 1727.

David Bushnell, an American inventor, is credited with building the first war submarine, used during the Revolutionary War. His vessel, called the *Turtle*, was made of wood with iron bands and covered in tar to stop leaks. It was a one-man vessel propelled by turning cranks attached to propellers. One propeller made the craft go forward or backward; the other lifted or lowered the craft—depending on which way the cranks were turned. The operator opened a valve letting water into a tank to submerge the craft. A hand pump was used to force the water out when the operator wanted to surface. The *Turtle* had enough air to stay under water for 30 minutes, and could dive to 20 feet. A glass tube with a floating cork told the depth, and a compass reported direction. The instruments were painted with phosphorus to be seen while under water. The *Turtle* would approach an anchored ship to attach a timed charge to its hull, then move away. The first attack was in 1776 at New York against the British ship HMS *Eagle*, but the charge exploded harmlessly in the river.

The first effective submarine was the CSS *Hunley* designed by H. L. Hunley in 1863. It was powered by eight men cranking a shaft connected to the propeller. Catastrophe plagued this vessel: it sank twice in heavy seas, then failed to surface during a drill, killing Hunley and the crew he was training. The refloated sub finally achieved results by sinking the Union warship USS *Housatonic*, but the resulting wave also took the *Hunley* to its doom with all hands. This marked the first time a submarine sank an enemy ship.

The United States Navy commissioned the USS *Holland* in 1900. It was the first submarine to use a gasoline engine on the surface and electric power when submerged. It had a primitive periscope and carried three torpedoes. This vessel validated the submarine as a legitimate weapon for war, and by World War I all major navies had submarines. Early use was limited to coastal operations, duties that included mine laying and supply. Germany, however, would begin using U-boats (*Unterseeboote*, literally "underseaboats") instead of surface vessels to attack shipping, and the British developed antisubmarine submarines to counter the threat. Thus, the submarine established its role as an effective weapon of war.

Submarines improved considerably in World War II. They had long range, could patrol for weeks at a time, and became very lethal. American submarines were assigned less than 2 percent of all navy personnel but accounted for 55 percent of enemy shipping destroyed in the Pacific Ocean. Submarines were also dangerous for the crews. Forty thousand German sailors served in submarines and 30,000 of them were lost. All submariners were considered special for these reasons. Promotions came quickly, and military procedures tended to be more relaxed for them. German submarine crews could grow beards with the captain's approval and wear nonuniform apparel; some sported bowler hats or ski caps. A German captain could paint insignias on the U-boat's conning tower. These insignias came from various sources: family crests, coats of arms, and good luck symbols like a horseshoe or black cat. The insignia had special meaning to the crew. To boost morale, U-boat crews also painted on the conning tower their total tonnage of shipping sunk.

Submarine life was demanding. A submarine might patrol as long as 90 days, and the crew had no contact with their families. The craft ran submerged in daytime and surfaced at night to recharge batteries, so the crew would see little daylight. Men stood lookout in all types of weather, and were always wet. American submarines were heated but German submarines were not. Germans wore leather uniforms to stay warm. Food would spoil, so no fresh fruit or vegetables were available after a few weeks at sea. Americans had refrigerators for meat, and made bread daily. Germans, with no refrigerators, ate canned meat and carried many loaves of bread that soon grew moldy; the German submariners called this bread "white rabbit" when mold grew on the loaf. American submariners had saltwater showers, but Germans bathed only in sea spray when allowed on deck. Men shared the same bunks, due to lack of space, by alternating when changing watches. This procedure is called "hot bunking" because the mattress is still warm from the last occupant. Japanese submarines were even less accommodating than German subs, for they used no bunks at all and efficiency suffered greatly as a result.

The United States, Germany, and Japan were the main submarine powers in World War II. German submarines were very effective in the Atlantic Ocean due to strategy developed by Admiral Karl Doenitz (1891–1980). He invented the technique for U-boats known as the wolf pack. A U-boat would locate an enemy convoy and radio others to come and—like wolves—to join in the kill. The United States' main submarine campaign was in the Pacific Ocean attacking Japanese shipping. Japanese submarines were also formidable in the Pacific. The "I class" submarine could reach the United States coast, but heavy losses of men and equipment diminished their effectiveness. Japan resorted to human torpedoes (called *kyokoku heiki*, meaning "national salvation weapon," later called *kaiten*, or "heaven-shaker") in 1944, but the end of the war came before they could influence the outcome.

The Japanese submariners were going to certain doom. American submariners also faced doom, but theirs was uncertain. This doom took the form of faulty torpedoes, which ran too deep, or worse, would fail to

USS Porpoise *and* Shark, *two submarines in drydock with the crews posted on the bows, early 1900s*

explode, leaving the submarine detected and vulnerable to counterattack. A new magnetic warhead, supposed to explode in close proximity to a ship's hull, was no better. Washington officials even blamed the crews for failing to use the torpedoes properly. The trouble was discovered in late 1943. Torpedoes were dropped from a crane onto a steel plate to simulate hitting a target. The investigation showed that firing pins were bending instead of striking the charge and exploding. The problem was rectified and the American subs became deadly hunters. It is a tribute to submarine crews that they carried out patrols with faulty torpedoes, knowing they may have been risking their lives in vain. This dedication to duty is what confers on these men a well- deserved place in history.

Many men contributed to the American submarine service but one who stands out is Admiral Hyman G. Rickover (1900–1986). He helped develop the nuclear-powered submarine USS *Nautilus*, launched in 1954. This began the era of nuclear-powered submarines, which are specifically designed to travel under water at all times. The nuclear submarine, by leaving port and remaining submerged until returning to base, established new tactics in submarine warfare. Its mission is one of deterrence and prevention of nuclear war, and is an important factor in keeping the peace. A nuclear sub is able to deliver ballistic missiles on enemy targets anywhere in the world. The missiles can reach targets in less than 15 minutes because no location on land is far from an ocean. For these warriors, however, a successful mission is returning to base with no shots fired.

Nuclear submarine crew members are also different from their predecessors. Instead of hunting ships to sink, they patrol to locate and monitor the movement of other vessels, while keeping their submarine at full readiness. This highly complex craft requires fully one half of the crew to be assigned to engineering and maintenance. This technical work requires much training because the entire crew may depend on one individiual doing the job correctly. A nuclear submarine dive alone requires more than 200 operational checks. The typical sailor goes through exhaustive physical and psychological screening and experiences a couple of years of training before being assigned to a nuclear sub. An officer must have a science or engineering degree and more than five years of training before being awarded supervisory duties. Once aboard the sub, all men have to pass their qualifications in order to earn their "Dolphins" pin. This pin is worn by all submariners who have completed training in their job categories. Officers are awarded gold and enlisted sailors wear silver dolphins. Men are rated in different areas and are qualified in many fields to be able to do many jobs if needed. School is conducted on the submarine while on patrol and training never stops. One rating, for example, is the ELT (Engineering Laboratory Technician). This sailor's duties require monitoring personnel for radiation and maintaining primary and secondary reactor chemistry. This person is trained in chemistry, radiology, and radiation. Another series of ratings held by an officer could be in sonar, propulsion, chemistry and radiation, and torpedo and fire control.

Routine aboard a nuclear submarine can be described as quiet. The term "Silent Service," denoting a submarine's underwater stealth, has new meaning in the electronic age. Detection by sound is a submarine's enemy. Listening devices can hear a sub miles away. Silence is so important that the hull is covered in rubber plates that absorb electronic signals, and acoustic sensors inside the sub report excessive internal noises to the crew. Submarines are now quieter than the surrounding ocean.

American submarines have two crews, called Blue and Gold, to reflect traditional navy colors. One crew is on shore duty while the other is at sea. They rotate every four months. Crews at sea work six hours on watch and 12 hours off watch. Off-watch crews train, do maintenance, or conduct drills. Sleeping is done in short periods and enlisted ranks, where required, use hot bunking. Food is the best the navy can offer; the traditional meal halfway through the cruise is steak and crab. Fresh eggs are available by putting wax on the shells for preservation. There are also soda and ice cream machines on board. Still, fresh fruit ranks high on a sailor's list upon returning to shore. Crew members each get a 40-word "familygram" each week, but send out no messages. The sub has a library, and videos are available on closed-circuit TV.

Submarines are an elite service with many hardships but also many rewards. Crews are highly trained in very technical fields. Besides constant schooling and having to maintain their ratings, submariners also go to battle, fight, and demonstrate courage as do all soldiers. Men who choose submarine duty seldom transfer. They know few can do this job and it is important. The ability to travel undetected and deliver a strike anywhere in the world with this sophisticated weapon is a credit to the crews who man them, and a significant factor for world peace.

—John Stephen Drake

References: Clancy, Tom. *Submarine: A Guided Tour Inside a Nuclear Warship* (New York: Berkley Books, 1993); McKay, Ernest A., *Undersea Terror: U-Boat Wolf Packs in World War II* (New York: Julian Messner, 1982); Weller, George Anthony, *The Story of Submarines* (New York: Random House, 1962).

Swedes of Gustavus Adolphus

The dominant army in the Thirty Years War (1618–1648) responsible for many military innovations, as well as establishing the first modern professional army.

Much of northern Europe went to war in 1619 for political and religious reasons. The Diet of Augsburg in 1555 had decreed that a prince could mandate a particular religion within the borders of his domain. This applied to Lutherans as well as Catholics. It did not, however, include Calvinists. As Calvinism grew in popularity with many in the lower classes, it also became more distasteful to many princes. In 1619 Ferdinand of Bohemia, a staunch Catholic, rose to the position of Holy Roman Emperor. Although placed in that position by the seven electors whose duty it was to choose the emperor, Ferdinand had but two days prior to his election been deposed by his Bohemian subjects in favor of a Calvinist ruler, Frederick V of the Palatinate. In order to regain his Bohemian throne and crush the Calvinists he despised, Ferdinand brought the power of the Holy Roman Empire to bear on Calvinists in his homeland and on Protestants in northern Europe in general. Thus began the Thirty Years War.

Throughout the 1620s the Catholic imperial forces pillaged their way through Protestant territory, the armies led by Johann Tilly and Albrecht von Wallenstein. These two generals raised forces through force, principally by devastating a region so thoroughly that the only alternative for the survivors was to join the army and be paid in loot. With an army driven by blood lust more than principle, the Catholics defeated Frederick V and gave his homeland of the Palatinate to a Catholic monarch. They then defeated Danish forces raised by King Christian IV that entered the war in 1625. By 1628, however, the Catholic armies had stretched their forces too thin and ran into trouble when attempting to besiege the port city of Stralsund on the Baltic Sea.

A few days prior to the beginning of the siege, the city of Stralsund concluded a treaty with Swedish King Gustavus Adolphus. Gustavus's army was the best of its era and was molded completely by its commander. With this army Gustavus acquired the provinces of Estonia and Latvia after defeating the forces of both Poland and Russia between 1604 and 1617. It was an army unlike any other of its day, and Gustavus embarked for Stralsund to both protect his newly acquired provinces and to fight for the Protestant cause.

The armies of Europe at that time were primarily mercenary. The core of the force typically consisted of professionals who hired out their services, while the rank and file would be whatever manpower could be obtained. Such an army was therefore lacking in discipline and cohesion, but if well led could be devastating. Gustavus, however, created his army strictly from Swedes, and did so by mandating that every tenth man in each parish was liable for military service. This created a national army of citizen-soldiers such as had not been seen in Europe since the fall of Rome. It was also the first standing army since the Roman Empire, for Gustavus kept 20,000 men under arms at all times. Seventy percent of Sweden's budget was dedicated to this army, and it was one of the few armies of the age regularly and fairly paid. Gustavus instilled in his men a spirit that combined nationalism and religion, and it was an army that was motivated, disciplined, well prepared, and well equipped.

Although all the armies of the seventeenth century were equipped with firearms, Gustavus improved his weaponry with mobility in mind. The standard formations of the day were large squares based upon the system developed by the Spaniards some decades earlier. The standard square was made up of a mixture of pikemen and musketeers, who used a heavy wheel-lock musket. The Swedish musket was redesigned by Gustavus to lighten it from the standard 25 pounds to a more manageable 11 pounds. This made the standard forked support used by other armies unnecessary. He also created the cartridge, a paper package with a premeasured amount of gunpowder and a musket ball. This made for much quicker reloading, hence much greater firepower. The musketeers were deployed in ranks six deep, unlike the ten ranks used in other armies. The front three would face the enemy with ranks successively kneeling, crouching, and standing. They would volley fire, then countermarch to the rear to reload while the other three ranks moved forward to deploy and fire. Although the standard formation of other armies called for a greater number of pikemen to act as defenders for the musketeers, the Swedes introduced a 150-man company that included 72 musketeers to only 54 pikemen. The smaller company could be used much more flexibly than the large square formation.

Gustavus also improved his artillery. Most guns of the time shot a 33-pound ball and were so heavy that they were arranged to stay in one place all day. The Swedish artillery was much lighter. Most fired only six- or 12-pound balls while the smallest (which could be easily moved by a single horse or three men) fired only a three-pound ball. Constant training that only a standing army could provide made Gustavus's artillerists able to fire their cannon eight times while the enemy musketeers could fire but six times in the same span. Again, this meant increased fire power for the Swedes. By quickly moving light field pieces around the battlefield and using smaller infantry units to outflank the bulky enemy squares, the Swedish rate of fire was designed to take advantage of the large target the enemy formations presented.

Finally, Gustavus remolded the cavalry. The standard European horseman was little more than a semimobile gun platform. He would ride to a position on the battlefield, usually on the flanks of the infantry squares, and deploy with the same large musket the men in the squares carried. The cavalry was trained to fight in much the same fashion as Gustavus's infantry, with a line of horsemen delivering a volley of pistol fire, then riding to the rear to reload as another line advanced. The Swedish cavalry was again more lightly armed, with carbines (shortened muskets) and pistols. In the early years of his reign, Gustavus's cavalry fought as dragoons, mounted infantry who dismounted to fight in order to capture positions before the arrival of the infantry. In later times they were equipped with sabres and fought from the saddle. The Swedish horsemen would charge the enemy cavalry, which had to maintain its formation in order to maintain its fire, and the speed and shock of the Swedish assault shattered whatever cohesion the enemy may have had. Then the close-range pistol fire, coupled with the cold steel of the sabres, proved more than most horsemen could withstand. The coordination necessary among cavalry, infantry, and artillery only came from the constant training that a regular standing army could provide.

All of this fire power and coordination needed direction, however, and Gustavus provided that as well. He proved himself in battle (which always endears men to their leader) but ruled his army with an iron hand. Unlike the pillaging and looting encouraged in the armies of Tilly and Wallenstein, the Swedish army was banned from any action against civilians. Hospitals, schools, and churches were strictly off-limits as targets. Anyone caught looting or harming a civilian was punished by death, the sentence for violating about a quarter of Gustavus's regulations. Gustavus apparently believed that if one fought for religious reasons, one should behave in a more religious manner.

Thus, it was a thoroughly professional army that Gustavus Adolphus brought to the continent to assist the city of Stralsund in 1628. Although he was forced to recruit replacements while on campaign, he tended to hire individuals and not mercenary units. This brought the new man into an already organized unit with an existing identity, and he became part of the Swedish army rather than remaining a part of a mercenary band. The Swedes arrived on the coast of Pomerania in 1630 but, rather than welcoming them, the hard-pressed Protestants viewed Gustavus's forces at first with suspicion. In the fall of 1631 Gustavus finally found an ally in the Elector of Saxony, and in September the allied force met and defeated Tilly's imperial force at Breitenfeld, near Leipzig. In three hours, the entire momentum of the war was reversed. Thirteen thousand of Tilly's 40,000 men were killed or wounded and the army of the Holy Roman Empire fled, abandoning all their artillery. This victory helped unite the Protestants into an army that numbered almost 80,000 by the end of the year.

The following spring Gustavus defeated Tilly again, and the imperial commander died of wounds a few weeks later. The Protestant army liberated much of southern Germany, but in the process extended their supply lines too far. Wallenstein took advantage of this by moving a new army into Saxony, threatening Gustavus's rear. Wallenstein occupied a strongly fortified position at Alte Veste, which the Protestants failed to take after a two-day battle in September 1632. When Wallenstein dispersed his men into winter quarters in November, Gustavus seized his opportunity. He attacked with 18,000 men against Wallenstein's 20,000 at Leuthen, about 20 miles from Breitenfeld. Again the forces of the empire were forced to retreat, but Gustavus was killed in the battle.

The army command fell to Prince Bernhard of Saxe-Weimar, who led it during the majority of the battle at Leuthen, but Gustavus was irreplaceable. Luckily for the Protestants, however, Wallenstein failed to follow up on the advantage of having killed Gustavus. Instead, he entered into a variety of political machinations that ultimately lost him his job and then his life. With the deaths of Wallenstein and Tilly, the empire's armies were left without talented leadership. Nevertheless, the war dragged on until the Peace of Westphalia in 1648. The Protestants (including the Calvinists) won significant concessions in the peace treaty, and religious war came to an end in Europe for a long time. The reforms implemented by Gustavus had a great effect on the other armies of Europe. Professional standing armies became the norm and civilians remained out of the way of the battlefield until the nineteenth century. Nationalism, which had been growing for two hundred years, began to take serious root in Europe. Gustavus Adolphus's professional military was the standard by which others were created until the development of the completely nationalist armies engendered by the French Revolution.

References: Addington, Larry, *Patterns of War through the Eighteenth Century* (Bloomington: University of Indiana Press, 1990); Roberts, Michael, *Gustavus Adolphus: A History of Sweden,* 2 vols. (New York: Longman, 1953–1958); Wedgewood, C.V., *The Thirty Years War* (Gloucester, MA: P. Smith, 1969 [1938]).

T

Terry's Texas Rangers

A partisan unit operating as part of the Confederate army during the American Civil War (1861–1865).

One of the Confederacy's best-known cavalry units was informally created on board a stagecoach between Austin and Brenham, Texas, in March 1861. Benjamin F. Terry, Thomas Lubbock, and John Wharton, all representatives at Texas's secession convention, decided among themselves to organize a cavalry regiment for service in the war they were sure would not be long in coming. Terry was a wealthy planter from the Houston area, Lubbock was a Houston merchant and a veteran of the Texas revolution, and Wharton was a lawyer born in Tennessee but brought to Texas as an infant. These men, all financially secure and socially respectable, did what many Southerners did in early 1861: They voluntarily raised their own forces for service to their country.

The unit was not organized immediately, however. Confederate President Jefferson Davis, overwhelmed by pleas for command and rank, rejected the Texans' offer because he was sure the war would be short and that transportation of units from Texas would be unnecessary and costly. Terry and Lubbock, however, traveled to Virginia on their own and managed to wrangle assignments to General James Longstreet's staff for the battle at Bull Run in July 1861. There they impressed influential people in the Confederate command and were granted permission to raise their unit. They quickly returned to Texas and advertised for volunteers. Each man was to bring his own horse and weapons, and the term of enlistment was for the duration of the war. Four thousand men arrived in Houston and Terry was obliged to turn some of them away, finally accepting almost 1,200 men into his command. The men were immediately sworn into the Confederate army, but Terry delayed formally organizing the regiment until they arrived in Virginia. Although he was the unit's organizer, he refused to take any rank until elections were held by the men.

The Texans traveled to Beaumont, where Terry directed the horses to be sent back. The men marched through Louisiana to New Iberia, then floated down the Mississippi to New Orleans, arriving in September 1861. The experience was not pleasant, for the men were not prepared to march and the weather turned cold. It was a small foretaste of future misery. In New Orleans, the recruits were referred to as the Texas Rangers, the local population believing they were indeed that frontier organization. Although the Texas Rangers did not officially organize any forces during the war, the appellation stuck to Terry's command. Also in New Orleans Terry received word from his old friend Albert Sydney Johnston, now commander of Confederate forces in the west. Johnston notified Terry that the cavalry were to travel to Kentucky and join his forces. Johnston promised the best horses Kentucky could provide and that the Texans would operate as an independent command as long as he was in charge. Serving under a Texan and being offered quality free horses was too good an offer to refuse, and in October 1861 the regiment boarded trains for Columbus, Kentucky.

In Tennessee, the population also believed the Texas Rangers had arrived, and the Texans either could not or would not convince them otherwise. Although they were welcomed by the citizens of Nashville, the Texans suffered their first casualties; they were not from combat, but from disease and sickness, including measles, various fevers, and respiratory infections. After ten days in Nashville, the Texans were transferred to Bowling Green, Kentucky. Here the ten companies were officially organized into a regiment and the Confederate government designated them the Eighth Texas Cavalry. Had Terry officially organized his regiment upon its creation, they almost certainly would have been designated the First Texas Cavalry. As it was, seven units had been organized before his. Not happy with the later number, the unit took to calling themselves what the civilians had: Terry's Texas Rangers. In Bowling Green, elections were held and Terry now officially became a colonel, with Lubbock his second in command. They were now a real regiment, but little else about them was regulation. There were no consistent uniforms or weapons, each man wearing and shooting whatever he brought with him. Pistols and shotguns were the preferred weapons, with Bowie knives chosen over sabres. Johnston provided the horses as promised.

In the field the first few months of the regiment's existence were dreary. The weather was cold and damp and the numbers of sick rose steadily. Outbreaks of measles and respiratory infections disabled and killed so many that by January 1862 only half the men were available for duty. Eighty-four men died that winter, but only five owing to enemy action. Still, the unit did see some action. On 17 December Terry led his men on reconnaissance to Woodsonville, Kentucky. There they engaged elements of the Thirty-second Indiana Regiment. It was a short and relatively inconsequential skirmish, but Terry was killed. A man widely respected by his command and potentially a great cavalry commander, Terry was struck down early in the war before he could prove himself. Lubbock took command, but he too was killed a month later. This established a pattern for command in the Rangers: The officers at all levels were regularly wounded or killed. Such is the fate of leaders who lead rather than direct. Command fell to the third inhabitant of that stagecoach almost two years earlier, John Wharton. The Rangers continued to operate patrols in Kentucky throughout February, but withdrew to Corinth, Mississippi, after the Union capture of Forts Henry and Donelson in northwestern Tennessee in midmonth.

The Rangers were involved in the battle at Shiloh in early April 1862 but most of their work came covering the Confederate retreat. Wharton was wounded in the battle and turned command over to Major Thomas Harrison, who was considered by the men to be something of a gun-shy martinet. He was to prove them wrong. Joined with Tennessee cavalry under the command of Nathan Bedford Forrest, the Rangers were detailed to slow the close Union forces pressing on the retreat. The Rangers led the attack and stunned the Union with the ferocity of their charge. At close range with buckshot-loaded shotguns they dispersed the Union forces trying to stand against them. They then chased them all the way back to the main Union body, securing the retreat of the main Confederate army. The action cost the regiment three company commanders wounded.

After some raiding and scouting into central Tennessee in early summer 1862, the new Confederate commander, P. G. T. Beauregard, ordered Forrest to unite the cavalry commands into one unit under Forrest's direction. Under the command of one of the finest cavalry generals in all of history, the Texans shone. At Murfreesboro in mid-July they captured 1,200 Union troops, along with much-needed supplies, artillery, and horses. Forrest's brigade harassed Union supply lines throughout the summer and fall of 1862 creating havoc for Union General Buell. In September, Wharton returned to duty and was given command of the brigade. Forrest was ordered to create another similar unit. With Wharton's promotion, Thomas Harris was elevated to command of the Ranger regiment. The Texans continued to harass Union supply columns for the remainder of the year, developing a reputation with the Union as well as their own forces. Regimental strength, however, now barely reached 700, although returning wounded and a dribble of recruits from home kept the Rangers stronger than many other Confederate regiments.

The Rangers again did good work around Murfreesboro in early January 1863 at the battle of Stones River. After this battle Harrison resigned his command to be replaced by L. N. Rayburn, who was soon succeeded by Gustave Cook. The spring and summer of 1863 brought more scouting and harassment of Union supply lines in Tennessee, with a number of trains captured or destroyed. In July the Rangers were able to withdraw to Georgia and spend two months resting and refitting, but their numbers were now just over 400. At Chickamauga they covered a Confederate flank and captured 136 members of a cavalry brigade commanded by General Thomas Crook, who went on to fame after the war as an Indian fighter. In the autumn they were back to their raiding, destroying large amounts of Union supplies in eastern Tennessee, but the pro-Union population of that area, coupled with the constant riding and fighting, took its toll on the unit. By spring of 1864 Terry's Texas Rangers were back in Georgia, preparing for General William Sherman's offensive toward Atlanta. They fought Sherman's men, sometimes as cavalry and sometimes dismounted as infantry. They were detailed to an attack on Sherman's supply lines in late July, but strong Union forces in the rear lessened the effect of their raiding. Meanwhile, Sherman occupied Atlanta. The Rangers did what they could to harass Sherman's flanks as his army staged the infamous "March to the Sea" in November and December, but they could not do much to limit the destruction. After Savannah fell in December 1864 the Rangers continued to fight and harass Sherman's command as he marched into the Carolinas, and Sherman singled the Texans out as particularly bothersome to his progress.

The regiment made its last major charge at Bentonville, North Carolina, on 19 March 1865. Gustave Cook, in command for almost two years, was wounded and replaced by J. F. Matthews, who oversaw the surrender of the Rangers. In late April 1865 Matthews gave each company commander permission to do what he would with his company, withdraw or surrender. The regiment now numbered a mere 248 men. Like the rest of the Confederate army, they took their paroles and went home.

— Melvin C. (Mel) Wheat

References: Cutrer, Thomas, ed., *Terry's Texas Rangers* (Austin: State House Press, 1996); Fitzhugh, Lester Newton, *Terry's Texas Rangers,* unpublished memoirs (Austin: Barker Center Archives); Fletcher, William, *Rebel Private, Front and Rear* (New York: Penguin, 1995).

Teutonic Knights

A religious and political group of knights operating in Eastern Europe and the Middle East during the thirteenth through sixteenth centuries.

Many crusades followed the first crusade of the western Christians against the Muslims in the Holy Land in the year 1095. Many of these campaigns, which spanned centuries, had nothing to do with the eastern Mediterranean shores and the Holy Land. Europe sought to correct aberrant Christian behavior in Bohemia against the Hussites, in southern France against the Albingensians, in England against the Lollards, and even in the Near East, when Christian crusaders in the Fourth Crusade attacked their fellow Christians of the Byzantine Empire and conquered

Constantinople (Istanbul) in 1204. But, one of the last and longest crusades (1226-1525) was that conducted by The Order of the Hospital of the Blessed Virgin Mary of the German House of Jerusalem—more commonly known as the Order of the Teutonic Knights (in German *Deutsche Ritterorden*).

During this period of three centuries, the Teutonic Knights waged war in the name of Christ against the peoples of the southern shores of the Baltic, from what is now northeast Germany to northwest Russia. This land includes portions of the present countries of Germany, Poland, Lithuania, Latvia, Estonia, and Russia. Although many historians have made much of the theory that this was an aggressive and deliberate strategy on the part of the Knights, it would seem that the Knights' activities were motivated more by the personal interests of the leaders of the order than by religious or nationalistic reasons.

A historian of warfare in the Middle Ages, Maurice Keen, discussed the role played by the Knights in the spectrum of both the Crusades specifically and medieval warfare in general: "In these wars, the Teutonic Knights relied heavily on the voluntary aid of visiting knights from other parts of Europe; and Prussia and Lithuania became, in consequence, a principal center of crusading activity for western knighthood in the fourteenth century" (Keen, 1984). Before the fourteenth century, as well as later in the fifteenth and early sixteenth centuries, the Knights not only relied heavily on support from 'western Christianity' but eagerly sought such support by appeals to individual knights, and even negotiated alliances with various monarchs and noblemen in northeastern and central Europe.

In fact the very presence of the Teutonic Knights in northeastern Europe was predicated on an invitation from one of the various dukes of Poland in the last quarter of the thirteenth century. Duke Konrad of Mazovia invited the Knights to help conquer and Christianize the pagan and unruly Prussians, who inhabited the lands north of Konrad's principality and blocked his access to the Baltic Sea. Actually, in the first quarter of the thirteenth century, the Knights had already begun diversifying their crusading efforts into other geographic areas because of the deteriorating Christian situation in the Holy Land. In 1223 King Andrew II of Hungary expelled them, as he had strong indications that they were attempting to create their own principality in Transylvania at his expense. Fortunately, Konrad's invitation had arrived as the Knights' tenure in both the Near East and Transylvania became strained.

To understand why the Knights emerged as a major aggressive force in northeastern Europe, an explanation of their origins is necessary. The Teutonic Knights first emerged in the Near East as an offshoot of a hospital confraternity composed of Germans (*Domus hospitalis sanctae Mariae Teutonicorum*), which had been formed in 1128 in the Latin Kingdom of Jerusalem. German knights, stranded by the death of Emperor Frederick I during the Third Crusade (1189-1192), had begun to affiliate with this confraternity, which had moved to Acre after Jerusalem fell in 1187. A large number of the German knights decided not to return home and, after copying the example of the Knights of the Hospital of St. John, were incorporated in 1198 as a military order. At that time the Teutonic Knights were recognized by Amalric, King of Jerusalem, and Pope Innocent III. Emperor Henry VI's chancellor, Conrad of Hildesheim, recognized the potential of this new knightly order, as did other German magnates, and helped them accrue large estates in areas of the Holy Roman Empire. These acquisitions provided them with substantial revenue that helped to finance many of their subsequent efforts, both in the Holy Land and in the Baltic.

The Knights reciprocated the favor bestowed on them by the politically most powerful elements in Germany by serving as a vital support for German efforts after the Third Crusade, including accompanying German-led expeditions in the Holy Land. Beginning in Acre, they expanded their re-

Marienburg, the chief fortress and seat of the Order of Teutonic Knights, begun in 1276

sources by accepting feudal lands and castles belonging to King Leo III of Armenia in Cilicia (present day southern Turkey) in 1212 and by adding the castle of Montfort, near Tyre, in 1227. In the early years of the thirteenth century Hermann Bardt, the grand master (*Hochmeister*) and his successor, Hermann von Salza, were both mentioned prominently in the records of activities in the Holy Land. Von Salza (Hochmeister from 1210 to 1239) negotiated the acquisition of the Turkish castles, negotiated and planned the subsequent activities in Transylvania, accepted Konrad of Mazovia's invitation to establish the Knights on the Baltic shores, and united with the Livonian Knights in 1237. In fact, he was such a recognized force in the spectrum of German politics that Holy Roman Emperor Frederich II appointed him to the position of imperial chancellor and also made him a prince of the empire.

Von Salza's agenda for the Knights in Transylvania apparently was a prelude to later attitudes and strategies as they established themselves in northeastern Europe. King Andrew II of Hungary had requested their aid in his efforts to deal with the non-Christian Cumans in his eastern lands and also in his confrontations with the Byzantine Empire in 1211. Thirteen years later in 1223 he realized that the Knights he had called on for help were establishing an independent principality in his territory, so he expelled them. This pattern of styling themselves as the bulwark of Christianity in eastern and northeastern Europe while organizing de facto self-governing "colonies" of Knights was to repeat itself many times.

The Knights remained active in the Holy Land even while they began to develop opportunities for expansion into new lands. Several historians have labeled their efforts as a willingness to sell their services "to any ruler who was willing to pay them to fight *pagans and infidels*" (Keen, 1984). However, long after Lithuanians, Poles, Prussians, and Russians had been "Christianized," the Knights continued their aggression. After accepting Konrad of Mazovia's invitation to aid his efforts to open up Mazovia's access to the

Baltic Sea, they continued assaults on Christians and non-Christians alike in the Baltic lands.

Despite their aggressiveness, the Teutonic Knights were not always noted for distinction in battle. In 1197 while assisting in the siege of the fortress of Toron in Galilee, the crusaders where informed that an army from Egypt had marched across the Sinai Peninsula and was nearing the fortress. The leaders of the crusaders and the various orders of the monastic knights (including the Teutonic Knights) fled Toron, deserting the helpless foot soldiers, who were left to their own destiny. During the Fifth Crusade, the Knights set fire to food and other supplies during a retreat and thereby alerted the Muslim forces who immediately attacked and decimated the crusading army. In 1242 the Teutonic Knights, together with their brethren the Livonian Knights and their momentary allies the Lithuanians, were defeated by Alexander Yaroslavski, Prince of Novgorod, at the battle of Lake Peipus. The mounted Knights had charged in full armor across the frozen surface of the lake and the ice could not bear their weight.

The most famous defeat of the Knights occurred in 1410 when a combined force of Poles, Lithuanians (together with their Tartar allies), Czechs, Hungarians, and Wallachians under the leadership of King Jogaila confronted them at Grunwald (Tannenberg). For that battle, the Hochmeister, Ulric von Jungingen, had summoned assistance from many Christian countries of western Europe. However, the Knights and their allies were outnumbered with 27,000 men to an estimated 39,000 men on the side of the confederated forces. In many respects, the Teutonic Knights never recovered from this defeat. The Hochmeister, grand marshall, grand commander, and half the Knights were killed. After the battle, the remnants of the defeated army retreated to Marienburg, their magnificent castle/headquarters in Gdansk where they were besieged for several months. The Teutonic Knights never again regained the initiative against the various peoples allied against them. From 1410 forward they were engaged in efforts merely to maintain their existence.

The Teutonic Knights carved out a feudal principality that included most of the Baltic coastline from Gdansk (Poland) to Riga (Latvia) and included portions of present-day Germany, Poland, Lithuania, Latvia, Estonia, and western Russia, where it is estimated that they founded over 1,400 villages and 93 towns. Several historians have noted that their strength resided in their tenacity. Most historians acknowledge that they were very effective—albeit ruthless—administrators and colonizers. Rather than referring to their efforts as a focused policy of "Drang nach Osten" (Drive to the East) some historians have described it as being similar to the less organized evolution of "Manifest Destiny" in the United States. The Knights moved inexorably east against various peoples they chose to consider as theologically unacceptable; or, they engaged in politically expedient reasoning.

The chronology of the Knights' evolution in northeastern Europe is ultimately one of expediency. They were the products and exponents of feudalism, cloaked with the white robe and the red cross, patterned after that of the Knights Templar (who were thereby incensed). They later replaced the red cross with the black cross (the same iron cross adopted by a later German army), but otherwise did not emulate the Templars. Unlike the Templars, they created a feudal state, which became the inspiration for the Knights of the Hospital of St. John (Hospitallers or Knights of Rhodes/Malta) who created principalities in Rhodes and later in Malta. Civil and church authorities and conquerors were busily creating principalities in the thirteenth through the fifteenth centuries throughout Europe.

During the three centuries of the Knights' existence on the Baltic coast, they relied on the support of the Holy Roman Emperor, German magnates within the empire, aspirants to the imperial crown, the papacy, and the nobility of much of western and central

Europe. They were also able to depend on their own substantial financial resources accrued over the years from bequests from the German nobility. In 1400 the Knights depended on their *Wehrpflichtige* (mobilized or conscripted forces), which included 426 knights, 3,200 serving men, 5,872 sergeants, 1,963 troops (conscripted from the towns they ruled), and some 1,500 additional levies from the abbeys in their principality. Hochmeisters represented several of the major ruling families of German principalities and the imperial families, including Habsburgs, Hohenzollerns, Wettins, and others. The Knights also attracted to their crusading efforts such knightly luminaries as Henry Grosmont, duke of Lancaster; Henry of Bolingbroke (later King Henry IV of England); Gaston-Phoebus of Foix; and Duke Albert III of Austria (a Habsburg).

From 1226 to 1525 the various grand masters of the order virtually ignored the subsequent Christianization of numerous Baltic peoples or the authority of vested rulers in the different lands they subjected, or sought to subject, to their authority. During these three centuries they also engaged in activities that were designed to defend or even expand their territories, fighting numerous battles with Poland, Lithuania, or both. The Teutonic Knights approached the sixteenth century unalterably opposed to acknowledging any authority other than their own and continued to refuse to swear homage to Poland-Lithuania. In 1511 Albrecht von Hohenzollern-Ansbach, who was both grandson of Casimir IV of Poland and the elector of Brandenberg, became Hochmeister. In 1525 he acknowledged the sovereignty of the Kingdom of Poland-Lithuania in his new capacity as duke of Prussia. His descendants (the Hohenzollern family, who ultimately became kings of Prussia and then the Kaisers of Germany) were to continue to confront Poland for 250 years and eventually assumed control of major portions of western and northern Poland in the eighteenth century.

—Robert Burke

References: Halecki, O., *A History of Poland* (New York: David McKay Company, 1981); Johnson, Lonnie R., *Central Europe* (New York and Oxford: Oxford University Press, 1996); Keen, Maurice, *Chivalry* (New Haven and London: Yale University Press, 1984); Wandycz, Piotr, *The Price of Freedom: A History of East Central Europe from the Middle Ages to the Present* (London: Routledge, 1992).

Texas Rangers

The Texas Rangers are an organization difficult to describe. They started as protectors of the frontier, later served as soldiers under the command of the federal government, and finally became a law enforcement agency. This quite possibly makes them unique in all history.

In the early 1820s Mexico gained its independence from Spain. In need of citizens to protect the country should Spanish troops return, and in need of a buffer between Mexican citizens and hostile Plains Indians, the Mexican government advertised for settlers to move from the United States. Empresarios (basically immigrant brokers) contracted with the Mexican government to bring in Anglo settlers in return for large tracts of land. The first and most successful operation was that conducted by Stephen F. Austin, who oversaw the creation of the Rangers in May 1823. The Americans moving to the northern Mexican province of Texas settled along the Colorado and Brazos Rivers and stayed, for the most part, east of the lands dominated by the warlike Comanche tribe. But the frontier between Anglo and Indian lands was close enough to cause friction, and the Rangers were given the task not only of protecting the frontier from attack, but launching punitive expeditions as well.

The Rangers were largely a haphazard organization, but when the Texans broke away from Mexico in the autumn of 1835 the fledgling Texas provisional government officially gave them the title "Texas Rangers." At first the Rangers provided their own horses and weapons, with ammunition and supplies furnished irregularly by the new government of the Republic of Texas after 1836. The Rangers spent the next nine years not only protecting the settlements from the Indians, but also taking reprisals against Mexican army expeditions sent to harass Texas. They had no more than a few hundred men in their ranks at any time. It was in this period of the Republic that the Rangers developed a fearsome reputation among the Indians and the Mexicans for determination, bravery, and marksmanship.

The first major battle they fought with the Comanche came in 1840. During a meeting in San Antonio in which some Comanche were discussing peace and returning hostages, the Indians were ambushed and slaughtered by local citizens. The Comanche came back for vengeance a few months later, raiding and pillaging almost to the Texas coast, where they burned every farmhouse they passed and stole every horse they found. Slowed by the 3,000 horses they had accumulated, the Comanche were caught by a Ranger unit under one of the organization's early legends, Ben McCulloch. At the battle of Plum Creek on 11 August 1840 the Rangers inflicted a severe defeat on the Comanches. This fight marked the first use of Colt repeating pistols, and they proved so effective that the United States Army took notice and mandated those sidearms for their cavalry from that point forward. Indeed, the Rangers were the first organization to purchase revolvers and use them in combat.

When the United States annexed Texas in 1845, the Mexican government disputed the border the Texans had claimed: the Rio Grande River from mouth to source. When the United States recognized that border, the Mexicans threatened war. War came in April 1846 just north of the lower Rio Grande, where Mexican cavalry captured and killed some American dragoons in the force occupying the disputed territory. The army commander, General Zachary Taylor, called on the Texas government to provide him with volunteer forces, and the Texas Rangers were the first to respond. This unit, commanded by John Coffee Hays, served under Taylor's command when he invaded Mexico in September 1846 and fought with him at the capture of Monterrey and in the defeat of General Santa Anna's Mexican army at Buena Vista the following February. The Rangers transferred to General Winfield Scott's command for the assault on Vera Cruz and served as scouts and in antiguerrilla action during the cross-country march on Mexico City in 1847. The already-established reputation for ruthlessness among Mexicans was reinforced during this war, but there were reports of atrocities on the part of the Rangers. Most of these were later proven to be untrue, but the allegations did result in some damage to the Rangers' reputation. The Rangers' abilities in stealth and reconnaissance, however, proved invaluable for both Taylor and Scott.

Once the Mexican-American War was over and Texas was part of the United States, the Rangers' duties focused more on fighting Indians but also began to include more general law enforcement. The western half of Texas was inhabited largely by Indians and outlaws, and the Rangers learned to operate on their terms and beat them at their own games. It was at this time that the Texas Rangers developed their unofficial motto: "Ride like a Mexican, track like an Indian, shoot like a mountain man, fight like the devil." They did all of these much better than their enemies. With each ranger armed with at least two pistols, a rifle, and a knife, they operated in small groups that could move quietly and strike quickly.

During the Civil War, Rangers did not join the Confederate army as complete units, as they had done in the Mexican-American War, but virtually all of them served in the Confederate cause. One of the most respected of the Ranger captains, John "Rip" Ford, commanded a cavalry unit in South Texas made up of Texans too young or too old to join the army. His force of no more than 1,500 men almost never operated as a complete unit, but in small groups managed to clear the lower

Rio Grande Valley of Union soldiers, capture Brownsville from a much larger force, and fight the last battle of the war at Palmito Ranch, a Confederate victory that came on 12–13 May 1865, four weeks after the war had ended at Appomattox Court House, Virginia. They lived off the land and outfought the Union troops at every turn, just as Ford had done in his fighting against the Indians.

The Rangers not only tracked down Indians and outlaws, but were called upon to maintain peace as range wars and ethnic conflicts broke out in the post–Civil War era. Often they quelled disturbances merely by their presence and reputation. "One riot, one Ranger" has become a modern slogan. In the twentieth century they have become strictly a law enforcement agency with high standards, but their methods are still controversial. At times criticized for possibly racist or sexist attitudes (although they now admit racial minorities and women to their ranks), the Texas Rangers are regarded nevertheless as an elite law enforcement organization, with a standard of conduct on the job that recalls the discipline and tenacity of the roughest days on the frontier.

References: Davis, John, *The Texas Rangers* (San Antonio: University of Texas Institute of Texan Cultures, 1975); Webb, Walter Prescott, *The Story of the Texas Rangers* (Austin: Encino Press, 1971); Wilkins, Frederick, *The Highly Irregular Irregulars: Texas Rangers in the Mexican War* (Austin: Eakin Press, 1990).

U

United States Marines

Troops trained in amphibious warfare, known for intense pride of service.

The Marine Corps, like the navy and army, was created during the American Revolutionary War. The Marines were formed on 10 November 1775, seven months after the first shots were fired at Lexington and Concord, Massachusetts. For the first 20 years of their existence they did what all marines did: served aboard ships in the equal role of enforcing discipline among the crew and engaging enemy marines in combat. The warships of the time, after blasting each other with artillery fire, would often close and grapple onto an enemy ship. Marines acted both as snipers from the rigging and as members of the boarding parties, both to fight the enemy and to secure possession of the captured vessel.

American Marines had little to do after the Revolution, for the United States Navy did not exist. Merchant ship protection from pirates was the main role the Marines served. In the 1790s conflict in Europe over the French Revolution had repercussions in America. In need of ships to enlarge their navy, the French began seizing American vessels. The British reacted to American privateers operating under French letters of marque by capturing and incorporating American ships into the Royal Navy. Without warships the United States had no ability to respond to these indignities, so in 1794 Congress appropriated money for the construction of six warships. They came to service too late to keep the United States from being forced to sign a treaty paying tribute to pirates along North Africa's Barbary Coast. In 1798 Congress passed legislation enlarging the Marine Corps to 500 men and ordering their use aboard ships.

The early Marine Corps had no traditions or esprit de corps upon which to build, and the early recruits were not of the highest quality. They soon showed themselves to be excellent fighters, however. Within a matter of months in 1798 American ships and Marines were driving off French warships in the Caribbean as well as landing shore parties that attacked French coastal fortifications. The amphibious nature of the Marines was thus begun. The first major conflict in which they took part was the first serious international fighting U.S. forces had engaged in since the Revolution: an attack on the Barbary pirates. After Stephen Decatur rescued American hostages from North Africa in February 1804, a force of eight Marines, accompanied by about 500 European mercenaries and commanded by U.S. Army General William Eaton, landed in Egypt and marched 600 miles along the coast to attack the pirate stronghold at Derna, in modern Libya. On the morning of 27 April 1805 with support from American ships bombarding the fort, Eaton's force attacked. The Marines were under the command of Lieutenant Presley O'Bannon, and they not only captured the cannons defending the pirate fort but turned them on the commander's headquarters and forced his surrender after a two-hour cannonade. For a total loss of 13 dead, including two Marines, the fortress was captured and its garrison captured or scattered. O'Bannon received from the pirate commander a sword patterned after the style of that used by Egyptian Mameluke troops, and that sabre became the one upon which Marine dress swords have been patterned ever since.

During the War of 1812 the U.S. Navy began to show its abilities, and the Marines enhanced their reputation for mobility and fighting well under difficult conditions. They continued to fight enemy sailors and marines in ship-to-ship actions and were again landed on British-held Caribbean islands for attacks on shore facilities. In the decades that followed, the Marines were used in antislaving operations and piracy suppression. In 1847 they were involved in the American attack on Mexico City alongside forces of the U.S. Army. A force of Marines under command of Army Colonel Robert E. Lee was responsible for attacking and capturing a force of insurrectionists under the leadership of John Brown, who seized an arsenal at Harper's Ferry, Virginia, in 1859 and planned to provoke slave rebellions in the American South. As the American (Union) navy did little during the Civil War except for blockade duty, the Marines saw little action, but after the war, as the government severely reduced the size of both army and navy, the Marines became the instrument of American "force projection" abroad. They were used extensively in expeditions to Caribbean islands and Central American nations to maintain the peace or protect American interests and lives, as well as in the Philippines, suppressing the insurrection against the American occupation after the Spanish-American War of 1898–1901.

During World War I, Marines served under the control of the U.S. Army, as the traditionally small American military establishment needed trained soldiers to be committed to France as quickly as possible and the Marines provided a ready-made contingent. One fifth of the U.S. force in France in World War I were Marines. In the 1920s the Marines saw a need to become amphibious. This was not only to be able to "project force" into an enemy country but also to give the Marines a specialty no other branch of the military had, thus ensuring their continued funding and even their continued existence as an independent force. After the British disaster at Gallipoli in 1915–1916 many thought that amphibious warfare was impracticable, but the Marines spent the next two decades devising methods and doctrine. It was fortunate that they did, for it proved to be the only way to take the war to the Japanese in the Pacific theater of operations during the Second World War.

It was during World War II that the Marines achieved their highest status. As an all-volunteer force, they had maintained strict recruitment standards that made them the most professional and highly trained force the United States possessed at the outset of hostilities. Thus, the Marines were the first American troops to engage enemy ground forces. On 7 August 1942 the United States took the offensive against Japan by landing marines on the island of Guadalcanal in the Solomon Islands northeast of Australia. The First Marine Division learned how to fight the Japanese and deal with jungle warfare as the battle progressed. It was a learning experience for which prewar training had not equipped them, except in the ability to adapt and overcome. This was also the first large-scale amphibious operation the United States had ever undertaken. The Marines, and later the army, learned valuable lessons in jungle warfare that would serve them well on other South Pacific islands. Not all islands were covered with jungle, however, and the Marines fought on coral atolls with little cover, mountainous islands strewn with well-defended caves, or islands consisting of nothing but volcanic ash and sand. In all these battles, the Marines fought entrenched Japanese forces that always were in superior numbers, and each island battle was an American victory.

During World War II, amphibious tactics

were perfected as the Marines staged landing after landing on hostile beaches. Also developed at this time was the use of close air support, and the Marine Air Wing came into being. Neither of these were used to any great extent in the Marines' next major conflict in Korea, 1950–1953. Only at Inch'on in September 1950, did an amphibious landing take place, but the Marines were in the thick of the fighting throughout the war. When the Communist Chinese staged their massive counteroffensive in November 1950 Marine units were surrounded and in some cases overwhelmed. The Marine Corps creed not to abandon anybody, living or dead, to the enemy, meant extremely difficult operations wherein the Marines had to fight not only a determined enemy but subfreezing temperatures as well. Chosin Reservoir became another battle added to the ever-growing list of Marine honors. This was the scene of the famous comment by one Marine commander, "Retreat, hell! We're just attacking in a different direction." Once again, as in World War I, Marines served as ground troops under overall army command.

That same duty fell to them again during the American conflict in Vietnam. No landings took place against hostile beaches, but the Marines were once again the first combat troops committed to action in March 1965. The professional, all-volunteer force reached a psychological low point in its existence, as did all branches of the American military, in a war with ever-changing goals that proved frustrating for all involved. Having to defend entrenched positions against attacking forces was anathema to Marine doctrine, and the morale problems associated with the inability to successfully implement their training and dealing with a hostile populace at home and in Southeast Asia proved extremely demoralizing. After the American withdrawal, Marine recruiting suffered, to the point that organizations such as the Brookings Institution theorized disbanding the force.

However, the type of "small wars" that the Marines had fought so successfully throughout the nineteenth century reappeared and the need to project force kept the Marines not only in existence, but busy. Marines fought in American operations in Grenada, Panama, Somalia, and the Gulf War. The new American doctrine of rapid response forces, able to move quickly anywhere in the world by sea or air, fit well into traditional Marine operational views. Currently the Marines are part of the Fleet Marine Forces, which include the navy's transport and supply ships. The Marine contingent is made up of four parts: (1) ground combat elements with infantry, armor, artillery, and engineers; (2) air support; (3) command and control for planning and directing operations; and (4) service support to maintain the necessary supplies. Although paratroopers can deploy more quickly than any other force, the Fleet Marine Forces are necessary to continue the missions that the airborne forces start.

Marines believe that their standard training is virtually the equivalent of that provided for special forces like the Green Berets and the SEALs. Basic training is a three-month affair. The first month is dedicated to physical conditioning, code of conduct, and history—an area to which the Marines believe they are the most dedicated of services. The second month is dedicated to weapons training and surviving outdoors. The final month finds the recruits engaged in more physical training and combat training. About 10 percent of the recruits do not make it to the end of basic training. Those that take the Officer Candidate Course find the same things they found in basic training, but even more intense. Almost half the officer candidates do not finish the course.

The final product is a soldier who believes he or she has become a part of the best and toughest branch of the American military. As one officer put it, "You aren't afraid of death or of getting wounded so much as the horror of letting the other Marines on your left and right down. It isn't the enemy so much as that 217-year-old tradition of the Corps. People expect a lot from us—and we expect more from each other. *That's* the difference between us and the other services" (Halberstadt, 1993). Those with experience with the Corps believe that there are no ex-Marines, only those no longer wearing the uniform.

References: Alexander, Joe, et.al., *A Fellowship of Valor* (New York: HarperCollins, 1997); Halberstadt, Hans, *US Marine Corps* (Osceola, WI: Motorbooks International, 1993); Millett, Allan, *Semper Fidelis* (New York: Macmillan, 1980).

V

Vandals

A northern European population that settled in North Africa during the decline of the Roman Empire.

The Vandals were one of the tribes that migrated from the area below the Baltic Sea during the late Roman Empire. They were of the same racial stock as the Goths but travelled across Germany more directly than did the Goths, who migrated at the same time but took a more southerly route before moving westward across Europe. Little is known of their early history, but the Vandals crossed into Germany about the time Rome was loosening its grip on the area in the mid-300s A.D. The Vandals were actually the leaders of a group of tribes, and were themselves divided into two groups, the Asdings and the Silings. They conquered and incorporated the Sueves, another Germanic tribe, and the Alans, who were a non-Germanic people driven into Europe by the advance of the Huns.

The Vandal coalition moved across Germany as the western Goths (Visigoths) were occupying northern Italy and Dacia, and the two fought each other in the mid-fourth century. The Visigoths had the better of the encounter and the Vandals seemed to disappear for a time, but emerge again in 406 when they led their forces across the Rhine River. Their passage into western Europe was bloody as the Vandals pillaged through Gaul, areas covered by modern-day Belgium, Holland, and northern France, then turned south and cut a wide swath of destruction to the Pyrenees. This was all officially territory of the Roman Empire, and the emperor tried to convince his Visigothic allies/mercenaries to save Gaul, but by the time they turned to face the Vandal threat, the tribes had moved into northern Spain in 409.

The Vandals, like the Goths, were Arian Christians. The two peoples were of the same heritage and spoke a similar language. The Goths, however, had established themselves in Italy as occasional allies to what remained of the Roman Empire. They therefore went to Spain to regain control of the area for Rome and to carve out whatever good lands they could acquire for themselves, even if it meant making war against people much like themselves. The four Vandalic tribes had spread quickly over much of central and western Iberia, and the Goths operated out of the eastern part of the peninsula. After a failed attempt to cross over to North Africa, the Goths made war against the Vandalic tribes. After a few defeats, the Vandals appealed to Rome for protection; the emperor played one tribe against another by granting or denying favors. That imperial aid went mainly to the Asdings and the Suevians, so the Goths continued to fight the Silings and the Alans. The Silings were virtually exterminated and the Alans, after losing their king, retreated westward to join the Asdings. The ruler of this remainder came to be called "King of the Vandals and the Alans."

Once the Visigoths went about establishing their own claims, the remaining Vandals were left to themselves. An argument soon arose between the Vandals and the Sueves and, after a battle, they parted company. The Sueves stayed in northwest Iberia; the Vandals and Alans moved to the south. They fought and defeated a Roman force on their way south and established themselves in the province of Baetica. The Vandal king, Gunderic, raided into other areas of Spain and possibly across the Mediterranean into Mauritania. His brother and successor, Gaiseric, saw the potential of the farmland of North Africa, which had long been Rome's primary food source. He was leader of the Vandals when chance called them to Africa.

The general commanding Roman forces in Africa was Boniface, loyal to Rome and a strong Christian. He took a second wife, however, who was an Arian and that placed him in opposition to the Roman Catholic Church. He refused to return to Rome to answer to the government, and Boniface defeated the first army that came after him. The second one defeated him, however, and Boniface fled to the Vandals. He invited them to come to Africa and fight alongside him and he would reward them with land. Boniface provided shipping and some 80,000 people crossed the Mediterranean, of which some 15,000 were fighting men.

The Vandals proved to be unmerciful in their treatment of the Mauritanian population. They killed people and looted towns and churches, caring nothing for Catholic shrines or priests. Gaiseric proved an able military leader and a cunning diplomat. His treatment of Roman citizens encouraged other groups that disliked Rome to join in the fray: Moors and Egyptian Donatists attacked eastward along the Mediterranean shore, and other groups branded as heretics saw a chance to take some vengeance on their Roman oppressors. Attempts to negotiate with Gaiseric proved futile, and he not only fought the Roman armies sent against him but he turned on Boniface as well and drove him back into Roman arms. In 430 the Vandals invaded Numidia and besieged the city of Hippo, home to St. Augustine, which held out for a year. When Boniface joined with an army sent from Constantinople in 431 Gaiseric defeated them as well, then turned back and captured Hippo.

In Rome, internal power struggles kept the government from any effective resistance to Gaiseric. Finally, the Visigoth general Aetius was able to speak for Rome and convince the Vandals to stop fighting. In 435 they were ceded the Mauritanian provinces and part of Numidia in return for acknowledging the overlordship of the Roman government. Gaiseric consolidated his hold on northwestern Africa but continued to consider his options. Basing himself in Carthage, Gaiseric built a fleet and began raiding at sea. His forces raided Italy and occupied Sicily and Sardinia. The Vandals did not long survive Gaiseric, however. Roman forces ultimately returned and reconquered the area, bringing the Vandal tribe to an end in 533.

Although the Vandals' power lasted about a century, they left behind little cultural heritage. Their time in Spain was sufficiently brief that they had no impact there, and even in North Africa they built little and contributed little. The effect of the Vandal migrations and conquests was not small, however. By their very presence in North Africa, controlling the grain-producing lands that had for centuries fed Italy, the declining power of Rome declined even faster. Without the logistical support of Africa, Roman forces could not aggressively respond to threats in Europe, mostly in Gaul. The advances of the Huns and the Ostrogoths, then of the Franks, came about more easily because Rome could not support enough troops in the field. Roman power fell more quickly and German influence rose more quickly in Europe because the Vandals, at Rome's back door, split the attention of the fading empire.

References: Bury, J.B., *The Invasion of Europe by the Barbarians* (New York: Russell and Russell, 1963); Isadore of Seville, *The History of the Goths, Vandals and Suevi*, trans. Guido Donini and Gordon Ford (Leiden: E.J. Brill, 1970);

Thompson, E.A., *Romans and Barbarians: The Decline of the Western Empire* (Madison: University of Wisconsin Press, 1982).

Varangian Guard

An elite unit of household guards in the Byzantine Empire between the ninth and fourteenth centuries.

In the latter part of the tenth century, the Byzantine emperor Basil II recruited a number of Varangians, reputedly Norsemen from Russia, as a personal bodyguard. The term Varangian comes from the Norse *var*, meaning "pledge," and denotes one of a band of men who pledged themselves to work together for profit. Usually this meant in trade, but the oath of loyalty to each other certainly had more than commercial meaning, for they were bound to fight for each other's safety as members of a merchant band. As "merchant adventurer" describes a Viking fairly well, such bands were not uncommon. The term also refers to men who hired themselves into the service of an overlord for set period of time, as the Norsemen did for the lords of Novgorod and Kiev in Russia. Thus, the term *Varangian* does not necessarily mean "Viking" or "Scandinavian," although most of them were from that part of the world. Generally, however, it refers to the Scandinavian Russian empire led by the city-states of Kiev and Novgorod.

Varangians fought southward down the Volga toward territory under Byzantine control, raiding the area around Constantinople in 865. As the Byzantine emperors fought to protect their northern frontiers, they gained firsthand knowledge of the fighting abilities of these men. In 911 Prince Oleg of Russia concluded a trade agreement with Constantinople, and it was through these more peaceful contacts that Emperor Basil II began to hire Varangians for his personal guard, starting an organization that lasted until at least the 1300s. Basil made use of his new soldiers immediately, taking them with him on an expedition into Bulgaria, where the Varangians so distinguished themselves that Basil separated them from the remainder of the army in order to give them a larger share of the loot. They also served under his command in Anatolia and Georgia, continuing to fight ferociously and earn the emperor's respect. In the Balkans, the Varangians fought one of the most determined of Byzantine foes, the Pechenegs. The Pechenegs' defeat led to a peace treaty with Constantinople in 1055. After another defeat at Varangian hands in 1122 they served the emperor's army as light cavalry.

Although the Varangians served in the army that fought in Byzantine army campaigns, their service as a palace guard was most important to the various emperors. They had three main functions. First, they guarded the safety of the emperor, standing at the entrance to his bedchamber and in the reception hall. Second, they occasionally were known to have guarded the imperial treasury, over the funds of which they apparently thought they exercised some control. Third, late in their tenure, they acted as prison guards and probably as torturers. The Varangian Guard was best known for its weaponry, for they carried axes, sometimes described as single-bladed and sometimes as double. "The imperial axe-bearers" is a common description of them.

The Varangian Guard's top commanders seem to have been Byzantine, although smaller units had foreign commanders. By the latter stages of their service, larger numbers of Anglo-Saxons, especially from England, entered the Guard. One source refers to an "axe-bearing Keltikon," and Celt seems to have become a standard description of the Guard members by the late eleventh and early twelfth centuries, especially after the capture of England by William the Conqueror. Icelandic sagas tell tales of their natives serving in the Guard as well.

The primary characteristic of Guard members, apparently, was their loyalty. The Byzantine Empire was a virtual breeding ground of intrigue and the emperors seemed always to be under threat of overthrow or assassination. By hiring foreign troops and paying them very well, the rulers hoped to avoid the problems of subversion and infiltration by local political factions. This was a successful strategy, but often put the Varangians themselves in difficulty. The generally accepted view of overthrow and assassination in the Byzantine Empire was a variation on the Chinese concept of the "Mandate of Heaven." If an individual came to the throne, it was through God's will. If he was removed, violently or otherwise, that was also God's will. Thus, the Varangians had to accept an ever-changing political situation and be prepared to fight to the death for one emperor but immediately support his successor against whom they may have fought hours earlier. The record of the lavish gifts and bonuses given to the Varangian Guard upon the succession of a new emperor shows the Guard's ability to adapt to, and indeed profit from, this power shift.

The best known of the Varangians was Harald Sigurdson, also known as Harald Hardraada, who served in Constantinople as a young man before returning to his homeland and leading forces defeated by King Harold of England at Stamford Bridge in 1066. Harald fled his homeland at age fifteen after his family, rulers of Norway, was defeated in battle. He served in the military in Russia, where he seems to have fallen in love with the daughter of an aristocrat, Yaroslav. She apparently was in the royal court in Constantinople and he followed her there. Yaroslav wanted more than royal blood for his son-in-law, so he bade Harald make a name for himself before he could have the daughter's hand in marriage. Harald arrived in Constantinople in 1034 and entered into the service of the newly crowned Emperor Michael IV. The Icelandic saga penned by Snorri Sturluson tells Harald's tale and describes him as an outstanding military leader, determined and clever, and always able to end a battle with lots of plunder. Contemporary accounts written by Byzantine observers confirm his abilities in campaigns in Sicily and Bulgaria.

After the Byzantine defeat at the hands of the Turks at Manzikert in 1071 the Byzantine army became even more dependent on mercenaries, and the Varangians served as the loyal core of the military. They were not always victorious, however. By 1082 the Guard was becoming increasingly Anglo-Saxon, and it was the descendants of the Norsemen, the Normans of France, who ironically were the instrument of a Guard disaster. The great Norman leader Robert Guiscard aspired to become the emperor of the Byzantine Empire, so he led his forces out of Sicily across the Adriatic Sea. He laid siege to the city of Durazzo on the island of Corfu in 1081 but was forced to lift the siege upon the arrival of the Byzantine emperor, Alexius Comnenus, with 50,000 men. The Varangian Guard, some of whose members had fought the Normans at Hastings in 1066, couldn't wait for the bulk of the army to position itself. They flung themselves at the Norman position and succeeded in forcing a hasty retreat, but their pause to plunder the Norman base gave their enemy time to regroup and counterattack. Surrounded, the Guard fought to the last man.

The Guard also distinguished itself in a losing effort in 1204 when the Fourth Crusade attacked Constantinople instead of Muslim targets further inland. The Varangians defended the walls of the city for two days until Venetian ships flung incendiaries over the walls and set the city afire. In the ensuing melee, the Varangian Guard was virtually wiped out. The final references to Varangians in Constantinople occur in 1395 and 1400 when some appeared to have been serving in administrative, rather than military, capacities in the Byzantine government.

References: Bartusis, Mark C., *The Late Byzantine Army* (Philadelphia: University of Pennsylvania Press, 1992; Davidson, H. R. Ellis, *The Viking Road to Byzantium* (London: George Allen & Unwin, 1976).

Viet Minh

A guerrilla force resisting French colonization in Southeast Asia in the 1940s and 1950s.

Southeast Asia has long been a region dominated by foreign power. The Chinese Han dynasty imposed its will on the area in 208 B.C. They found, like every other power trying to occupy Vietnam, that the country might be occupied but the population would not be absorbed. The land that the Chinese called *Nam Viet* ("land of the southern Viets") was the eastern coastal region of Southeast Asia along the South China Sea, composed of three provinces: Tonkin in the north, Annam in the center, and Cochin China in the south. The people of these three provinces resisted Chinese authority constantly, staging revolts and dislodging the invaders, only to be reoccupied later. Still they fought on, and the Vietnamese people developed a warrior cult that worshipped military virtues and accomplishments. The leaders that fought the Chinese were national heroes above and beyond any other. Over time Chinese dynasties came and went, but they all tried to dominate Vietnam. The people accepted portions of Chinese governmental and social concepts, but continually rejected assimilation.

In the 1600s a power struggle within Vietnam broke out between two aristocratic families, the Nguyens and the Trinhs. The Trinhs won the power struggle and came to dominate Tonkin in the north, while the Nguyens retreated southward and established a power base in Cochin China and Annam. The two regions began to develop different personalities. The south, where the Mekong River provided periodic flooding for regular crops, developed into an easy-going society that could prosper without too much work. In the north, the Red River was too unpredictable to provide such a lifestyle, and the people needed a centralized governmental system to build dikes and wrest a living from the soil. The southerners also embraced Indian Buddhism, which taught of a future Nirvana achieved after life cycles of suffering. The northerners practiced Chinese Buddhism, which taught that anyone could achieve the status of a Buddha and live a peaceful and rewarding life in the present. The northerners achieved a society that depended on hard work and at the same time the ability to enjoy a life of personal satisfaction. The southerners enjoyed an easier physical life but without the immediate internal satisfaction. Thus, the north was more aggressive; the south, more accepting of what life had to offer.

In northern Annam, a region that seemed to embody elements of both northern and southern Vietnam, lay the province of Nghe An. The land provided scanty sustenance, but the people were intellectual, creative, and stubborn. The population of Nghe An produced the best poets and artists in Vietnam, but also the most discontented radicals. When France established a colonial presence in Southeast Asia in the middle 1800s it was Nghe An that produced the first dissidents demanding independence. Just as the Vietnamese had spent centuries resisting Chinese rule, of which they were finally free in 938, they had not forgotten the stories of their military past and would just as tenaciously resist French rule. Into a family of anti-French agitators was born in 1890 Nguyen Sinh Cung. His sister became a well-known balladeer, singing songs protesting colonialism. His brother joined a conspiracy to poison French military officers. His father, an employee of the ruling mandarin class through which the French ruled, was vehemently anti-French, a stance that ultimately got him fired from his civil service position. In such a family it is not surprising that Nguyen Sinh Cung became a revolutionary himself.

Unhappy with life in Vietnam, Nguyen left in 1912 aboard a French steamer on which he worked as a messboy. He sailed the world and saw the effects of colonialism everywhere: French Algeria and British South Africa in particular. He spent some time in the United States and was impressed with the democratic system and the ideas of the American founding fathers. He was working in a London restaurant when World War I broke out, and moved to Paris in 1918. There he found a large Vietnamese immigrant community and he frequented their restaurants and became well-known. His dormant political senses returned and he joined the French Socialist Party. In 1919 as the Allies were meeting in Versailles to dictate the fate of Germany and much of the rest of the world, he composed a manifesto calling for the recognition of individual rights in Vietnam and the treatment of Vietnamese as equals within the French empire. He gained official notice, even if his demands did not. He turned away from the socialists and became one of the founding members of the French Communist Party. He had been given some of the writings of Vladimir Lenin and he saw in them the path to Vietnamese liberation.

In Paris Nguyen Sinh Cung began calling himself *Nguyen Ai Quoc*, or "Nguyen the Patriot." He traveled to the Soviet Union in 1923 then served as an advisor to the Soviet envoy to China in 1924. He met more Vietnamese immigrants, including exiles who had fled the French after revolutionary activities at home got them in trouble. In Canton he organized a communist youth committee, then returned to Moscow. He traveled in communist circles in Europe, then in 1928 spent time in Bangkok organizing Vietnamese immigrants into communist organizations. In 1929 he went to Hong Kong, where he met two people who would assist him and Vietnam immensely over the next decades: Le Duc Tho and Vo Nguyen Giap. They were both from upper class families but both had come to despise French rule.

In 1930 discontented peasants in Nghe An province marched to protest high taxes. The French government called in aircraft to strafe the column and killed some 175 people, then another 15 who later came to look for survivors among the bodies. This, more than any other incident, coalesced resistance to the French ruling elite. Although the mandarins through whom they had ruled had been abolished as a class, the French now governed through Vietnamese who embraced French culture by becoming Catholics and speaking French. They saw in a popular peasant rising the end of their preferential treatment, should the French be removed, and the French saw the potential for a mass movement that could lead to the loss of a colony. The French began rounding up anyone with revolutionary tendencies and Nguyen Ai Quoc fled to Hong Kong. There British authorities imprisoned him. He escaped in 1932 and spent five years in the Soviet Union before returning to China. He secretly entered his homeland in 1941 with Vo Nguyen Giap and established a headquarters in a cave in the north. Japan had succeeded the French as occupiers of his country, and he would fight them as well. In 1941 Nguyen Ai Quoc created the Viet Nam Doc Lap Dong Minh Hoi (League for Vietnamese Independence), or Viet Minh. He also changed his name yet again to the one for which he became world famous: *Ho Chi Minh*, or "He Who Enlightens."

He sought aid from Chiang Kai-shek in China, but was imprisoned for his trouble. Released in 1943 when the Chinese decided he may be of some assistance fighting the Japanese, he returned home to where Giap was organizing and fighting a guerrilla war against the Japanese and the French colonial infrastructure that still remained. Ho sought and obtained the support of the American Office of Strategic Services, getting weapons in return for information on Japanese troop movements and aid in returning downed U.S. pilots. When Japan was defeated in 1945 Ho thought that all his work had paid off. The Japanese were gone and so were the French, but new troubles emerged. Chinese troops occupied territory in the north and in order to remove them diplomatically rather than militarily it was necessary to cooperate with France. That, however, brought the French colonial system back into Vietnam. Appeals to the United States for political assistance to convince France to grant Vietnamese independence gained sympathetic words but little else.

Ho Chi Minh went back to fighting his

guerrilla war, now against the French. Giap proved to be an able military mind and the hit-and-run tactics that had served them so well against the Japanese continued to work through the late 1940s and into the 1950s. French public opinion favored an end to colonialism in Vietnam, but the renewed interest of the United States, now dedicated to fighting communists anywhere, kept France in the country and in the fight. The Viet Minh over time not only continued to harm the French military, but gained continued popular support and a growing recruitment. In 1954 the Viet Minh did what every successful guerrilla campaign ultimately accomplishes: Build enough strength to beat the enemy at his own game, in a head-to-head pitched battle. In May 1954 the French base at Dien Bien Phu fell as French and Vietnamese negotiators in Geneva were discussing peace.

France promised to withdraw completely within two years, with national elections to be held in 1956 to elect a popular government. The United States, however, knew that Ho Chi Minh could not lose a popular election, so they unilaterally supported the creation of a government in the south based on the old French hierarchy and held it in place with American financial and military aid. The south, although socially different from the north, had always been part of a Vietnamese "nation," but after 1956 a distinct Republic of South Vietnam was created to formally separate the two regions. Ho Chi Minh and his followers, with their primary control and popular support among the northerners, responded by creating their own government. Most of the communists in the south (some 10,000) moved north, while those in the north with French connections fled south to avoid retribution. In reality this exchange of populations ended the Viet Minh, for the military force under the control of Ho Chi Minh and Vo Nguyen Giap became the North Vietnamese army, a regular military force. The communists in the south came to be referred to as the Viet Cong, or Vietnamese Communists.

Ho Chi Minh, 1969

The southerners, who had lived longer under French rule but for the most part were more amenable to it, provided only some communist party strength. As the ruler of South Vietnam, Ngo Dinh Diem, proved to be as oppressive as the pro-French Vietnamese had been during French rule. The communists began to gain recruits. What started as a nationalist attempt to free Vietnam from foreign rule became an ideological war between Ho Chi Minh's communist training and organization on the one hand and the anticommunist determination of the United States. Although the United States threatened to abandon South Vietnam because of the oppressive policies Ngo Dinh Diem imposed on his people (mainly religious in nature), the administration of President Lyndon Johnson in the United States brought ideological concerns to military fruition. The guerrilla tactics that the Viet Minh had used against both French and Japanese worked just as well against the Americans, who brought massive logistical superiority and a colonial superiority complex. American Secretary of State Henry Kissinger once commented that he refused to believe the United States could be beaten by a group of farmers in black pajamas. That was much the same attitude held by the Chinese, French, and Japanese. It was also, ironically, the same attitude held by the British government when confronted with a group of farmers in the American colonies in the 1770s. Ho Chi Minh did not live to see the formation of an independent Vietnam, but it was created nonetheless. Communism no longer holds the sway it once did in the country, but the Vietnamese once again proved to be impossible for a foreign power to assimilate.

References: Davidson, Phillip, *Vietnam at War* (New York: Oxford University Press, 1988); Olson, James, and Randy Roberts, *Where the Domino Fell* (New York: St. Martin's Press, 1996); Short, Anthony, *The Origins of the Vietnam War* (New York: Longman, 1989).

Vikings

An aggressive Scandinavian population known for ruthlessness, raiding, commerce, and widespread settlement during the eighth through eleventh centuries.

The Vikings came out of Scandinavia in the latter years of the eighth century to attack and plunder whatever source of wealth they could find. It was this raiding that possibly gave the Vikings their name, for *vikingr* translates as "sea-rover" or "pirate." It is also possible, however, that it denotes the region from which they originated, for the Vik is the stretch of water also known as the Skagerrak, the straits between the North and the Baltic seas. Whatever its origin, the name came to mean terror for residents of northern Europe, the British Isles, and even the Mediterranean.

The first Viking raid of consequence was at the Northumbrian abbey of Lindisfarne in 793. Abbeys, monasteries, and churches were regular Viking targets because they were defended lightly, if at all, and contained large amounts of wealth. What precipitated this onslaught into the European world is a matter of some debate. It probably had to do with growing population pressures in the Scandinavian countries, where farmland was at a premium. It also could have been aided by the defeat of the Frisians by Charlemagne in the late eighth century. The Frisians, living in modern Belgium/Holland, had dominated the waters of the North Sea. But now, with Frisian power broken, the Vikings were no longer bottled up in their homelands. In addition, raiding was easier and more profitable for some time in Britain, because Charlemagne and his son, Louis the Pious, maintained a stout defense of continental Europe. When Louis's sons began a dynastic struggle for the Holy Roman Empire after Louis's death, the internal struggle diverted the military from the outside threat. It is also possible that Scandinavian mercenaries fought for Louis's son Lothar.

Whatever the reason, targets of opportu-

Vendel warrior's iron helmet with impressed bronze sheets; Viking, seventh century, from Uppland, Sweden (Statens Historiska Museet, Stockholm)

nity were plentiful, and the Vikings took advantage of them all. Their raiding was so effective because of their transport, the Viking longship. Built with a shallow draft and a wide beam, these vessels were powered by both sail and oars. They were seaworthy, but with a shallow enough draft to allow them to land on any flat stretch of beach. Harbors were unnecessary, and so the Vikings were able to arrive without warning, attack before a defense could be mounted, and withdraw before reinforcements could arrive. As pillage was their pay, it was the civilian population that suffered the most from these forays, and the prayer "God deliver us from the fury of the Northmen" was commonly spoken in the ninth and tenth centuries. Indeed, the only way to spare a town from pillage was by bribery, and *danegeld* (literally translated as "Danish money," but meaning bribes initially, and, later, legal fines or compensation for damages) was collected in huge amounts. Usually this totaled hundreds if not thousands of pounds of silver. This usually bought immediate, but temporary, protection, because other Viking bands could arrive within months.

The Vikings laid out spheres of influence, with the Swedes directing their attention eastward to the settlement of towns along the Volga, from which the nation of Russia ultimately formed. The Danes spent most of their energies in Britain and Ireland, while the Norse focused more on continental Europe. The Danes soon replaced raiding with conquest, for a time dominating northern England and most of Ireland. The Norse established settlements at the mouths of the major French rivers, from which they rowed upriver for attacks in the interior. Paris was a popular target, often attacked or held for the danegeld ransom. The Norse success was so great that land along the northeastern coast was offered to them as a permanent settlement if the settlers would prevent other Vikings from sailing up the Seine. Thus, the Norsemen became Normans; and Normandy, their home.

Most Vikings were armed alike, wearing a conical helmet (without horns or wings) and sometimes chain mail. They carried a sword or axe and a round wooden shield with a central metal boss to protect the hand. The axe could be either single or double bladed and usually bore carved decorations in the metal. The sword was on the Frankish pattern, common in Europe, being almost always double-bladed and fairly broad, of varying length. The sword fight consisted of hacking at one another's shield until an opening could be forced, with the point of the sword rarely used. They also carried spears with poles of ash that could be used for throwing or like a pike for fighting closer in. Bows were sometimes used, but apparently it was a weapon of the lower classes. The Vikings fought hand to hand and developed a reputation for ferocity. Among the Viking ranks were those called *berserkers* who would, through trance or other self-motivation, become unthinking killing machines until battle's end, when they would collapse from the output of adrenalin. When occasionally unable to reach their ships for rapid retreat, the Vikings showed themselves quite able to quickly build strong defensive positions that usually proved unassailable.

The Vikings followed their kings or other aristocrats, and the soldier was referred to as a *hird*, or *huscarl*. The king or *jarl* (earl) would call out his men for campaign, and the standard period of duty was four months per year. Mercenaries were also employed, and often the danegeld was collected to pay them, the rest of the plunder going to the regular soldiers. The smallest unit in the army was the ship's crew, and the smallest ship allowed was 26 oars. Most ships tended to number between 32 and 50 oars, though the largest ships were probably used for transport nearer home rather than sea-going journeys. The ship carried the necessary number of soldier/oarsmen and additional troops up to twice that number, although one ship is recorded to have carried 574 men. The fleets could be just a few ships, depending on the target, but fleets in the scores or hundreds were much more common. King Cnut in the early eleventh century was reputed to have had a fleet of 850 ships in one flotilla.

Although the Vikings were also traders, it was as fighters that they made their reputation. Their settlements spread across Europe from the Atlantic to Russia, and Vikings fought for themselves or as mercenaries in the Mediterranean and as far east as Constantinople. There the Varangian Guard of Vikings was created as a personal guard for the Byzantine Emperor in the 900s, a unit that lasted until 1400. Other Viking settlers explored further west, establishing populations in Iceland and Greenland that exist to this day, as well as exploring the east coast of North America in the year 1000. The end of their reign of terror came in the 1100s through a combination of absorption by the conquered populations and a widespread conversion to Christianity from previously pagan beliefs.

References: Arbman, Olger, *The Vikings* (New York: Frederick Praeger, 1961); Jones, Gwyn, *A History of the Vikings* (New York: Oxford University Press, 1984 [1968]); Norman, A. V. B., *The Medieval Soldier* (New York: Thomas Crowell, 1971).

W

Waffen SS

An elite force operating in the Nazi army during World War II

The *Schutzstaffeln* (Protection Squads), or SS, have an unusual reputation. They are regarded by many as outstanding soldiers who put forth the best performances of German soldiers in World War II. They are also hated as butchers and torturers of civilians, both in and out of concentration camps. As will be seen, the SS bears responsibility for many of the horrors of German actions in World War II, but the Waffen SS achieved positive reviews as a separate branch of the overall organization.

The SS had its roots in the early days of the Nazi Party with bodyguards chosen to drive and protect Adolph Hitler. This was a personal guard that was recruited in major cities where Hitler traveled and rarely numbered more than 20 in a local group and less than 300 in total nationwide. This group differed from the *Sturmabteilung* (Storm Troops), or SA, which were the paramilitary arm of the Nazi Party. Organized to protect party functions and attack the gathering of rival parties, the SA grew inordinately through the 1920s and became a fearsome group. Unfortunately for Hitler, they also came to be fearsome within the party. Under the leadership of Ernst Roehm, the SA was dominated by street thugs operating with some legitimacy within the Nazi organization. However, by the end of the decade they had grown too large and too independent. Their brutality, which had been effective in the early days when the Nazi Party was being established, now reflected badly on a party establishing itself as a major player in German politics. Hitler began depending more and more on the SS, under its director Heinrich Himmler.

Himmler received training in agriculture and attempted to raise chickens, but found his experience in the Nazi Party more successful. Without an intimidating presence, he seemed an unlikely role model for a "protection" organization, but his subservient manner and utter devotion to Hitler filled the bill. Himmler viewed the SS as not just a bodyguard group, but as an adjunct to the army that would incorporate the best of German manhood. It would serve as an advertisement for Aryan supremacy by accepting only what Himmler considered to be perfect specimens of tall, blond, muscular young men with impeccable breeding—that is, no Jewish or Slavic ancestors.

When Hitler rose to the position of chancellor of Germany in January 1933 the SA became a liability. Roehm's group continued to act like thugs and became less responsive to Hitler's will; so much so that Hitler feared Roehm's personal ambition to turn the SA into the new German army. The SA expanded from 300,000 in January 1933 to 3,000,000 in early 1934, incorporating other nationalist paramilitary groups and unemployed men looking for authority and income. Himmler had meanwhile expanded the SS to about 50,000 and had convinced

Hitler to make him head of the Berlin secret police. Himmler had already gained control of most of the police forces in major cities around Germany, so the number of men under his control was much greater than just the SS. Himmler was aided in this expansion by Reinhard Heydrich, who came to operate Himmler's *Sicherheitsdienst* (Security Service), or SD.

In talks with the army high command, Hitler was given an ultimatum: Get rid of the SA or lose the support of the army, one of Germany's most powerful and respected organizations. The SS received orders to assassinate Roehm and the inner circle of his advisors. Starting on the night of 30 June 1934 the SS began the killing in what was called the Blood Purge or, later, the Night of the Long Knives. The total number of SA killed is unknown (estimates go as high as 2,000), but its leaders all died, along with some of Himmler's personal rivals. The SA was officially disbanded and the SS came to be the elite troops of the Third Reich. The army was glad to see the SA removed, but surprised that the SS had emerged as a more serious rival. The SS was loyal not to Germany, but to Hitler, for each member (especially of the *Leibstandarte Adolph Hitler*, Hitler's personal guard) swore this oath: "I swear to you, Adolph Hitler, as Führer and Reich Chancellor, loyalty and bravery. I vow to you, and to those you have named to command me, obedience unto death, so help me God."

Men of the SS stand around a collection of captured communist placards.

The SS remained a political tool with military duties and was involved in Germany's reoccupation of the Rhineland in 1936 and the *Anschluss*, or joining, of Germany and Austria in March 1938. That same year Hitler put control of Germany's armed forces under his direct command and, while stating that the SS would remain a political unit, ordered it armed and trained to assist the army in times of need. The SS participated in the occupation of Czechoslovakia in spring 1939 by which time its members were training with the army and dressed in the same field gray uniforms, although with their own collar tabs and other insignia. They were at division strength, with the addition of artillery, in September 1939 when World War II started in Poland.

Although their performance in the Polish invasion was not stellar, it was sufficiently good for Himmler to ask for, and receive, permission to expand the SS from one division to three. In order to build quickly and have men with some experience, Himmler drafted the policemen who had been under his control for some years. He also began to recruit among the *Volksdeutsch*, the Germans who lived in the newly acquired Polish and Slovakian territories. Through the months of winter 1939–1940, Himmler consolidated the training units, bodyguard, cadet schools, and reserves under the umbrella designation *Waffen* (Weapons) SS, which were the fighting units, as opposed to the concentration camp SS guards.

The new organization's first remarkable performance came in the campaign against France in spring 1940. The Waffen SS distinguished itself by driving 135 miles through Dutch resistance on the first day and was involved in the surrender of Rotterdam. Transferred south into France, the SS saw action in the attack on British forces around Dunkirk. Here, an SS company commander accepted the surrender of almost 100 British soldiers, then massacred them. Although not accepted policy, this was to be the first of many random acts of terror perpetrated by some SS commanders.

After the successful German campaigns against Holland, Belgium, Denmark, and Norway, Himmler began to recruit new soldiers from these occupied countries. Although not Germans, they were of acceptable Aryan stock and had already formed paramilitary right-wing organizations in the late 1930s. By summer 1941, SS strength stood at five divisions, and they were divided among the three prongs of the Nazi advance into the Soviet Union in June. Because of the fact that all were motorized divisions and because they had gained a reputation as good fighters motivated by their status and racial indoctrination, the SS units were often in the news. They became even better known once the invasion was well under way, when the underground Russian partisan movement began harassing the German supply lines. Waffen SS units were detailed to engage in counterinsurgency and often did so with gusto, establishing their reputation for ruthlessness in their treatment of suspected partisans. It was also during the autumn of 1942 that SS divisions were withdrawn from the Eastern Front and relocated temporarily to France to receive and train with new equipment. The SS divisions became panzer grenadiers, not just motorized, but in tracked vehicles with newly added tank units.

More experience on the Eastern Front enhanced the SS divisions' reputations and they were rewarded with the best and newest equipment. This was used to good effect in the counteroffensives around Stalingrad in February 1943 but in the summer of that year the Waffen SS units were mauled along with the rest of the German forces at the massive tank battle at Kursk. From this point on, the SS and their compatriots were on the defensive. As the tide turned against the Germans, Himmler was obliged to abandon his ethnic views and recruit new SS units from other occupied countries, including what he considered "subhuman" Slavic populations. These foreign units consisted of troops from Hungary, the Caucasus, Bosnia-Herzegovina, Turkmenistan, and even captured Indian troops. Unlike their western European counterparts, they performed consistently badly for the Germans. The recruitment of troops from the Baltic states, Ukraine, and other provinces that disliked communism came too late to be of effective use.

On the Western Front the SS were active in attempts to blunt Allied thrusts out of the Normandy region. The armored units performed well, outfighting their Allied counterparts, but were unable to overcome Allied air superiority and an ever-decreasing amount of supplies from Germany. Although badly mauled in the fighting near Mortain in northern France in August 1944, SS tank units won a hard-fought victory a month later over British and American airborne forces attempting to establish a bridgehead over the Rhine at the Dutch town of Arnhem. In December, Hitler once again called on his SS forces, in which he had had the greatest faith through the years, to launch a surprise counteroffensive through British and American lines in Luxembourg. The Ardennes offensive, to break through the Allied positions and capture the huge amount of supplies collecting in Antwerp, got off to a good start in the bad weather of mid-December, but once again the Germans could not stand up to Allied air superiority or a flanking attack by George Patton's Third Army cutting them off from the south. In this campaign SS units again became notable for the execution of prisoners.

For the remainder of the war, SS units could do little better than other units in the German army. Hitler continued to order them to where the fighting was thickest, but their increasing lack of equipment and manpower spelled their ultimate doom. An SS guard was on hand at the end of April 1945 to carry Hitler's body to the surface above his bunker in Berlin and to destroy it. The führer had died a suicide.

The SS leaders were brought up on war crimes charges after the war and with justification. Some SS units actively engaged in activity well beyond the pale of decency—even in war, including the suppression of the Jewish uprising in Warsaw and the execution of partisans in the Soviet Union. There were also regular transfers of soldiers between front-line and concentration camp duties, where the worst of the crimes against humanity took place. Still, most of the Waffen SS performed well and honorably in combat, with a relative few engaging in war crimes. Because their creed from the beginning of their existence was racial purity, they drew upon themselves after the war a full measure of blame for the awful acts perpetrated upon concentration camp victims.

References: Höhne, Heinz, *The Order of the Death's Head*, trans. Richard Barry (London: Coward, McCann & Geoghegan, 1969); Keegan, John, *Waffen SS: The Asphalt Soldiers* (New York: Ballantine, 1970).

White Company

A unit of mercenaries operating in medieval Italy, 1361–1364.

Among the many groups of condottieri, the mercenary troops of Italy in the 1300s through the 1500s, one of the best known was the White Company. Its leader, John Hawkwood, was probably the best known of the captains-general of the era. The White Company got its name from the fact that the soldiers serving in it went to great lengths to make sure their armor was highly polished (often using goat bone marrow), so the Italians gave it the name *Compagnia Bianca*.

Hawkwood and most of the White Company were from the British Isles. They had served in the army of the English king in the waning years of the Hundred Years War and found themselves unemployed when the Treaty of Bretigny brought the war to an end in 1360. Many of the knights had served both English and French monarchs in that conflict, but had no domains of their own to which they could return. Therefore, they banded together to continue their previous practice of living off the land. This naturally brought the anger of the French king, who appealed to English King Edward III to rid his country of these "free companies." Edward had mixed success in complying with this request, but the free companies found that work could be had in the employ of Italian city-states. Most of Hawkwood's compatriots left France for Italy in 1361 but Hawkwood stayed behind for a few months. The White Company first organized itself under the leadership of a German knight, Albert Stertz, who spoke Italian and had served in Italy before. He got the group its first commission and led the members in their first combat as the White Company, but when Hawkwood joined the Company in 1362 the men voted him their new commander. Stertz became second-in-command and proved invaluable in negotiations in the early days before Hawkwood became fluent in Italian.

The White Company was made up predominantly of knights who, together with their squires and pages, formed the basic unit, called the "lance." In combat, however, these knights tended to fight on foot. While in the service of King Edward III, Hawkwood had learned firsthand the massive destruction that could be dealt by bowmen to heavily armored knights on horseback. Thus, in combat Hawkwood's men used their lances like pikes: Encountering this defense in a square, no charging cavalry could survive the pikes, while on offense the massive hedgehog formation recalled the Greek phalanx. This strategy was at variance with the normal condottieri units that relied on heavy cavalry. In Hawkwood's Company horses were used for pursuit once the enemy had broken (the page would come running with the knight's mount) or for retreat if the battle went badly. As auxiliaries, Hawkwood commanded a force of English archers. Their longbows had proven the key ingredient in English victories at Agincourt and Crecy, and their quickly shot arrows could penetrate armor. The Company also had slingers as well as men carrying flint, steel, and tinder for setting afire defensive positions and dwellings. Burning houses aided in the spread of panic among defenders.

The White Company's first action took place shortly after their entrance into Italy in 1361. As they marched out of the Piedmont area into Lombardy, the city of Milan sought to bribe them to keep peaceful. Stertz pretended to accept the offer to negotiate, then attacked the countryside around the city during New Year's Eve celebrations. His men grabbed all the loot they could and 600 nobles. As was customary at the time, the nobles were not harmed but held for ransom. The White Company made 100,000 gold florins for their night's work. Indeed, it was the ability to march and fight at night that distinguished not just the White Company but all English troops. Used to harsher weather conditions at home, the Italian nights bothered them little.

For all its fame, the life of the White Company was short. The word of the English escapade at Milan had reached Pisa, and Hawkwood's men were contracted to that city-state in its conflict with Florence when they went into action in February 1364. The campaign did not start well, as Florentine forces (mostly German mercenaries) bested Hawkwood's unit in a few skirmishes. In April, reinforced, Hawkwood led his Company and the remainder of forces under Pisan hire in an attack on Florence. They were blocked 12 miles from the city at the town of Prato. Hawkwood drew back and tried another route, negotiating rough terrain to secure the town of Fiesole, from whose heights he could look down on Florence. Hawkwood and his advisors decided the best time to attack would be 1 May, hoping to take advantage of the city's May Day revelry as they had on New Year's Eve. The Pisan force successfully occupied the suburbs of Florence, but could make no headway against the city walls. Still, there was sufficient loot to justify their attack as well as enough destruction to please their employers. After a night of their own revelry back in Fiesole, they proceeded to harass and pillage the countryside, attacking Florence just often enough to keep the defenders from sallying out.

Unable to defeat Hawkwood's command by force, the Florentines tried bribery. It was successful. They convinced a portion of the attacking army to change sides, and the White Company took money to declare a five-month truce. When offered another large sum to abandon the Pisans for Florentine employment, Hawkwood refused. He stood by his bargain with Pisa, but a number of his men found the idea a good one. Many left the White Company, including Stertz, and Hawkwood was left with only 800 men. This effectively ended the attack on Florence.

Stertz reformed some of those who had changed sides into a new unit, the Company of the Star, which soon was in the employ of Siena. Hawkwood later fought for Milan and was for a while employed by the Catholic Church. His final and longest-lasting employer was Florence, which he served faithfully until his death in 1394. He was given a public funeral and treated as a hero. Hawkwood had not only fought well for his employers, he profited well, as did the men under his command. From his time in service with Pisa Hawkwood had acquired the nickname Giovanni Acuto (John the Sharp), partly because of the difficulty in transcribing "Hawkwood" phonetically into Italian (which lacks the "h" and "w" sounds), but mainly because of his ability to drive a hard bargain. Hawkwood's service and reputation for loyalty, in a time and place where fidelity was rare, made his reputation grander than any of the White Company with whom he had originally served.

References: Deiss, Joseph Jay, *Captains of Fortune* (New York: Thomas Crowell Company, 1967); Trease, Geoffrey, *The Condottieri* (New York: Holt, Rinehart and Winston, 1971).

Wild Geese

Irish exiles fighting with French and Spanish armies in the seventeenth and eighteenth centuries.

It seems as though the Irish and English have always been mutually antagonistic, certainly since the Norman conquest of Ireland in the late eleventh century. Resistance to English domination has been a regular facet of their relationship, and has shown itself in a number of ways. The Wild Geese were exiled from Ireland following the failed attempt by the Stuart dynasty to reclaim the throne of England and reestablish Catholic rule. James II led an uprising in Ireland in 1689 which was countered by English troops sent over by King William III. After his forces were defeated at the Boyne River in July 1690 James fled to France. A year later the rebellion was completely crushed. Although William proposed leniency for the Irish, including safe transport of their soldiers to France, the Protestant-dominated Irish Parliament instead adopted a harsh anti-Catholic penal code. These laws discriminated against the Irish in their own homeland, including denying them the ability to enlist in the British army. Although that may seem an option Irishmen would not have exercised anyway, inclusion of Irish troops could well have mitigated the flavor of foreign military rule on the island. Many Irishmen took the transport offer and went to France, hoping someday to return to their home victorious.

Through the first half of the eighteenth century, Irish soldiers settled in France, joining the army while marrying French women and having half-French children. They came to be called the Wild Geese, for they had flown far from home and seemed to be perpetually wandering. In 1745 they received an opportunity to fight the English once more. By this time the men in command of the Irish regiments were second-generation Frenchmen, named Dillon, Lally, and Clare. James Dillon, called by the French Chevalier de Dillon, at age 46 commanded one of the regiments. At age 43, Arthur de Lally de Tollendal commanded a second. In command of a third, and in overall command of the brigade, was the sixth viscount Clare and ninth earl of Thomond, whose residence outside Ireland apparently meant little to him in claiming those titles. These men had relatives who had made their peace with the English and lived in Ireland, but these three had been raised by the brigade and knew no other home.

The latest Stuart pretender to the English throne, Prince Charles Edward, in 1745 again hoped that with French aid he could restore the Stuart dynasty. Europe was in the midst of the War of the Austrian Succession, wherein France and Bavaria were aiding Frederick of Prussia against the empress of Austria, Maria Therese, in her bid to inherit her father's throne. Supporting the empress were the German states of Saxony and Hanover (English King George II's homeland), the Spanish Netherlands, and England. With English troops on the continent, Irish troops in the service of French King Louis XV looked for the opportunity to draw some English blood.

Their time to shine came in May 1745 in Flanders at the battle of Fontenoy. The French General Maurice de Saxe, one of the most talented generals France has produced, laid siege to the Flemish town of Tournai. The duke of Cumberland, George II's son, led a combined Anglo-Dutch-Hanoverian force to relieve the city. Saxe left some 18,000 men to maintain the siege and placed the remaining 52,000 troops at the town of Fontenoy, on Cumberland's path. Saxe had his army dig a long line of entrenchments stretching from the Scheldt River on his right at the town of Anthoin, some two miles to the town of Fontenoy, then past that to Barri Wood. Between the towns and the woods he constructed three redoubts within which he placed most of his artillery. Cumberland would have to detour widely to bypass the French force, or attack it head-on. Saxe was banking on the latter choice, and Cumberland obliged. Saxe did have two conditions that hampered his performance, however. He was suffering from dropsy to such an extent that he had to have his swollen body hauled around the battleground in a cart; he also had King Louis XV in camp. Louis was little problem, but his army of courtiers wore Saxe's nerves thin.

Cumberland's army numbered 50,000, of which 12,000 were British infantry and another 3,000 cavalry, 8,000 Hanoverians, and the remainder Dutch and Austrians in whom he had little faith. Although he realized the difficulty of attacking prepared positions in a frontal assault, Cumberland trusted his infantry. His redcoats were renowned for their discipline and tenacity, and both were sorely tested on 10 May 1745. After watching Dutch cavalry fruitlessly charge French positions on the flanks then turn and flee the field, Cumberland massed his infantry in a huge square, British in the lead and Hanoverians covering the rear. His attack on the center of the French line allowed the French artillery in the redoubts on his flanks to continually rake his force, and both grapeshot and roundshot tore massive holes in the lines.

The British infantry closed ranks and pressed on, losing men at each step. When the British were within 50 yards of their entrenchments, the French infantry rose and loosed a massive volley that again wiped out ranks of redcoats. The British pressed on. At 30 yards away, they halted. Almost all firing on the field stopped. The British dressed their ranks, then Lieutenant Colonel Lord Charles Hay stepped in front of his men and faced the French. He took out a silver flask, toasted the French with an inflammatory remark about their poor performance in the last battle between the French and English, then saluted the French and returned to his men as they gave him three cheers. The French returned the salute and, as they were doing so, found themselves mowed down by the first volley of English musket fire. From that point on the redcoats stood and fired volley after volley, one rank firing as the next two reloaded then took their place. Wave after wave of French soldiery died in repeated attempts to come to grips with the British, but the disciplined fire upon which Cumberland had depended proved its worth. Panicked French cavalry, turned back by the awful fire, streamed to the rear past their king, who refused to evacuate.

Deadly as their fire was, the British and Hanoverians remained under constant French bombardment from the front and both flanks, and their numbers continued to dwindle. Then, Saxe sent in the Wild Geese. They had taken some casualties in the opening British volleys, but nothing like they took in this charge that broke the British assault. Although the first wave of Irish were mowed down, the second and successive waves closed and fought hand to hand with the redcoats. It was melee fighting at its worst and the Irish took the highest casualties of any unit in the French army that day. Unable to withstand the fury of the Irish and the pounding of the artillery, the British conducted an orderly withdrawal, firing and holding back any serious pursuit.

The Wild Geese lost 270 dead, including 13 officers, and another 400 wounded—one sixth of their force. These were among the 7,200 reported French casualties. Their enemy had left behind at least 7,500 dead and wounded, and Cumberland had to withdraw from the field. Within weeks Saxe had not only brought about the fall of Tournai, but had gone on to capture almost all of Flanders. Lally, the Irish brigade commander, was promoted for his efforts at Fontenoy, but was transferred to India to fight the British there in a losing cause that brought about his disgrace in the eyes of the French government. The French finally executed him after years of imprisonment. Such treatment of one of their heroes infuriated the Irish, who began to look at the French with a more jaundiced eye, especially in 1745, when the Stuart cause was crushed as the French monarchy stood idly by. Within a few months of Fontenoy, Prince Charles Edward failed in his bid to invade England. His defeat at Culloden marked the end of any hope of a restoration of Catholic rule. The British government learned from this battle, however, the quality of the Irish as fighting men and soon opened recruiting in Ireland. Although Anglo-Irish troubles remain, in times of emergency Irish troops have joined the British colors while both sides keep quiet about their differences for the duration of the conflict.

It has been suggested that while in French service, from 1691 to 1745, the Irish lost 450,000 dead. Although the Irish in French service were the best-known exile troops, Irish emigres served across Europe. They were only occasionally in completely Irish units, however, more often being incorporated into existing organizations of the host country's army. Irish soldiers served in several regiments in the Spanish army, fighting alongside British forces under the Duke of Wellington against Napoleon's troops in Spain. One of those regiments later moved to Italy to serve the Kingdom of Naples as the Regimiento del Rey, or the King's Regiment. In possibly the best example of the freedom of movement of the Wild Geese, one regiment served alternately for the Duchy of Lorraine, Brandenburg-Anspach, Saxony-Poland, Brandenburg again, and finally in British imperial service.

References: Hennessey, Maurice, *The Wild Geese: The Irish Soldier in Exile* (London: Sidgwick & Jackson, 1973); Smith, Robert Barr, *Men at War* (New York: Avon, 1997).

Z

Zealots

A radical Jewish sect resisting Roman occupation in the first century A.D.

The Zealots were a revolutionary faction in Israel during the Roman occupation, active in the first century A.D. Although the Romans rarely did anything to hamper the Jews of Israel in the practice of their religion, the Roman practice of their own religion offended many Jews. The affront they felt to their faith, coupled with a series of harsh Roman rulers, set off a revolt that had ruinous consequences for the Jewish people.

The first mention of a leader of resistors to Roman rule is that of Judas of Galilee in 6–7 A.D. He preached resistance to the census ordered by the Romans, possibly the same one mentioned in the biblical Book of Luke. He was killed in this revolt, and his death gave rise to the Zealots. They were not only politically active against Roman rule, but were fundamentalist in their interpretation of the Jewish law. They followed the teachings of Shammai, a member of the Sanhedrin, the semigoverning body of interpreters of Jewish law. Shammai took an extremely conservative view of Jewish law and objected to anyone converting to the faith who was not born a Jew, and any Israelite that cooperated with Rome became a target for his wrath. A small faction of the Zealots, the Sicarii (from *sica*, a dagger), became assassins, attacking not only Romans but Jews who cooperated with them. For a time the Zealots remained a religious faction, preaching their conservative values, but they came to the fore in 41 A.D. when the Romans attempted to place a statue of the emperor in the temple in Jerusalem. Later, a synagogue in the neighborhood was violated in the wake of an attack on a Roman patrol. Such incidents could well have been blown out of proportion and used to inflame the population. Nevertheless, the uprisings remained limited until the appointment of Gessius Florus as procurator for Israel in 67 A.D.

Florus was unusually corrupt and made no attempt to take Jewish sensibilities into account in his actions. It is reported by Josephus (the only recorder of these incidents) that Florus provoked the Jews so he could bring in the troops and use the disturbances as an excuse for looting. Florus's high-handed activities, coupled with a division within the Jewish ranks over how to respond, led to violence. When the population of Jerusalem publicly jeered Florus, he let loose his legionaries to ransack the city. He then provoked the people further by demanding that they welcome two arriving Roman cohorts. When the Jews did so and their actions not fully appreciated, they again vented their vocal ire on Florus. Again the troops were set loose and fighting took place throughout the city. The Romans occupied the temple and the Zealots began taking over the abandoned forts of Masada and Herodion, built decades earlier by King Herod, which still held sizable armories.

The leading citizens of Jerusalem saw the

ultimate impossibility of defeating Rome and counseled moderation, but many of the Jewish religious leaders supported the rebellion. The area governor, Agrippa II, sent troops to Jerusalem but they proved too few to recapture the city. To further seal their fate, the rebels massacred a Roman garrison granted safe passage out of the city. Throughout Israel the Zealots and their supporters seized population centers, with only a few remaining in Roman control. The Roman legate in Syria, C. Cestius Gallus, marched to Israel with a legion and regained much of the countryside, but was not strong enough to besiege Jerusalem. He withdrew northward but was ambushed and those Romans not killed fled, abandoning their weapons. Any hope of a negotiated peace was gone, but the Zealots could not capitalize on their early success. Instead, they quarreled among themselves, to the point of combat, and did little to prepare themselves for a war. They were rebels, not soldiers, and the leadership and discipline necessary to train and prepare a real fighting force did not exist.

When word of the revolt reached Rome, Emperor Nero reinforced the military with troops under the command of Vespasian, a general who had proven his worth in campaigns in Britain. He again reestablished Roman control over the countryside but hesitated to attack Jerusalem, not only owing to its difficulty but because of the power struggle in Rome that followed Nero's death. Finally Vespasian himself was named caesar and returned to Rome, leaving his son Titus in command of operations against the Zealots. In the months that Vespasian waited for news from Rome, the Zealots did not put the time to good use but continued to fight among themselves.

Titus laid siege to Jerusalem in the spring of 70 A.D. with four legions and auxiliary troops on hand. He weakened the city's defenses by allowing pilgrims to enter to celebrate Passover, then bottling them up inside to strain the food supply. In the face of the Roman enemy, the defenders buried their differences and held fast even though conditions in the city grew progressively desperate. With their experience in siege warfare, the Romans made steady progress against the successive walls the Jews defended, capturing them at the rate of one a month throughout the summer. In September the last of the city fell to Roman soldiers and was almost completely razed.

The Zealots continued to hold out in the fortresses at Herodion, Macherus, and Masada. The task of capturing them fell to Governor Barrus, sent by Vespasian. Herodion fell immediately, but Macherus resisted until its commander, Eleazar, fell prisoner to the Romans. Barrus scourged Eleazar and made ready to crucify him in sight of the garrison, which offered its surrender in return for its leader's life. Barrus agreed, then proceeded to slaughter 1,700 men and boys among the surrendered garrison. The women and children he sold into slavery. At Masada, according to Josephus, the 1,000 Zealot defenders resisted to the very last and then committed mass suicide rather than give in to Roman captivity. This story has been challenged by some scholars, especially those that point out that the Zealots were fundamentalists, and one of the greatest of sins in the Jewish faith is suicide. Could such a conservative group go against one of its most strongly held beliefs? Certainly a siege took place there for the siege ramp still exists, but the ultimate fate of those inside is recorded again only by Josephus, whose veracity is doubted on many points. Suicide or not, the Roman conquest was costly for the Jews, who suffered (according to both Josephus and Tacitus) 600,000 dead or as much as one quarter of the population. Perhaps another quarter was sold into slavery.

The Zealot movement officially ended with the fall of Masada in 73 A.D., but those who managed to escape earlier from Jerusalem or other battles spread their discontent to surrounding countries and fomented anti-Roman movements from Persia to Egypt. A last gasp of Zealot resistance was a movement in Cyrenaica (modern Libya) led by one Jonathan, who led a mass of the lower classes into the Libyan desert on the promise of divine deliverance. The Jewish authorities, by now afraid of Roman retribution, turned Jonathan over to the Romans. He was sent to Rome, scourged, and burned alive. Possibly one Zealot group escaped to Arabia and established a community at Medina, reportedly lasting until the seventh century.

References: Graetz, Heinrich, *History of the Jews*, vol. II (Philadelphia: The Jewish Publication Society of America, 1893); Soggin, J. Alberto, *A History of Ancient Israel*, trans. John Bowden (Philadelphia: Westminster Press, 1984); Yadin, Yigael, *Herod's Fortress and the Zealots's Last Stand* (New York: Random House, 1966).

Zouaves

Moroccan and Algerian troops fighting in French service in 1830–1891, and American units copying their uniform style.

The original Zouave troops were North African soldiers of the Zouaoua tribe recruited by the French during their campaigns in Algeria and Morocco in 1830. They developed a reputation not only as outstanding soldiers but also for their attire. Most notable were the *serouels*, the baggy pants reminiscent of the Arabian Nights. These were combined with a short coat and a fez, creating a thoroughly Middle Eastern look. The French *Military Annual* of 1831 describes them as wearing "jacket with sleeves and waistcoat closed in front, in blue cloth. Moorish pants in wine-colored cloth. Turban and red riding breeches." Considering the usual uniforms of the day, these were not really more colorful, although the cut was certainly distinctive.

The French formed local forces in North Africa into the *Armee d'Afrique*, not only because of the need for soldiers but because local recruiting created a bond (they hoped) between the population and the occupying power. The Zouaves were originally at a strength of two battalions, but because of their early success and their rapidly gained reputation for dash and courage, the unit was much in demand by commanding generals in Algeria. That, coupled with the strong desire of soldiers to join an elite and distinctive unit, led to the expansion of the Zouaves until they ultimately numbered ten regiments that served not only in North Africa, but everywhere the French army fought. Although they attracted sufficient volunteers from the French army to fill the ranks of noncommissioned officers and officers, the rank and file remained Algerian. There was no lack of volunteers, and therefore no lack of replacements for the high number of casualties the units incurred. As once source states, "Most of the officers became generals; four died under fire or from overwork" (Detaille, 1992).

After meritorious service in North Africa, Zouave regiments served with the French expedition to Russia during the Crimean War in 1854. They suffered immense losses, as did most units in this war, not only from combat but from disease—notably cholera. The Zouaves distinguished themselves in every battle in which they took part, but the number of dead and wounded French officers was high. They also made a name for themselves in Russia as *bon vivants*. One Zouave hijacked a flock of sheep kept by the British commander, so that the French always had plenty of fresh meat; they did, however, share this with British troops, and stories are told of French Zouaves and Scottish Highlanders sharing British mutton cooked by French soldiers. The Zouaves also became well known for their "theater." In the evenings men would dance and sing music hall numbers, giving rise to the comment that the Zouaves were at the same time Parisian and Arab.

After the Crimean War they returned to action in Africa, when the entire *Armee d'Afrique* fought with French forces in Italy in 1859. Some regiments fought in Syria while others were sent along with Maximillian's ill-fated expedition to Mexico from 1863 to 1866. They also served in France during the Franco-Prussian War in 1870–1871. Although later troops were of lesser quality, the officer corps always remained first-rate and the spirit of the regiments immediately infused those who transferred in. "A simple Zouave thought himself and knew himself to be an individual. With his *chechia* set back on his head, he surveyed from the heights of his grandeur everything that was not Zouave" (Detaille, 1992). "All those in the army who had the ambition and the fanaticism of his profession dreamed of joining the Zouaves. All dreamed of this but not everyone got there despite the fact that death harshly ravaged the chosen" (Detaille, 1992).

The reputation earned by the Zouaves in French service became well known in the United States in the 1850s. Most impressed was a New Yorker named Elmer Ellsworth, who had had a lifelong fascination with things military. While attending law school in Chicago he joined the Illinois state militia and formed his own unit called the United States Zouave Cadets. He drilled his men to perfection, ultimately taking them to the East Coast where they toured several cities, giving demonstrations of their marching skill that no other military unit could match. The intricacies of their maneuvering led to fanciful stories published in contemporary newspapers, and both the soldiers and their commander became popular public figures. Finally, however, the maintenance of the unit proved too expensive and the Zouave Cadets were disbanded in 1860. Ellsworth returned to Illinois where he entered into law practice with Abraham Lincoln. When Lincoln was elected president, he invited Ellsworth to Washington to work in the War Department.

When the Civil War broke out in April 1861 Ellsworth resigned his position and went to New York City. There he was determined to raise a new Zouave unit and went looking for recruits. He found them in the New York Fire Department. The firemen remembered his Cadets and embraced the idea of forming such a unit, so the New York Fire Zouaves were created, officially the Eleventh New York Regiment. Marching into Virginia in May 1861, Ellsworth entered a tavern in Alexandria to remove a Confederate flag. The tavern owner killed him. Thus, when the Zouaves went into combat at the first battle of Bull Run in June, they were under the command of Noah Farnham. Their performance in combat was no better or worse than most of the rest of the untrained Union army, although some individuals did distinguish themselves. The unit was disbanded a few months later.

The romance of the French Zouave troops and the exotic uniform motivated many units on both sides of the war to adopt the Zouave heritage. Most of the early units on the Union side were from New York and many contained French immigrants, even some who had served in French Zouave units. Over time, the idea spread westward and Zouave units were formed in Ohio and Indiana. The most famous of the Indiana units was the Eleventh Indiana Volunteer Infantry, known as Wallace's Zouaves. Their commander was Lewis Wallace, the youngest Union soldier to hold the commission of major general, but more famous for his postwar accomplishment of writing *Ben-Hur*. The Eleventh started the war as mounted soldiers, unusual for Zouaves, and distinguished themselves in a sharp fight with Confederate cavalry at Romney, Virginia, when a detachment fought off a cavalry unit through an afternoon and evening and inflicted 28 casualties on the Confederates for a loss of but one of their own killed. Wallace, like Ellsworth, prided himself on having the best-drilled unit in Indiana and they fought throughout the war in campaigns such as Fort Donelson, Shiloh, Champion's Hill, Vicksburg, and in the Shenandoah Valley.

The South had Zouave units as well, not surprisingly originating in Louisiana. The best known was Wheat's Tigers (First Special Battalion, Louisiana Infantry), named for their commander, Roberdeau Wheat. Wheat's Tigers made their debut at the first battle of Bull Run in 1861, where they fought well. They had a reputation for wildness that was only partially curbed when Wheat was tem-

A Zouave sergeant, 1846

porarily replaced (due to a wound received at Bull Run). His second in command, Charles de Choiseul, executed two men for attacking an officer; he sought to establish a more disciplined unit. Both the battalion and Wheat were subdued by this action. They fought with General Thomas "Stonewall" Jackson in the Shenandoah Valley campaign in the summer of 1862 making up his famous "foot cavalry" known for their rapid marches. The Zouaves' last great battle was in that summer at Gaines's Mill east of Richmond, where Wheat was killed. His men were heartbroken at his death and many stopped fighting immediately and left the battlefield. Some men went home and the remainder were transferred to other units.

Another famous Louisiana unit was the First Battalion Louisiana Zouaves, commanded by wealthy New Orleans socialite George Auguste Gaston de Coppens. These Zouaves earned a reputation for wildness far outstripping that of Wheat's men. They terrorized every town through which their train travelled on its way to Richmond, Virginia, in the summer of 1861. That same ferocity showed itself during and after battles as well, as they engaged in widespread burning of buildings in the first town they captured. Called "the most rakish and devilish looking beings I ever saw" by one Confederate soldier, Coppens's Zouaves proved themselves in battle at Seven Pines in June 1862 then later at Gaines' Mill with Wheat's Zouaves. They suffered severe losses at the second battle at Bull Run in August, and their last major battle was Antietam in September 1862. Coppens was killed there and the unit was so badly decimated it was withdrawn from combat for reorganization. It saw no serious fighting for the remainder of the war.

One other aspect of Zouave units should be mentioned, and that is the position of *vivandiere*, a mixed French and Latin word literally meaning "hospitality giver." The vivandiere was a woman, often the wife of one of the men in the unit, who acted as sort of an unofficial (and later official) commissary. She wore a skirted uniform, and marched with the men on campaign. She was responsible for acquiring "necessaries" such as tobacco, liquor, extra food, etc., for the troops. The vivandiere tradition started with the French Zouaves and the women travelled to French battlefields in the Crimea, Italy, and Mexico. In some cases women fought and were decorated for valor, although they usually stayed out of combat. Vivandieres also travelled with the American Zouave formations on both sides.

More than 50 regiments were formed in the American Civil War and American Zouaves had uniforms that were variations on those worn by French Zouaves: Officers usually did not wear the baggy pants, but red and blue were the primary colors. The uniform coats were usually decorated with contrasting piping sewn into elaborate clover leaf designs and with *tambeaus*, or false pockets. The hats varied from fezzes to kepis to turbans to stocking caps. Wheat's Tigers wore baggy white pants with blue pinstripes, but most were either solid or trimmed red or blue. After the war, some militia units continued to wear the Zouave uniforms, but with the adoption of more subdued uniforms in armies worldwide, men in such elaborate and decorative garb never saw combat again.

References: Detaille, Edouard, *L'Armée Francaise*, trans. Maureen Reinertsen (New York: Waxtel & Hasenauer, 1992); McAfee, Michael, *Zouaves: The First and the Bravest* (Dallas: Thomas Publishing, 1994); Smith, Robin, *Zouaves of the American Civil War* (London: Stackpole, 1996).

Zulus

A tribe dominating southern Africa in the early nineteenth century, known for the toughness of their warriors.

The Zulu nation began in southeastern Africa as a vassal to the neighboring Mtetwa tribe. The Mtetwa first began to rise to prominence under the leadership of Dingiswayo, who became chief in 1795 at the age of 25. Dingiswayo began the practice of organizing his population along regimental lines, establishing a military framework for his tribe. After training them intensively he went on campaign, beginning a series of wars called the Mfecane. Dingiswayo refused to allow his warriors to slaughter captives, preferring to unify the tribes through intermarriage. He defeated virtually every tribe in the region and made them tributaries. The subject tribes were incorporated into a confederation with the Mtetwa as the leaders. The one tribe that Dingiswayo failed to bring totally under his control was the Ndwande, whose chief, Zwide, would prove to be Dingiswayo's undoing.

Dingiswayo took under his tutelage a young exile from the Zulu tribe who had escaped with his mother to the Mtetwa. This young man was Shaka, illegitimate son of the Zulu chief, who had fled his homeland to escape persecution from his half-brothers. Shaka distinguished himself in combat, gained Dingiswayo's attention, and rose to the highest ranks. He became one of the tribe's leading figures through his fighting skill and his devotion to Dingiswayo. Shaka disagreed with his mentor on the appropriate policy for dealing with defeated enemies; he believed the warriors should be killed and the remainder of the tribe forcibly integrated, rather than follow Dingiswayo's more peaceful method. As a subordinate, however, he continued to faithfully follow his chief's lead.

In 1810 Shaka learned that his father had died and had been succeeded by one of Shaka's half-brothers. Shaka wanted his father's position and arranged for the new chief's assassination. Dingiswayo then appointed Shaka to fill the position. Shaka thus came to lead his old tribe in 1816 at the age of 32. The Zulus remained vassals to the Mtetwa and Shaka continued to fight under Dingiswayo's command. Three of these campaigns were fought against the Ndwande tribe and the Mtetwa were victorious. The defeated Chief Zwide swore fealty to Dingiswayo, but secretly plotted against him. In 1818 Zwide captured Dingiswayo in battle and executed him. By this act he hoped to succeed to overall command of the confederation, but the tribesmen recognized Shaka as the new chief instead.

Zwide led his Ndwande tribe against Shaka when, in April 1818 Zwide's army invaded Zululand. At the battle of Qokli Hill a force of some 4,300 Zulus defeated a force twice their size, but the retreating Ndwande stole a large number of Zulu cattle. A second invasion occurred 14 months later. This time Shaka ordered his people to hide all available supplies, then he withdrew his troops before an ill-supplied invading Ndwande army of some 18,000. After leading his enemies deep into Zululand and wearing them down, Shaka attacked. The Zulus scored a major victory and immediately advanced on Zwide's capital. Zwide escaped capture, but was never again to bother the new chief. Shaka proceeded to put down any other resistance to his rule while incorporating the tribes he inherited from Dingiswayo into the Zulu nation.

Shaka now became the leader of all the tribes of the Natal area of southeastern Africa. He built on Dingiswayo's idea of organizing his population along military lines and ultimately created one of the most powerful military forces in history. At its height, the Zulus numbered 600,000 men and Shaka's empire covered 11,500 square miles. He established a training program second to none, whereby warriors were forbidden to wear sandals in order to toughen their feet. They developed the stamina to travel long distances at a run, covering as much as 50 miles a day, and then go straight into combat. He also developed a new weapon for his warriors, the *iklwa*. This is a stabbing spear with a blade about ten inches long in a leaf shape, fastened on a three-foot-long haft. The name comes from the sound the blade makes upon being removed from an enemy body. Another favorite weapon was the knobkerrie, or *iwisa,* a club made of ironwood. The shields they carried were of hardened cowhide in an oval shape 4.5 by 2.5 feet. Each shield was painted with the identifying marks of the warrior's unit. Each unit was also designated by a particular decorative piece of clothing, like an armband made of feathers. Necklaces were crafted in such a fashion as to indicate the number of enemy killed in battle. When the Europeans arrived and became aggressive the Zulus adopted firearms, but they were rarely very skilled with them and preferred the traditional melee style of fighting.

Shaka also developed the traditional formation employed by the Zulus, based upon the body of a bull. The army would form into four units, with three of the units forming up side-by-side. The central unit of the formation was the chest, which engaged the enemy head-on. Units to the right and left of the chest were regarded as the horns, and these were used to outflank the enemy force in a double-envelopment. Directly behind the chest unit was a reserve unit called the loins.

All Zulu males were raised from childhood to become warriors and learned to fight with Shaka's weapons and in his attack formation. Boys ages 13 through 18 were organized into military groups in which they served three years as cadets, practicing mili-

Zulu warriors, ca. 1870

tary skills while herding the cattle that were the major source of wealth and influence in the Zulu society or working in the fields. When their training was over, they went to a regiment assigned to them by the king, where they would await his permission to marry. This would usually come around age 35, at which point a warrior could leave his regiment and begin a family.

The principle reason for war was cattle. Cattle played an important part of Zulu life by providing milk, food, and raw materials. All cattle captured in battle became the property of the king, who distributed them to men who had reached marrying age and had proved themselves in battle. The importance of putting age restrictions on marriage is thus shown. Had there been no restrictions, there would not have been enough cattle available for all those who wanted to marry; Zulu society would have broken down.

Ironically, It was this military and social system that was a key factor in bringing about the decline of Zulu power. When the Dutch settlers of South Africa began to move northward toward Zulu territory in the 1830s and 1840s they often found themselves in bloody conflict with the Zulu population. As the British administration stretched into the region in the 1870s they became arbitrators in Zulu-Boer disputes. The British governor, Sir Henry Bartle Frere, ran into a dilemma when a border commission ruled in favor of Zulu claims against the Boer state of the Transvaal. Already at odds with the Boers, Frere did not want to further anger them by enforcing the commission's decision. He also heard the taunts of other native tribes that the British had never fought the Zulus, inferring a British fear of them. Frere decided a war against the Zulus would impress the natives and appease the Boers. Frere provoked a conflict by demanding that the Zulu king dismantle his military and allow the adult males to marry when they pleased. He also demanded an immediate reply that would not give the tribe sufficient time to gather and discuss the ultimatum.

The Zulu King Cetshwayo could not comply. To allow men to marry early would deplete the cattle supply while the inability to go to war would make it impossible to acquire sufficient new cattle. As Cetshwayo put it, he felt like a man "trying to ward off a falling tree." The British deadline passed on 11 January 1879 and British troops were almost immediately on the move. Lord Chelmsford, in command of British troops, invaded Zululand along a 200-mile front with his three columns directed to converge at the Zulu capital of Ulundi. Cetshwayo mobilized his army to defend his country, and his forces scored the initial victory at Ishandlwana on 22 January. There 20,000 Zulus overran a British camp defended by 1,300 British and native soldiers; all were slaughtered by the time-honored strategy of the Zulu bull formation. Overwhelming numbers and bravery had allowed the Zulu *iklwas* to overcome the British Martini-Henry rifles. Ishandlwana was the worst defeat the British ever suffered in one battle during their entire imperial experience. The small British outpost at Rorke's Drift was attacked that evening, but the 130-man contingent managed to survive a number of Zulu onslaughts.

After Ishandlwana the Zulu fortunes began to turn. The disciplined defense at Rorke's Drift forced the withdrawal of their far larger force, while a defeat at the hands of another one of the attacking British columns at Inyezane River the same day began to shake Zulu morale. They thus refrained from directly attacking a British force at the mission at Eshowe, but surrounded it and attacked patrols and supply columns. The Zulus were badly defeated by a force marching to Eshowe and the garrison was relieved in early April 1879 after more than two months under siege. The Zulus regained some momentum with victories over a supply column at Intombe River and a British unit at Hlobane Mountain, but after those battles the British gained the upper hand. On 29 March and 2 April the British dealt serious defeats to larger Zulu forces, then captured the capital at Ulundi on 4 July. British forces by that time were under the command of Sir

Garnet Wolseley, who oversaw the destruction of Zulu power and independence. Cetshwayo was captured a month after the battle at Ulundi and was sent to England, where he met with Queen Victoria. After two years there he was returned to Zululand as king, but as little more than a figurehead. In 1897 Zululand was annexed into Natal Province. The Zulus made a final attempt to regain their freedom in 1906 but the rebellion was quickly crushed. The Zulus, who had once dominated southeastern Africa, became just another native tribe under British rule. They maintain to this day a strong tribal heritage. Although they played a significant role in the Republic of South Africa's first postapartheid elections in 1994, their trademark cowhide shields and short stabbing spears are now more tourist items than the weapons of war that temporarily shocked the British nation in 1879.

References: Farwell, Byron, *Queen Victoria's Little Wars* (New York: Harper and Row, 1972); Ritter, E.A., *Shaka Zulu; the Rise of the Zulu Empire* (London: Longman, 1960); Roberts, Brian, *The Zulu Kings* (New York: Scribner, 1974).

Bibliography

Adamec, Ludwig. *Dictionary of Afghan Wars, Revolutions, and Insurgencies* (Lanham, MD: Scarecrow Press, 1996).

Adcock, Frank. *Greek and Macedonian Art of War* (Berkeley: University of California Press, 1974).

Addington, Larry. *Patterns of War through the Eighteenth Century* (Bloomington: University of Indiana Press, 1990).

Aeschylus. *Persians*, trans. Edith Hall (Warminster: Aris & Phillips, 1996).

Alden, John. *The American Revolution* (New York: Harper & Row, 1954).

Alexander, Joe, *et al. A Fellowship of Valor* (New York: HarperCollins, 1997).

Arbman, Olger. *The Vikings* (New York: Frederick Praeger, 1961).

Ashley, James. *The Macedonian Empire* (Jefferson, NC: McFarland & Co., 1997).

Baines, J., and J. Malek. *Atlas of Ancient Egypt* (New York: Facts on File, Inc., 1980).

Barker, Geoffrey. *A Concise History of the United States Airborne* (Brandon, FL: Anglo-American Publishing, 1989).

Barnett, Correlli. *The Desert Generals* (Bloomington: University of Indiana Press, 1982).

———. *The Swordbearers* (New York: Morrow, 1964).

Bartha, Antal. *Hungarian Society in the 9th and 10th Centuries*, trans. K. Baazs (Budapest: Akademiai Kiado, 1975).

Bartos, Frantisek. *The Hussite Revolution* (Boulder, CO: East European Monographs, 1986).

Bartusis, Mark C. *The Late Byzantine Army* (Philadelphia: University of Pennsylvania Press, 1992).

Bary, William Theodore de, *et al.* eds. *Sources of Chinese Tradition* (New York: Columbia University Press, 1960).

Bianco, Richard. *Rommel, the Desert Warrior* (New York: Julian Messner, 1982).

Bickers, Richard Townshend. *Von Richthofen: The Legend Evaluated* (Annapolis, MD: Naval Institute Press, 1996).

Bidwell, Shelford. *The Chindit War* (New York: Macmillan, 1980).

Bilgrami, Ashgar. *Afghanistan and British India* (New Delhi: Sterling Press, 1972).

Bishop, Edward. *Better to Die* (London: New English Library, 1976).

Bjorge, Gary. "Merrill's Marauders: Combined Operations in Northern Burma in 1944," in *Army History*, Spring/Summer 1995.

Bona, Istvan. *The Dawn of the Dark Ages: The Gepids and the Lombards* (Budapest: Corvina Press, 1976).

Brander, Michael. *The Scottish Highlanders and Their Regiments* (New York: Barnes & Noble, 1996).

Brion, Marcel. *Attila: The Scourge of God* (New York: Robert McBride and Company, 1929).

Burns, Thomas. *A History of the Ostrogoths* (Bloomington: University of Indiana Press, 1984).

Bury, J. B. *The Invasion of Europe by the Barbarians* (New York: Russell and Russell, 1963).

Caidin, Martin. *The Ragged, Rugged Warriors* (New York: E. P. Dutton, 1966).

Campbell, George. *The Knights Templars, Their Rise and Fall* (New York: Robert McBride, 1937).

Carroll, John M. *The Black Military Experience in the American West* (New York: Liveright, 1971).

Center of Military History. *Merrill's Marauders* (Washington, D.C.: Historical Division, War Department, 1945).

Ceram, C. W. *The Secret of the Hittites*, trans. Richard Winston and Clara Winston (New York: Alfred A. Knopf, 1956).

Cervens, Thierry de. "The French Foreign Legion" (www.instantweb.com/l/legion).

Chaliand, Gerald, ed. *Guerrilla Strategies* (Berkeley: University of California Press, 1982).

Chambers, James. *The Devil's Horsemen* (New York: Atheneum, 1979).

Chandler, David. *The Campaigns of Napoleon* (New York: Macmillan, 1966).

Chandler, David, and I. F. W. Beckett. *Oxford Illustrated History of the British Army* (London: Oxford University Press, 1994).

Clancy, Tom. *Submarine: A Guided Tour inside a Nuclear Warship* (New York: Berkley Books, 1993).

Coppa, Frank. *The Origin of the Italian Wars of Independence* (New York: Longman, 1992).

Cowles, Virginia. *The Phantom Major* (New York: Harper and Bros. 1958).

Crankshaw, Edward. *Bismarck* (New York: Viking, 1981).

Cunliffe, Barry. *The Ancient Celts* (Oxford: Oxford University Press, 1997).

Curtin, Jeremiah. *The Mongols: A History* (Westport, CT: Greenwood Press, 1972).

Cutrer, Thomas, ed. *Terry's Texas Rangers* (Austin, TX: State House Press, 1996).

Davidson, H. R. Ellis. *The Viking Road to Byzantium* (London: George Allen & Unwin, 1976).

Davidson, Phillip. *Vietnam at War* (New York: Oxford University Press, 1988).

Davis, John. *The Texas Rangers* (San Antonio: University of Texas Institute of Texan Cultures, 1975).

Davis, Ralph H. C. *The Normans and Their Myth* (London: Thames and Hudson, 1976).

Dear, E. D. S., and M. R. D. Foot, eds. *Oxford Companion to World War II* (Oxford: Oxford University Press, 1995).

Deiss, Joseph Jay. *Captains of Fortune* (New York: Thomas Crowell Company, 1967).

Delbruck, Hans. *History of the Art of War* (Lincoln: University of Nebraska Press, 1991).

DePolnay, Peter. *Garibaldi, the Man and the Legend* (New York: T. Nelson, 1961).

Descola, Jean. *The Conquistadors*, trans. Malcolm Barnes (London: George Allen and Unwin, 1957).

Detaille, Edouard. *L'Armée Francaise*, trans. Maureen Reinertsen (New York: Waxtel & Hasenauer, 1992).

Diner, Helen. *Mothers and Amazons* (New York: The Julian Press, 1965).

Dower, John. *War Without Mercy* (New York: Pantheon, 1986).

Downey, Fairfax. *The Buffalo Soldiers in the Indian Wars* (New York: McGraw-Hill, 1969).

Drews, Robert. *The End of the Bronze Age* (Princeton, NJ: Princeton University Press, 1996).

Dudley, Donald. *The Romans* (New York: Alfred Knopf, 1970).

Dupuy, Colonel Trevor N. *A Genius for War* (New York: Prentice-Hall, 1977).

———. "Burma: The Drive from the North," in *History of the Second World War,* vol. 71 (London: BBC Publications, 1966).

Durant, Will, and Ariel Durant. *Rousseau and Revolution* (New York: Simon and Schuster, 1967).

Eby, Cecil. *Between the Bullet and the Lie* (New York: Holt, Rinehart & Winston, 1969).

Edwards, I. E. S., ed. *The Cambridge Ancient History* (Cambridge: Cambridge University Press, 1980).

Ellis, John. *Cassino: The Hollow Victory* (New York: McGraw-Hill, 1984).

Erman, Adolf. *Life in Ancient Egypt*, trans. H. M. Tirard (New York: Dover Publications, 1971 [1894]).

Fabing, Howard D. "On Going Berserk: A Neurochemical Inquiry," in *Scientific Monthly*, vol. 83 (November 1956)

Fage, J. D. *A History of West Africa* (London: Cambridge University Press, 1969).

Farwell, Byron. *The Gurkhas* (New York: Norton, 1984).

———. *Queen Victoria's Little Wars* (New York: Harper & Row, 1972).

Featherstone, Donald. *Colonial Small Wars* (Newton Abbot, Devon: David & Charles, 1973).

Ferrill, Arther. *The Origins of War* (London: Thames and Hudson, 1985).

Firkins, Peter. *The Australians in Nine Wars* (London: Robert Hale & Co., 1972).

Fischer, David Hackett. *Paul Revere's Ride* (New York: Oxford University Press, 1995).

Fitzhugh, Lester Newton. *Terry's Texas Rangers*, unpublished memoirs (Austin: Barker Center Archives).

Fletcher, William. *Rebel Private, Front and Rear* (New York: Penguin, 1995).

Foote, Shelby. *The Civil War, a Narrative*, 3 vols. (New York: Vintage Books, 1958–1972).

Ford, Daniel. *Flying Tigers: Claire Chennault and the American Volunteer Group* (Washington, DC: Smithsonian Institution Press, 1991).

Forrest, W. G. *A History of Sparta, 950–192 B.C.* (New York: Hutchinson, 1968).

Freidel, Frank. *The Splendid Little War* (Boston: Little, Brown and Company, 1958).

Fuentes, Patricia de. *The Conquistadors: First Person Accounts of the Conquest of Mexico* (New York: Orion, 1963).

Fuller, J. F. C. *The Generalship of Alexander* (Westport, CT: Greenwood, 1981).

Gabriel, Richard. *From Sumer to Rome* (New York: Greenwood Press, 1991).

———. *The Culture of War* (New York: Greenwood Press, 1990).

Gann, Lewis H. *Guerrillas in History* (Stanford, CA: Hoover Institution Press, 1971).

Gibbons, Floyd. *The Red Knight of Germany* (London: Cassell, 1932).

Gies, Frances. *The Knight in History* (New York: Harper & Row, 1984).

Ginouves, Rene, and Giannes Akamates.

Macedonia: From Philip II to the Roman Conquest (Princeton: Princeton University Press, 1994).

Glubb, John Bagot. *Soldiers of Fortune: The Story of the Mamlukes* (London: Stein & Day, 1957).

Gokhale, Balkrishna. *Ancient India: History and Culture* (Bombay and New York: Asia Publishing House, 1959).

Goodwin, Godfrey. *The Janissaries* (London: Saqi, 1994).

Graetz, Heinrich. *History of the Jews*, vol. II (Philadelphia: The Jewish Publication Society of America, 1893).

Grant, Michael. *The Army of the Caesars* (New York: Scribner, 1974).

Gregory of Tours. *History of the Franks*, trans. Ernest Brehaut (New York: Norton, 1969).

Guttman, John, "Poland's Winged Warriors," in *Military History*, vol. 10, no. 5 (December 1993).

Hackett, General Sir John. *Warfare in the Ancient World* (London: Sidgwick & Jackson, 1989).

Halberstadt, Hans. *US Marine Corps* (Osceola, WI: Motorbooks International, 1993).

Halecki, O. *A History of Poland* (New York: David McKay Company, 1981).

Hallenbeck, Jan. *Pavia and Rome: The Lombard Monarchy and the Papacy in the Eighth Century* (Philadelphia: American Philosophical Society, 1982).

Hallett, Robin. *Africa to 1875* (Ann Arbor: University of Michigan Press, 1970).

Hamilton, Allen. *Sentinel of the Southern Plains* (Fort Worth, TX: TCU Press, 1987).

Hanson, Lawrence. *Chinese Gordon* (New York: Funk and Wagnalls, 1954).

Hassig, Ross. *Aztec Warfare: Imperial Expansion and Political Control* (Norman: University of Oklahoma Press, 1995).

Hayes, W. *The Scepter of Egypt* (Cambridge, MA: Harvard University Press, 1959).

Heather, Peter. *Goths and Romans* (Oxford: Clarendon, 1991).

Heidler, David Stephen. *Old Hickory's War* (Mechanicsburg, PA: Stackpole, 1996).

Heiferman, Ron. *Flying Tigers: Chennault in China* (New York: Ballantine, 1971).

Hennessey, Maurice. *The Wild Geese: The Irish Soldier in Exile* (London: Sidgwick & Jackson, 1973).

Herodotus. *The Histories,* trans. Aubrey de Selincourt (Baltimore: Penguin, 1954).

Hibbert, Christopher. *Garibaldi and His Enemies* (London: Longman, 1965).

———. *Redcoats and Rebels* (New York: Norton, 1990).

Hickey, Michael. *Out of the Sky* (New York: Scribner, 1979).

Höhne, Heinz. *The Order of the Death's Head*, trans. Richard Barry (London: Coward, McCann & Geoghegan, 1969).

Hough, Richard, and Denis Richards. *The Battle of Britain* (New York: Norton, 1989).

How, W. W. "Arms, Tactics, and Strategy in the Persian War," in *Journal of Hellenic Studies*, vol. LXIII.

Hoyt, Edwin. *SEALs at War* (New York: Bantam Doubleday Dell, 1993).

Innes, Hammond. *The Conquistadors* (New York: Knopf, 1969).

Inoguchi, Rikihei, Tadashi Nakajima, and Roger Pineau. *The Divine Wind* (Annapolis: United States Naval Institute Press, 1958).

Irwin, Robert. *The Middle East in the Middle Ages* (Carbondale: Southern Illinois University Press, 1986).

Isadore of Seville. *The History of the Goths, Vandals and Suevi*, trans. Guido Donini and Gordon Ford (Leiden: E. J. Brill, 1970).

Isby, David. *Ten Million Bayonets* (London: Arms and Armour Press, 1988).

Jimenez, Ramon. *Caesar against the Celts* (New York: Sarpedon Publishers, 1995).

Johnson, Lonnie R. *Central Europe* (New York and Oxford: Oxford University Press, 1996).

Jones, Gwyn. *A History of the Vikings* (New York: Oxford University Press, 1984 [1968]).

———. *Eirik the Red and Other Icelandic Sagas* (New York: Oxford University Press, 1961).

Jones, Virgil Carrington. *Gray Ghosts and Confederate Raiders* (New York: Henry Holt & Co., 1956).

Kaminsky, Howard. *A History of the Hussite Revolution* (Berkeley: University of California Press, 1967).

Keegan, John. *A History of Warfare* (New York: Random House, 1993).

———. "Ashanti," in *War Monthly*, no. 7, 1974.

———. *Waffen SS: The Asphalt Soldiers* (New York: Ballantine, 1970).

Keen, Maurice. *Chivalry* (New Haven and London: Yale University Press, 1984).

Kelly, Orr. *Brave Men, Dark Waters* (Novato, CA: Presidio Press, 1992).

Kelly, Ross. *Special Operations and National Purpose* (Lexington, MA: Lexington Books, 1989).

Kennedy Shaw, Major W. B. "Britain's Private Armies," in *History of the Second World War,* vol. 28 (London: BBC Publishing, 1966).

Kenrick, John. *Ancient Egypt under the Pharaohs* (New York: John B. Alden, 1883).

King, Michael. *Rangers* (Ft. Leavenworth, KS: Combat Studies Institute, 1985).

King, Winston. *Zen and the Way of the Sword* (New York: Oxford University Press, 1993).

Kinross, Patrick. *The Ottoman Centuries* (New York: Morrow, 1977).

Kipling, Rudyard. "Fuzzy Wuzzy," from *The Complete Verse* (London: Kyle Cathie, 1995).

Kwanten, Luc. *Imperial Nomads* (Philadelphia: University of Pennsylvania Press, 1979).

Lasko, Peter. *The Kingdom of the Franks* (New York: McGraw-Hill, 1971).

Lawson, Don. *The Abraham Lincoln Brigade* (New York: Thomas Crowell, 1989).

Lehman, Johannes. *The Hittites: People of a Thousand Gods*, trans. J. M. Brownjohn (New York: Viking Press, 1977).

Lindsay, Jack. *The Normans and Their World* (New York: St. Martin's Press, 1975).

Longworth, Philip. *The Cossacks* (New York: Holt, Rinehart and Winston, 1970).

Lord, Walter. *The Good Years* (New York: Harper & Bros. 1960).

Lowell, E. J. *The Hessians and the German Auxiliaries of Great Britain in the Revolutionary War* (New York: Harper & Bros. 1884).

Loyn, H. R. *Anglo-Saxon England and the Norman Conquest* (New York: Longman, 1991).

Luttwak, E. N. *The Grand Strategy of the Roman Empire* (Baltimore: Johns Hopkins University Press, 1977).

Macartney, C. A. *The Magyars in the Ninth Century* (Cambridge: Cambridge University Press, 1968).

MacKinnon, Charles. *Scottish Highlanders* (London: Robert Hale, Ltd., 1984).

Macksey, Kenneth. *Invasion* (New York: Macmillan, 1969).

MacMunn, G. F. *The Armies of India* (London: Adam and Charles Black, 1911).

MacPherson, James. *Ordeal by Fire* (New York: McGraw-Hill, 1982).

Macqueen, J. G. *The Hittites and Their Contemporaries in Asia Minor* (London: Thames and Hudson, 1968).

Majdalany, Fred. *The Battle of Cassino* (New York: Houghton Mifflin, 1957).

Mao Tse-tung. *On Guerrilla Warfare*, trans. Samuel B. Griffith (New York: Praeger, 1961).

Mason, Herbert Malloy. *The Lafayette Escadrille* (New York: Random House, 1964).

Mason, Herbert Malloy. *The Rise of the Luftwaffe, 1918–1940* (New York: Dial Press, 1973).

Mason, Philip. *A Matter of Honour* (London: Jonathan Cape, 1974).

McAfee, Michael. *Zouaves: The First and the Bravest* (Dallas: Thomas Publishing, 1994).

McCormick, T. J. *China Market: America's Quest for Informal Empire* (Chicago: Quadrangle Books, 1967).

McKay, Ernest A. *Undersea Terror: U-Boat Wolf Packs in World War II* (New York: Julian Messner, 1982).

McLeave, Hugh. *The Damned Die Hard* (New York: Saturday Review Press, 1973).

Millett, Allan. *Semper Fidelis* (New York: Macmillan, 1980).

Millis, Walter. *Martial Spirit* (New York: Houghton Mifflin, 1931).

Mitcham, Samuel. *Rommel's Desert War: The Life and Death of the Afrika Korps* (New York: Stein and Day, 1982).

Moorehead, Alan. *Gallipoli* (London: H. Hamilton, 1956).

Muir, William. *Mameluke, or Slave Dynasty of Egypt* (New York: AMS, 1973).

Mulroy, Kevin. *Freedom on the Border* (Lubbock, TX: Texas Tech University Press, 1993).

Naito, Hatsuho. *Thunder Gods* (New York: Kodansha International USA Ltd., 1989).

Nolan, Alan T. *The Iron Brigade: A Military History* (Indianapolis: Indiana University Press, 1961).

Norman, A. V. B. *The Medieval Soldier* (New York: Thomas Y. Crowell, 1971).

Nuttingham, Anthony. *Scramble for Africa: The Great Trek to the Boer War* (London: Constable, 1970).

Olmstead, A. T. *History of the Persian Empire* (Chicago: University of Chicago Press, 1948).

Olson, James, and Randy Roberts. *Where the Domino Fell* (New York: St. Martin's Press, 1996).

Oman, C. W. G. *The Art of War in the 16th Century* (New York: AMS Press, 1979 [1937]).

Oman, Charles. *A History of the Art of War in the Middle Ages* (Ithaca, NY: Cornell University Press, 1953 [1885]).

Pakenham, Thomas. *The Scramble for Africa: White Man's Conquest of the Dark Continent* (New York: Random House, 1991).

Paret, Peter. "Napoleon and the Revolution in War," in *Makers of Modern Strategy* (Princeton: Princeton University Press, 1986).

Parke, H. W. *Greek Mercenary Soldiers* (Chicago: Ares, 1981 [1933]).

Partner, Peter. *The Murdered Magicians: The Templars and Their Myth* (New York: Oxford University Press, 1982).

Paul the Deacon. *History of the Langobards*, trans. W. D. Foulke

(Philadelphia: University of Pennsylvania Press, 1974).

Payne, Chuck. "'Rangers Lead the Way': The History of the U.S. Army Rangers" (http://users.aol.com/armysof1/Ranger.html).

Pitt, Barrie. *1918: The Last Act* (New York: Ballantine, 1963).

Plutarch. *The Age of Alexander*, trans. Ian Scott-Kilvert (Middlesex: Penguin Books, 1986).

Porch, Douglas. *The French Foreign Legion* (New York: HarperCollins, 1991).

Reid, Stuart. *British Redcoat, 1740-1793* (London: Reed International, 1996).

———. *British Redcoat, 1793-1815* (London: Reed International, 1997).

Reitz, Deneys. *Commando: A Boer Journal of the Boer War* (London: Faber & Faber, 1929).

Richthofen, Baron Manfred von, *Der Rote Kampfflieger* (Berlin: Ullstein, 1917).

Ritter, E.A. *Shaka Zulu; the Rise of the Zulu Empire* (London: Longman, 1960).

Roberts, Brian. *The Zulu Kings* (New York: Scribner, 1974).

Roberts, Michael. *Gustavus Adolphus: A History of Sweden*, 2 vols. (New York: Longman, 1953-1958).

Roberts, P. E. *History of British India* (London: Oxford University Press, 1952).

Rooney, David. *Burma Victory* (London: Arms and Armour Press, 1992).

Roosevelt, Theodore. *The Rough Riders* (New York: Charles Scribner's Sons, 1924 [1899]).

Rosenstone, Robert. *Crusade of the Left* (New York: Pegasus, 1969).

Rothenberg, Gunther. *The Art of Warfare in the Age of Napoleon* (Bloomington, IN: University of Indiana Press, 1978).

Sage, Michael. *Warfare in Ancient Greece* (London: Routledge, 1996).

Sahagun, Bernardino de. *The War of Conquest*, trans. Arthur Anderson and Charles Dibble (Salt Lake City, UT: University of Utah Press, 1978).

Sandars, N. K. "The Sea Peoples," in Cotterell, Arthur. *The Encyclopedia of Ancient Civilizations* (London: Rainbird Publishing, 1980).

Seaton: Albert. *The Horsemen of the Steppes* (London: Hippocrene, 1985).

Secoy, Frank. *Changing Military Patterns of the Great Plains Indians* (Lincoln, NE: University of Nebraska Press, 1992).

Shaw, Stanford. *The History of the Ottoman Empire and Modern Turkey*, 2 vols. (Cambridge: Cambridge University Press, 1976-1977).

Short, Anthony. *The Origins of the Vietnam War* (New York: Longman, 1989).

Siepel, Kevin. *Rebel: The Life and Times of John Singleton Mosby* (New York: St. Martin's Press, 1983).

Silberman, Neil Asher. "The Coming of the Sea Peoples," in *Military History Quarterly*, vol. 10, no. 2 (Winter, 1998).

Simons, Anna. *The Company They Keep* (New York: Free Press, 1997).

Simpson, Harold. "Hood's Texas Brigade at Appomattox," in Wooster, Ralph, ed. *Lone Star Blue and Gray: Essays on Texas in the Civil War* (Austin: Texas State Historical Association, 1995).

Singh, Khushwant. *A History of the Sikhs*, 2 vols. (Princeton, NJ: Princeton University Press, 1963-1966).

Slim, Field Marshal William, *Defeat into Victory* (London: Cassell and Company, 1956).

Smith, Page, *A New Age Now Begins* (New York: McGraw-Hill. 1976).

Smith, Page. *Trial by Fire* (New York: McGraw-Hill, 1982).

Smith, Robert Barr. *Men at War* (New York: Avon, 1997).

Smith, Robin. *Zouaves of the American Civil War* (London: Stackpole, 1996).

Soggin, J. Alberto. *A History of Ancient Israel*, trans. John Bowden (Philadelphia: Westminster Press, 1984).

Starr, Chester. *A History of the Ancient World* (New York: Oxford University Press, 1965).

Stearns, Peter, *et al*. *World Civilizations* (New York: HarperCollins, 1992).

Stilwell, Joseph W. *The Stilwell Papers*, Theodore H. White, ed. (New York: William Sloane Associates, 1948).

Strabo. *Geography*, trans. Horace Leonard Jones (Cambridge: Harvard University Press, 1966).

Sullivan, George. *Elite Warriors* (New York: Facts on File, 1995).

Swinson, Arthur. *The Raiders: Desert Strike Force* (New York: Ballantine, 1968).

Thomas, Hugh. *The Spanish Civil War* (New York: Harper and Row, 1961).

Thompson, E. A. *Romans and Barbarians* (Madison, WI: University of Wisconsin Press, 1982).

Thomson, Alastair. *ANZAC Memories* (New York: Oxford University Press, 1994).

Time-Life series, *The Third Reich: Fists of Steel* (Alexandria, VA: Time-Life, 1988).

Toland, John. *No Man's Land* (New York: Doubleday, 1980).

Townsend, Richard. *The Aztecs* (London: Thames and Hudson, 1992).

Trease, Geoffrey. *The Condottieri* (New York: Holt, Rinehart, and Winston, 1971).

Trench, Charles Chenevix. *The Road to Khartoum* (New York: Norton, 1978).

Trimingham, J. S. *Islam in West Africa* (London: Oxford University Press, 1962).

Tuker, Lt.-Gen. Sir Francis. *Gorhka: The Story of the Gurkhas of Nepal* (London: Constable, 1957).

Turnbull, Stephen. *The Samurai: A Military History* (New York: Macmillan, 1977).

———. *The Book of the Medieval Knight* (New York: Crown, 1985).

———. *Samurai Warriors* (New York: Sterling Publishing, 1991).

Utley, Robert. *Frontiersmen in Blue* (New York: Macmillan, 1967).

Vambery, Arminius. *Hungary in Ancient, Medieval, and Modern Times* (Hallandale, FL: New World Books, 1972).

Van Seeters, J. *The Hyksos* (New Haven, CT: Yale University Press, 1966).

Walker, Greg. "Elite SEAL Units," in *International Combat Arms*, vol. 7, no. 6 (November 1989).

Wandycz, Piotr. *The Price of Freedom: A History of East Central Europe from the Middle Ages to the Present* (London: Routledge, 1992).

Ward, Christy. "Description of the Berserk," (www.realtime.com/~gunnora).

Warry, John. *Warfare in the Classical World* (London: Salamander Books, 1980).

Watson, G. R. *The Roman Soldier* (Ithaca, NY: Cornell University Press, 1969).

Webb, Walter Prescott. *The Story of the Texas Rangers* (Austin, TX: Encino Press, 1971).

Wedgewood, C. V. *The Thirty Years War* (Gloucester, MA: P. Smith, 1969 [1938]).

Weeks, John. *Assault from the Sky* (New York: Putnam, 1978).

Weller, George Anthony. *The Story of Submarines* (New York: Random House, 1962).

Wheeler, Radha. *Early India and Pakistan* (New York: Praeger, 1959).

Whitehouse, Arch. *Legion of the Lafayette* (New York: Doubleday, 1962).

———. *The Years of the Sky Kings* (New York: Doubleday, 1964).

Wilkins, Frederick. *The Highly Irregular Irregulars: Texas Rangers in the Mexican War* (Austin, TX: Eakin Press, 1990).

Wilson, Andrew. *The Ever Victorious Army* (Edinburgh: Blackwood, 1868).

Winderbaum, Larry. *The Martial Arts Encyclopedia* (Washington, DC: Inscape Corp. 1977).

Wise, Terence. *Ancient Armies of the Middle East* (London: Osprey Publishing, 1981).

Wiseman, D. J. "The Assyrians," in *Warfare in the Ancient World*, John Hackett, ed. (London: Sidgwick and Jackson, 1989).

Wolfram, Herwig. *History of the Goths* (Berkeley: University of California Press, 1988).

Wolpert, Stanley. *India* (Englewood Cliffs, NJ: Prentice-Hall, 1965).

Wood, Derek, and Derek Dempster. *The Narrow Margin* (New York: Coronet, 1969).

Woolman, David. "The Day the Hadendowa Broke the British Square—or Did They?," in *Military History*, vol. 11, no. 2 (June, 1994).

Wright, J. Leitch. *Creeks and Seminoles* (Lincoln, NE: University of Nebraska Press, 1996).

Yadin, Yigael. *Herod's Fortress and the Zealots' Last Stand* (New York: Random House, 1966).

Young, John Robert. *French Foreign Legion* (New York: Thames and Hudson, 1984).

Young, Marilyn. *The Rhetoric of Empire: American China Policy, 1895-1901* (Cambridge: Harvard University Press, 1968).

Illustration Credits

3 Archive Photos

13 From the collections of the Library of Congress

18 From the collections of the Library of Congress

20 From the collections of the Library of Congress

25 Reprinted from *War Sketches in Color*, London, 1903.

29 Corbis-Bettmann

33 Reprinted from *The Arms of India*, London, 1911.

35 From the collections of the Library of Congress

37 Werner Forman/Art Resource, NY

44 Erich Lessing/Art Resource, NY

46 Erich Lessing/Art Resource, NY

55 Alinari/Art Resource, NY

56 From the collections of the Library of Congress

64 From the collections of the Library of Congress

66 From the collections of the Library of Congress

68 Erich Lessing/Art Resource, NY

74 Archive Photos

77 Archive Photos

82 Reuters/Corbis-Bettmann

87 Corbis-Bettmann

95 Earl Young/Archive Photos

104 Corbis-Bettmann

108 Erich Lessing/Art Resource, NY

114 The National Archives/Corbis

121 Corbis-Bettmann

128 Erich Lessing/Art Resource, NY

132 UPI/Corbis-Bettmann

135 From the collections of the Library of Congress

150 Erich Lessing/Art Resource, NY

162 Library of Congress/Corbis

164 From the collections of the Library of Congress

168 Giraudon/Art Resource, NY

174 Early Young/Archive Photos

176 Erich Lessing/Art Resource, NY

179 SEF/Art Resource, NY

182 From the collections of the Library of Congress

186 UPI/Corbis-Bettmann

190 From the collections of the Library of Congress

191 Reuters/Richard Ellis/Archive Photos

195 From the collections of the Library of Congress

198 Alinari/Art Resource, NY

204 Archive Photos

209 Werner Forman/Art Resource, NY

213 Navy photo by Chris Vickers

215 From the collections of the Library of Congress

219 Reprinted from *The Armies of India*, London, 1911.

224 Reuters/Archive Photos

230 From the collection of the Library of Congress

239 Erich Lessing/Art Resource, NY

255 Hulton-Deutsch Collection/Corbis

256 Werner Forman/Art Resource, NY

260 Imperial War Museum/Archive Photos

271 Baldwin H. Ward/Corbis-Bettmann

273 From the collections of the Library of Congress

Index

Page numbers in bold refer to main reference.